MICROSOFT® OFFICE EXCEL® 2007
QuickSteps

JOHN CRONAN

New York Chicago San Francisco
Lisbon London Madrid Mexico City
Milan New Delhi San Juan
Seoul Singapore Sydney Toronto

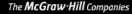
MICROSOFT® OFFICE EXCEL® 2007 QUICKSTEPS

Copyright © 2007 by Matthews Technology. All rights reserved. Printed in the United States of America. Except as permitted under the Copyright Act of 1976, no part of this publication may be reproduced or distributed in any form or by any means, or stored in a database or retrieval system, without the prior written permission of publisher, with the exception that the program listings may be entered, stored, and executed in a computer system, but they may not be reproduced for publication.

567890 CCI CCI 10

ISBN-13: 978-0-07-226372-5
ISBN-10:   0-07-226372-5

SPONSORING EDITOR / Roger Stewart

EDITORIAL SUPERVISOR / Jody McKenzie

PROJECT MANAGER / Samik Roy Chowdhury

SERIES CREATORS AND EDITORS / Marty and Carole Matthews

ACQUISITIONS COORDINATOR / Carly Stapleton

TECHNICAL EDITOR / Marty Matthews

COPY EDITOR / Lisa McCoy

PROOFREADER / Joette Lynch

INDEXER / Valerie Perry

PRODUCTION SUPERVISOR / Jim Kussow

COMPOSITION / International Typesetting and Composition

ILLUSTRATION / International Typesetting and Composition

SERIES DESIGN / Bailey Cunningham

ART DIRECTOR, COVER / Jeff Weeks

COVER DESIGN / Pattie Lee

To the Neighbors (Nanci, Sharon, Tom & Barb, and Doug & Lois)…

…thanks for sharing your time, wine, and dine with us.
You all add immeasurably to the quality and enjoyment of our
journey through life…and it's a ride we look forward to continuing with you!

—John (and Faye)

Acknowledgments

It doesn't get any easier to write a book, but working with great people certainly helps!

Marty Matthews, technical editor and series co-creator, provided great consul (as usual), kept me honest (as usual), and is to thank for the technical quality of this book.

Lisa McCoy, copy editor, ensured readable, grammatically correct text, and in consideration to the reader, removed most of my attempts at humor.

Valerie Perry, indexer, who comes in late in the process and under a tight deadline, adds tremendous value to the overall usability of the book.

Jody McKenzie, **Samik Roy Chowdhury**, and **Carly Stapleton**, project editors, provided the gentle "nudges" to keep me on task and on schedule.

Roger Stewart, sponsoring editor, championed this title at the publisher level and didn't call me names (at least to my face—LOL) as deadlines were stretched.

About the Author

John Cronan was introduced to computers in college over 30 years ago, and has maintained a close relationship with them in personal and professional endeavors ever since. Over the years, John has worked on dozens of books and software product manuals, performed several technical reviews of other authors' works, runs his own technical services business, and reclaims furniture for his wife's antiques business.

Recent books he has worked on published by McGraw-Hill include *Build an eBay Business QuickSteps*, *Adobe Acrobat 7 QuickSteps*, and *Microsoft Office FrontPage 2003 QuickSteps*.

John and his wife, Faye, (and cat, Little Buddy) live in the historic mill town of Everett, WA.

Contents at a Glance

Chapter 1 **Stepping into Excel** 1
Start Excel, open workbooks, use the ribbon, understand new file
formats and compatibility, get help, save workbooks, exit Excel

Chapter 2 **Entering and Editing Data** 25
Enter text, enter numeric data, format numbers, edit cells,
copy and paste data, use Paste Special, verify spelling

Chapter 3 **Formatting a Worksheet** 45
Add and remove rows, columns, and cells; add comments; use
themes and styles; view multiple workbooks

Chapter 4 **Using Formulas and Functions** 75
Reference cells, find named cells, create formulas, format
conditionally, use functions, check for errors, evaluate formulas

Chapter 5 **Viewing and Printing Data** 103
Add headers and footers, adjust margins, work with zoom, print
comments, use print areas, preview before printing

Chapter 6 Charting Data 129
Choose a chart type, select data for charting, add titles,
format chart items, create your own chart type, print a chart

Chapter 7 Working with Shapes and Pictures 155
Add shapes and pictures, organize clip art, create an organization
chart with SmartArt, use WordArt, format and position graphics

Chapter 8 Managing Data 185
Create and modify tables, add a total row, validate data,
sort and filter data, create an AutoFilter, use outlines

Chapter 9 Analyzing and Sharing Data 213
Use Goal Seek, scenarios, and Solver; lay out a PivotTable;
create a PivotTable chart; share and protect workbooks

Chapter 10 **Extending Excel** 243
Add external data from text files, Access, and the Web; manage data
connections; save data for the Web; create hyperlinks; record macros

Index 265

Contents

Acknowledgments iv

Introduction xii

Chapter 1 **Stepping into Excel** 1
     Opening Excel 3
     Get Started with Excel 3
      Explore the Excel Window 3
      Create a Workbook 3
     Understanding the Ribbon 7
      Open an Existing Workbook 7
      Change the Appearance of New Workbooks 8
      Customize the Quick Access Toolbar 10
     Get Help 14
      Open Help 15
      Use the Excel Help Window 16
     Understanding Excel's XML File Formats 18
     Close Your Excel Workbook 18
      Save a Workbook Automatically 18
      Save a Workbook Manually 21
      Save a Copy of Your Workbook 22
      Add Identifying Information 22
     Understanding Excel File Compatibility 24
      Exit an Excel Session 24

Chapter 2 **Entering and Editing Data** 25
     Understanding Data Types 26
     Enter Data 26
      Enter Text 26
      Enter Numeric Data 29
     Completing an Entry 30
      Enter Dates 30
      Use Times 31
     Formatting Numbers 32
     Understanding Excel Dates and Times 34
     Edit Data 35
      Edit Cell Data 35
     Adding Data Quickly 36
      Remove Cell Contents 36
      Copy and Paste Data 38
     Selecting Cells and Ranges 39
      Use Paste Special 39
      Find and Replace Data 39
      Verify Spelling 42
      Modify Automatic Corrections 44

1

2

3 Chapter 3 **Formatting a Worksheet** 45
    Adding and Removing Rows, Columns, and Cells...................................46
    Work with Cells, Rows, and Columns...46
        Adjust Row Height..46
        Adjust Column Width...47
        Hide and Unhide Rows and Columns...48
        Change Cell Borders..49
        Add a Comment..51
    Formatting Comments..53
    Apply Formatting 53
    Understanding Excel Formatting..54
        Apply Themes...54
        Create Custom Themes..59
    Searching for Themes..60
        Use Cell Styles...60
        Change Fonts..64
        Change Alignment and Orientation...65
        Add a Background...66
        Transfer Formatting...68
    Arrange and Organize Worksheets 69
        Lock Rows and Columns..69
        Split a Worksheet 71
    Working with Worksheets 72
        View Worksheets from Multiple Workbooks.................................72
        Compare Workbooks...72

4 Chapter 4 **Using Formulas and Functions** 75
    Understanding Cell Referencing Types..76
    Reference Cells...76
        Change Cell References..76
        Change to R1C1 References 76
        Name Cells...77
    Using Cell Reference Operators 79
        Go to a Named Cell 79
    Build Formulas...79
        Create a Formula..79
    Working with Cell Names 80
        Edit a Formula..82
        Move Formulas 83
    Using Formulas 84
        Copy Formulas...84
        Recalculate Formulas 85
        Use External References in Formulas 85
    Understanding the Trust Center...87
        Format Conditionally...91
    Using Functions Quickly...95
    Use Functions..95
        Enter a Function 95
        Enter a Sum in Columns or Rows Quickly 98

Find and Correct Errors 98
    Check for Errors 98
    Trace Precedent and Dependent Cells 100
    Watch a Cell 100
    Evaluate a Formula in Pieces 101

Chapter 5 Viewing and Printing Data 103
    Understanding Excel Views 104
    Lay Out a Worksheet 104
        Add Headers and Footers...104
    Adding Content to Headers and Footers 109
        Add Pictures to Headers and Footers...109
        Change Margins..110
        Select Page Orientation 112
        Use Headers as Page Titles 112
    Working with Zoom 114
    Print the Data..115
        Change the Order in Which Pages Print 115
    Choosing Worksheet Print Options...116
        Print Comments 116
        Use Print Areas...116
    Choosing What to Print 118
        Preview the Print Job...119
        Scale Your Data Before Printing..125
        Output the Print Job 125

Chapter 6 Charting Data 129
    Building a Chart...131
    Create and Design a Chart...131
        Choose a Chart Type 131
    Selecting Data for Charting 134
        Choose a Chart Location..134
        Modify How the Data Is Plotted..137
        Apply a Chart Layout 139
        Change a Chart's Style 140
    Selecting Chart Elements 141
    Modify Chart Elements 141
        Add Titles...141
        Show or Hide Axes...142
        Add or Remove Gridlines...142
    Identifying Chart Elements 143
        Show or Hide a Legend 143
        Add Data Labels...143
        Display the Data Table 145
        Create Your Own Chart Type...145
        Add a Second Value Axis...146
        Format Chart Elements...147
    Working with Charts 148
    Use Charts 149
        Add Charts Elsewhere 149
        Analyze Charts...150
        Print a Chart 153

5

6

Chapter 7 Working with Shapes and Pictures 155

Understanding Shapes 156
Add Shapes, Pictures, and Text...156
  Add Shapes...156
Working with Curves 157
  Insert Pictures..158
Using Pictures...163
  Organize Pictures..163
  Add Text...167
  Use SmartArt 169
Changing SmartArt 171
Working with Shapes...171
  Select, View, and Delete Shapes......................................171
Using Handles and Borders to Change Shapes......................173
  Crop Pictures...174
  Position Shapes 175
Combining Shapes by Grouping 177
Formatting Shapes and Text...177
  Use Styles...177
  Apply Styling Elements to Pictures 178
Changing a Picture's Attributes...180
  Change a Shape's Fill 180
  Add WordArt Styling to Text 181
  Make Detailed Formatting Changes 184

Chapter 8 Managing Data 185

Understanding Excel Tables 186
Build Tables..186
  Create a Table 186
Adding Rows and Columns to a Table 189
  Delete Rows and Columns Within a Table......................189
  Add a Total Row 189
  Apply Styles to a Table...190
Working with Tables 192
  Validate Data...195
Locating Validation Data 197
Organize Data..198
  Sort Data by Columns 199
  Sort Data by Rows 202
Removing Filters 203
  Create an AutoFilter 203
Setting Up Criteria and Extract Ranges.................................206
  Use Advanced Filtering 206
  Outline Data Automatically 207
Using Outlines...208
  Outline Data by Manually Grouping..............................210
  Add Subtotals..210
  Add Styles to an Outline...211

Chapter 9 **Analyzing and Sharing Data**..................................... 213
   Get the Results You Want..213
      Use Goal Seek 214
      Compare Alternatives Using Scenarios 216
      Use Multiple Variables to Provide a Result 219
      Save Solver Results and Settings 222
      Changing Solver Settings...224
   Work with PivotTables 224
      Create a PivotTable 224
      Understanding PivotTable Terms..225
      Create the PivotTable Layout..225
      Style a PivotTable..229
      Using PivotTables 231
      Create a PivotTable Chart 231
   Work with Other Users 234
      Protect Workbooks with Passwords...234
      Share a Workbook 235
      Working with Changes in a Shared Workbook 237
      Protect a Shared Workbook 237
      Discontinue Sharing a Workbook...238
      Work with Views...240
      Protect Worksheet and Workbook Elements...............................241

Chapter 10 **Extending Excel** 243
   Acquire Data..244
      Convert Text to Data...244
      Add a Table from an Access Database 246
      Get Data from the Web...247
      Add External Data from Existing Connections 248
      Setting External Data Range Properties....................................249
      Manage Connections 249
   Use Excel with Web Technology 252
      Understanding the Difference Between Save and Publish 253
      Save a Workbook as a Web Page...253
      Publish Workbook Items as a Web Page....................................255
      Understanding Excel Services..256
      Use Hyperlinks...256
   Automate Excel...260
      Use Recorded Macros...260
      Edit a Macro..262

Index 265

9

10

Introduction

QuickSteps books are recipe books for computer users. They answer the question "how do I…" by providing a quick set of steps to accomplish the most common tasks with a particular operating system or application.

The sets of steps are the central focus of the book. QuickSteps sidebars show how to quickly perform many small functions or tasks that support the primary functions. Notes, Tips, and Cautions augment the steps, and are presented in a separate column so as not to interrupt the flow of the steps. The introductions are minimal, and other narrative is kept brief. Numerous full-color illustrations and figures, many with callouts, support the steps.

QuickSteps books are organized by function and the tasks needed to perform that function. Each function is a chapter. Each task, or "How To," contains the steps needed for accomplishing the function, along with the relevant Notes, Tips, Cautions, and screenshots. You can easily find the tasks you want to perform through:

- The table of contents, which lists the functional areas (chapters) and tasks in the order they are presented

- A How To list of tasks on the opening page of each chapter

- The index, which provides an alphabetical list of the terms that are used to describe the functions and tasks

- Color-coded tabs for each chapter or functional area, with an index to the tabs in the Contents at a Glance (just before the Table of Contents)

Conventions Used in This Book

Microsoft Office Excel 2007 QuickSteps uses several conventions that are designed to make the book easier for you to follow. Among these are:

- A 🌐 or a 🚫 in the table of contents or the How To list in each chapter references a QuickSteps or QuickFacts sidebar in a chapter.

- **Bold type** is used for words on the screen that you are to do something with, like "…click the **File** menu, and click **Save As**."

- *Italic type* is used for a word or phrase that is being defined or otherwise deserves special emphasis.

- Underlined type is used for text that you are to type from the keyboard.

- SMALL CAPITAL LETTERS are used for keys on the keyboard, such as ENTER and SHIFT.

- When you are expected to enter a command, you are told to press the key(s). If you are to enter text or numbers, you are told to type them.

How to...

- Opening Excel
- Explore the Excel Window
- Create a Workbook
- Understanding the Ribbon
- Open an Existing Workbook
- Change the Appearance of New Workbooks
- Customize the Quick Access Toolbar
- Open Help
- Use the Excel Help Window
- Understanding Excel's XML File Formats
- Save a Workbook Automatically
- Save a Workbook Manually
- Save a Copy of Your Workbook
- Add Identifying Information
- Understanding Excel File Compatibility
- Exit an Excel Session

Chapter 1
Stepping into Excel

Excel 2007 is Microsoft's premier spreadsheet program. While maintaining the core features and functionality of Excel from years past, this version adds features that support everyone—from the casual user who simply wants to set up a household budget to the high-end user who wants to programmatically connect Excel data to Web services. If you have used earlier versions of Excel, your first indication that this version is something out of the ordinary is your first look at the new *ribbon* and other user interface items (this collection of screen elements allows you to use and navigate the program). Gone is the familiar menu structure you might have grown accustomed to with Microsoft Office programs, replaced with a new organizational scheme to better connect tools to tasks. In addition, a new workbook file format allows tight integration with XML (eXtensible Markup Language) Web services, though it does so transparently to users and maintains a compatibility path with earlier versions.

This chapter explains how to open Excel, use the ribbon and the new user interface, and then set it up to meet your own needs. You will learn how to get Help, online or offline. This chapter will also show you how to end an Excel session and save a workbook.

Figure 1-1: The classic way to start Excel is from All Programs.

NOTE

The terms *worksheet*, *sheet*, and *spreadsheet* all refer to the same row-and-column matrix that comprises the working area of Excel. These terms are used interchangeably throughout this book.

QUICKSTEPS

OPENING EXCEL

Excel can be started by several methods. The method you choose depends on convenience, personal style, and the appearance of your desktop.

USE THE START MENU TO START EXCEL

Normally, the surest way to start Excel is to use the Start menu.

1. Start your computer, if it is not running, and log on to Windows, if necessary.

2. Click **Start**. The Start menu opens.

3. Click **All Programs**, click **Microsoft Office**, and click **Microsoft Office Excel 2007**, as shown in Figure 1-1.

LOAD EXCEL FROM THE KEYBOARD

1. Press the **WINDOWS FLAG** key (between **CTRL** and **ALT** keys on most keyboards), or press **CTRL+ESC**.

2. Press the **DOWN ARROW** key several times until **All Programs** is selected, and then press the **RIGHT ARROW** key to open it.

3. Press the **UP ARROW** or **DOWN ARROW** keys until **Microsoft Office** is selected; press **RIGHT ARROW** to display the list of programs.

4. Press **DOWN ARROW** until **Microsoft Office Excel 2007** is selected; press **ENTER** to start it.

Continued . . .

Get Started with Excel

You can quickly get to work in Excel, but before you get too far, you might want to look over the information on the Excel window, including the new ribbon, to familiarize yourself with this retooled navigation scheme. You will do that in this section. You will also learn how to personalize Excel to your way of working.

Explore the Excel Window

The Excel window has many features to aid you in performing calculations, adding visual objects, and formatting your work to target your audience. The container for Excel *worksheets*—the grid where numbers, text, inserted objects, and formulas reside and calculations are performed—is a file called a *workbook* with a default file name of Book1 (see the "Understanding Excel File Compatibility" QuickFacts and "Understanding Excel's XML File Formats" for more information on file formats and extensions). When Excel is started, an existing workbook displays or a new workbook is created and displays a blank worksheet, as shown in Figure 1-2. The principal features of the Excel window are introduced in Table 1-1 and will be described further in this and other chapters of this book.

Create a Workbook

You can create new workbooks, whether you are working inside or outside of Excel.

CREATE A NEW WORKBOOK IN EXCEL

When Excel is started, you can just start typing on the first sheet of the workbook that is displayed, you can create another blank workbook, or you can choose to create a workbook based on a previous workbook.

1. Open Excel using one of the methods described in the "Opening Excel" QuickSteps.

2. Click the **Office Button**, and click **New**. The New Workbook dialog box, shown in Figure 1-3, is displayed. (Your Office Online section will probably look different from the one shown in the figure.)

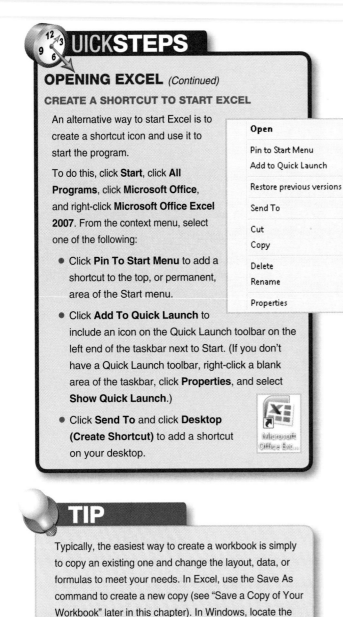

QUICKSTEPS

OPENING EXCEL *(Continued)*

CREATE A SHORTCUT TO START EXCEL

An alternative way to start Excel is to create a shortcut icon and use it to start the program.

To do this, click **Start**, click **All Programs**, click **Microsoft Office**, and right-click **Microsoft Office Excel 2007**. From the context menu, select one of the following:

- Click **Pin To Start Menu** to add a shortcut to the top, or permanent, area of the Start menu.

- Click **Add To Quick Launch** to include an icon on the Quick Launch toolbar on the left end of the taskbar next to Start. (If you don't have a Quick Launch toolbar, right-click a blank area of the taskbar, click **Properties**, and select **Show Quick Launch**.)

- Click **Send To** and click **Desktop (Create Shortcut)** to add a shortcut on your desktop.

Context menu:

Open

Pin to Start Menu
Add to Quick Launch

Restore previous versions

Send To ▶

Cut
Copy

Delete
Rename

Properties

TIP

Typically, the easiest way to create a workbook is simply to copy an existing one and change the layout, data, or formulas to meet your needs. In Excel, use the Save As command to create a new copy (see "Save a Copy of Your Workbook" later in this chapter). In Windows, locate the workbook you want to copy, right-click the file, and click **Copy**. Navigate to where you want the new workbook located, right-click the folder or the desktop, and click **Paste**.

3. Select one of the following options in the Blank And Recent area (double-click an icon or click a link to perform the action):

   - **Blank Workbook** allows you to create one or more worksheets from scratch and save them in a separate file.

   - **My Templates** provides access to templates or models of workbooks you've created and stored on your computer.

   - **New From Existing** opens the New From Existing Workbook dialog box, where you can browse for an existing workbook. Then you can modify it to suit your current purposes.

4. Alternatively, from the left pane, you can access templates provided by Excel (Installed Templates) or templates available from Office Online. Select a category (and subcategory, if applicable), click the template on which to base your workbook, and click **Create** (for templates stored on your computer) or click **Download** (for templates stored at Office Online).

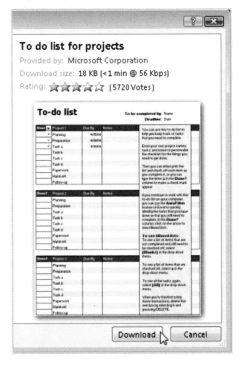

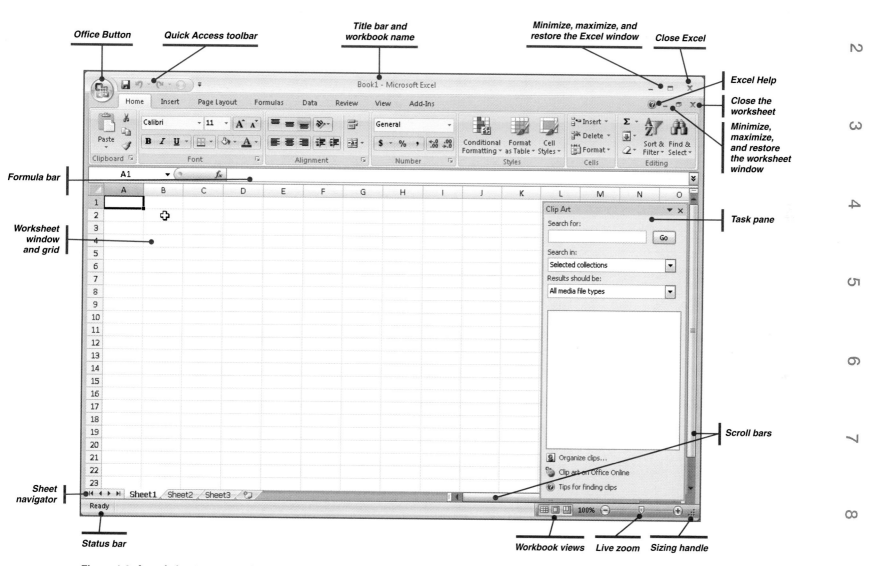

Office Button

Quick Access toolbar

Title bar and workbook name

Minimize, maximize, and restore the Excel window

Close Excel

Excel Help

Close the worksheet

Minimize, maximize, and restore the worksheet window

Formula bar

Worksheet window and grid

Task pane

Sheet navigator

Scroll bars

Status bar

Workbook views

Live zoom

Sizing handle

Figure 1-2: *A worksheet, supported by groups of tools, panes, and navigation controls, is the main focus of an Excel workbook.*

FEATURE	DESCRIPTION
Title bar and workbook name	Displays the workbook file name and can be dragged to move the window
Office Button	Opens a menu of commands that allow you perform actions on a workbook, such as Open, Save, and Print
Quick Access toolbar	Provides easy access to favorite tools
Ribbon	Container for available tools
Tabs	Organize groups of tools into areas of use
Group	Contains tools with common functionalities
Dialog box launcher	Opens a dialog box that provides further options
Help	Opens the Excel Help window, the gateway to online and offline assistance
Minimize, maximize, and restore the Excel window	Minimizes the Excel window to an icon on the Windows taskbar, maximizes the window to full screen, or restores the window to its previous size
Close Excel	Prompts you to save any unsaved work, exits Excel, and closes the window
Minimize, maximize, and restore the workbook window	Minimizes the workbook window to an icon at the bottom of the Excel window, maximizes the window to full size, or restores the window to its previous size
Formula bar	Displays a cell's contents and contains features for working with formulas and functions
Gallery	Displays visual examples of available options
Live preview	Displays results of options on a worksheet as you select or point to them
Worksheet grid	Provide the row-and-column structure where text, formulas, data, and supporting objects are added
Worksheet navigator	Allows easy access to all worksheets in a workbook
Scroll bars	Move the contents of the window in the direction they are clicked or dragged
Task pane	Contains controls for certain features in a pane that can be dragged around your screen and remain on top or "floating" on other screen elements
Status bar	Displays information on several workbook parameters, such as the sum of selected numbers, page numbers, and whether your CAPS LOCK key is enabled
Workbook views	Provides shortcuts for Normal, Page Layout, and Page Break Preview views
Live zoom	Displays the current zoom level and interactively changes the appearance of the worksheet as you click the Zoom button or drag the slider
Sizing handle	Sizes the window by dragging in one or two dimensions

Table 1-1: *Principal Features of the Excel Window*

UNDERSTANDING THE RIBBON

Where are the familiar menus? They've gone the way of black-and-white televisions and 40-MB hard drives. The original menu and toolbar structure used in Office products from the late '80s and early '90s (File, Edit, Format, Window, Help, and other menus) was designed in an era of fewer tasks and features that has simply outgrown its usefulness. Microsoft's solution to the increased number of feature enhancements is the *ribbon*, the container at the top of most Office program windows for the tools and features you are most likely to use to accomplish the task at hand (see Figure 1-4). The ribbon collects tools you are likely to use in *groups*. For example, the Font group provides the tools to work with text. Groups are organized into tabs, which bring together the tools to work on broader tasks. For example, the Insert tab contains groups that allow you to add components, such as tables, links, and charts, to your spreadsheet (or slide presentation or document).

Each Office program has a default set of tabs and additional tabs that become available as the context of your work changes. For example, when working on a picture, a Picture Tools-Format tab displays. The ribbon provides more screen real estate so that each of the tools (or commands) in the groups has a labeled button you can click. Depending on the tool, you are then presented with additional options in the form of a list of commands, a dialog box or task pane, or galleries of choices that reflect what you'll see in your work. Groups that contain more detailed tools than there is room for in the ribbon include a *dialog launcher* icon that takes you directly to these other choices.

The ribbon also takes advantage of slick new Office 2007 features, including a live preview of many potential changes

Continued . . .

CREATE A NEW WORKBOOK OUTSIDE OF EXCEL

Workbooks saved as templates (see "Save a Workbook Manually" and its associated Tip later in this chapter) and stored on your computer or network can be located in Windows and used to create a new workbook, which you can then open in Excel.

1. In Windows, use Search tools, Windows Explorer, or the desktop (if you have template files stored on it) to locate the template on which you want your workbook based.

2. Right-click the file and click **New**. Excel starts (if it is not already open) and displays a new workbook based on the template.

New
Open
Print
Open With...

Open an Existing Workbook

Opening an existing workbook is a simple matter of navigating to the file, within or outside of Excel.

OPEN AN EXISTING WORKBOOK IN EXCEL

1. Click the **Office Button**, and click **Open**. The Open dialog box appears, as shown in Figure 1-5.

2. In the Open dialog box, use the address bar or the navigation pane containing your favorite links and folders to browse to the folder that contains the workbook you want.

3. When you have located it, double-click the workbook.

   –Or–

   Click the workbook to select it, and click **Open**.

In either case, the workbook opens in Excel.

UNDERSTANDING THE RIBBON (Continued)

(for example, you can select text and see the text change color as you point to various colors in the Font Color gallery). Other new features that are co-located with the ribbon include the Office Button and the Quick Access toolbar. The Office Button menu (similar to the old File menu) lets you work *with* your document (such as saving it), as opposed to the ribbon, which centers on working *in* your document (such as editing and formatting). The Quick Access toolbar is similar to the Quick Launch toolbar in the Windows taskbar, providing an always-available location for your favorite tools. It starts out with a default set of tools, but you can add to it. See the accompanying sections and figures for more information on the ribbon and the other elements of the Excel window.

OPEN AN EXISTING WORKBOOK OUTSIDE OF EXCEL

1. In Windows, use Search tools, Windows Explorer, or the desktop (if you have template files stored on it) to locate the workbook you want to open.

2. Right-click the file and click **Open**. Excel starts (if it is not already open) and displays the workbook.

Change the Appearance of New Workbooks

You can customize how new workbooks are set up, saving you time otherwise spent manually adjusting several settings.

1. Click the **Office Button**, and click **Excel Options** at the bottom of the pane.

Excel Options   Exit Excel

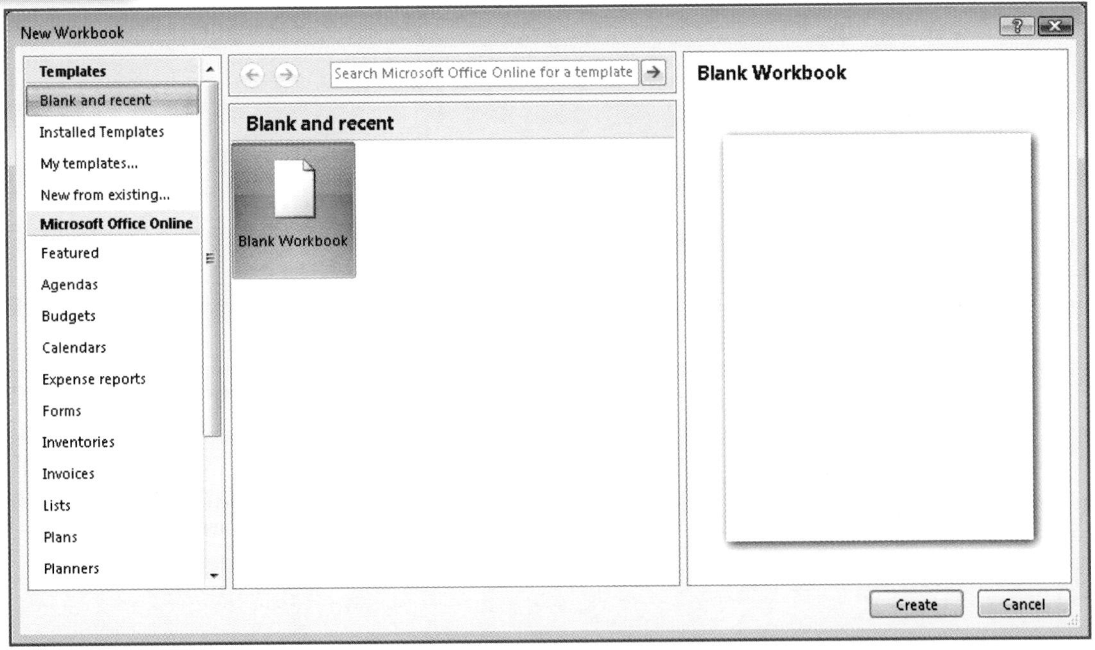

Figure 1-3: The New Workbook dialog box provides several ways to create a new workbook.

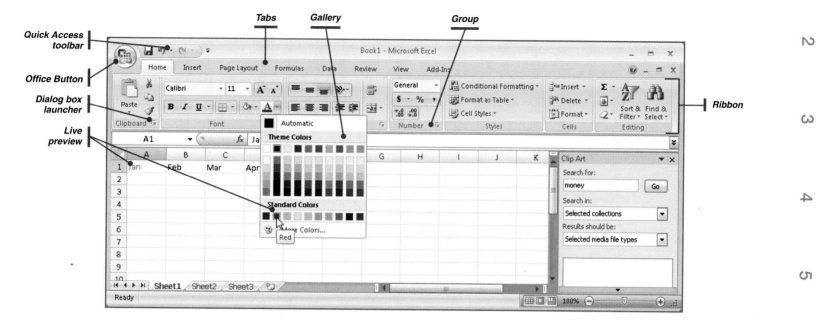

Quick Access toolbar

Office Button

Dialog box launcher

Live preview

Tabs **Gallery** **Group**

Ribbon

Figure 1-4: *The ribbon, containing groups of the most common tools, replaces the familiar Office menu and toolbar structure.*

TIP

The ribbon adapts to the size of your Excel window and your screen resolution, changing the size and shape of buttons and labels. See for yourself by maximizing the Excel window and noticing how the ribbon appears, and then clicking the **Restore** button on the title bar. Drag the right border of the Excel window toward the left, and see how the ribbon changes to reflect its decreasing real estate.

2. In the Excel Options dialog box, shown in Figure 1-6, click **Popular** in the left pane, and use the **When Creating New Workbooks** area to change one or more of the following settings:

- Click the **Use This Font** down arrow to display and select the font you want.

- Click the **Font Size** down arrow to display and select the text size you want (text size is listed by points; there are 72 points in an inch).

- Click the **Default View For New Sheets** down arrow to display and select an alternate view (see Chapter 5 for information on how you can change your layout to facilitate printing).

- Click the **Include This Many Sheets** spinner to increase or decrease the number of sheets included in the workbook. (You can easily add or remove sheets after a workbook is created—Chapter 3 describes how.)

3. Click **OK** when finished.

2

3

4

5

6

7

8

9

10

Navigation pane   Address bar

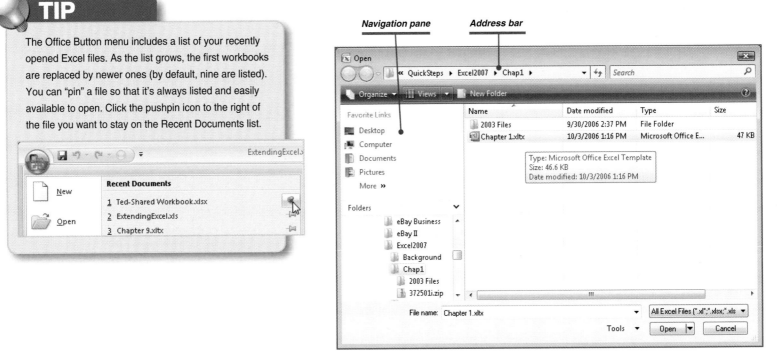

Figure 1-5: *The Open dialog box allows you to browse to an existing workbook.*

Customize the Quick Access Toolbar

You can provide one-click access to your favorite Excel tools by adding them to the Quick Access toolbar, which, by default, is to the right of the Office Button. The starter kit of tools includes Save, Undo, and Redo.

ADD OR REMOVE TOOLS FROM A LIST

1. Click the down arrow ⚊ to the right of the Quick Access toolbar, and click **More Commands**.

   –Or–

   Click the **Office Button**, click **Excel Options**, and click **Customize**.

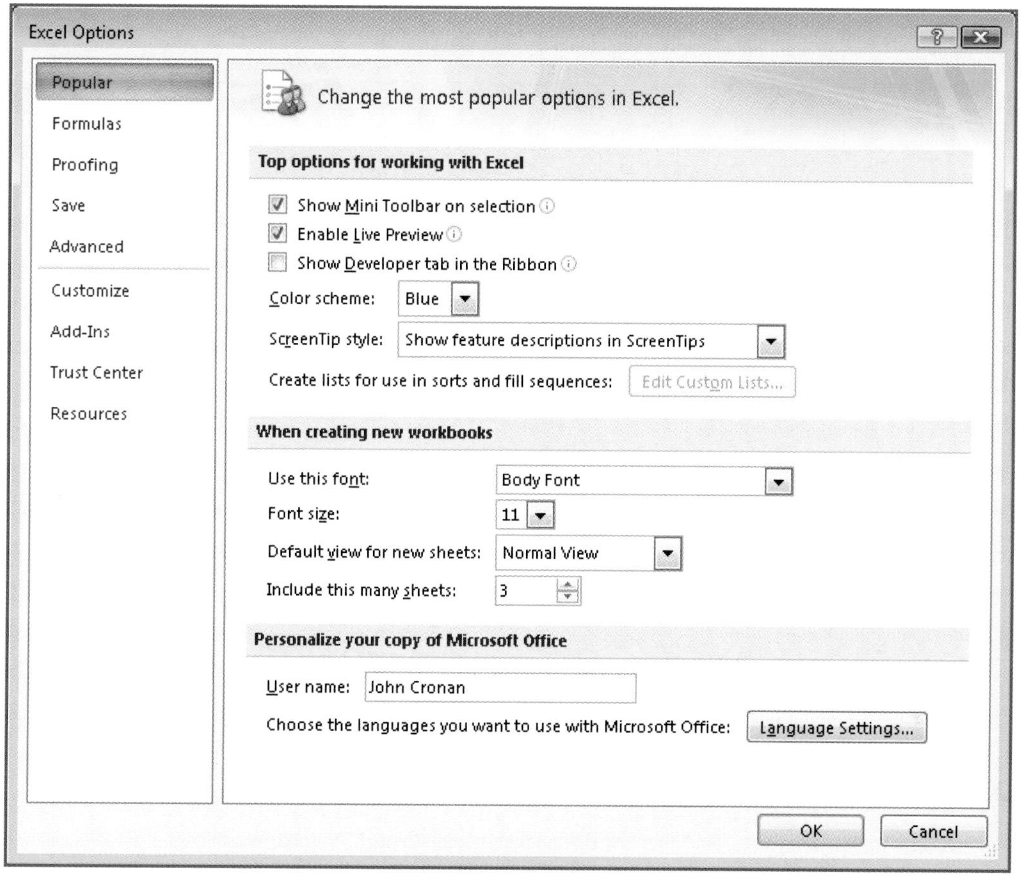

Figure 1-6: *You can create new workbooks to appear more to your liking.*

In either case, the Excel Options dialog box appears with the Customize options displayed, as shown in Figure 1-7.

2. Click the **Choose Commands From** down arrow, and click the tab or other option from the drop-down list to find the tool you are looking for.

3. Click the tool to select it, and click **Add** in the middle of the right pane. The tool appears in the list of current toolbar tools to the right.

4. To remove a tool from the toolbar, select it from the list on the right, and click **Remove**.

5. Click **OK** when finished.

2

3

4

5

6

7

8

9

10

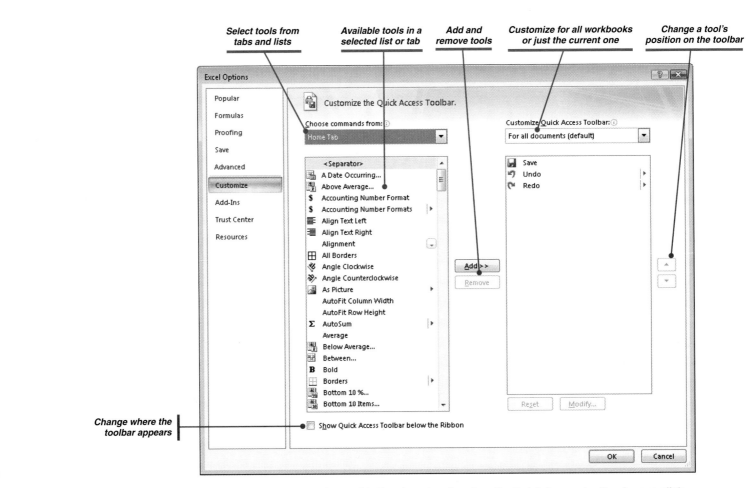

Select tools from tabs and lists

Available tools in a selected list or tab

Add and remove tools

Customize for all workbooks or just the current one

Change a tool's position on the toolbar

Change where the toolbar appears

Figure 1-7: *Any command or tool in Excel can be placed on the Quick Access toolbar for one-click access.*

ADD OR REMOVE TOOLS DIRECTLY ON THE TOOLBAR

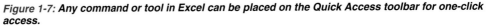

- To add a tool to the Quick Access toolbar, right-click a tool on the ribbon, and click **Add To Quick Access Toolbar**.

- To remove a tool from the Quick Access toolbar, right-click the tool and click **Remove From Quick Access Toolbar**.

TIP

You can hide the tools on the ribbon and show only the list of tabs, thereby providing more "real estate" within the Excel window for the worksheet. Right-click a tool on the Quick Access toolbar or on the ribbon, and click **Minimize The Ribbon**. Click a second time to restore the ribbon to its full height. Alternatively, double-click a tab name to minimize the ribbon; double-click a second time to restore it.

Book1 - Microsoft Excel

| Home | Insert | Page Layout | Formulas | Data | Review | View | Add-Ins |

A1

RELOCATE THE QUICK ACCESS TOOLBAR

You can display the Quick Access toolbar at its default position (above the ribbon) or directly below the ribbon using one of the following methods:

- Right-click a tool on the Quick Access toolbar or on the ribbon, and click **Place Quick Access Toolbar Below The Ribbon** (once located below the ribbon, you can move it above the ribbon in the same manner).

  –Or–

- In the Customize pane (click **Customize** in the Excel Options dialog box), click the **Show Quick Access Toolbar Below The Ribbon** check box, and click **OK** (to return the toolbar above the ribbon, open the pane and clear the check box).

CUSTOMIZE THE QUICK ACCESS TOOLBAR FOR A WORKBOOK

By default, changes made to the Quick Access toolbar are applicable to all workbooks. You can create a toolbar that only applies to the workbook you currently have open.

1. In the Customize pane, click the **Customize Quick Access Toolbar** down arrow.

2. Click the option that identifies the workbook the toolbar will apply to.

Customize Quick Access Toolbar: ⓘ

For all documents (default)

For all documents (default)

For Products Data.xlsx

3. Click **OK** when finished.

REARRANGE TOOLS ON THE QUICK ACCESS TOOLBAR

You can change the order in which tools appear on the Quick Access toolbar.

1. In the Customize pane, select the tool in the list on the right whose position you want to change.

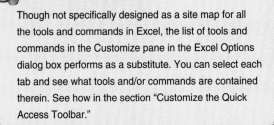

TIP

Though not specifically designed as a site map for all the tools and commands in Excel, the list of tools and commands in the Customize pane in the Excel Options dialog box performs as a substitute. You can select each tab and see what tools and/or commands are contained therein. See how in the section "Customize the Quick Access Toolbar."

TIP

You can check for new updates for Office, activate your copy of Office, attempt to repair problems, and contact Microsoft technical support from one handy location (see Figure 1-8). Click the **Office Button**, click **Excel Options**, click the **Resources** option, and click the button next to the service you want.

2. Click the up or down arrows to the right of the list to move the tool. Moving the tool up moves it to the left in the on-screen toolbar; moving it down the list moves it to the right in the on-screen toolbar.

3. Click **OK** when finished.

Get Help

Microsoft provides a vast amount of assistance to Excel users. If you have Internet access, you can automatically access the greater breadth of information available at the Microsoft Web site. When offline, information is limited to what is stored on your computer. Also, new to Excel 2007 are "super" tooltips that provide much more detailed explanatory information about tools when the mouse pointer is hovered over them.

Format Painter

Copy formatting from one place and apply it to another.

Double-click this button to apply the same formatting to multiple places in the document.

⊘ **Press F1 for more help.**

Figure 1-8: You can get assistance from Microsoft technical support on Excel and other Office programs.

Excel Options

Popular
Formulas
Proofing
Save
Advanced
Customize
Add-Ins
Trust Center
Resources

Contact Microsoft, find online resources, and maintain health and reliability of your Microsoft Office programs.

get updates   Check for Updates
Get the latest updates available for Microsoft Office.

run Microsoft Office Diagnostics   Diagnose
Diagnose and repair problems with your Microsoft Office programs.

contact us   Contact Us
Let us know if you need help, or how we can make Microsoft Office better.

activate Microsoft Office   Activate
Activation is required to continue using all the features in this product.

go to Microsoft Office Online   Go Online
Get free product updates, help, and online services at Microsoft Office Online.

about Microsoft Office Excel 2007   About
Microsoft® Office Excel® 2007

OK   Cancel

Open Help

You are never far from help on Excel. Access it using one of these techniques:

- Click the **Excel Help** question mark icon above the rightmost end of the ribbon.

  –Or–

- Press **F1**.

In either case, the Excel Help window opens, as shown in Figure 1-9.

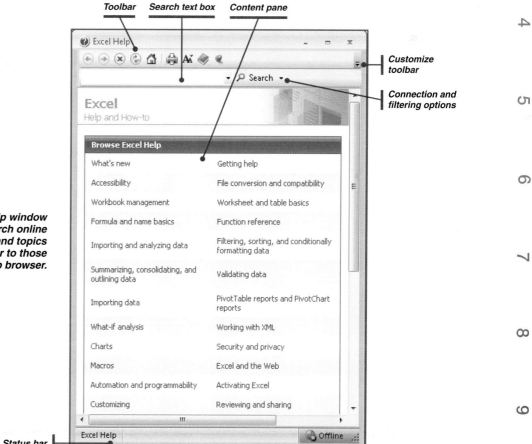

Figure 1-9: The Excel Help window allows you to search online and offline articles and topics using tools similar to those in a Web browser.

TIP

The first time you open the Excel Help window, it opens to a default position and size. You can reposition and resize the window, and Excel will remember your changes the next time you open Help.

TIP

Once you start down a path to locate information, you can easily lose track of where you are in the Help system. Instead of backing out of your current location, page by page, you can directly hop to the level from where you want to resume your search. Below the Search text box, a navigation bar indicates where you are in the Help hierarchy. Each level is a link that you can click to take a shortcut to the level you want.

Use the Excel Help Window

The Excel Help window provides a simple, no-nonsense gateway to volumes of topics, demos, and lessons on using Excel. The main focus of the window is a search box, supported by a collection of handy tools.

SEARCH FOR INFORMATION

1. Open the Excel Help window by clicking the **Excel Help** icon or pressing **F1**.

2. In the text box below the toolbar, type keywords that are relevant to the information you are seeking.

3. Click the **Search** down arrow to view the connection and filtering options for the search:

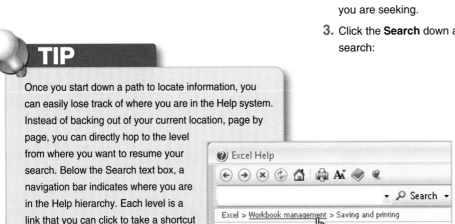

- **Connection options** allow you to choose between options from online (Content From Office Online) or offline (Content From This Computer) information. If you have an active Internet connection, Help automatically assumes you want online content each time you open the Help window.

- **Filtering options** let you limit your search to categories of information. For example, if you only want a template to create a family budget, under the online content heading, click **Excel Templates**. Your search results will only display templates.

4. Click the **Search** button when you are ready for Excel to search for your keywords.

You can have the list of top-level Help headings displayed in the initial Help page always available to you in the Help window. Click **Show Table Of Contents** on the toolbar. A Table of Contents pane displays to the left of the content pane.

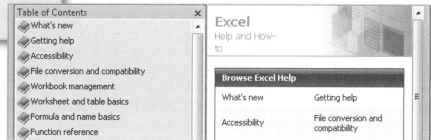

BROWSE FOR HELP

The initial Help window (shown in Figure 1-9) displays a list of Help categories similar to a table of contents. Click any of the headings to display a list of available topics and articles and/or subcategories of information. Continue following the links to drill down to the information you seek.

USE HELP TOOLS

Several tools are available to assist you in using Excel Help. The first collection of buttons contains standard Web browser tools. Table 1-2 describes these and the other Excel Help tools.

The Keep On Top tool only works in relationship to Office programs. If you are multitasking with non-Office programs, they will move to the forefront (on top) when active.

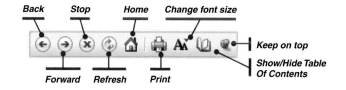

2   3   4   5   6   7   8   9   10

QUICK**FACTS**

UNDERSTANDING EXCEL'S XML FILE FORMATS

XML (eXtensible Markup Language) is rapidly becoming the de facto standard for a data-exchange format throughout modern computing. XML does for data what HTML (Hypertext Markup Language) did for the formatting of Web pages. By providing a consistent set of *tags* (or identifiers) for data, along with a road map of how that data is structured (a *schema*) and a file format that *transforms* the data from one use to another, documents can easily exchange information with Web services, programs, and other documents. XML was introduced to Office in its 2003 release, but it is fully embedded in Office 2007 programs. A key feature of the new file formats (identified by the "x" in the file extension, such as .xlsx) is how a file is now organized. Previously, a workbook was a single binary file, such as MyBudget.xls. Office 2007 XML files are actually a collection of several files and folders that all appear as a single file, such as the workbook, MyBudget.xlsx, or the template, MyBudgetTemplate.xltx (see Figure 1-10). XML provides several key advantages over binary files in addition to data parsing. XML files are:

- **Smaller**—They use ZIP compression to gain up to a 75 percent file size reduction.

- **More secure**—Executable code, such as VBA (Visual Basic for Applications), used in macros and ActiveX controls is segregated into more secure file packages, such as macro-enabled workbooks (.xlsm) and macro-enabled templates (.xltm).

- **More easily recovered**—Individual XML files can be opened in text readers such as Notepad, so it's not an all-or-nothing proposition when opening a corrupted file.

Continued . . .

TOOL	DESCRIPTION
Back and Forward	Allows you to move from the current Help page, one page at a time, in the respective direction
Stop	Halts the current attempt at loading a Help page (useful when loading an online demo if you have a slow connection speed)
Refresh	Reloads the current page to provide the most recent information
Home	Displays the Excel Help home page
Print	Opens a Print dialog box from which you can choose common printing options
Change Font Size	Opens a menu that lets you increase or decrease the size of text displayed in Help pages
Show/Hide Table Of Contents	Displays or removes a pane showing the list of highest-level Help categories
Keep/Not On Top	Keeps the Help window on top of the Excel (and other Office programs) window or allows it to move to the background when switching to the program

*Table 1-2: **Tools to Enhance Your Search for Excel Help***

Close Your Excel Workbook

When you are finished with your workbook, you need to save it and exit Excel. One way to make this more efficient is to get Excel to do save things automatically while you work.

Save a Workbook Automatically

As you work with a workbook, it is important to periodically save it. Having Excel do it automatically using AutoRecover will reduce the chance of losing data in case of a power failure or other interruption. To save your file automatically:

QUICKFACTS

UNDERSTANDING EXCEL'S XML FILE FORMATS *(Continued)*

So what does all this have to do with you if you simply want to create a worksheet to track your monthly cash flow? Fortunately, very little. All this XML tagging and multiple file organizing is done behind the scenes. As far as you're concerned, you have one file per workbook or template to save, copy, delete, or perform any standard file-maintenance actions upon.

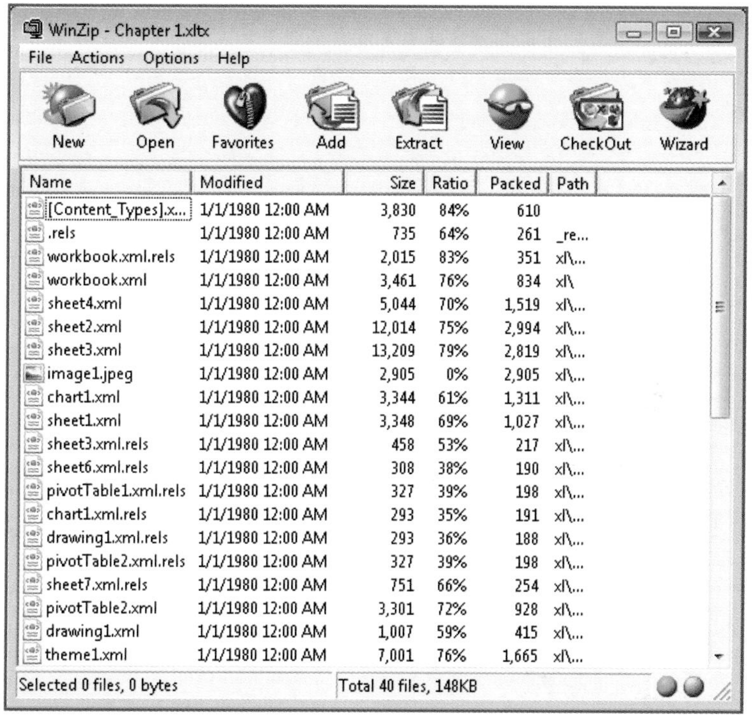

Figure 1-10: The default Excel workbook file format is a container for a myriad of XML files.

1. Click the **Office Button**, click **Excel Options**, and click the **Save** option. The Save settings are shown in Figure 1-11.

2. Under **Save Workbooks**, select the following settings:

   - Click the **Save Files In This Format** down arrow, and select the default file format in which to save workbooks (see the "Understanding Excel File Compatibility" and "Understanding Excel's XML File Formats" QuickFacts for more information on Excel file formats).

   - Ensure the **Save AutoRecover Information Every** check box is selected, and click the **Minutes** spinner to establish how often Excel will save your work. The shorter time selected will ensure you lose less work in the event of a problem, though you will find it a bit annoying if you decrease the time too much. Stay with the default and see how it works for you.

- Review the paths in the **AutoRecover File Location** and **Default File Location** text boxes. The AutoRecover file location is where you will find open files that are saved after a program or system problem. The Default file location is the initial file location that will appear in the Save As dialog box.

- If you want to remove AutoRecover protection for any open workbook, click the **AutoRecover Exceptions For** down arrow, and select the workbook. Click the **Disable AutoRecover For This Workbook Only** check box.

3. Click **OK** when finished.

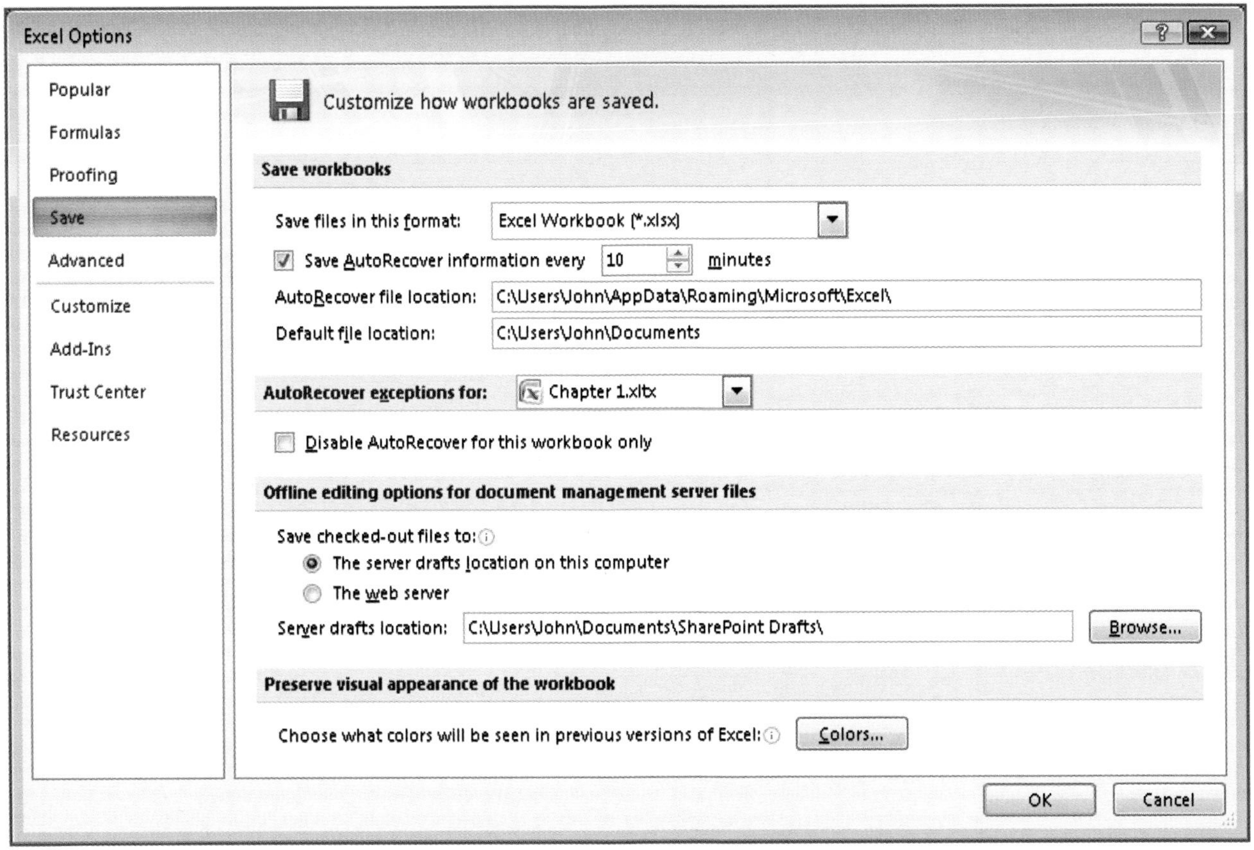

Excel Options

Popular
Formulas
Proofing
Save
Advanced
Customize
Add-Ins
Trust Center
Resources

Customize how workbooks are saved.

Save workbooks

Save files in this format: Excel Workbook (*.xlsx)

☑ Save AutoRecover information every 10 minutes

AutoRecover file location: C:\Users\John\AppData\Roaming\Microsoft\Excel\

Default file location: C:\Users\John\Documents

AutoRecover exceptions for: Chapter 1.xltx

☐ Disable AutoRecover for this workbook only

Offline editing options for document management server files

Save checked-out files to:
◉ The server drafts location on this computer
○ The web server

Server drafts location: C:\Users\John\Documents\SharePoint Drafts\   Browse...

Preserve visual appearance of the workbook

Choose what colors will be seen in previous versions of Excel: Colors...

OK   Cancel

Figure 1-11: Save settings let you fine-tune how AutoRecover automatically saves your Excel files.

Save a Workbook Manually

Even if you use AutoRecover, it's good practice to manually save your workbook after you have done any significant work. To save a workbook file:

- Click the **Office Button**, and click **Save**.

  –Or–

- Click the **Save** button on the Quick Access toolbar (see "Customize the Quick Access Toolbar" earlier in this chapter).

  –Or–

- Press **CTRL+S**.

If you haven't previously saved the workbook, the Save As dialog box will appear, as shown in Figure 1-12.

1. In the Save As dialog box, use the address bar or the navigation pane containing your favorite links and folders to browse to the folder where you want to save the workbook,

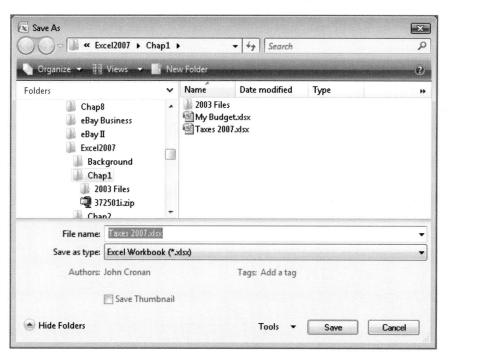

Figure 1-12: Give a workbook a name, location, and identifying information in the Save As dialog box.

TIP

To save a workbook as a template, an easily recognizable format on which to base future workbooks, follow the same steps as saving a workbook (see "Save a Workbook Manually"), but select **Excel Template (.xltx)** from the Save As Type drop-down list. (Templates, by default, are saved in a special Templates folder for Microsoft programs, C:\Users\ *currentusername*\AppData\Roaming\Microsoft\Templates.)

NOTE

A popular way to share documents is to convert them to a graphics-based format, such as Adobe PDF, that can be viewed by anyone using a free viewer program. Microsoft is introducing its own portable format, XPS (XML paper specification), and viewer. You can save Excel workbooks in the PDF or XPS formats from the Save As Type drop-down list in the Save As dialog box, but first you need to download a free add-in program from the Microsoft Office web site. Chapter 10 contains more information on PDF and XPS files.

Save a copy of the document

Excel Workbook
Save the workbook in the default file format.

Excel Macro-Enabled Workbook
Save the workbook in the XML-based and macro-enabled file format.

Excel Binary Workbook
Save the workbook in a binary file format optimized for fast loading and saving.

Excel 97-2003 Workbook
Save a copy of the workbook that is fully compatible with Excel 97-2003.

PDF or XPS
Publish a copy of the workbook as a PDF or XPS file.

if different from the default location. (If you don't see a navigation pane on the left side of the dialog box, click **Browse Folders**.)

2. Type a name for the workbook in the File Name text box.

3. Ensure the Save As Type box displays the correct file type. If not, click its down arrow, and select the file type you want.

4. Change or add identifying information. (More detailed document information can be added using a Document Information panel. See "Add Identifying Information" later in the chapter.)

5. Click **Save** when finished.

Save a Copy of Your Workbook

When you save a workbook under a different name, you create a copy of it. Both the original workbook and the newly named one will remain. To create a copy with a new name:

1. Click the **Office Button**, and click **Save As**.

2. In the Save As dialog box, use the address bar or the navigation pane containing your favorite links and folders to browse to the folder where you want to save the copy of the workbook, if different from the default location. (If you don't see a navigation pane on the left side of the dialog box, click **Browse Folders**.)

3. Type a name for the new workbook in the File Name text box.

4. Change any identifying information, and click **Save**.

Add Identifying Information

You can add identifying information to a workbook to make it easier to find during searches and when organizing files, especially in a shared environment (see Chapter 9 for more information on sharing Excel files).

1. Click the **Office Button**, click **Prepare**, and click **Properties** in the right pane. A Document Information panel containing standard identifiers displays under the ribbon, as shown in Figure 1-13.

2. Type identifying information, such as title, subject, and keywords (words or phrases that are associated with the workbook).

3. To view more information about the workbook, click **Standard** in the panel's title bar, and click **Advanced Properties**. Review each tab in the Properties dialog box to see the information available and make any changes or additions. Close the Properties dialog box when finished.

4. When finished with the Document Information panel, click the **Close** button (the "X") at the rightmost end of the panel's title bar to close it.

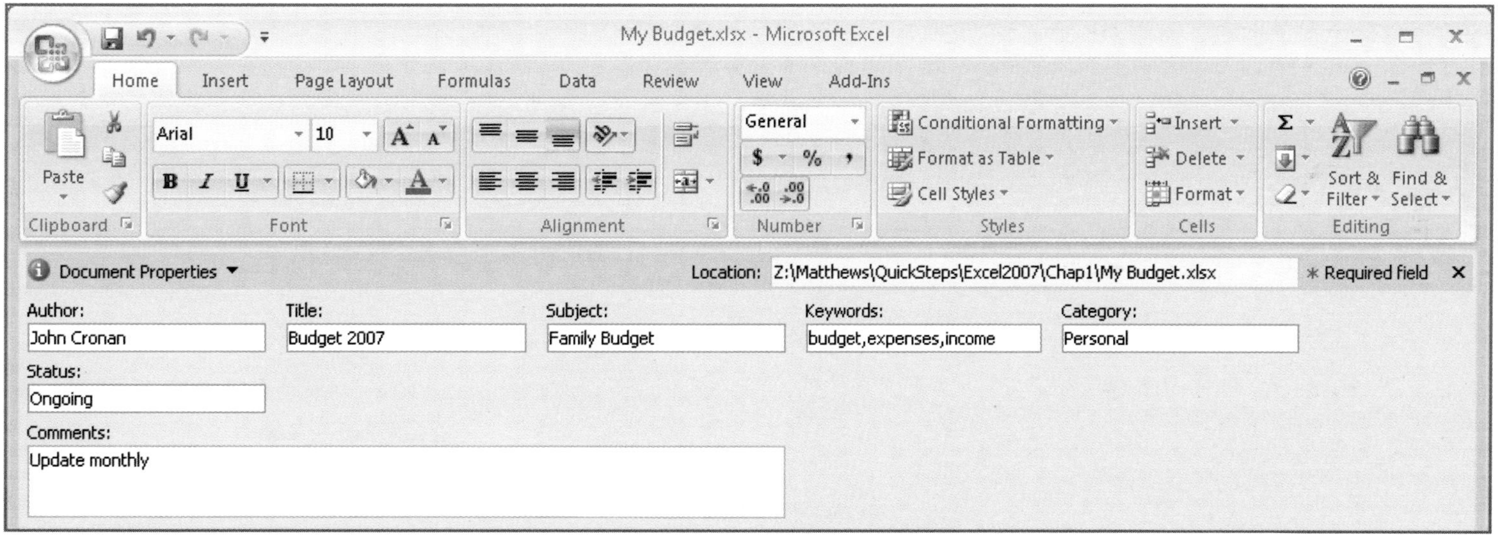

Figure 1-13: **You can more easily locate a workbook using search tools if you add identifying data.**

UNDERSTANDING EXCEL FILE COMPATIBILITY

Any time a version of Office is released with a new file format, sales of the antacid Maalox spike higher for several months (from anecdotal evidence, LOL). The default XML workbook in Excel 2007 is backward-compatible all the way to Excel 5.0/95, although Excel 2007 formatting and features will not be available. If you will be opening an Excel 2007 workbook in a more recent version of Excel (one that uses the Excel 97-2003 file format), you have a couple of options to do that. You can save a copy of your Excel 2007 workbook (.xlsx) in the Excel 97-2003 format (.xls) using the Save As dialog box. This option is preferable if you have no control over the computers the file will be used on. If you have control over the computer environment, you can install a File Format Compatibility Pack (available from the Microsoft Office Web site) on the computers running earlier versions of Excel. This set of updates and converters will allow those computers to open, edit, and save files in the Excel 2007 .xlsx format without manually creating a separate file copy.

Legacy Excel files opened in Excel 2007 can be edited and saved in their original format. Excel lets you know you are working with a workbook in an earlier file format by adding the words "Compatibility Mode" to the end of the workbook name in the Excel window title bar. Saving the file will keep the file in the legacy format, or you can convert the file to the Excel 2007 file format using the Save As Type drop-down list in the Save As dialog box.

ExtendingExcel.xls [Compatibility Mode] - Microsoft Excel

Exit an Excel Session

After you have saved the most recent changes to your workbook, you can close the workbook and exit Excel.

CLOSE THE WORKBOOK

1. Click the **Office Button**, and click **Close**.

2. If asked, click **Yes** to save any unsaved work. If you haven't previously saved the workbook, the Save As dialog box will appear so that you can locate where you want the file stored and name it (see "Save a Workbook Manually" earlier in the chapter).

EXIT EXCEL

- Click the **Office Button**, and click the **Exit Excel** button in the lower-right corner of the pane.

Excel Options   ✕ Exit Excel

–Or–

- Click the **Close** icon in upper-right corner of the Excel window.

—   ☐   **X**

How to...

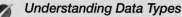 *Understanding Data Types*

• *Enter Text*

• *Enter Numeric Data*

Completing an Entry

• *Enter Dates*

• *Use Times*

Formatting Numbers

Understanding Excel Dates and Times

• *Edit Cell Data*

Adding Data Quickly

• *Remove Cell Contents*

• *Copy and Paste Data*

Selecting Cells and Ranges

• *Use Paste Special*

• *Find and Replace Data*

• *Verify Spelling*

• *Modify Automatic Corrections*

Chapter 2
Entering and Editing Data

Data is the heart and soul of Excel, yet before you can calculate data, chart it, analyze it, and otherwise *use* it, you have to place it on a worksheet. Data comes in several forms—such as numbers, text, dates, and times—and Excel handles the entry of each form uniquely. After you enter data into Excel's worksheets, you might want to make changes. Simple actions—such as removing text and numbers, copying and pasting, and moving data—are much more enhanced in Excel than the standard actions most users are familiar with.

In addition, Excel provides several tools to assist you in manipulating your data. You can have Excel intelligently continue a series without having to manually enter the sequential numbers or text. Automatic tools are available to help you verify accuracy and provide popups—small toolbars related to the task Excel you're working on. These, and other ways of entering and editing data, are covered in this chapter.

QUICK**FACTS**

UNDERSTANDING DATA TYPES

Cells in Excel are characterized by the type of data they contain. *Text* is comprised of characters that cannot be used in calculations. For example, "Quarterly revenue is not meeting projection." is text, and so is "1302 Grand Ave." *Numbers* are just that: numerical characters that can be used in calculations. *Dates* and *times* occupy a special category of numbers that can be used in calculations, and are handled in a variety of ways. Excel lets you know what it thinks a cell contains by its default alignment of a cell's contents; that is, text is left-aligned and numbers (including dates and times) are right-aligned by default.

Text–left-aligned   Number–right-aligned

	A	B
1	Supplies	23567
2		

D9

TIP

It is quite easy to lose track of the address of the cell you are currently working in. Excel provides several highly visible identifiers for the active cell: the Name box at the left end of the Formula bar displays the address; the column and row headings are highlighted in color; the Formula bar displays cell contents; and the cell borders are bold.

Enter Data

An Excel worksheet is a matrix, or grid, of lettered *column headings* across the top and numbered *row headings* down the side. The first row of a typical worksheet is used for column *headers*. The column headers represent categories of similar data. The rows beneath a column header contain data that is further categorized either by a row header along the leftmost column or listed below the column header. Figure 2-1 shows examples of two common worksheet arrangements. Worksheets can also be used to set up *tables* of data, where columns are sometimes referred to as *fields* and each row represents a unique *record* of data. Tables are covered in Chapter 8.

Each intersection of a row and column is called a *cell*, and is referenced first by its column location and then by its row location. The combination of a column letter and row number assigns each cell an *address*. For example, the cell at the intersection of column D and row 8 is called D8. A cell is considered to be *active* when it is clicked or otherwise selected as the place in which to place new data.

Enter Text

In an Excel worksheet, text is used to identify, explain, and emphasize numeric data. It comprises characters that cannot be used in calculations. You enter text by typing, just as you would in a word-processing program.

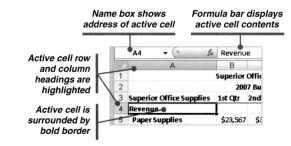

Name box shows
address of active cell

Formula bar displays
active cell contents

Active cell row and column headings are highlighted

Active cell is surrounded by bold border

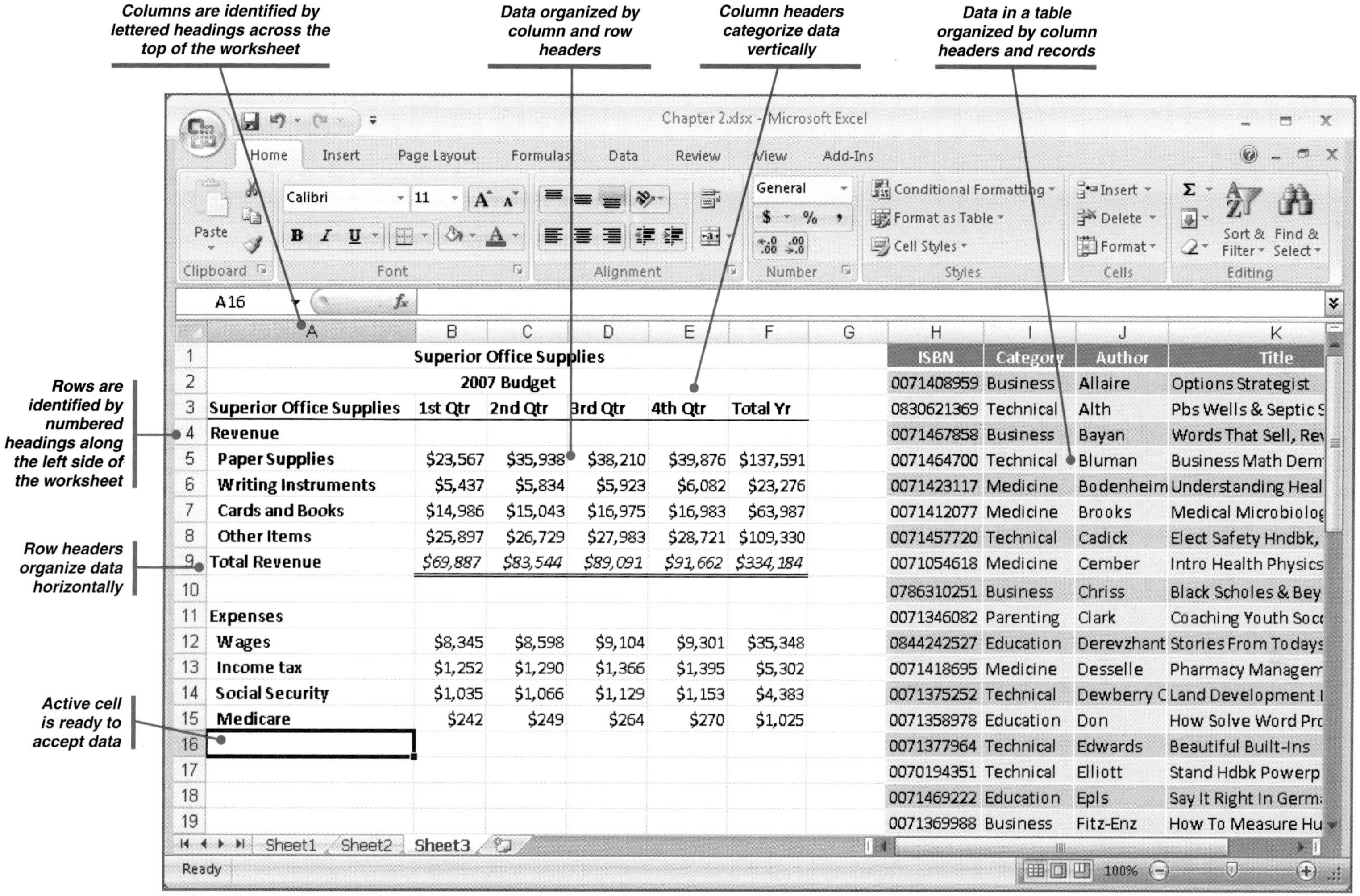

Figure 2-1: *The grid layout of Excel worksheets is defined by several components.*

Columns are identified by lettered headings across the top of the worksheet

Data organized by column and row headers

Column headers categorize data vertically

Data in a table organized by column headers and records

Rows are identified by numbered headings along the left side of the worksheet

Row headers organize data horizontally

Active cell is ready to accept data

	A	B	C	D	E	F	G	H	I	J	K
1		Superior Office Supplies						ISBN	Category	Author	Title
2		2007 Budget						0071408959	Business	Allaire	Options Strategist
3	Superior Office Supplies	1st Qtr	2nd Qtr	3rd Qtr	4th Qtr	Total Yr		0830621369	Technical	Alth	Pbs Wells & Septic S
4	Revenue							0071467858	Business	Bayan	Words That Sell, Rev
5	Paper Supplies	$23,567	$35,938	$38,210	$39,876	$137,591		0071464700	Technical	Bluman	Business Math Dem
6	Writing Instruments	$5,437	$5,834	$5,923	$6,082	$23,276		0071423117	Medicine	Bodenheim	Understanding Heal
7	Cards and Books	$14,986	$15,043	$16,975	$16,983	$63,987		0071412077	Medicine	Brooks	Medical Microbiolog
8	Other Items	$25,897	$26,729	$27,983	$28,721	$109,330		0071457720	Technical	Cadick	Elect Safety Hndbk,
9	Total Revenue	$69,887	$83,544	$89,091	$91,662	$334,184		0071054618	Medicine	Cember	Intro Health Physics
10								0786310251	Business	Chriss	Black Scholes & Bey
11	Expenses							0071346082	Parenting	Clark	Coaching Youth Socc
12	Wages	$8,345	$8,598	$9,104	$9,301	$35,348		0844242527	Education	Derevzhant	Stories From Todays
13	Income tax	$1,252	$1,290	$1,366	$1,395	$5,302		0071418695	Medicine	Desselle	Pharmacy Managem
14	Social Security	$1,035	$1,066	$1,129	$1,153	$4,383		0071375252	Technical	Dewberry C	Land Development
15	Medicare	$242	$249	$264	$270	$1,025		0071358978	Education	Don	How Solve Word Pro
16								0071377964	Technical	Edwards	Beautiful Built-Ins
17								0070194351	Technical	Elliott	Stand Hdbk Powerp
18								0071469222	Education	Epls	Say It Right In Germa
19								0071369988	Business	Fitz-Enz	How To Measure Hu

D14			fx		
	A	B	C	D	E
1					
2		$ 543			
3					
4		Cost of Goods Sold (Seattle property)			
5					
6		Cost of Goods Sold (Seattle property)			
7					
8					

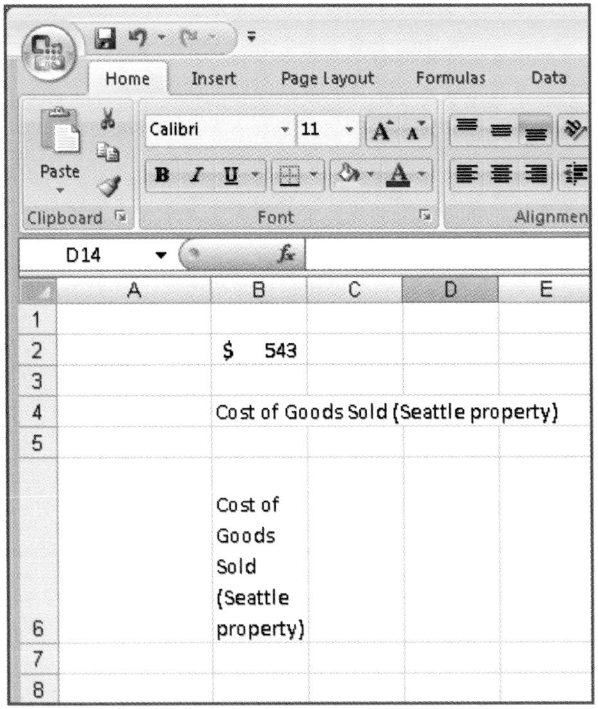

Figure 2-2: Text in a cell can cover several cells or be placed on multiple lines.

ENTER TEXT CONTINUOUSLY

Text (and numbers) longer than one cell width will appear to cover the adjoining cells to the right of the active cell. The covered cells have not been "used"; their contents have just been hidden, as shown in Figure 2-2. To enter text on one line:

1. Click the cell where you want the text to start.

2. Type the text. The text displays in one or more cells. (See Chapter 3 for more information on changing cell width.)

3. Complete the entry. (See the "Completing an Entry" QuickSteps later in the chapter for several ways to do that.)

WRAP TEXT ON MULTIPLE LINES

You can select a cell and wrap text at the end of its column width, much like how a word-processing program wraps text to the next line when entered text reaches its right margin.

1. Click the cell where you want to enter text.

2. Type all the text you want to appear in a cell. The text will continue to the right, overlapping as many cells as its length dictates (see row 4 in Figure 2-2).

3. Press **ENTER** to complete the entry. (See the "Completing an Entry" QuickSteps later in the chapter.) Click the cell a second time to select it.

4. Click the **Home** tab at the left end of the ribbon. In the Alignment group, click the **Wrap Text** button. The text wraps within the confines of the column width, increasing the row height as necessary (see row 6 in Figure 2-2).

CONSTRAIN TEXT ON MULTIPLE LINES

When you want to constrain the length of text in a cell:

1. Click the cell where you want to enter text.

2. Type the text you want to appear on the first line.

NOTE

See Chapter 3 for ways to increase column width to accommodate the length of text in a cell.

TIP

If you are a keyboard junkie, you'll love the new KeyTips to access tools on the ribbon. Start by pressing **ALT** to place lettered KeyTips on the first level of tools on the ribbon. Press a letter corresponding to the tab or tool you want and if there are additional tools available, they will display. For example, press **ALT** to display KeyTips for the tabs on the ribbon. Press **N** to see the KeyTips available on the Insert menu. Press **T** to insert a table. Remove the KeyTips by pressing **ALT** a second time.

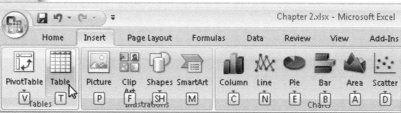

NOTE

The *beginning cell* is in the same column where you first started entering data. For example, if you started entering data in cell A5 and continued through E5, pressing **TAB** between entries A5 through D5 and pressing **ENTER** in E5, the active cell would move to A6 (the first cell in the next row). If you had started entering data in cell C5, after pressing **ENTER** at the end of that row of entries, the active cell would move to C6, the cell below it.

TIP

You can cause a number to be interpreted by Excel as text by typing an apostrophe (') in front of it and completing the entry. The "number" is left-aligned as text and a green triangle is displayed in the upper-left corner of the cell (the apostrophe is not displayed). When selected, an error icon displays next to the cell, indicating a number is stored as text.

3. Press **ALT+ENTER**. The insertion point moves to the beginning of a new line.

4. Repeat steps 2 and 3 for any additional lines of text. (See row 6 in Figure 2-2.)

5. Complete the entry. (See the "Completing an Entry" QuickSteps.)

Enter Numeric Data

Numbers are numerical data, from the simplest to the most complex. Excel provides several features to help you more easily work with numbers used to represent values in various categories, such as currency, accounting, and mathematics.

ENTER NUMBERS

Enter numbers by simply selecting a cell and typing the numbers.

1. Click the cell where you want the numbers entered.

2. Type the numbers. Use decimal places, thousands separators, and other formatting as you type, or have Excel format these things for you. (See the "Formatting Numbers" QuickSteps later in this chapter).

3. Complete the entry. (See the "Completing an Entry" QuickSteps.)

G	H
	ISBN
◇	0071408959

TIP

You can convert a number to scientific notation from the Home tab Number group on the ribbon. Click the **Number Format** down arrow, and click **Scientific** near the bottom of the list. To set the number of decimal places, click the **Increase Decimal** or **Decrease Decimal** buttons at the bottom of the Number group.

UICKSTEPS

COMPLETING AN ENTRY

You can complete an entry using the mouse or the keyboard, and control where the active cell goes next.

STAY IN THE ACTIVE CELL

To complete an entry and keep the current cell active, click **ENTER** on the Formula bar.

MOVE THE ACTIVE CELL TO THE RIGHT

To complete the entry and move to the next cell in the same row, press **TAB**.

MOVE THE ACTIVE CELL TO THE NEXT ROW

To complete the entry and move the active cell to the next row, press **ENTER**. The active cell moves to the *beginning cell* in the next row.

Continued ...

ENTER NUMBERS USING SCIENTIFIC NOTATION

Exponents are used in scientific notation to shorten (or round off) very large or small numbers. The shorthand scientific notation display does not affect how the number is used in calculations.

1. Click the cell where you want the data entered.
2. Type the number using three components:
   - **Base.** For example: 4, 7.56, -2.5.
   - **Scientific notation identifier.** Type the letter "e" to represent the number is based on powers (exponents) of 10.
   - **Exponent.** The number of times 10 is multiplied by itself. Positive exponent numbers increment the base number to the right of the decimal point, negative numbers to the left. For example, scientific notation for the number 123,456,789.0 is written to two decimal places as 1.23×10^8. In Excel you would type 1.23e8, and it would display as: 1.23E+08
3. Complete the entry. (See the "Completing an Entry" QuickSteps.)

Enter Dates

If you can think of a way to enter a date, Excel can probably recognize it as such. For example, Table 2-1 shows how Excel handles different ways to make the date entry using the date of March 1, 2007 (assuming it is sometime in 2007) in a worksheet.

In cases when a year is omitted, Excel assumes the current year.

TYPING THIS...	DISPLAYS THIS AFTER COMPLETING THE ENTRY
3/1, 3-1, 1-mar, or 1-Mar	1-Mar
3/1/07, 3-1-07, 3/1/2007, 3-1-2007, 3-1/07, or 3-1/2007	3/1/2007
Mar 1, 07, March 1, 2007, 1-mar-07, or 1-Mar-2007	1-Mar-07

*Table 2-1: **Examples of Excel Date Formats***

UICKSTEPS

COMPLETING AN ENTRY *(Continued)*

CHANGE THE DIRECTION OF THE ACTIVE CELL

1. Click the **Office Button**, click **Excel Options**, and click the **Advanced** option.

2. Under Editing Options, click **After Pressing Enter, Move Selection** to select it if it is not already selected.

3. Click the **Direction** down arrow, and click a direction. Down is the default.

4. Click **OK** when finished.

MOVE THE ACTIVE CELL TO ANY CELL

To complete the entry and move the active cell to any cell in the worksheet, click the cell you want to become active.

Editing options

☑ After pressing Enter, move selection
Direction: Down ▾
☐ Automatica Down   ecimal point
Places: Right
☑ Enable fill h Up   ell drag-and-drop
            Left
☑ Alert before overwriting cells

NOTE

Formatting also can be applied to cells in advance of entering numbers (or text) so that the attributes are displayed as you complete the entry. Simply select the cells, and apply the formatting. See the "Selecting Cells and Ranges" QuickSteps later in the chapter for ways to select cells.

TIP

In Excel, you can tell what short date setting is currently in use by clicking a cell with a date in it and seeing what appears in the Formula bar.

	fx	12/4/2006
	B	C
		4-Dec

CHANGE THE DEFAULT DISPLAY OF DATES

Two common date formats (long and short) are displayed by default in Excel from settings in the Windows Regional And Language Options feature in Control Panel, shown in Figure 2-3.

1. In Windows Vista, click **Start** and click **Control Panel**.

2. In Control Panel Home's Category view, click the **Clock, Language, And Region** category, and then click **Regional And Language Options**.

   –Or–

   In Classic view, double-click **Regional And Language Options**.

3. On the Formats tab, click **Customize This Format**.

4. Click the **Date** tab, click the **Short Date Format** down arrow, and select a format. Similarly, change the long date format, as necessary.

5. Click **OK** twice and close Control Panel.

FORMAT DATES

You can change how a date is displayed in Excel by choosing a new format.

1. Right-click the cell that contains the date you want to change. (See the "Selecting Cells and Ranges" QuickSteps later in the chapter to see how to apply formats to more than one cell at a time.)

2. Click **Format Cells** on the context menu. The Format Cells dialog box appears with the Date category selected in the Number tab, as shown in Figure 2-4.

3. Select a format from the Type list. You can see how the new date format affects your date in the Sample area. Click **OK** when finished.

Use Times

Excel's conventions for time are as follows:

- Colons (:) are used as separators between hours, minutes, and seconds.
- AM is assumed unless you specify PM or when you enter a time from 12:00 to 12:59.

UICKSTEPS

FORMATTING NUMBERS

Numbers in a cell can be formatted in any one of several numeric categories by first selecting the cell containing the number. You can then use the tools available in the Home tab Number group or have the full range of options available to you from the Format Cells dialog box.

DISPLAY THE NUMBER TAB

Click the **Dialog Box Launcher** arrow in the lower-right corner of the Number group. The Format Cells dialog box appears with the Number tab displayed (shown in Figure 2-5).

ADD OR DECREASE DECIMAL PLACES

1. On the Number tab of the Format Cells dialog box, choose the appropriate numeric category (Number, Currency, Accounting, Percentage, or Scientific) from the Category list box.

2. In the Decimal Places text box, enter a number or use the spinner to set the number of decimal places you want. Click **OK**.

   –Or–

   In the ribbon's Home tab Number group, click the **Increase Decimal** or **Decrease Decimal** buttons.

ADD A THOUSANDS SEPARATOR

On the Number tab of the Format Cells dialog box, click the **Number** category, and click **Use 1000 Separator (,)**. Click **OK**.

–Or–

In the ribbon's Home tab Number group, click the **Comma Style** button in the Number group.

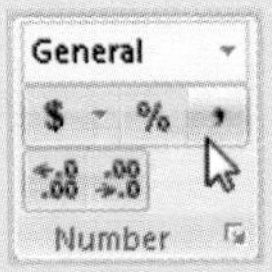

Continued . . .

- AM and PM do not display in the cell if they are not entered.
- You specify PM by entering a space followed by "p," "P," "pm," or "PM."
- Seconds are not displayed in the cell if not entered.
- AM, PM, and seconds are displayed in the Formula bar of a cell that contains a time.

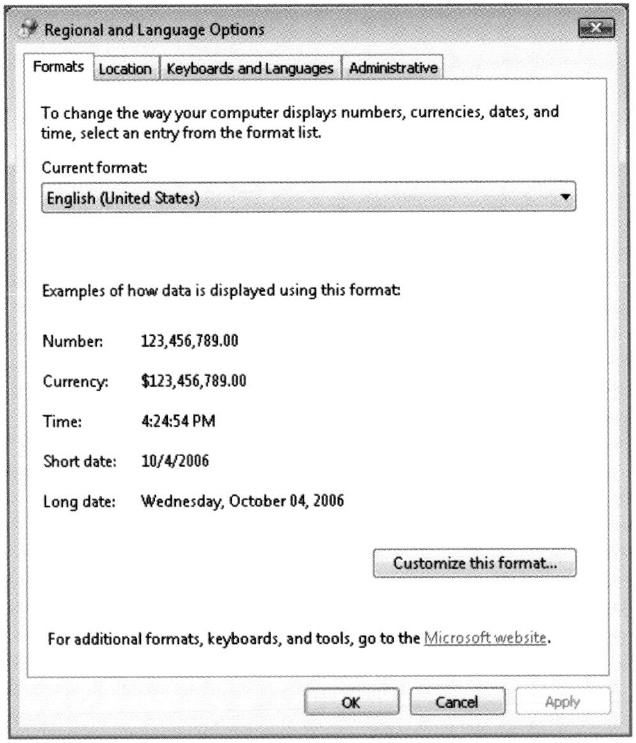

Figure 2-3: Use Windows to change how Excel and other Windows programs display dates.

ENTER TIMES

1. Select the cell in which you want to enter a time.
2. Type the hour followed by a colon.
3. Type the minutes followed by a colon.
4. Type the seconds, if needed.

FORMATTING NUMBERS (Continued)

ADD A CURRENCY SYMBOL

1. On the Number tab, choose the appropriate numeric category (Currency or Accounting) from the Category list box.

2. Click **OK** to accept the default dollar sign ($), or choose another currency symbol from the Symbol drop-down list, and click **OK**.

   –Or–

   Click the **Accounting Number Format** button in the Number group. (You can change the currency symbol by clicking the down arrow next to the current symbol and choosing another one.)

CONVERT A DECIMAL TO A FRACTION

1. On the Number tab, click the **Fraction** category.

2. Click the type of fraction you want. View it in the Sample area, and change the type if needed. Click **OK**.

CONVERT A NUMBER TO A PERCENTAGE

1. On the Number tab, click the **Percentage** category.

2. In the Decimal Places text box, enter a number or use the spinner to set the number of decimal places you want. Click **OK**.

   –Or–

   Click the **Percent Style** button in the Number group.

FORMAT ZIP CODES, PHONE NUMBERS, AND SSNS

1. On the Number tab, click the **Special** category.

2. Select the type of formatting you want. Click **OK**.

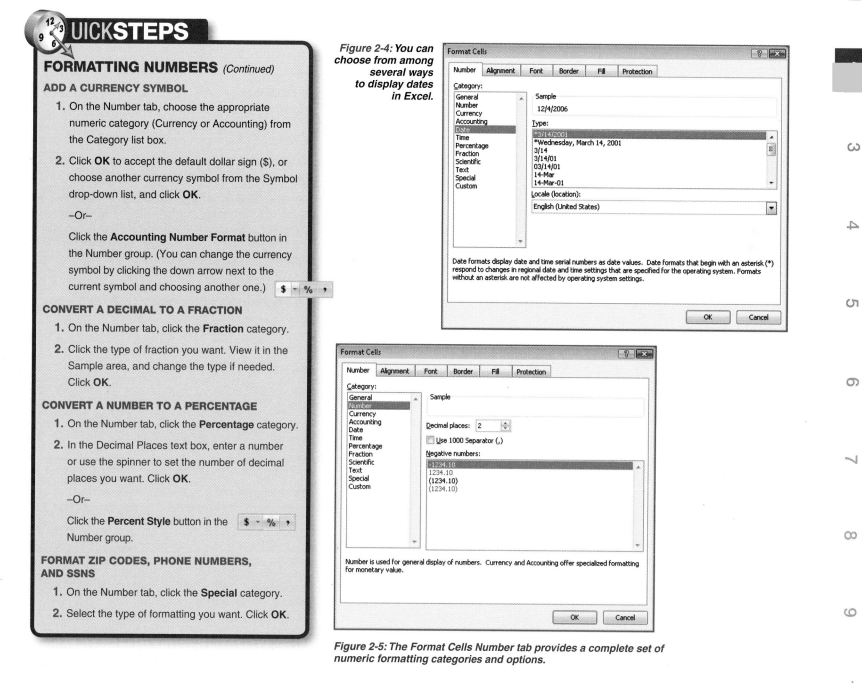

Figure 2-4: You can choose from among several ways to display dates in Excel.

Figure 2-5: The Format Cells Number tab provides a complete set of numeric formatting categories and options.

5. Type a space and PM, if needed.

6. Complete the entry.

CHANGE THE DEFAULT DISPLAY OF TIMES

Times are displayed by default in Excel from settings configured in the Windows Regional And Language Options feature of Control Panel. To change the default settings:

1. In Windows Vista, click **Start** and click **Control Panel**.

2. In Category view, click the **Clock**, **Language**, **And Region** category, and then click **Regional And Language Options**.

–Or–

In Classic view, double-click **Regional And Language Options**.

3. On the Formats tab, click **Customize This Format**.

4. Click the **Time** tab, click the **Time Format** down arrow, and select a format. Similarly, change the AM and PM format, as necessary.

Time format:	h:mm:ss tt	▼
AM symbol:	AM	▼
PM symbol:	PM	▼

5. Click **OK** twice and close Control Panel.

FORMAT TIMES

You can change how a time is displayed in Excel by choosing a new format.

1. Select the cell that contains the time you want to change. (See the "Selecting Cells and Ranges" QuickSteps later in the chapter for how to apply formats to more than one cell at a time.)

2. Click the **Dialog Box Launcher** arrow in the Home tab Number group. The Format Cells dialog box appears with the Number tab displaying the Time category.

3. Under Type, select a format. You can see how the new time format will affect your time in the Sample area. Click **OK** when finished.

Edit Data

The data-intensive manner of Excel necessitates easy ways to change, copy, or remove data already entered on a worksheet. In addition, Excel has facilities to help you find and replace data and check the spelling.

Edit Cell Data

You have several choices on how to edit data, depending on whether you want to replace all the contents of a cell or just part of the contents, and whether you want to do it in the cell or in the Formula bar.

EDIT CELL CONTENTS

To edit data entered in a cell:

- Double-click the text in the cell where you want to begin editing. An insertion point is placed in the cell. Type the new data, use the mouse to select characters to be overwritten or deleted, or use keyboard shortcuts. Complete the entry when finished editing. (See the "Completing an Entry" QuickSteps earlier in the chapter.)

  January

  –Or–

- Select the cell to edit, and then click the cell's contents in the Formula bar where you want to make changes. Type the new data, use the mouse to select characters to overwrite or delete, or use keyboard shortcuts. Click **Enter** on the Formula bar or press **ENTER** to complete the entry.

  –Or–

- Select the cell to edit, and press **F2**. Edit in the cell or on the Formula bar using the mouse or keyboard shortcuts. Complete the entry.

ADDING DATA QUICKLY

Excel provides several features that help you quickly add more data to existing data with a minimum of keystrokes.

USE AUTOCOMPLETE

Excel will complete an entry for you after you type the first few characters of data that appears in a previous entry in the same column. Simply press **ENTER** to accept the completed entry. To turn off this feature if you find it bothersome:

1. Click the **Office Button**, click **Excel Options**, and click the **Advanced** option.

2. Under Editing Options, click **Enable AutoComplete For Cell Values** to remove the check mark.

FILL DATA INTO ADJOINING CELLS

1. Select the cell that contains the data you want to copy into adjoining cells.

2. Point to the fill handle in the lower-right corner of the cell. The pointer turns into a cross.

3. Drag the handle in the direction you want to extend the data until you've reached the last cell in the range you want to fill.

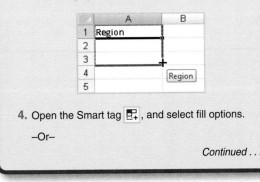

4. Open the Smart tag, and select fill options.

–Or–

Continued . . .

REPLACE ALL CELL CONTENTS

Click the cell and type new data. The original data is deleted and replaced by your new characters.

CANCEL CELL EDITING

Before you complete a cell entry, you can revert back to your original data by pressing **ESC** or clicking **Cancel** on the Formula bar.

Remove Cell Contents

You can easily delete cell contents, move them to other cells, or clear selective attributes of a cell.

DELETE DATA

Remove all contents (but not formatting) from a cell by selecting it and pressing **DELETE**. You can delete the contents of more than one cell by selecting the cells or range and pressing **DELETE**. (See the "Selecting Cells and Ranges" QuickSteps for more information on selecting various configurations.)

MOVE DATA

Cell contents can be removed from one location and placed in another location of equal size. Select the cell or range you want to move. Then:

- Place the pointer on any edge of the selection, except the lower-right corner, until it turns into a cross with arrowhead tips. Drag the cell or range to the new location.

11	Expenses				
12	Wages	$8,345	$8,598	$9,104	$9,301	$35,348
13	Income tax	$1,252	$1,290	$1,366	$1,395	$5,302
14	Social Security	$1,035	$1,066	$1,129	$1,153	$4,383
15	Medicare	$242	$249	$264	$270	$1,025
16						
17						

–Or–

QUICKSTEPS

ADDING DATA QUICKLY *(Continued)*

Select the contiguous cells you want to fill in with the data in a cell (see the "Selecting Cells and Ranges" QuickSteps later in the chapter). In the Home tab Editing group, click the **Fill** button ⬇▾.

CONTINUE A SERIES OF DATA

Data can be *logically* extended into one or more adjoining cells. For example, 1 and 2 extend to 3, 4...; Tuesday extends to Wednesday, Thursday...; January extends to February, March...; and 2004 and 2005 extend to 2006, 2007....

1. Select the cell or cells that contain a partial series. (See the "Selecting Cells and Ranges" Quick-Steps later in the chapter for more information on selecting more than one cell.)

2. Point to the fill handle in the lower-right corner of the last cell. The pointer turns into a cross.

3. Drag the handle in the direction you want until you've reached the last cell in the range to complete the series.

	A	B
1	January	
2		
3		
4		March
5		

–Or–

1. Select the partial series, and continue the selection to as many contiguous cells you want. In the Home tab Editing group, click the **Fill** down arrow, and click **Series**.

2. Verify the series parameters are what you want (see Figure 2-6), and click **OK**.

Continued . . .

- On the Home tab Clipboard group, click **Cut**. Select the new location, and click **Paste** in the Clipboard group. (See "Copy and Paste Data" and "Use Paste Special" later in this chapter for more information on pasting options.)

REMOVE SELECTED CELL CONTENTS

A cell can contain several components, including:

- **Formats**—Consisting of number formats, conditional formats (formats that display if certain conditions apply), and borders.

- **Contents**—Consisting of formulas and data.

- **Comments**—Consisting of notes you attach to a cell.

1. Choose which cell components you want to clear by selecting the cell or cells.

2. On the Home tab Editing group, click the **Clear** button, and click the applicable item from the menu. (Clicking **Clear Contents** performs the same action as pressing **DELETE**.)

Figure 2-6: You can fine-tune how you want a series to continue.

QUICKSTEPS

ADDING DATA QUICKLY (Continued)

REMOVE THE FILL HANDLE

To hide the fill handle and disable AutoFill:

1. Click the **Office Button**, click **Excel Options**, and click the **Advanced** option.

2. Under Editing Options, click **Enable Fill Handle And Cell Drag And Drop** to remove the check mark.

ENTER DATA FROM A LIST

Previously entered data in a column is available to be selected from a list and entered with a click.

| Business |
| Education |
| Education |

| Business |
| Education |
| Medicine |
| Parenting |
| Technical |
| Business |

1. Right-click a cell in a column of data.

2. Select **Pick From Drop-Down List** from the context menu, and then click the data you want to enter in the cell.

TIP

To undo a data-removal action, even if you have performed several actions since removing the data, click **Undo** on the Quick Access toolbar next to the Office Button (or press **CTRL+Z**) for the most recent action. For earlier actions, continue clicking **Undo** to work your way back; or click the down arrow next to the button, and choose the action from the drop-down list.

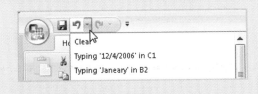

| Clear |
| Typing '12/4/2006' in C1 |
| Typing 'Janeary' in B2 |

Copy and Paste Data

Data you've already entered on a worksheet can be copied to the same or other worksheets, or even to other Windows applications (see Chapter 10 for information on using data with other programs). You first *copy* the data to the Windows Clipboard, where it is temporarily stored. After selecting a destination for the data, you *paste* it into the cell or cells. You can copy all the data in a cell or only part of it.

1. Select the cells that contain the data you want to copy; or double-click a cell, and select the characters you want to copy.

2. In the Home tab Clipboard group, click the **Copy** button, or press **CTRL+C**. The selected data is copied to the Clipboard and the border around the cells displays a flashing dotted line.

| Cards and Books | $14,986 | $15,043 |

3. Select the new location for the data. In the Clipboard group, click **Paste** or press **CTRL+V**. The selected data is entered into the new cells. (If you click the **Paste** down arrow, you will see a menu of other paste options. Most of these options are covered in "Use Paste Special," next, and the others are related to features described in other chapters in this book.)

4. Click the **Smart** tag next to the pasted data, and choose the formatting or other options you want.

○	Keep Source Formatting
◉	Use Destination Theme
○	Match Destination Formatting
○	Values and Number Formatting
○	Keep Source Column Widths
○	Formatting Only
○	Link Cells

5. Repeat steps 3 and 4 to paste the copied data to other locations. Press **ESC** when finished to remove the flashing border around the source cells.

TIP

To select larger numbers of adjacent cells, rows, or columns, click the first item in the group, and then press **SHIFT** while clicking the last item in the group.

QUICKSTEPS

SELECTING CELLS AND RANGES

The key to many actions in Excel is the ability to select cells in various configurations and use them to perform calculations. You can select a single cell, nonadjacent cells, and adjacent cells (or *ranges*).

SELECT A SINGLE CELL

Select a cell by clicking it, or move to a cell using the arrow keys or by completing an entry in a cell above or to the left.

SELECT NONADJACENT CELLS

Select a cell and then press **CTRL** while clicking the other cells you want to select.

SELECT A RANGE OF ADJACENT CELLS

Select a cell and drag over the additional cells you want to include in the range.

SELECT ALL CELLS ON A WORKSHEET

Click the **Select All** button in the upper-left corner of the worksheet, or press **CTRL+A**.

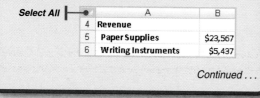

Continued . . .

Use Paste Special

Paste Special allows you to selectively include or omit formulas, values, formatting, comments, arithmetic operations, and other cell properties *before* you copy or move data. (See Chapter 4 for information on formulas, values, and arithmetic operations.) This tool offers more options than the Paste Smart tag used *after* you paste.

1. Select and then copy or cut the data you want.
2. Select the destination cell or cells to where you want the data copied or moved.
3. In the Home tab Clipboard group, click the **Paste** down arrow, and click **Paste Special**; or right-click the destination cells, and click **Paste Special**. The Paste Special dialog box appears, as shown in Figure 2-7.
4. Select the paste options you want in the copied or moved cells, and click **OK**.

Find and Replace Data

In worksheets that might span thousands of rows and columns (over one million rows and over 16,000 columns are possible), you need the ability to locate data quickly, as well as to find instances of the same data so that consistent replacements can be made.

FIND DATA

1. In the Home tab Editing group, click **Find & Select**, and click **Find**; or press **CTRL+F** to open the Find And Replace dialog box with the Find tab displayed, shown in Figure 2-8.

2. Type the text or number you want to find in the Find What text box.
3. Click **Options** to view the following options to refine the search:
   - **Format**—Opens the Find Format dialog box, where you select from several categories of number, alignment, font, border, patterns, and protection formats.
   - **Choose Format From Cell**—(From the Format drop-down list) lets you click a cell that contains the format you want to find.

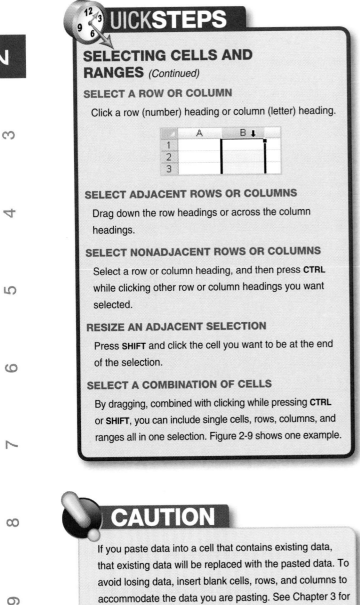

SELECTING CELLS AND RANGES *(Continued)*

SELECT A ROW OR COLUMN

Click a row (number) heading or column (letter) heading.

SELECT ADJACENT ROWS OR COLUMNS

Drag down the row headings or across the column headings.

SELECT NONADJACENT ROWS OR COLUMNS

Select a row or column heading, and then press **CTRL** while clicking other row or column headings you want selected.

RESIZE AN ADJACENT SELECTION

Press **SHIFT** and click the cell you want to be at the end of the selection.

SELECT A COMBINATION OF CELLS

By dragging, combined with clicking while pressing **CTRL** or **SHIFT**, you can include single cells, rows, columns, and ranges all in one selection. Figure 2-9 shows one example.

CAUTION

If you paste data into a cell that contains existing data, that existing data will be replaced with the pasted data. To avoid losing data, insert blank cells, rows, and columns to accommodate the data you are pasting. See Chapter 3 for more information on inserting cells, rows, and columns.

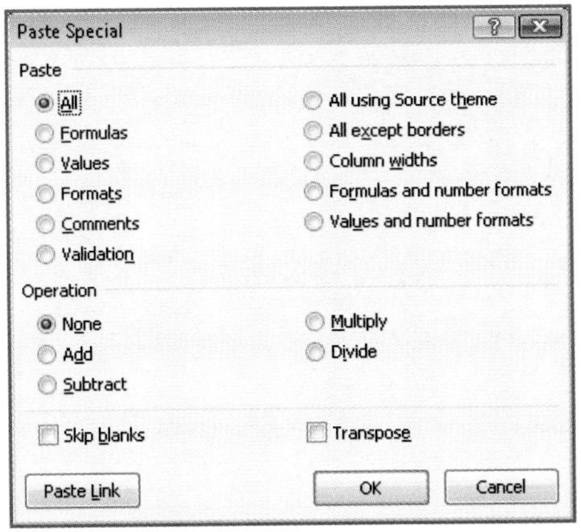

Figure 2-7: You can selectively add or omit many cell properties when you move or copy data.

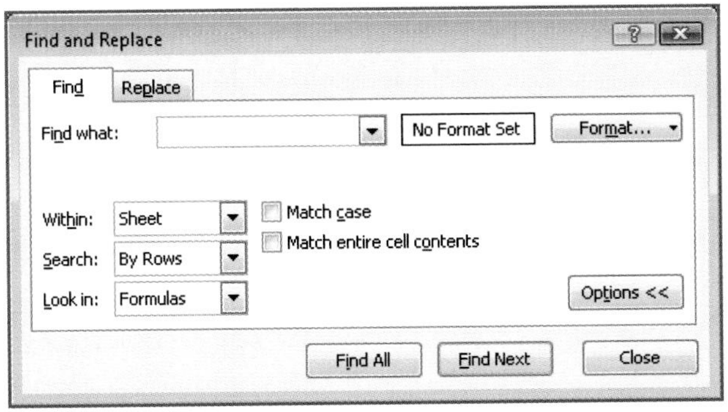

Figure 2-8: The Find tab lets you refine your search based on several criteria.

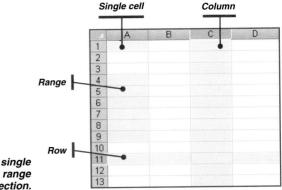

Figure 2-9: You can include a single cell, a row, a column, and a range all in one selection.

- **Within**—Limits your search to the current worksheet or expands it to all worksheets in the workbook.

- **Search**—Lets you search to the right by rows or down by columns. You can search to the left and up by pressing **SHIFT** and clicking **Find Next**.

- **Look In**—Focuses the search to just formulas, values, or comments.

- **Match Case**—Lets you choose between uppercase or lowercase text.

- **Match Entire Cell Contents**—Searches for an exact match of the characters in the Find What text box.

4. Click **Find All** to display a table of all occurrences, or click **Find Next** to find the next singular occurrence.

Book	Sheet	Name	Cell	Value	Formula
Chapter 2.xlsx	Sheet1		$B$2	Medicine	
Chapter 2.xlsx	Sheet1		$D$3	Medicine	
Chapter 2.xlsx	Sheet2		$E$2	Medicine	
Chapter 2.xlsx	Sheet3		$I$6	Medicine	
Chapter 2.xlsx	Sheet3		$I$7	Medicine	
Chapter 2.xlsx	Sheet3		$I$9	Medicine	
Chapter 2.xlsx	Sheet3		$I$13	Medicine	

10 cell(s) found

REPLACE DATA

The Replace tab of the Find And Replace dialog box looks and behaves similar to the Find tab covered earlier.

1. In the Home tab Editing group, click **Find & Select**, and click **Replace**; or press **CTRL+H** to open the Find And Replace dialog box with the Replace tab displayed.

2. Enter the text or number to find in the Find What text box; enter the replacement characters in the Replace With text box. If formatting or search criteria are required, click **Options**. See "Find Data" for the options' descriptions.

3. Click **Replace All** to replace all occurrences in the worksheet, or click **Replace** to replace occurrences one at a time.

🔍	Find...
ᵃᵇ꜀	Replace...
➡	Go To...
	Go To Special...
	Formulas
	Comments
	Conditional Formatting
	Constants
	Data Validation
▹	Select Objects
🔳	Selection Pane...

FIND SPECIFIC EXCEL OBJECTS

You can quickly locate key Excel objects, such as formulas and comments, without having to type any keywords. The objects you can directly search for are listed on the Find & Select drop-down menu.

1. In the Home tab Editing group, click **Find & Select**. The drop-down menu lists several categories of objects from which you can choose.

   Click the item whose instances you want selected. The first instance is surrounded by a light border, and all other instances in the worksheet are selected/highlighted (see Figure 2-10).

   –Or–

   Click **Go To Special** to open a dialog box of the same name, and select from several additional objects. Click **OK** after making your selection.

2. To remove the selection/highlight from found objects, click **Find & Select** again, and click **Select Objects** to turn off that feature.

Verify Spelling

You can check the spelling of selected cells—or the entire worksheet—using Excel's main dictionary and a custom dictionary you add words to (both dictionaries are shared with other Office programs).

1. Select the cells to check; to check the entire worksheet, select any cell.

2. In the Review tab Proofing group, click **Spelling** or press **F7**. When the spelling checker doesn't find anything to report, you are told the spelling check is complete. Otherwise, the Spelling dialog box appears, as shown in Figure 2-11.

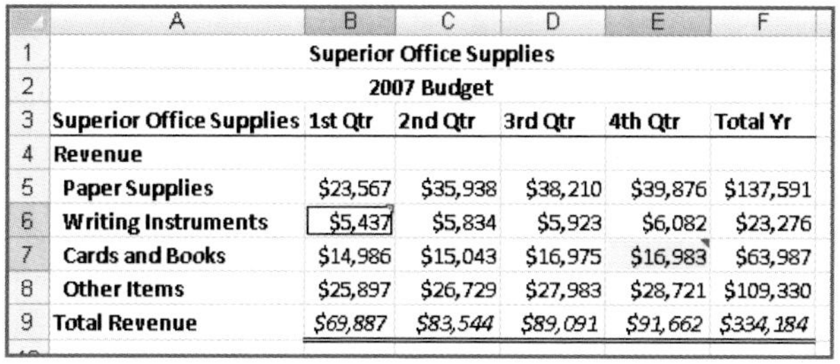

	A	B	C	D	E	F
1	Superior Office Supplies					
2	2007 Budget					
3	Superior Office Supplies	1st Qtr	2nd Qtr	3rd Qtr	4th Qtr	Total Yr
4	Revenue					
5	Paper Supplies	$23,567	$35,938	$38,210	$39,876	$137,591
6	Writing Instruments	$5,437	$5,834	$5,923	$6,082	$23,276
7	Cards and Books	$14,986	$15,043	$16,975	$16,983	$63,987
8	Other Items	$25,897	$26,729	$27,983	$28,721	$109,330
9	Total Revenue	*$69,887*	*$83,544*	*$89,091*	*$91,662*	*$334,184*

Figure 2-10: ***Certain Excel objects, such as comments, can be located and identified with just a few clicks.***

3. Choose to ignore one or more occurrences of the characters shown in the Not In Dictionary text box, or change the characters by picking from the Suggestions list.
4. Click **AutoCorrect** if you want to automatically replace words in the future. (See "Modify Automatic Corrections," next, for more information on using AutoCorrect.)
5. Click **Options** to change language or custom dictionaries and set other spelling criteria.

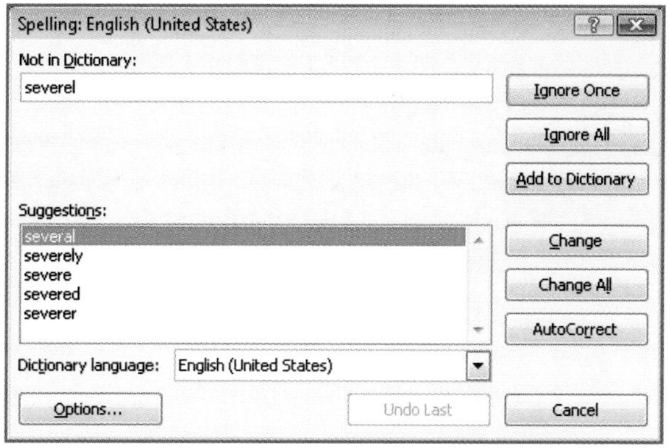

Figure 2-11: ***The Spelling dialog box provides several options to handle misspelled or uncommon words.***

Modify Automatic Corrections

Excel automatically corrects common data entry mistakes as you type, replacing characters and words you choose with other choices. You can control how this is done.

1. Click the **Office Button**, click **Excel Options**, click the **Proofing** option, and click **AutoCorrect Options**. The AutoCorrect dialog box appears, as shown in Figure 2-12. As appropriate, do one or more of the following:

   - Choose the type of automatic corrections you do or do not want from the options at the top of the dialog box.

   - Click **Exceptions** to set capitalization exceptions.

   - Click **Replace Text As You Type** to turn off automatic text replacement (turned on by default).

   - Add new words or characters to the Replace and With lists, and click **Add**; or select a current item in the list, edit it, and click **Replace**.

   - Delete replacement text by selecting the item in the Replace and With lists and clicking **Delete**.

2. Click **OK** when you are done.

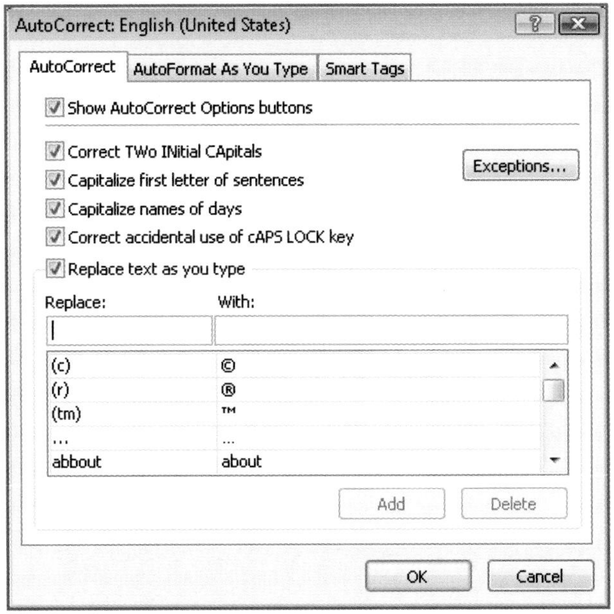

*Figure 2-12: **AutoCorrect provides several automatic settings and lets you add words and characters that are replaced with alternatives.***

How to...

- Adding and Removing Rows, Columns, and Cells
- Adjust Row Height
- Adjust Column Width
- Hide and Unhide Rows and Columns
- Change Cell Borders
- Add a Comment
- Formatting Comments
- Understanding Excel Formatting
- Apply Themes
- Create Custom Themes
- Searching for Themes
- Use Cell Styles
- Change Fonts
- Change Alignment and Orientation
- Add a Background
- Transfer Formatting
- Lock Rows and Columns
- Split a Worksheet
- Working with Worksheets
- View Worksheets from Multiple Workbooks
- Compare Workbooks

Chapter 3
Formatting a Worksheet

Arguably, the primary purpose of a worksheet is to provide a grid to calculate numbers, generally regarded as a rather boring display of numeric data. Excel provides you with the tools to adjust and rearrange the row-and-column grid to meet your needs, but it goes much further to bring emphasis, coordinated colors, and other features that let you add *presentation* to your data.

In this chapter you will learn how to add and delete cells, rows, and columns, and how to change their appearance, both manually and by having Excel do it for you. You will see how to change the appearance of text, how to use themes and styles for a more consistent look, and how to add comments to a cell to better explain important points. Techniques to better display workbooks and work with worksheets are also covered.

QUICKSTEPS

ADDING AND REMOVING ROWS, COLUMNS, AND CELLS

You can insert or delete rows one at a time or select adjacent and nonadjacent rows to perform these actions on them together. (See Chapter 2 for information on selecting rows, columns, and cells.)

ADD A SINGLE ROW

1. Select the row below where you want the new row.

2. In the Home tab Cells group, click **Insert**; or right-click a cell in the selected row, and click **Insert**.

ADD MULTIPLE ADJACENT ROWS

1. Select the number of rows you want immediately below the row where you want the new rows.

2. In the Home tab Cells group, click **Insert**; or right-click a cell in the selected rows, and click **Insert**.

ADD ROWS TO MULTIPLE NONADJACENT ROWS

1. Select the number of rows you want immediately below the first row where you want the new rows.

2. Hold down the **CTRL** key while selecting the number of rows you want immediately below any other rows.

3. In the Home tab Cells group, click the **Insert** down arrow, and click **Insert Sheet Rows**; or right-click any selection, and click **Insert**.

Continued . . .

Work with Cells, Rows, and Columns

Getting a worksheet to look the way you want will probably involve adding and removing cells, rows, and/or columns to appropriately separate your data and remove unwanted space. You might also want to adjust the size and type of cell border and add comments to provide ancillary information about the contents of a cell. This section covers these features and more.

Adjust Row Height

You can change the height of a row manually or by changing cell contents.

CHANGE THE HEIGHT USING A MOUSE

1. Select one or more rows (they can be adjacent or nonadjacent).

2. Point at the bottom border of a selected row heading until the pointer changes to a cross with up and down arrowheads.

3. Drag the border up or down to the row height you want.

CHANGE THE HEIGHT BY ENTERING A VALUE

1. Select the rows you want to adjust.

2. In the Home tab Cells group, click **Format**, and, under Cell Size, click **Row Height**; or right-click the cell, and click **Row Height**. The Row Height dialog box appears.

3. Type a new height in *points* (there are 72 points to an inch), and click **OK**. The cell height changes, but the size of the cell contents stays the same.

CHANGE ROW HEIGHT BY CHANGING CELL CONTENTS

1. Select one or more cells, rows, or characters that you want to change in height.

2. Change the cell contents. Examples of the various ways to do this include:

   - **Changing font size:** In the Home tab Font group, click the **Font Size** down arrow, and click a size from the drop-down list. (You can drag up and down the list of font sizes and see the impact of each on the worksheet without selecting one.)

ADDING AND REMOVING ROWS, COLUMNS, AND CELLS (Continued)

ADD A SINGLE COLUMN

1. Select the column to the right of where you want the new column.

2. In the Home tab Cells group, click **Insert**; or right-click a cell in the selected column, and click **Insert**.

ADD MULTIPLE ADJACENT COLUMNS

1. Select the number of columns you want immediately to the right of the column where you want the new columns.

2. In the Home tab Cells group, click **Insert**; or right-click a cell in the selected columns, and click **Insert**.

ADD COLUMNS TO MULTIPLE NONADJACENT COLUMNS

1. Select the number of columns you want immediately to the right of the first column where you want the new columns.

2. Hold down the **CTRL** key while selecting the number of columns you want immediately to the right of any other columns.

3. In the Home tab Cells group, click the **Insert** down arrow, and click **Insert Sheet Columns**; or right-click any selection and click **Insert**.

ADD CELLS

1. Select the cells adjacent to where you want to insert the new cells.

2. In the Home tab Cells group, click the **Insert** down arrow, and click **Insert Cells**, or right-click the cell and click **Insert**.

Continued . . .

- **Placing characters on two or more lines within a cell:** Place the insertion point at the end of a line or where you want the line to break, and press **ALT+ENTER**.

- **Inserting pictures or drawing objects:** See Chapter 7 for information on working with graphics.

When a selected object changes size or a new object is inserted, if its height becomes larger than the original row height, the height of all cells in the row(s) will be increased. The size of the other cell's contents, however, stays the same.

CHANGE ROW HEIGHT TO FIT SIZE OF CELL CONTENTS

Excel automatically adjusts row height to accommodate the largest object or text size added to a row. If you subsequently removed larger objects or text and want to resize to fit the remaining objects, you can do so using AutoFit.

- Double-click the bottom border of the row heading for a row or selected rows.

  –Or–

- Select the cell or rows you want to size. In the Home tab Cells group, click **Format** and click **AutoFit Row Height**.

The row heights(s) will adjust to fit the highest content.

Adjust Column Width

As with changing row height, you can change the width of a column manually or by changing cell contents.

CHANGE THE WIDTH USING A MOUSE

1. Select one or more columns (columns can be adjacent or nonadjacent).

2. Point at the right border of a selected column heading until the pointer changes to a cross with left and right arrowheads.

	Width: 7.43 (57 pixels)	
E		F
4th Qtr	**Total Yr**	
$39,876	$137,591	

3. Drag the border to the left or right to the width you want. The width is displayed in a ScreenTip.

ADDING AND REMOVING ROWS, COLUMNS, AND CELLS (Continued)

3. In the Insert dialog box, choose the direction to shift the existing cells to make room for the new cells. Click **OK**.

Insert dialog box:

Insert
- ○ Shift cells right
- ○ Shift cells down
- ○ Entire row
- ○ Entire column

[OK] [Cancel]

REMOVING CELLS, ROWS, AND COLUMNS

1. Select the single or adjacent items (cells, rows, or columns) you wish to remove. If you want to remove nonadjacent items, hold down the **CTRL** key while clicking them.

2. In the Home tab Cells group, click the **Delete** down arrow, and click the command applicable to what you want to remove; or right-click the selection, and click **Delete**.

3. When deleting selected cells, the Delete dialog box appears. Choose from which direction to fill in the removed cells, and click **OK**.

MERGE CELLS

Select the cells you want to combine into one cell.

1. In the Home tab Alignment group, click the **Merge And Center** down arrow. (If all you want to do is merge and center, click the button.)

Drop-down list:
- Merge and Center
- Merge Across
- Merge Cells
- UnMerge Cells

2. Click the applicable tool from the drop-down list.

You cannot change the width of a single cell without changing the width of all cells in the column.

CHANGE THE WIDTH BY ENTERING A VALUE

1. Select the columns you want to adjust.

2. In the Home tab Cells group, click **Format** and click **Column Width**; or right-click the cell, and click **Column Width**. The Column Width dialog box appears.

Column Width dialog box:

Column width: 8.43

[OK] [Cancel]

3. Type a new width, and click **OK**. The cell width changes, but the size of the cell contents stays the same.

CHANGE COLUMN WIDTH TO FIT SIZE OF CELL CONTENTS

● Double-click the right border of the column header for the column or selected columns.

–Or–

● Select the cell or columns you want to size. In the Home tab Cells group, click **Format** and click **AutoFit Column Width**.

The column width(s) will adjust to fit the longest entry.

Hide and Unhide Rows and Columns

Hidden rows and columns provide a means to temporarily remove rows or columns from view without deleting them or their contents.

HIDE ROWS AND COLUMNS

1. Select the rows or columns to be hidden (see Chapter 2).

2. In the Home tab Cells group, click **Format**, click **Hide & Unhide**, and click **Hide Rows** or **Hide Columns**; or right-click the selection, and click **Hide**.

–Or–

Drag the bottom border of the rows to be hidden *up*, or drag the right border of the columns to be hidden to the *left*.

The row numbers or column letters of the hidden cells are omitted, as shown in Figure 3-1. (You can also tell cells are hidden by the slightly darker border in the row or column headers between the hidden rows or columns.)

The default column width for a worksheet is determined by the average number of characters in the default font that will fit in the column (not in points, as is row height). For example, the Arial 10 pt. font provides a standard column width of 8.43 characters. If you want to change the default column width, in the Home tab Cells group, click **Format** and click **Standard Width**. Type a width and click **OK**. Columns at the original standard width will change to reflect the new value.

If you hide one or more rows or columns beginning with column A or row 1, it does not look like you can drag across the rows or columns on both sides of the hidden rows or columns to unhide them. However, you can by selecting the row or column to the right or below the hidden row or column and dragging the selection into the heading. Then when you click **Unhide**, the hidden object will appear. If you don't do this, you won't be able to recover the hidden row or column.

Darker heading border identifies hidden rows and columns

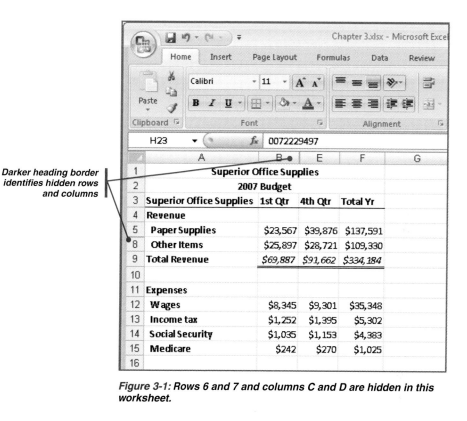

Figure 3-1: Rows 6 and 7 and columns C and D are hidden in this worksheet.

UNHIDE ROWS OR COLUMNS

1. Drag across the row or column headings on both sides of the hidden rows or columns.

2. In the Home tab Cells group, click **Format**, click **Hide & Unhide**, and click **Unhide Rows** or **Unhide Columns**.

   –Or–

   Right-click the selection and click **Unhide**.

Change Cell Borders

Borders provide a quick and effective way to emphasize and segregate data on a worksheet. You can create borders by choosing from samples or by setting them up in a dialog box. Use the method that suits you best.

PICK A BORDER

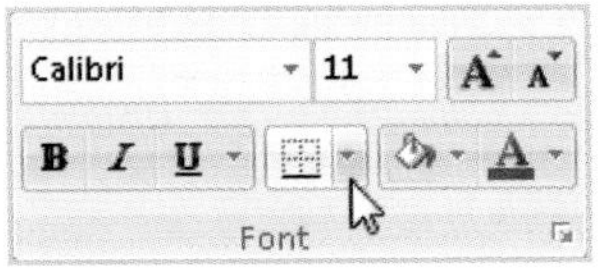

1. Select the cell, range, row, or column whose border you want modify.

2. In the Home tab Font group, click the **Border** down arrow, and select the border style you want. (The style you choose remains as the available border style on the button.)

3. To remove a border, select the cell(s), click the **Border** down arrow, and click **No Border**.

PREVIEW BORDERS BEFORE YOU CHANGE THEM

1. Select the cell, range, row, or column that you want modify with a border.

2. In the Home tab Font group, click the **Border** down arrow, and click **More Borders**.

   –Or–

   In the Home tab Font group, click the **Dialog Box Launcher**, or right-click the selection, and click **Format Cells**. Click the **Border** tab in the Format Cells dialog box.

   In any case, the Format Cells dialog box appears with the Border tab displayed, as shown in Figure 3-2.

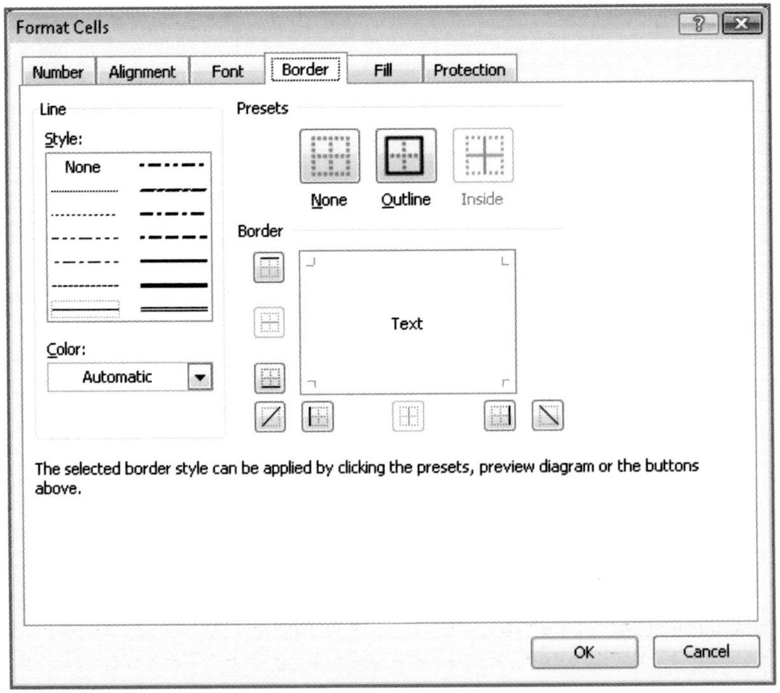

Figure 3-2: You can build and preview borders for selected cells in the Border tab.

3. In the Border area, you will see a preview of the selected cells. Use the other tools in the dialog box to set up your borders:

   - **Presets buttons**—Set broad border parameters by selecting to have no border, an outline border, or an inside "grid" border (can also be changed manually in the Border area).

   - **Line area**—Select a border style and color (see "Change Themed Colors" later in the chapter for information on color options).

   - **Border buttons**—Choose where you want a border (click once to add the border; click twice to remove it).

4. Click **OK** to apply the borders.

Add a Comment

A comment acts as a "notepad" for cells, providing a place on the worksheet for explanatory text that can be hidden until needed.

1. Select the cell where you want the comment.

2. In the Review tab Comments group, click **New Comment**.

   –Or–

   Right-click the cell, and click **Insert Comment**.

   In either case, a text box labeled with your user name is attached to the cell.

3. Type your comment and click anywhere on the worksheet to close the comment. An indicator icon (red triangle) in the upper-right corner of the cell shows that a comment is attached.

VIEW COMMENTS

You can view an individual comment, view them in sequence, or view all comments on a worksheet:

- To view any comment, point to or select a cell that displays an indicator icon (red triangle) in its upper-right corner. The comment stays displayed as long as your mouse pointer remains in the cell.

- To view comments in sequence, in the Review tab Comments group, click **Next**. The next comment in the worksheet, moving left to right and down the rows, displays until

The default behavior for comments is to show the indicator icon (red triangle) and display the comment text when the mouse pointer is hovered over a cell containing a comment. You can also choose to always show the comment text and indicators or to not show the indicators and text. Click the **Office Button**, click **Excel Options**, and click the **Advanced** option. In the Display area, under For Cells With Comments, Show, select the behavior you want, and click **OK**.

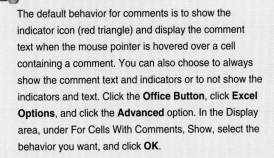

You can also delete comments by selectively clearing them from a cell. In the Home tab Editing group, click **Clear** ⊘ ˅ and click **Clear Comments**.

Moving a comment only moves the editing text box's position in relationship to its parent cell—it does not move the comment to other cells. The new location of moved comments only appears when editing the comment or when you display all comments in the worksheet; otherwise, when either the cell is selected or the mouse hovers over the cell, it appears in its default position.

you click another cell or press **ESC**. Click **Previous** in the Comments group to reverse the search direction.

- To keep the comment displayed while doing other work, select the cell that contains the comment. In the Review tab Comments group, click **Show/Hide Comment**; or right-click the cell, and click **Show/Hide Comments**. (Click either command to hide the comment.)

- To view all comments in a worksheet and keep the comment displayed while doing other work, in the Review tab Comments group, click **Show All Comments**. (Click the command a second time to hide all comments.)

EDIT A COMMENT

1. Select a cell that displays an indicator icon (red triangle) in its upper-right corner.
2. In the Review tab Comments group, click **Edit Comment**.

   –Or–

   Right-click the cell, and click **Edit Comment**.

3. Edit the text, including the user name if appropriate. Click anywhere in the worksheet when finished.

DELETE A COMMENT

1. Select the cell or cells that contain the comments you want to delete.
2. In the Review tab Comments group, click **Delete**.

   –Or–

   Right-click the cell, and click **Delete Comment**.

MOVE AND RESIZE A COMMENT

Open the comment (see "Edit a Comment"):

- To **Resize**, point to one of the corner or mid-border sizing handles. When the pointer becomes a double arrow-headed line, drag the handle in the direction you want to increase or decrease the comment's size.

- To **Move**, point at the wide border surrounding the comment. When the pointer becomes a cross with arrowhead tips, drag the comment to where you want it.

FORMATTING COMMENTS

You can apply several formatting techniques to comments, including changing text, borders, and color. These and other attributes are changed using the Format Comment dialog box, available after a comment is opened for editing (see "Edit a Comment").

CHANGE THE APPEARANCE OF COMMENT TEXT

1. To change the formatting of existing text, select the text first. If you do not select existing text, only new text you type will show the changes after you make them.

2. Right-click the interior of the comment, and click **Format Comment**. Make and preview the changes you want in the Font tab, and click **OK**. Alternatively, in the Home tab Font group, click the applicable control to change the font, size, and styling (see "Change Fonts" later in this chapter).

CHANGE A COMMENT'S COLOR AND BORDER

1. Right-click the border of the comment, and click **Format Comment**.

2. In the Format Comment dialog box, click the **Colors And Lines** tab.

3. Click the **Fill Color** down arrow to open the gallery. Click the new color you want (see "Change Themed Colors" later in the chapter for information on color options).

4. In the Line area, change the attributes that control the comment's border. Click **OK** when finished.

COPY A COMMENT

1. Select the cell that contains the comment you want to copy.

2. In the Home tab Clipboard group, click **Copy**.

   –Or–

   Right-click the cell, and click **Copy**.

   –Or–

   Press **CTRL+C**.

   In all cases, the cell is surrounded by a flashing border.

3. Select the cells to which you want the comment copied. Then, in the Clipboard group, click the **Paste** down arrow, and click **Paste Special**. In the Paste Special dialog box, under Paste, click **Comments**, and then click **OK**.

4. Repeat step 3 to paste the comment into other cells. When finished, press **ESC** to remove the flashing border.

Apply Formatting

Formatting gives life to a worksheet, transforming a rather dull collection of text and numbers into pleasing colors, shades, and variations in size and effects that bring attention to points you are trying to emphasize. You can apply or create *themes* (consistent use of color, fonts, and graphics effects) to give your worksheets a coordinated appearance. If you want more control, you can apply *styles* (consistent formatting parameters applicable to specific worksheet objects) and *direct formatting* (use of ribbon buttons and dialog boxes) to cells and text. (See the "Understanding Excel Formatting" QuickFacts for more information on these formatting types.) In addition, you can transfer formatting attributes from one cell to others.

UNDERSTANDING EXCEL FORMATTING

There are a plethora of ways you can change the appearance of text and worksheet elements. Without having a sense of the "method behind the madness," it's easy to become confused and frustrated when attempting to enhance your work. Excel (as well as Microsoft Word and Microsoft PowerPoint) operate on a hierarchy of formatting assistance (see Figure 3-3). The higher a formatting feature is on the stack, the broader and more automatic are its effects; the lower on the stack, the more user intervention is required, although you will have more control over the granularity of any given feature.

- **Themes** are at the top of the formatting heap. Themes provide an efficiently lazy way to apply professionally designed color, font, and graphic elements to a workbook. Each theme (with names like Office, Currency, and Solstice) includes 12 colors (four text colors, six accent colors, and two hyperlink colors), along with six shades of each primary theme color. Theme fonts are classified for headings and the body text (the default workbook theme is Office, which is where the new Calibri font comes from that you see in new workbooks). When you switch themes, all theme-affected elements are changed. You can modify existing themes and save them, creating your own theme.

Continued . . .

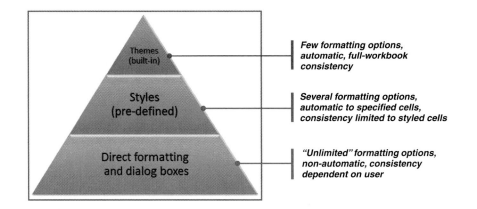

*Figure 3-3: **Excel provides three levels of formatting assistance.***

Apply Themes

Themes are the most hands-off way to add a coordinated look and feel to a worksheet. Built-in themes control the formatting of themed elements, such as the color of table headers and rows and the font used in chart text. In addition, you can change themes and modify themed elements (colors, fonts, and graphic effects).

CHANGE THE CURRENT THEME

By default, Excel applies the Office theme to new workbooks. You can easily view the effects from the other built-in themes and change to the one you prefer.

1. In the Page Layout tab Themes group, click **Themes**. A gallery of the available themes (built-in and custom) is displayed, as shown in Figure 3-4.

2. Point to each theme and see how colors, fonts, and graphics change in themed elements. The best way to view changes is to create a table and associated chart, and with it displayed, point to each theme in the gallery and see how the table and chart look (see Figure 3-4). Chapters 6 and 8 provide more information on charts and tables.

3. Click the theme you want, and save your workbook.

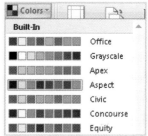

QUICKFACTS

UNDERSTANDING EXCEL FORMATTING *(Continued)*

- **Styles** occupy the middle tier of Excel formatting. Styles apply consistent formatting to directed Excel components, such as cells, tables, charts, and PivotTables. Styles, similar to themes, can be modified and saved for your own design needs. Both themes and styles are supported by several galleries of their respective formatting options, and provide a live preview by hovering your mouse pointer over each choice. Certain attributes of a style are *themed*, meaning they are consistent with the current theme and change accordingly.

- **Direct formatting** is the feature most of us have used to get the look we want, found in buttons on the ribbon and formatting dialog boxes divided into several tabs of options. Direct formatting provides the greatest control and access to formatting features, but even though Excel now provides live previews for many options, most still require you to accept the change, view the result in the workbook, and then repeat the process several times to get the result you want.

So how do you best put this hierarchy to work? Start at the top by applying a theme. If its formatting works for you, you're done! If you need more customization, try simply changing to a different theme. Need more options? Try applying a style to one of the style-affected components. Finally, if you need total control, use a component's formatting dialog box and ribbon buttons to make detailed changes. When you're all done, save all your changes as a new theme that you can apply to new workbooks, and also to your Word documents and PowerPoint presentations.

CHANGE THEMED COLORS

Each theme comes with 12 primary colors (see the "Understanding Excel Formatting" QuickFacts) affecting text, accents, and hyperlinks. You can choose a theme with different colors or modify each constituent color.

1. In the Page Layout tab Themes group, click **Colors**. The drop-down list displays the built-in themes and eight of the 12 colors associated with each theme.

2. At the bottom of the list, click **Create New Theme Colors**. The Create New Theme Colors dialog box displays each constituent theme color and a sample displaying the current selections (see Figure 3-5).

3. Click the theme color you want to change. A gallery of colors displays and provides three options from which you select a new color:

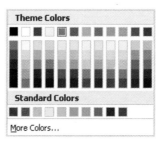

- **Theme Colors** displays a matrix of the 12 primary colors in the current theme and six shades associated with each. Click a color and see the change in the Sample area.

- **Standard Colors** displays the ten standard colors in the color spectrum (red through violet). Click the color you want.

- **More Colors** opens the Colors dialog box, shown in Figure 3-6, from where you can select a custom color by clicking a color and using a slider to change its **shading**, or by selecting a color model and entering specific color values. In addition, you can click the **Standard** tab, and select from a hexagonal array of Web-friendly colors.

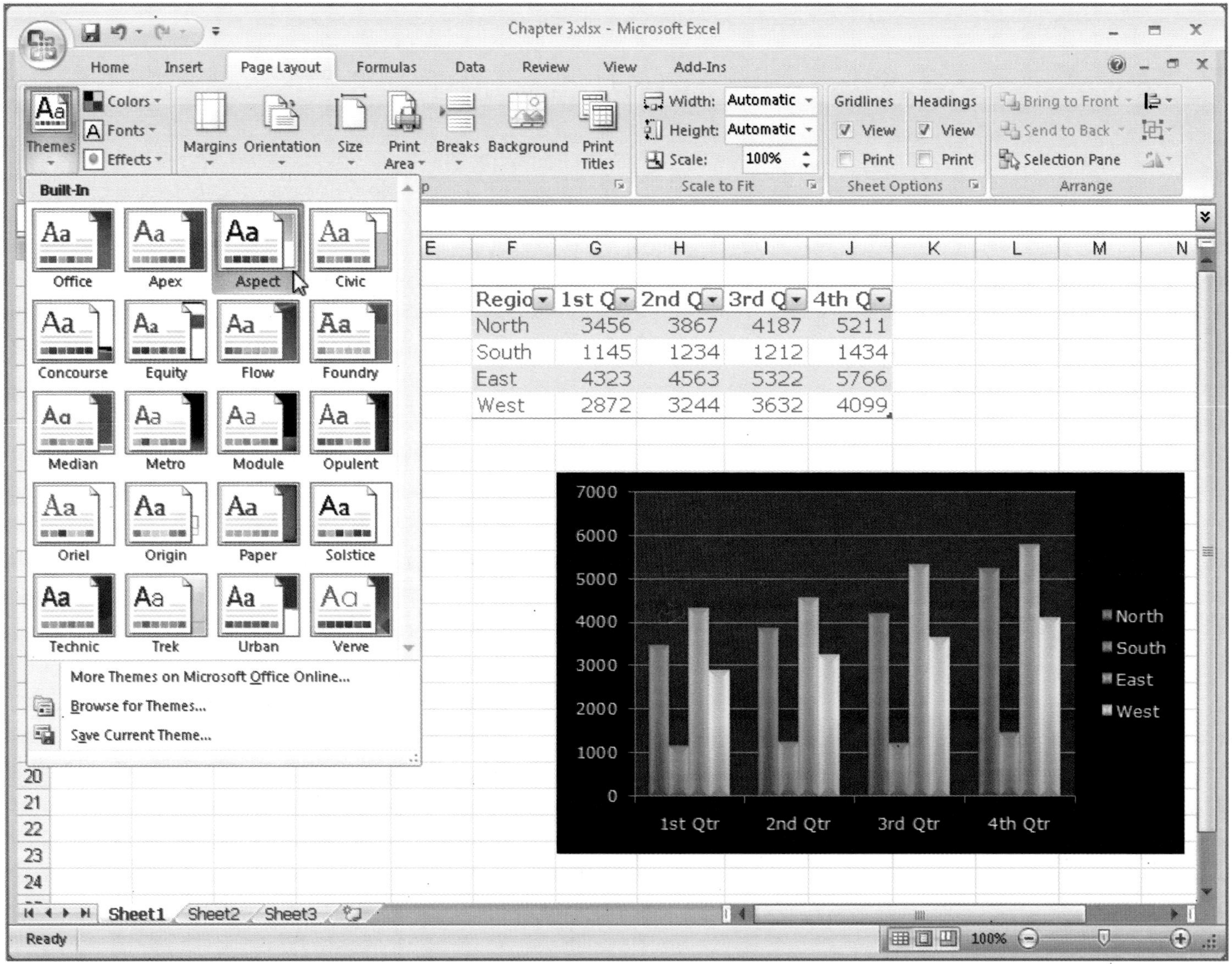

Figure 3-4: Excel provides 20 built-in professionally designed themes.

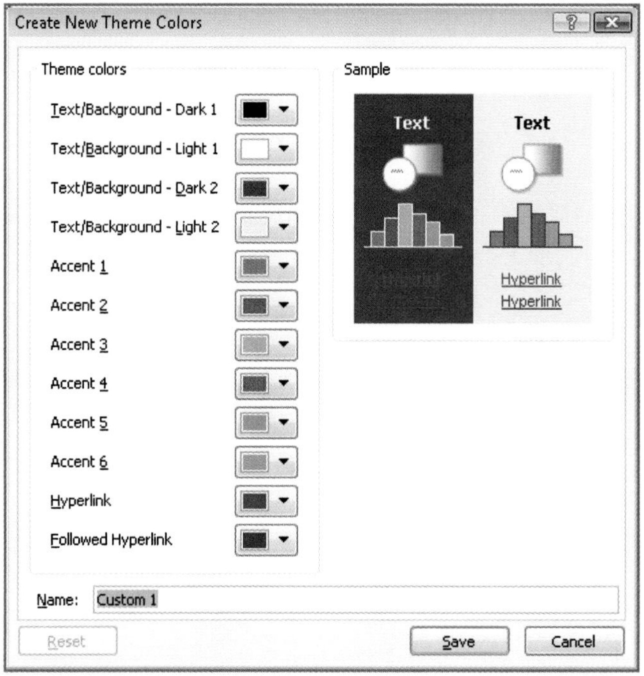

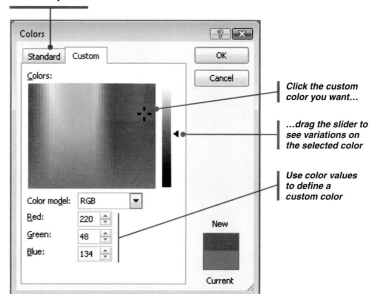

Figure 3-5: *Each theme color can be modified from an essentially infinite number of choices.*

Web-friendly colors

Click the custom color you want...

...drag the slider to see variations on the selected color

Use color values to define a custom color

Figure 3-6: *The Colors dialog box offers the greatest control of custom color selection, as well as a collection of standard Web-friendly colors.*

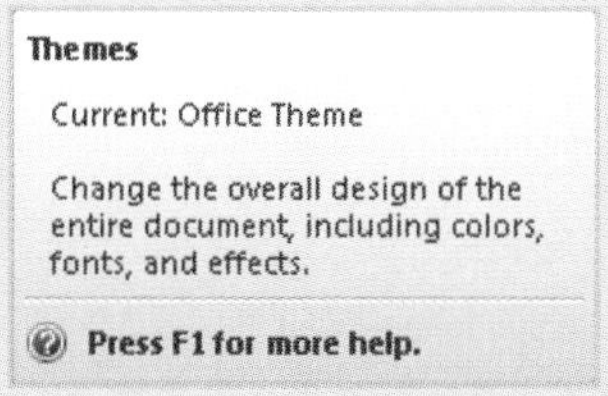

4. Repeat step 3 for any other theme color you want to change. If you get a bit far afield in your color changes, don't panic. Click **Reset** at the bottom of the Create New Theme Colors dialog box to return to the default theme colors.

5. Type a new name for the color combination you've selected, and click **Save**. Custom colors are available for selection at the top of the theme Colors drop-down list.

CHANGE THEMED FONTS

Each theme includes two fonts. The *body* font is used for general text entry (the Calibri font in the default Office theme is the body font). A *heading* font is also included and used in a few cell styles (see "Use Cell Styles" later in this chapter).

1. In the Page Layout tab Themes group, click **Fonts**. The drop-down list displays a list of theme font combinations (heading and body). The current theme font combination is highlighted.

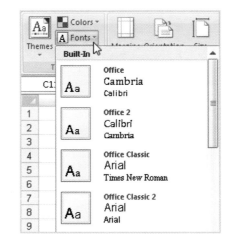

2. Point to each combination to see how the fonts will appear on your worksheet.

3. Click the combination you want, or click **Create New Theme Fonts** at the bottom of the drop-down list.

4. In the Create New Theme Fonts dialog box (see Figure 3-7), click either or both the **Heading Font** and **Body Font** down arrows to select new fonts. View the new combination in the Sample area.

Figure 3-7: You can choose a heading or body font from the fonts available in your Windows system.

5. Type a new name for the font combination you've selected, and click **Save**. Custom fonts are available for selection at the top of the theme Fonts drop-down list.

CHANGE THEMED GRAPHIC EFFECTS

Shapes, illustrations, pictures, and charts include graphic effects that are controlled by themes. Themed graphics are modulated in terms of their lines (borders), fills, and effects (such as shadowed, raised, and shaded). For example, some themes simply change an inserted rectangle's fill color, while other themes affect the color, the weight of its border, and whether it has a 3-D appearance.

1. In the Page Layout tab Themes group, click **Effects**. The drop-down list displays a gallery of effects combinations.

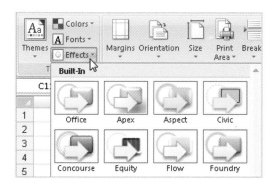

2. Point to each combination to see how the effects will appear on your worksheet, assuming you have a graphic or chart inserted on the worksheet (see Chapters 6 and 7 for information on inserting charts and graphics).

3. Click the effects combination you want.

Create Custom Themes

Changes you make to a built-in theme (or to a previously created custom theme) can be saved as a custom theme and reused in other Office 2007 documents.

1. Make color, font, and effects changes to the current theme (see "Apply Themes" earlier in the chapter).

2. In the Page Layout tab Themes group, click **Themes** and click **Save Current Theme**. In the Save Current Theme window, click **Browse Folders** to display the default Office themes folder, as shown in Figure 3-8.

3. Name the file and click **Save** to store the theme in the Office Document Themes folder.

–Or–

Name the file and browse to the folder where you want to store it. Click **Save** when finished.

CAUTION

Saved custom themes that are not stored in the default Document Themes folder will not be displayed in the Custom area of the Themes drop-down list. You will need to locate them to apply them (see the "Searching for Themes" QuickSteps).

QUICKSTEPS

SEARCHING FOR THEMES

You can quickly find individual theme files and themed documents, and apply them to your workbook. In addition, you can use prebuilt themes that are available from Microsoft Online.

LOCATE AND APPLY THEMES

You can apply themes from other files to your workbooks, either as individual theme files or from other Office 2007 files that have themes applied to them.

1. In the Page Layout tab Themes group, click **Themes** and click **Browse For Themes** at the bottom of the gallery.

2. In the Choose Theme Or Themed Document window, browse to the folder where the themes or themed documents are located. Only those documents will display. (*Themed documents* are Office 2007 files that contain a theme, such as Word files, Excel workbooks, PowerPoint presentations, and their respective templates.)

3. If you are only looking for theme files (.thmx), click **Office Themes And Themed Documents**, and click **Office Themes (.thmx)**.

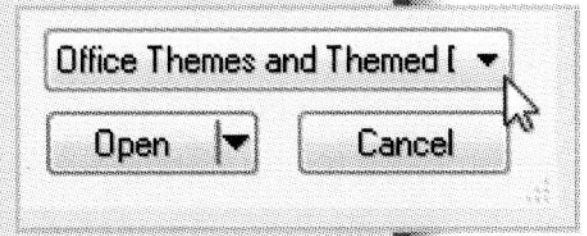

4. Select the Office document whose theme you want to apply or the theme file you want to apply, and click **Open**.

FIND THEMES ON OFFICE ONLINE

1. In the Page Layout tab Themes group, click **Themes** and click **More Themes On Microsoft Office Online**. Assuming you're connected to the Internet, the Microsoft Office Online Web site is displayed (see Figure 3-9).

Continued. . .

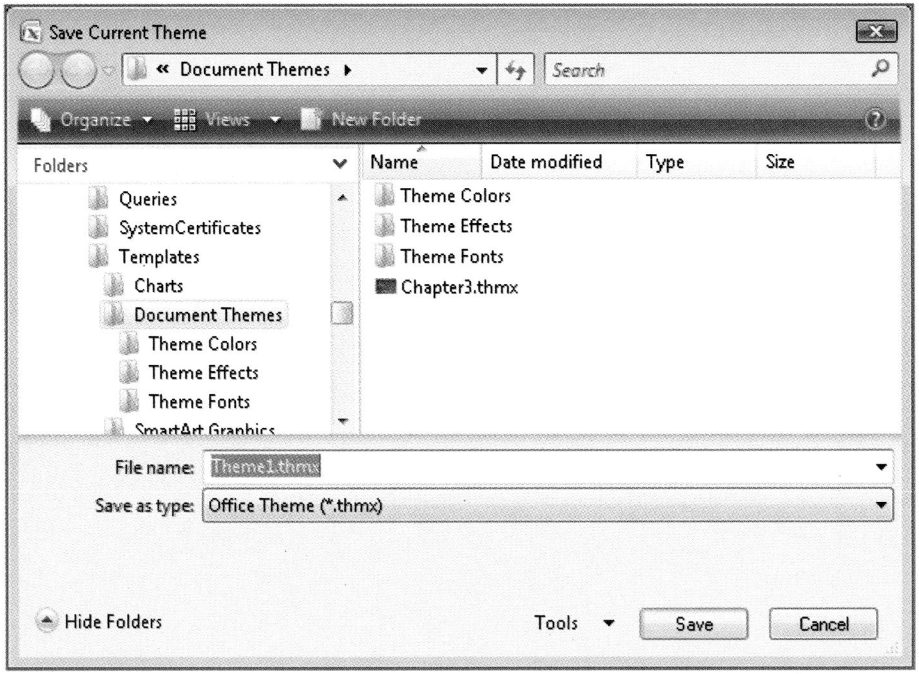

Figure 3-8: Custom themes are saved as individual files in the new Excel XML Office theme file format.

Use Cell Styles

Cell styles allow you to apply consistent formatting to specific cells, and let you make changes to styled cells with a few mouse clicks instead of changing each cell individually. Excel provides dozens of predefined styles, categorized by use. One category, themed cell styles, has the additional advantage of being fully integrated with the current theme. Colors associated with a theme change will automatically carry over to themed cell styles, preserving the coordinated appearance of your worksheet. Of course, you can modify any applied style and save the changes to create your own custom style.

QUICKSTEPS

SEARCHING FOR THEMES *(Continued)*

2. Use the options on the left sidebar or the Search tool to find the theme you want and download it to your system (you might have to download a template that includes the theme you want).

APPLY A STYLE

1. Select the cells you want to format with a style.

2. In the Home tab Styles group, click **Cell Styles**. A gallery of cell styles displays, as shown in Figure 3-10.

3. Point to several styles in the gallery to see how each style affects your selected cells.

4. Click the style that best suits your needs. The style formatting is applied to your selected cells.

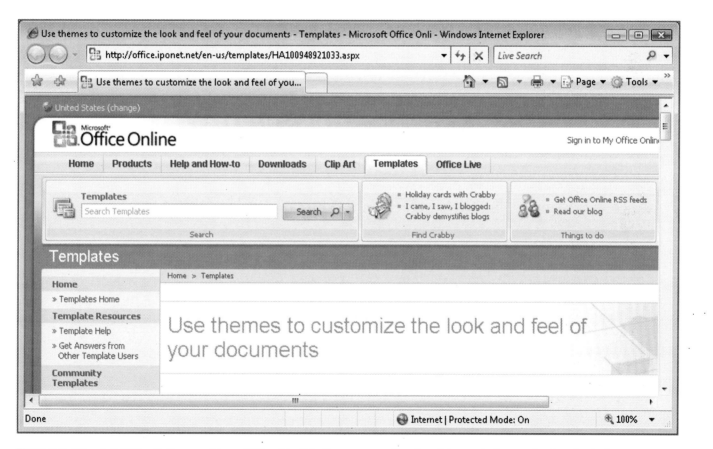

Figure 3-9: Microsoft Office Online provides additional built-in themes, as well as templates and other professionally designed content.

TIP

The easiest way to ensure a common look and feel to your Excel 2007 workbooks is to create or apply the theme you want and save the workbook as a template. In addition to the theme-controlled aspects of a workbook, the template allows you to consistently re-create formulas, tables, charts, and all else that Excel has to offer. Chapter 1 describes saving workbooks as templates.

NOTE

Styles also can be applied to charts, tables, and PivotTables. Using styles with these Excel components is covered in their respective chapters later in this book.

NOTE

The default font used in each style is derived from the current theme. When you change themes, the font used in styled cells will change according to the font used in the new theme. Themed cell styles, unlike other cell styles, will additionally change color as applicable to the new theme.

NOTE

Direct formatting using the ribbon and the Format Cells dialog box is discussed in other sections of this chapter.

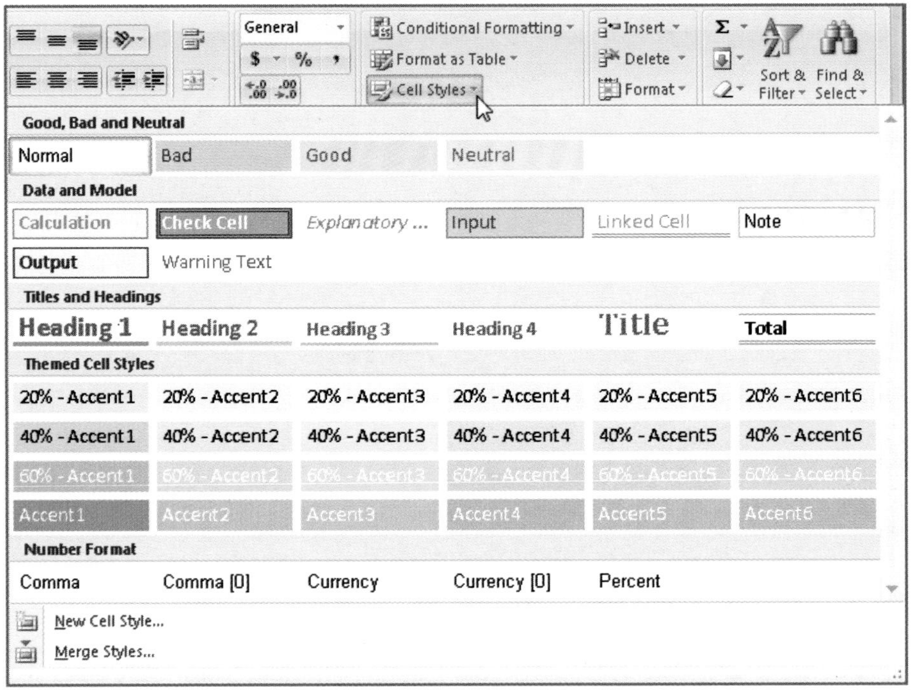

Figure 3-10: Excel's styles provide a broad swatch of cell styling possibilities.

CREATE A CUSTOM STYLE

You can create your own style by starting with a predefined style and making changes, or you can start from scratch and apply all formatting directly, using the formatting tools on the ribbon or in a formatting dialog box. In either case, you can save your changes as a custom style and apply it from the Cell Styles gallery.

1. Use one or more, or a combination, of the following techniques to format at least one cell as you want:
   - Apply a predefined style to the cell(s) you want to customize.
   - Use the formatting tools in the ribbon (Home tab Font, Alignment, and Number groups).
   - Right-click a cell to be styled, click **Format Cells**, and use the six tabs in the Format Cells dialog box to create the styling format you want. Click **OK** when finished.

Style

Style name: Style 1

Format...

Style Includes (By Example)

☑ Number   General

☑ Alignment   General, Bottom Aligned

☑ Font   Calibri (Body) 11

☑ Border   No Borders

☑ Fill   No Shading

☑ Protection Locked

OK   Cancel

2. In the Home tab Styles group, click **Cell Styles** and click **New Cell Style** at the bottom of the gallery.

3. In the Style dialog box, type a name for your style, and review the six areas of affected style formatting. If necessary, click **Format** and make formatting adjustments in the Format Cells dialog box. Click **OK** to apply formatting changes.

4. Click **OK** in the Style dialog box to create the style. The new custom style will be displayed in the Custom area at the top of the Cell Styles gallery.

CHANGE A CELL STYLE

1. In the Home tab Styles group, click **Cell Styles**.

2. Right-click a style (custom or predefined) in the gallery, and click **Modify**.

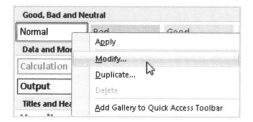

3. In the Style dialog box, click **Format** and make any formatting adjustments in the Format Cells dialog box. Click **OK** to apply the formatting changes.

4. Click **OK** in the Style dialog box to save changes to the style.

REMOVE A CELL STYLE

You can remove a style's formatting applied to selected cells, or you can completely remove the cell style from Excel (and concurrently remove all style formatting from affected cells):

● To remove style formatting from cells: Select the cells, click **Cell Styles** in the Styles group, and click the **Normal** style.

● To permanently remove a style: Click **Cell Styles** in the Styles group, right-click the cell style you want removed, and click **Delete**.

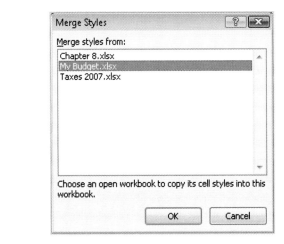

ADD CELL STYLES FROM OTHER WORKBOOKS

1. Open any workbooks whose styles you want to add and the workbook where you want the styles to be added.

2. In the View tab Window group, click **Switch Windows** and click the workbook to which you want the styles added, making it the active workbook.

3. In the Home tab Styles group, click **Cell Styles** and click **Merge Styles**.

4. In the Merge Styles dialog box, click the workbook from which you want to add styles. Click **OK**.

Change Fonts

Each *font* is comprised of a *typeface*, such as Arial; a *style*, such as italic; and a size. Other characteristics, such as color and super/subscripting, further distinguish text. Excel also provides several underlining options that are useful in accounting applications.

1. On a worksheet, select:
   - Cells to apply font changes to all characters
   - Characters to apply font changes to just the selected text and numbers

2. Use one of the following techniques to access font tools and options:
   - On the ribbon, click the **Home** tab, and click the appropriate Font group tools (see Figure 3-11).
   - Right-click a cell or selection, and use the font tools available on the mini-toolbar.

   - Click the Font group **Dialog Box Launcher** (located in the lower-right corner of group).
   - Right-click a cell or selection, click **Format Cells**, and then click the **Font** tab.

3. In the latter two cases, the Format Cells dialog box appears with the Font tab displayed, as shown in Figure 3-12. Make and preview changes, and click **OK** when finished.

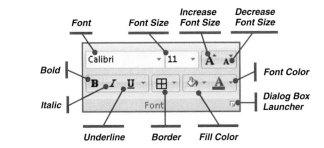

Figure 3-11: Font group tools apply formatting to text.

When selected, the Normal Font check box on the Font tab of the Format Cells dialog box resets font attributes to the defaults defined in the Normal template. The Normal template is an ever-present component of Excel (if you delete it, Excel will re-create another) that defines startup values in the absence of any other template.

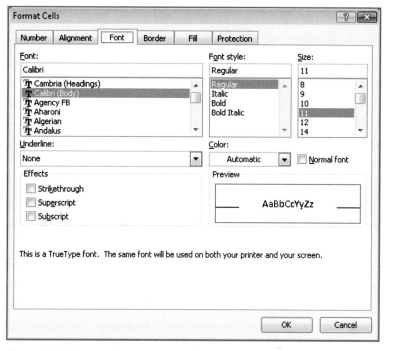

Figure 3-12: Change the appearance of text by changing its font and other characteristics.

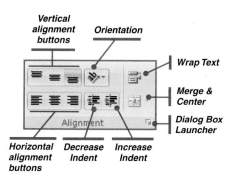

Figure 3-13: Alignment group tools allow you to reposition text.

Change Alignment and Orientation

You can modify how characters appear within a cell by changing their alignment, orientation, and "compactness."

1. Select the cells whose contents you want to change.

2. Use one of the following techniques to access font tools and options:

- On the ribbon, click the **Home** tab, and click the appropriate Alignment group tools (see Figure 3-13).

- Click the Alignment group **Dialog Box Launcher**.

- Right-click a cell or selection, click **Format Cells**, and then click the **Alignment** tab.

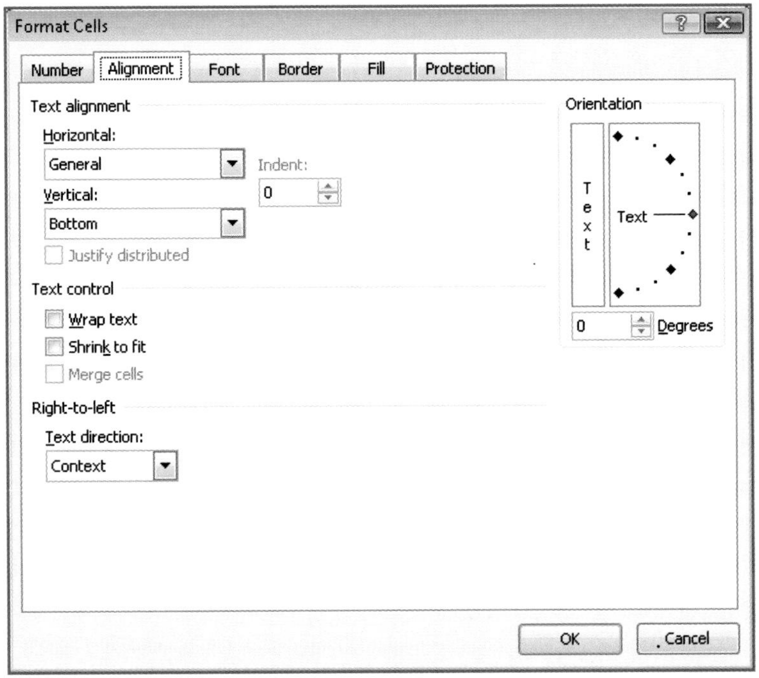

Format Cells
Number
Alignment
Font
Border
Fill
Protection
Text alignment
Horizontal:
General
Indent:
0
Vertical:
Bottom
Justify distributed
Text control
Wrap text
Shrink to fit
Merge cells
Right-to-left
Text direction:
Context
Orientation
Text
Text
0
Degrees
OK
Cancel

Figure 3-14: The Alignment tab provides detailed text-alignment options.

3. In the latter two cases, the Format Cells dialog box appears with the Alignment tab displayed, as shown in Figure 3-14. The specific features of the Alignment tab are described in Table 3-1.
4. Click **OK** when you are finished.

Add a Background

You can add color and shading to selected cells to provide a solid background. You can also add preset patterns, either alone or in conjunction with a solid background for even more effect.

1. Select the cell, range, row, or column that you want to modify with a background.
2. In the Home tab Alignment group, click its **Dialog Box Launcher**.

   –Or–

   Right-click the selection and click **Format Cells**.

   In either case, the Format Cells dialog box appears.
3. Click the **Fill** tab (see Figure 3-15), and choose colored and/or patterned fills.

USE SOLID COLORED BACKGROUNDS

1. In the Fill tab, click one of the color options in the Background Color area (see "Change Themed Colors" earlier in this chapter for information on the various color options), and select one of the color options.

   –Or–

   Click **Fill Effects** to apply blended fills, as shown in Figure 3-16. Preview your selections in the Sample area, and click **OK**.
2. Preview your selections in the larger Sample area at the bottom of the Fill tab, and click **OK** when finished.

USE PATTERNED BACKGROUNDS

1. In the Fill tab, click the **Pattern Style** down arrow to display a gallery of patterns. Click the design you want, and see it enlarged in the Sample area at the bottom of the Fill tab.

Pattern Style:

TIP

You can quickly add solid color and shading to selected cells from the Fill Color button in the Font group (see Figure 3-11). Click the button to apply the displayed color, or open a gallery by clicking the down arrow next to the button (see "Change Themed Colors" earlier in this chapter for information on the various gallery color options). The last color or shade selected remains on the Fill Color button until changed.

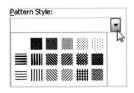

FEATURE	OPTION	DESCRIPTION
Text Alignment, Horizontal	General	Right-aligns numbers, left-aligns text, and centers error values; Excel default setting
	Left (Indent)	Left-aligns characters with optional indentation spinner
	Center	Centers characters in the cell
	Right (Indent)	Right-aligns characters with optional indentation spinner
	Fill	Fills cell with recurrences of content
	Justify	Justifies the text in a cell so that, to the degree possible, both the left and right ends are vertically aligned
	Center Across Selection	Centers text across one or more cells; used to center titles across several columns
	Distributed (Indent)	Stretches cell contents across cell width by adding space between words, with optional indentation spinner
Text Alignment Vertical	Top	Places the text at the top of the cell
	Center	Places the text in the center of the cell
	Bottom	Places the text at the bottom of the cell; Excel's default setting
	Justify	Evenly distributes text between the top and bottom of a cell to fill it by adding space between lines
	Distributed	Vertically arranges characters equally within the cell (behaves the same as Justify)
Orientation		Angles text in a cell by dragging the red diamond up or down or by using the Degrees spinner
Text Control	Wrap Text	Moves text that extends beyond the cell's width to the line below
	Shrink To Fit	Reduces character size so that cell contents fit within cell width (cannot be used with Wrap Text)
	Merge Cells	Creates one cell from contiguous cells, "increasing" the width of a cell without changing the width of the column(s)
Right To Left, Text Direction	Context	Text entry flows according to keyboard language in use
	Left To Right	Text entry flows from the left as in Western countries
	Right To Left	Text entry flows from the right as in many Middle Eastern and East Asian countries

Table 3-1: Text-Alignment Options in Excel

Format Cells

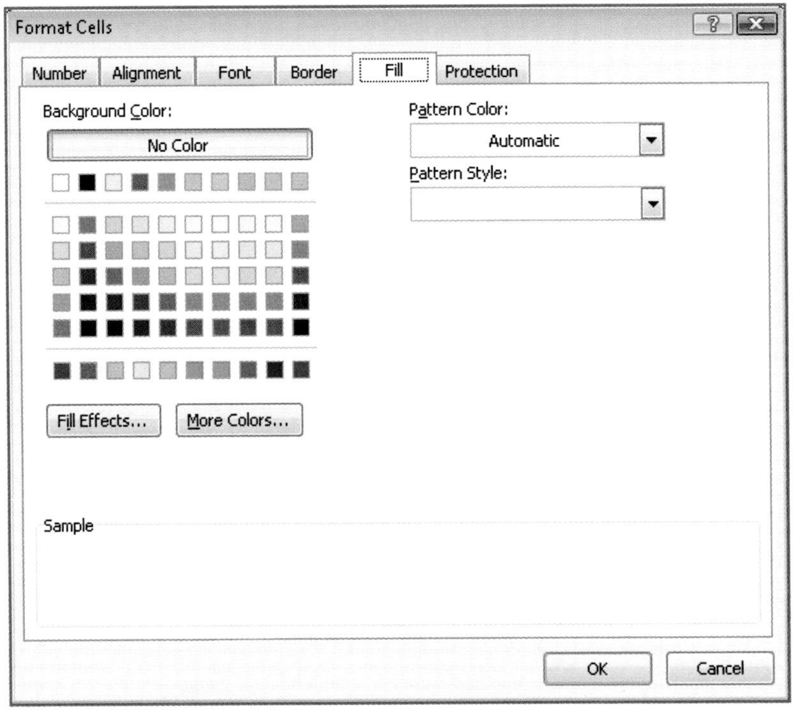

Figure 3-15: *Use the Fill tab to apply colored or patterned backgrounds to cells.*

2. If you want to colorize the pattern, click the **Pattern Color** down arrow to display the color gallery (see "Change Themed Colors" earlier in this chapter for information on the various color options), and select one of the color options.

3. Click **OK** when finished to close the Format Cells dialog box.

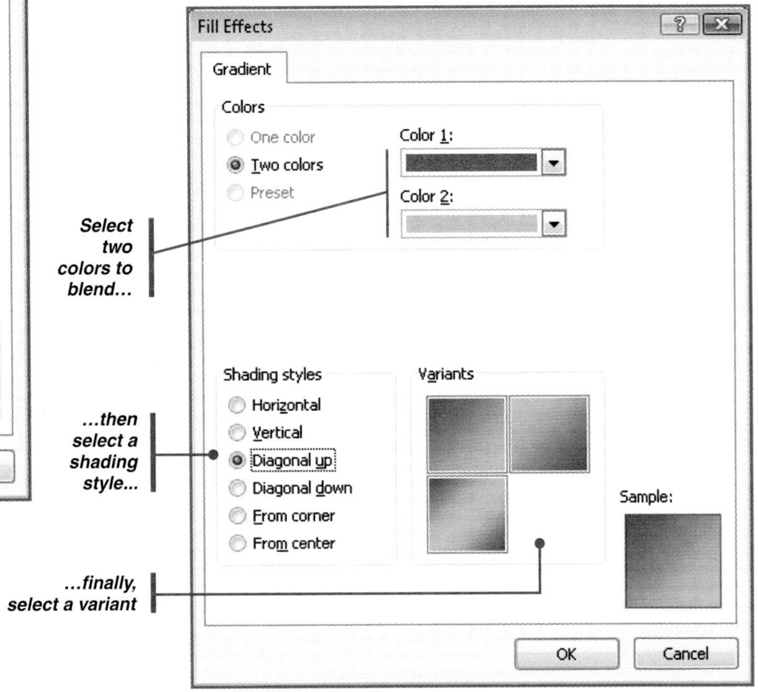

Select two colors to blend...

...then select a shading style...

...finally, select a variant

Figure 3-16: *You can add pizzazz to cell fills using gradient effects.*

NOTE

If you choose Automatic for the Pattern Color in the Format Cells Fill tab, the pattern is applied to the background color, but if you pick both a background color and a pattern color, the colors are merged.

Transfer Formatting

You can manually transfer formatting from one cell to other cells using the Format Painter, as well when you are inserting cells.

When the Format Painter is turned on by double-clicking it, every time you select an object on the worksheet, formatting will be applied to it. For this reason, be sure to turn off the Format Painter immediately after you are done transferring formats.

USE THE FORMAT PAINTER

1. Select the cell whose formatting you want to transfer.

2. In the Home tab Clipboard group, click the **Format Painter** once if you only want to apply the formatting one time.

   –Or–

   Double-click the **Format Painter** to keep it turned on for repeated use.

3. Select the cells where you want the formatting applied.

4. If you single-clicked the Format Painter before applying it to your selection, it will turn off after you apply it to your first selection; if you double-clicked the button, you may select other cells to continue transferring the formatting.

5. Double-click the **Format Painter** to turn it off or press ESC.

ATTACH FORMATTING TO INSERTED CELLS, ROWS, AND COLUMNS

Open the **Insert Options** Smart tag (the paintbrush icon that appears after an insert), and choose from which direction you want the formatting applied, or choose to clear the formatting.

- Format Same As **A**bove
- Format Same As **B**elow
- **C**lear Formatting

You can also copy formatting by using Paste Special and the Paste Options tag (see Chapter 2).

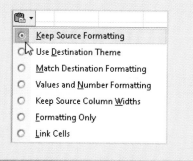

- **K**eep Source Formatting
- Use **D**estination Theme
- **M**atch Destination Formatting
- Values and **N**umber Formatting
- Keep Source Column **W**idths
- **F**ormatting Only
- Link Cells

Arrange and Organize Worksheets

Excel provides several features to help you work with and view worksheets. You can retain headers at the top of the worksheet window as you scroll through hundreds of rows, split a worksheet, and view worksheets from several workbooks. In addition, there are several techniques you can use to add, remove, copy, and organize worksheets (see Chapter 5 for features that allow you to adjust worksheet layout parameters that support pagination and printing).

Lock Rows and Columns

You can lock (or *freeze*) rows and columns in place so that they remain visible as you scroll. Typically, row and column headers are locked in larger worksheets, where you are scrolling through large numbers of rows or columns. You can quickly lock the first row and/or first column in a worksheet, or you can select the rows or columns to freeze.

NOTE

Freezing panes is not the same as freezing data. In an external data range, you can prevent the data from being refreshed, thereby freezing it. See Chapter 8 for more information on external data ranges.

TIP

You can save the arrangement of Excel windows you set up for future viewing in the workbook. After you have the layout looking as you want, in the View tab Window group, click **Save Workspace**. In the Save Workspace window, type a name for the workspace layout, and click **Save** to save the workspace file (.xlw). Open the saved workspace by using the Open dialog box as you would for a workbook file. To change the arrangement, resave a different layout and/or use the Arrange All tool to change how windows are displayed.

The first nine rows are locked as you scroll the rows below them

LOCK ROWS

- In the View tab Window group, click **Freeze Panes** and click **Freeze Top Row**. The top row (typically, your header row) remains in place as you scroll down.

  –Or–

- Select the row below the rows you want to lock, click **Freeze Panes** and click **Freeze Panes**. A thin border displays on the bottom of the locked row. All rows above the locked row remain in place as you scroll down.

	H	I	J	K	L	M
1	ISBN	Category	Author	Title	Publish Year	List Price
2	0071408959	Business	Allaire	Options Strategist	2003	$29.95
3	0830621369	Technical	Alth	Pbs Wells & Septic Systems	1991	$19.95
4	0071467858	Business	Bayan	Words That Sell, Revised	2006	$16.95
5	0071464700	Technical	Bluman	Business Math Demystified	2006	$19.95
6	0071423117	Medicine	Bodenheim	Understanding Health Polic	2004	$36.95
7	0071412077	Medicine	Brooks	Medical Microbiology, 23/E	2004	$52.95
8	0071457720	Technical	Cadick	Elect Safety Hndbk, 3/E	2005	$79.95
9	0071054618	Medicine	Cember	Intro Health Physics 3e	1996	$52.95
26	007146252X	Business	Krames	What The Best CEO's Know	2005	$14.95
27	0072231246	Technical	Meyers	A+ Guide To Operating Syst	2004	$60.00

LOCK COLUMNS

- In the View tab Window group, click **Freeze Panes** and click **Freeze First Column**. The leftmost column (typically, your header column) remains in place as you scroll to the right.

  –Or–

- Select the column to the right of the columns you want to lock, click **Freeze Panes** and click **Freeze Panes**. A thin border displays on the right side of the locked column. All columns to the left of the locked column remain in place as you scroll to the right.

Two locked columns

Two locked rows

	H	I	M
1	ISBN	Category	List Price
2	0071408959	Business	$29.95
3	0830621369	Technical	$19.95
4	0071467858	Business	$16.95
22	0071421947	Business	$14.95
23	0072229497	Technical	$24.99
24	007142251X	Technical	$59.95

LOCK ROWS AND COLUMNS TOGETHER

1. Select the cell that is below and to the right of the range you want to lock.

2. In the View tab Window group, click **Freeze Panes** and click **Freeze Panes**. A thin border displays below the locked rows and to the right of the locked columns. The range will remain in place as you scroll down or to the right.

UNLOCK ROWS AND COLUMNS

In the View tab Window group, click **Freeze Panes** and click **Unfreeze Panes**.

NOTE

Any changes you make in one pane are recorded simultaneously in the other—they are really the same worksheet.

Split a Worksheet

You can divide a worksheet into two independent panes of the same data, as shown in Figure 3-17.

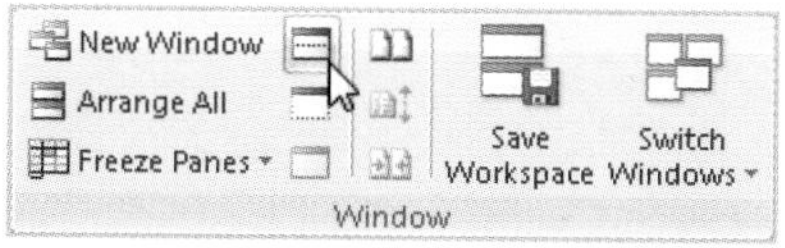

1. In the View tab Window group, click **Split**. Horizontal and vertical split bars are displayed across the worksheet. Remove the unwanted split bar by double-clicking it, leaving you with two panes.

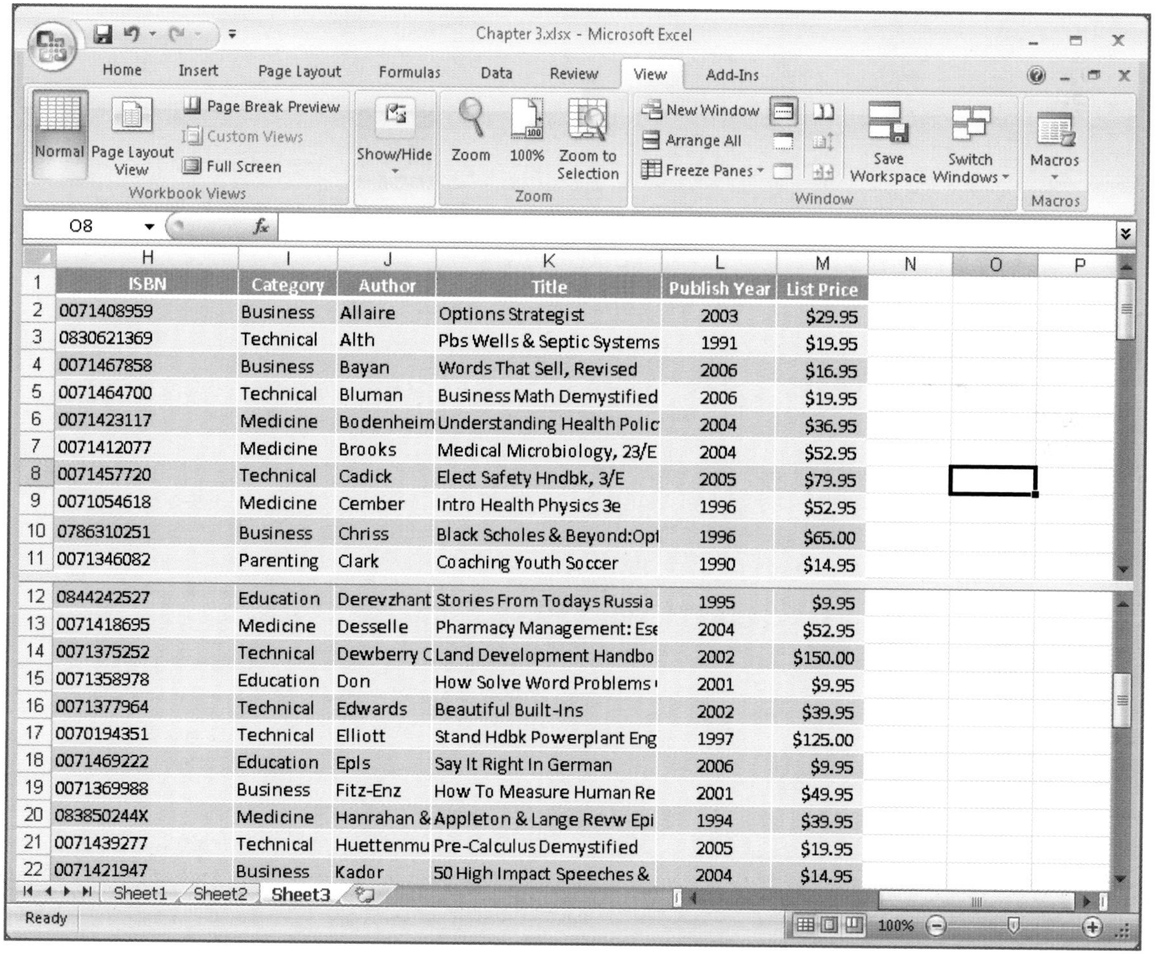

Figure 3-17: A split worksheet provides two independent views of the same worksheet.

2. Point at the split bar, and drag the bar up or down and/or left or right to proportion the two panes as you want.

3. Use the scroll bars to view other data within each pane. You may remove the split bar by double-clicking it.

View Worksheets from Multiple Workbooks

You can divide the Excel worksheet area so that you can view worksheets from multiple workbooks. This arrangement makes it easy to copy data, formulas, and formatting among several worksheets. (See Chapter 9 for information on sharing data.)

1. Open the workbooks that contain the worksheets you want to view. (See Chapter 1 for information on opening existing workbooks.)

2. In the View tab Window group, click **Arrange All**. The Arrange Windows dialog box appears.

3. Select an arrangement and click **OK**. (Figure 3-18 shows an example of tiling three workbooks.)

Compare Workbooks

Excel provides a few tools that allow easy comparison of two workbooks side by side.

1. Open the workbooks you want to compare.

2. In the View tab Window group, click **View Side By Side** 🔲. If you have only two workbooks open, they will appear next to one another. If you have more than

QUICKSTEPS

WORKING WITH WORKSHEETS

Excel provides several tools you can use to modify the number and identification of worksheets in a workbook.

ADD A WORKSHEET

Right-click the worksheet tab to the right of where you want the new worksheet, click **Insert**, and click **OK**.

–Or–

On the worksheet bar, click **Insert Worksheet**. A new worksheet is added to the right of any current tabs.

DELETE A WORKSHEET

Right-click the worksheet tab of the worksheet you want to delete, and click **Delete**.

MOVE OR COPY A WORKSHEET

You can move or copy worksheets within a workbook or between open workbooks by dragging a worksheet's tab. (See "View Worksheets from Multiple Workbooks" earlier in the chapter for steps to arrange multiple open workbooks to facilitate dragging objects between them.)

- To move a worksheet, drag the worksheet tab to the position on the worksheet bar where you want it to appear.

- To copy a worksheet, press and hold **CTRL**, and drag the worksheet tab to the position on the worksheet bar where you want it to appear.

Continued . . .

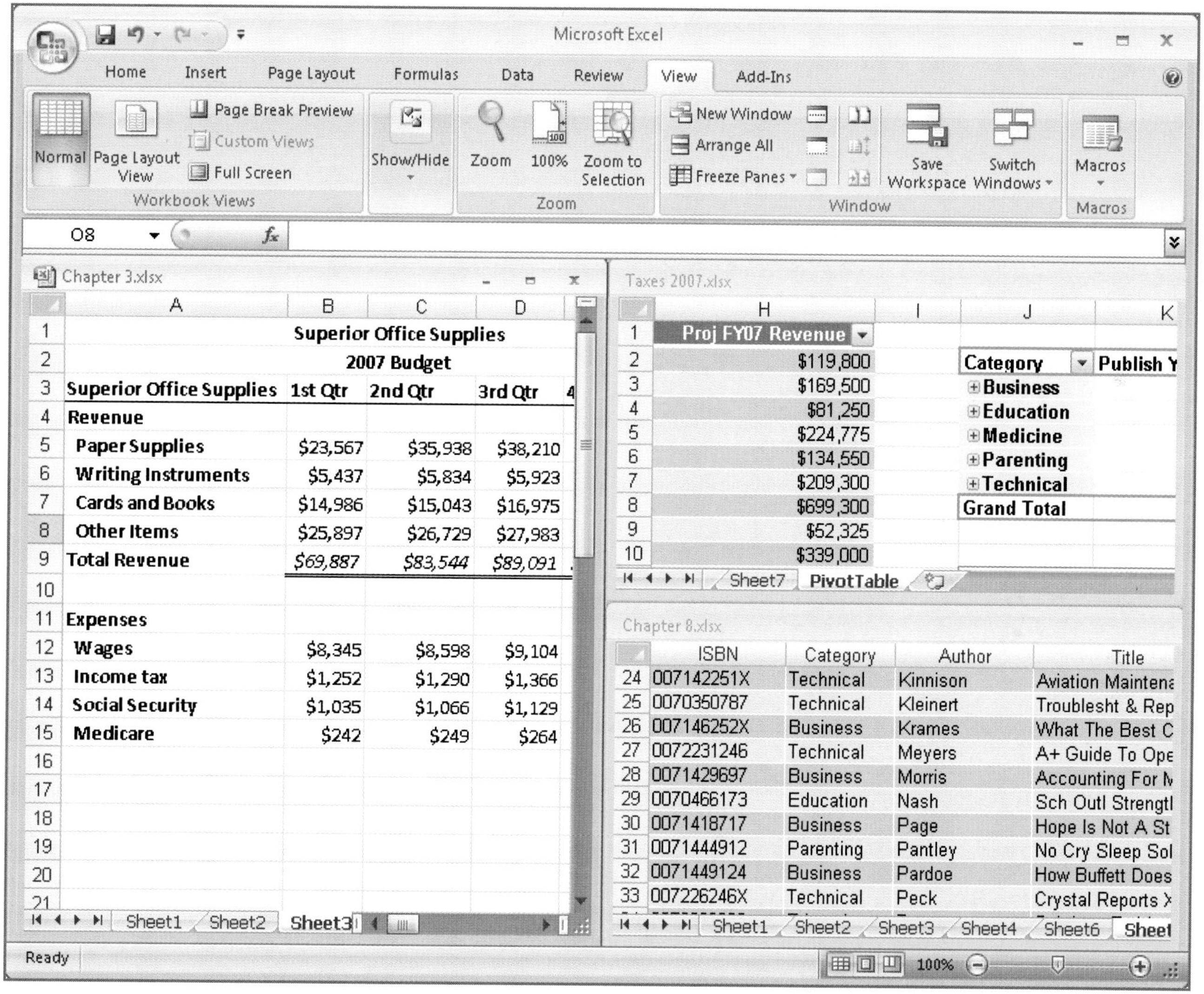

Figure 3-18: You can look at several workbooks at the same time to compare them or to transfer information among them.

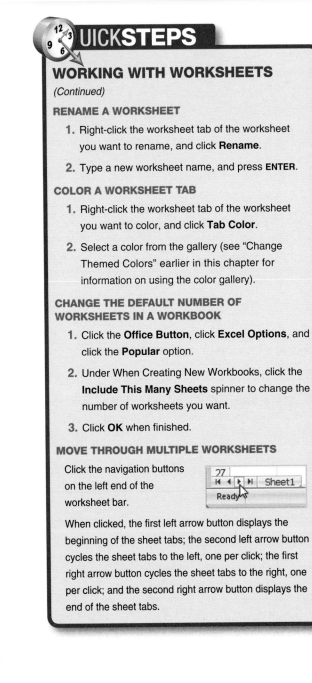

QUICKSTEPS

WORKING WITH WORKSHEETS

(Continued)

RENAME A WORKSHEET

1. Right-click the worksheet tab of the worksheet you want to rename, and click **Rename**.

2. Type a new worksheet name, and press **ENTER**.

COLOR A WORKSHEET TAB

1. Right-click the worksheet tab of the worksheet you want to color, and click **Tab Color**.

2. Select a color from the gallery (see "Change Themed Colors" earlier in this chapter for information on using the color gallery).

CHANGE THE DEFAULT NUMBER OF WORKSHEETS IN A WORKBOOK

1. Click the **Office Button**, click **Excel Options**, and click the **Popular** option.

2. Under When Creating New Workbooks, click the **Include This Many Sheets** spinner to change the number of worksheets you want.

3. Click **OK** when finished.

MOVE THROUGH MULTIPLE WORKSHEETS

Click the navigation buttons on the left end of the worksheet bar.

When clicked, the first left arrow button displays the beginning of the sheet tabs; the second left arrow button cycles the sheet tabs to the left, one per click; the first right arrow button cycles the sheet tabs to the right, one per click; and the second right arrow button displays the end of the sheet tabs.

---

two workbooks open, you can select the workbook to view along with the currently active workbook from the Compare Side By Side dialog box.

3. By default, both workbook windows will scroll at the same rate. To turn off this feature, click **Synchronous Scrolling** in the Window group.

How to...

- ⨂ *Understanding Cell Referencing Types*
- *Change Cell References*
- *Change to R1C1 References*
- *Name Cells*
- ⨂ *Using Cell Reference Operators*
- *Go to a Named Cell*
- *Create a Formula*
- ⌕ *Working with Cell Names*
- *Edit a Formula*
- *Move Formulas*
- ⌕ *Using Formulas*
- *Copy Formulas*
- *Recalculate Formulas*
- *Use External References in Formulas*
- ⨂ *Understanding the Trust Center*
- *Format Conditionally*
- ⌕ *Using Functions Quickly*
- *Enter a Function*
- *Enter a Sum in Columns or Rows Quickly*
- *Check for Errors*
- *Trace Precedent and Dependent Cells*
- *Watch a Cell*
- *Evaluate a Formula in Pieces*

Chapter 4

Using Formulas and Functions

4

Excel lets you easily perform powerful calculations using formulas and functions. Formulas are mathematical statements that follow a set of rules and use a specific syntax. In this chapter you will learn how to reference cells used in formulas, how to give cells names so that they are easily input, how to use conditional formatting to identify cells that satisfy criteria you specify, and how to build formulas. Functions—ready-made formulas that you can use to get quick results for specific applications, such as figuring out loan payments—are also covered. Finally, you will learn about several tools Excel provides to find and correct errors in formulas and functions.

Reference Cells

Formulas typically make use of data already entered in worksheets and need a scheme to locate, or *reference,* that data. Shortcuts are used to help you recall addresses as well as a *syntax*, or set of rules, to communicate to Excel how you want cells used.

Change Cell References

To change cell referencing:

1. Select the cell that contains the formula reference you want to change.

2. In the Formula bar, select the cell address, and press **F4** to switch the cell referencing, starting from a relative reference to the following in this order:

   - Absolute ($A$1)
   - Mixed (relative column, absolute row) (A$1)
   - Mixed (absolute column, relative row) ($A1)
   - Relative (A1)

   –Or–

   Edit the cell address by entering or removing the dollar symbol ($) in front of row or column identifiers.

Change to R1C1 References

You can change the A1 cell referencing scheme used by Excel to an older style that identifies both rows and columns numerically, starting in the upper-left corner of the worksheet, rows first, and adds a leading *R* and *C* for clarification. For example, cell B4 in R1C1 reference style is R4C2.

1. Click the **Office Button**, click **Excel Options**, and click the **Formulas** option.

2. Under Working With Formulas, click **R1C1 Reference Style** to select it.

3. Click **OK** when finished.

Working with formulas
☑ R1C1 reference style ⓘ
☑ Formula AutoComplete ⓘ
☑ Use table names in formulas

Name Cells

You can name a cell (MonthTotal, for example) or a range to refer to physical cell addresses, and then use the names when referencing the cell in formulas and functions. Names are more descriptive, easier to remember, and often quicker to enter than A1-style cell references. You can name a cell directly on the worksheet or use a dialog box and provide amplifying information.

To view formulas instead of cell values (see Figure 4-1), in the Formulas tab Formula Auditing group, click **Show Formulas** 🔢. Click the button a second time to return to a value display.

TIP

NAME A CELL OR RANGE DIRECTLY

1. Select the cells you want to reference.

2. Click the **Name Box** at the left end of the Formula bar.

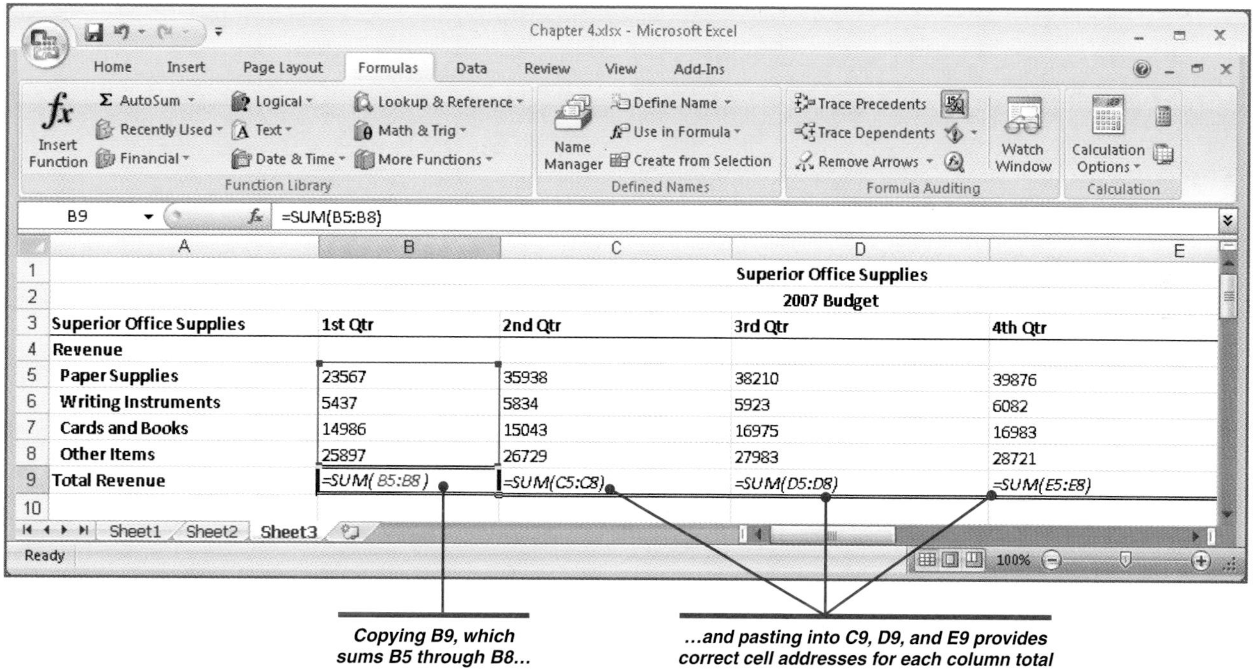

Copying B9, which
sums B5 through B8...

...and pasting into C9, D9, and E9 provides
correct cell addresses for each column total

Figure 4-1: Using relative references, Excel logically assumes cell addresses in copied formulas.

TIP

Absolute cell references are typically used when you want to copy the values of cells and are not interested in applying their formulas to other cells, such as in a summary or report where the relative references would be meaningless. Though you can apply absolute reference syntax to each cell reference, a faster way is to open the Paste Smart tag that displays next to the destination cells, and choose **Values Only** from the drop-down list. See "Copy Formulas" later in the chapter for more information on copying and pasting formulas.

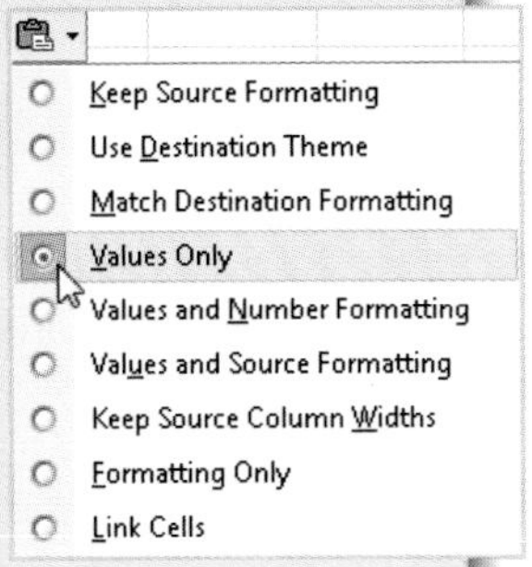

Keep Source Formatting
Use Destination Theme
Match Destination Formatting
Values Only
Values and Number Formatting
Values and Source Formatting
Keep Source Column Widths
Formatting Only
Link Cells

TIP

If a cell or range name is longer than what can be displayed in the Name Box, increase the width of the Name box by dragging the circle in the arc forming its right boundary to the right.

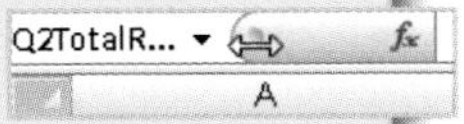

Q2TotalR...
A

CAUTION

Cell names need to adhere to a set of rules. Names are case-sensitive, and no spaces are allowed in a cell name, although multiple words can be joined by an underscore or period. Also, names must start with a letter, underscore (_), or backslash (\).

3. Type a name (see accompanying Caution for naming rules), and press **ENTER**. (See the "Working with Cell Names" QuickSteps for ways to modify cell names.)

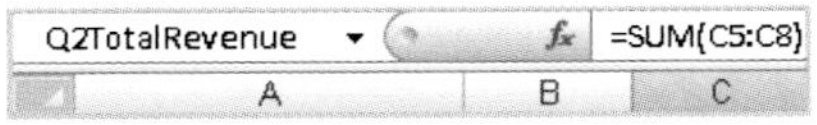

Q2TotalRevenue
=SUM(C5:C8)
A
B
C

NAME A CELL OR RANGE IN A DIALOG BOX

1. Select the cells you want to reference.
2. In the Formulas tab Defined Names group, click **Define Name**.

   –Or–

   Right-click the selection and click **Name A Range**.

   In the either case, the New Name dialog box appears, shown in Figure 4-2.

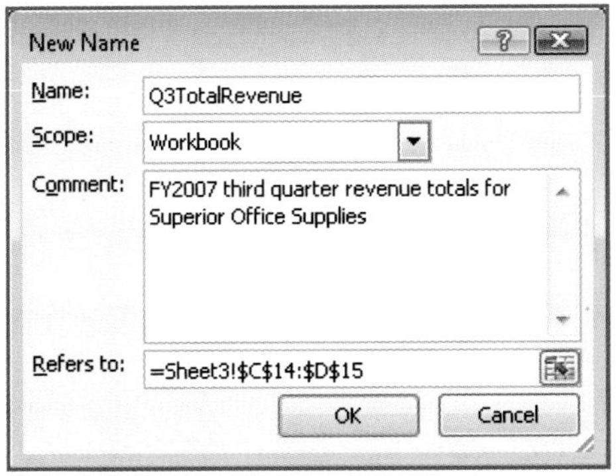

New Name
Name:
Q3TotalRevenue
Scope:
Workbook
Comment:
FY2007 third quarter revenue totals for Superior Office Supplies
Refers to:
=Sheet3!$C$14:$D$15
OK
Cancel

***Figure 4-2:** You can easily name cells and add descriptive information.*

3. Type a name for the cell or range (see the accompanying Caution for naming rules).
4. Click the **Scope** down arrow, and select whether the name applies to the entire workbook or to one of its worksheets.
5. If desired, type a comment that more fully explains the meaning of the named cells. Comments can be upward of 1,000 characters and will appear as a tooltip when the name is used in formulas and functions.

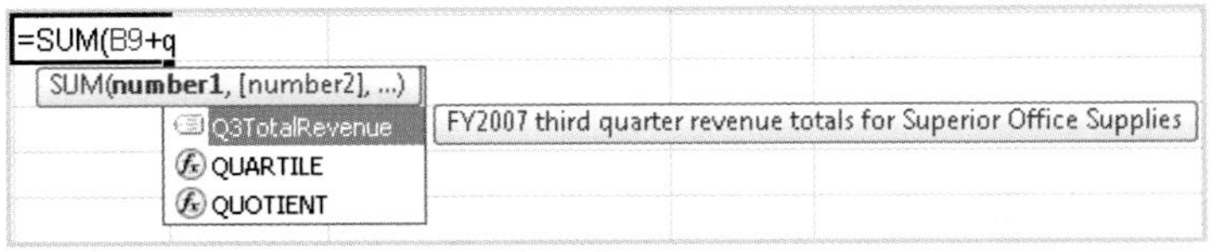

=SUM(B9+q
SUM(number1, [number2], ...)
Q3TotalRevenue
FY2007 third quarter revenue totals for Superior Office Supplies
QUARTILE
QUOTIENT

USING CELL REFERENCE OPERATORS

Cell reference operators (colons, commas, and spaces used in an address, such as E5:E10 E16:E17,E12) provide the syntax for referencing cell ranges, unions, and intersections.

REFERENCE A RANGE

A *range* defines a block of cells.

Type a colon (:) between the upper-leftmost cell and the lower-rightmost cell (for example, B5:C8).

=SUM(B5:C8)	
B	C
$23,567	$35,938
$5,437	$5,834
$14,986	$15,043
$25,897	$26,729

REFERENCE A UNION

A *union* joins multiple cell references.

Type a comma (,) between separate cell references (for example, B5,B7,C6).

=SUM(B5,B7,C6)	
B	C
$23,567	$35,938
$5,437	$5,834
$14,986	$15,043

REFERENCE AN INTERSECTION

An *intersection* is the overlapping, or common, cells in two ranges.

Type a space (press the **SPACEBAR**) between two range-cell references (for example, B5:B8 B7:C7). B7 is the common cell.

=SUM(B5:B8 B7:C7)	
B	C
$23,567	$35,938
$5,437	$5,834
$14,986	$15,043
$25,897	$26,729

To quickly open the Name Manager, press **CTRL+F3** or add the Name Manager icon to the Quick Access toolbar. (Chapter 1 describes how to add tools to the Quick Access toolbar.)

6. If you want to modify the cell or cells to be named, click the **Refers To** text box, and type the reference (starting with the equal (=) sign), or reselect the cells from the worksheet.

7. Click **OK** when finished.

Go to a Named Cell

Named cells are quickly found and selected for you.

- Click the **Name Box** down arrow to open the drop-down list, and click the named cell or range you want to go to.

G19	▾
Q2TotalRevenue	
Q3TotalRevenue	
Table2	
Books	

–Or–

- In the Home tab Editing group, click **Find & Select** and click **Go To**. In the Go To dialog box, double-click the named cell or range you want to go to.

Build Formulas

Formulas are mathematical equations that combine *values* and *cell references* with *operators* to calculate a result. Values are actual numbers or logical values, such as True and False, or the contents of cells that contain numbers or logical values. Cell references point to cells whose values are to be used, for example, E5:E10, E12, and MonthlyTot. Operators, such as + (add), > (greater than), and ^ (use an exponent), tell Excel what type of calculation to perform or logical comparison to apply. Prebuilt formulas, or *functions*, that return a value also can be used in formulas. (Functions are described later in this chapter.)

Create a Formula

You create formulas by either entering or referencing values. The character that tells Excel to perform a calculation is the equal sign (=) and must precede any combination of values, cell references, and operators.

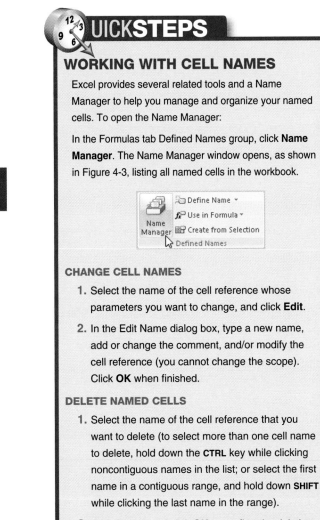

QUICKSTEPS

WORKING WITH CELL NAMES

Excel provides several related tools and a Name Manager to help you manage and organize your named cells. To open the Name Manager:

In the Formulas tab Defined Names group, click **Name Manager**. The Name Manager window opens, as shown in Figure 4-3, listing all named cells in the workbook.

CHANGE CELL NAMES

1. Select the name of the cell reference whose parameters you want to change, and click **Edit**.

2. In the Edit Name dialog box, type a new name, add or change the comment, and/or modify the cell reference (you cannot change the scope). Click **OK** when finished.

DELETE NAMED CELLS

1. Select the name of the cell reference that you want to delete (to select more than one cell name to delete, hold down the **CTRL** key while clicking noncontiguous names in the list; or select the first name in a contiguous range, and hold down **SHIFT** while clicking the last name in the range).

2. Click **Delete** and click **OK** to confirm the deletion.

Continued . . .

Figure 4-3: The Name Manager provides a central location for organizing, creating, and modifying named cells.

Excel formulas are calculated from left to right according to an ordered hierarchy of operators. For example, exponents precede multiplication and division, which precede addition and subtraction. You can alter the calculation order (and results) by use of parentheses; Excel performs the calculation within the innermost parentheses first. For example, =12+48/24 returns 14 (48 is divided by 24, resulting in 2; then 12 is added to 2). Using parentheses, =(12+48)/24 returns 2.5 (12 is added to 48, resulting in 60; then 60 is divided by 24).

ENTER A SIMPLE FORMULA

1. Select a blank cell, and type an equal sign (=). The equal sign displays in the cell and in the Formula bar.

2. Type a value, such as <u>64</u>.

3. Type an operator, such as <u>+</u>.

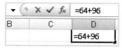

QUICKSTEPS

WORKING WITH CELL NAMES (Continued)

SORT AND FILTER NAMED CELLS

If you have several named cells in a workbook, you can easily view only the ones you are interested in:

- To sort named cells, click a column heading to change the sort order from ascending (numerals first 0-9, then A-Z) to descending (Z-A, numerals last 9-0). Click the heading a second time to return to the original order.

- To see only specific categories of named cells, click **Filter** and click the category of named cells you want to see. Only named cells that belong in the category you select will appear in the list of cell names.

    - Clear Filter
    - Names Scoped to Worksheet
    - Names Scoped to Workbook
    - Names with Errors
    - Names without Errors
    - Defined Names
    - Table Names

- To return a filtered list to a complete list of named cells, click **Filter** and click **Clear Filter**.

VIEW MORE DATA

The default width of the Name Manager and its columns might not readily display longer cell names, references, or comments:

- To increase a column width, drag the right border of the column heading to the right as far as you need.

- To increase the width of the dialog box, drag either the dialog box's right or left border to the left or right, respectively.

---

4. Type a second value, such as 96.

5. Complete the entry by pressing **ENTER** or clicking **Enter** on the Formula bar; or add additional values and operators, and then complete the entry. The result of your equation displays in the cell. (See Chapter 2 for other methods to complete an entry.)

USE CELL REFERENCES

1. Select a blank cell, and type an equal sign (=). The equal sign displays in the cell and in the Formula bar.

2. Enter a cell reference:

    - Type a cell reference (for example, B4) that contains the value you want.
    - Click the cell whose value you want. A blinking border surrounds the cell.
    - Select a named cell. In the Formulas tab Defined Names group, click **Use In Formula**, and click the named cell you want.

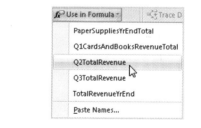

3. Type an operator.

4. Enter another cell reference or a value.

5. Complete the entry by pressing **ENTER**; or add additional cell references, values, and operators, and then complete the entry. The result of your formula is displayed in the cell, as shown in Figure 4-4.

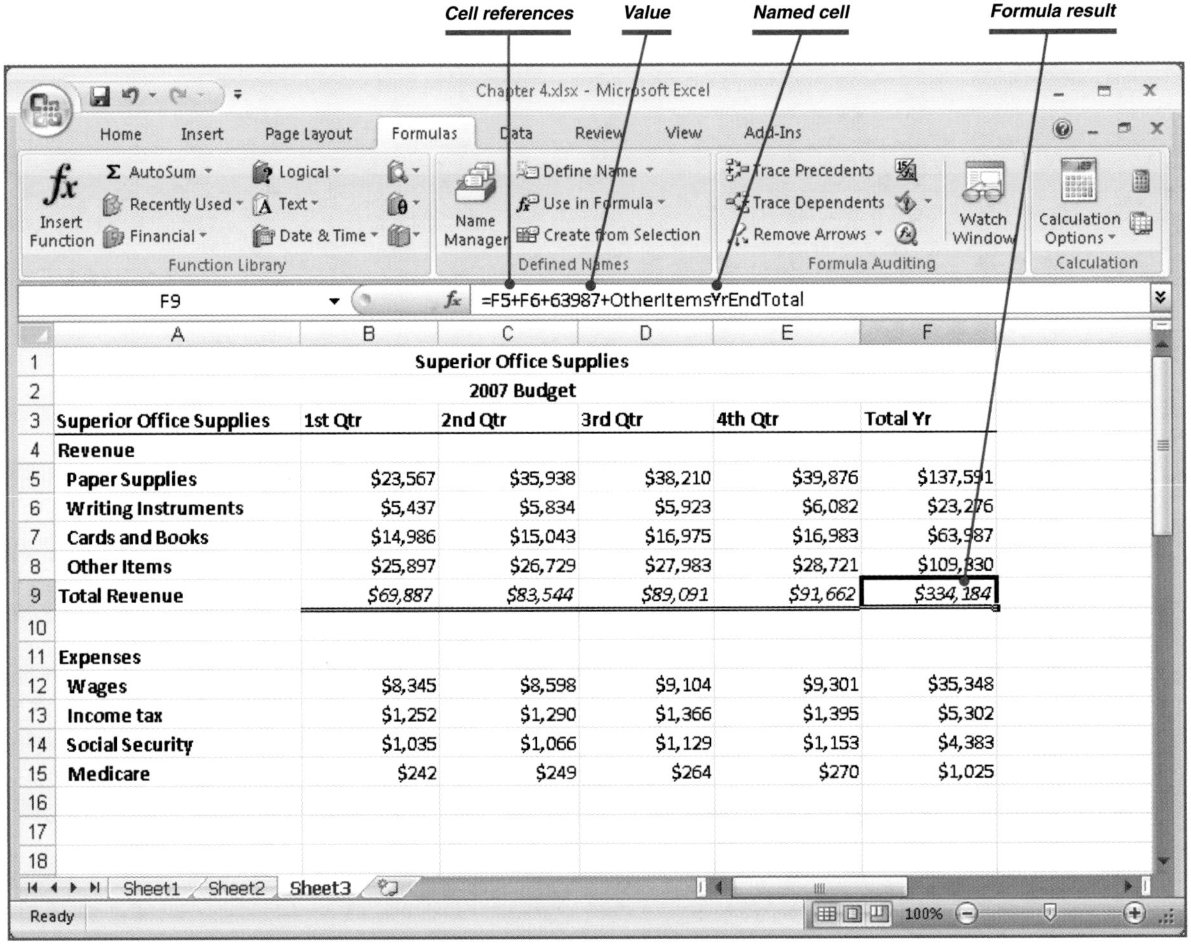

Figure 4-4: A formula in Excel is comprised of cell references, values, and named cells.

Edit a Formula

You can easily change a formula after you have entered one.

1. Double-click the cell that contains the formula you want to change. The formula is displayed in the cell and in the Formula bar. Cell references for each cell or range are color-coded.

TIP

Excel provides several concessions for users who are transitioning to Excel from Lotus 1-2-3. For example, when creating a formula, you can type a plus sign (+) instead of the equal sign to denote a formula. Excel will change the plus sign to an equal sign if a number follows it, or Excel will add the equal sign to a plus sign that is followed by a cell reference. In any case, be sure not to type a leading space before either the plus or the equal sign, as the characters that follow will be interpreted as text instead of as a formula. To enable Lotus transitioning, click the **Office** button, click **Excel Options**, and click the **Advanced** option. Under Lotus Compatibility Settings, click **Transition Formula Entry**, and click **OK**.

CAUTION

When creating a formula, be careful not to click any cells that you do not want referenced in the formula. After you type the equal sign, Excel interprets any selected cell as being a cell reference in the formula.

		=F5+F6+63987+OtherItemsYrEndTotal
D	E	F
plies		
3rd Qtr	**4th Qtr**	**Total Yr**
$38,210	$39,876	$137,591
$5,923	$6,082	$23,276
$16,975	$16,983	$63,987
$27,983	$28,721	$109,330
$89,091	$91,662	=F5+F6+63987+OtherItemsYrEndTotal

2. Edit the formula by:

- Making changes directly in the cell or on the Formula bar
- Dragging the border of a colored cell or range reference to move it to a new location
- Dragging a corner sizing-box of a colored cell or range reference to expand the reference

3. Complete the entry by pressing **ENTER**.

Move Formulas

You move formulas by cutting and pasting. When you move formulas, Excel uses absolute referencing—the formula remains exactly the same as it was originally with the same cell references. (See "Change Cell References" earlier in the chapter for more information on cell referencing.)

1. Select the cell whose formula you want to move.

2. In the Home tab Clipboard group, click **Cut** or press **CTRL+X**.

   –Or–

   Right-click the cell whose formula you want to move, and click **Cut**.

3. Select the cell where you want to move the formula.

4. In the Home tab Clipboard group, click **Paste** or press **CTRL+V**.

   –Or–

   Right-click the cell where you want to move the formula, and click **Paste**.

Copy Formulas

When you copy formulas, relative referencing is applied. Therefore, cell referencing in a formula will change when you copy the formula, unless you have made a reference absolute. If you do not get the results you expect, click **Undo** on the Quick Access toolbar, and change the cell references before you copy again.

COPY FORMULAS INTO ADJACENT CELLS

1. Select the cell whose formula you want to copy.

2. Point at the fill handle in the lower-right corner of the cell, and drag over the cells where you want the formula copied.

COPY FORMULAS INTO NONADJACENT CELLS

1. Select the cell whose formula you want to copy.

2. In the Home tab Clipboard group, click **Copy** 📋 or press **CTRL+C**.

   –Or–

   Right-click the cell you want to copy, and click **Copy**.

3. Copy formatting along with the formula by selecting the destination cell. Then, in the Home tab Clipboard group, click **Paste** or press **CTRL+V**.

   –Or–

   Right-click the destination cell, and click **Paste**.

4. Copy just the formula by selecting the destination cell. Then, in the Home tab Clipboard group, click the **Paste** down arrow, and click **Formulas**.

Recalculate Formulas

By default, Excel automatically recalculates formulas affected by changes to a value, to the formula itself, or to a changed named cell. You also can recalculate more frequently using the tips presented in Table 4-1.

To turn off automatic calculation and select other calculation options:

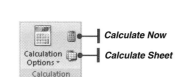

Calculate Now

Calculate Sheet

1. In the Formulas tab Calculation group, click **Calculation Options**.

2. In the Options drop-down menu, click **Manual**. You can also force an immediate calculation in the Calculation group by clicking **Calc Now** to recalculate the workbook or clicking **Calc Sheet** to recalculate the active worksheet.

TO CALCULATE...	IN...	PRESS...
Formulas, and formulas dependent on them, that have changed since the last calculation	All open workbooks	F9 (or click **Calculate Now** in the Calculation group)
Formulas, and formulas dependent on them, that have changed since the last calculation	The active worksheet	SHIFT+F9 (or click **Calculate Sheet** in the Calculation group)
All formulas, regardless of any changes since the last calculation	All open workbooks	CTRL+ALT+F9
All formulas, regardless of any changes since the last calculation, after rechecking dependent formulas	All open workbooks	CTRL+SHIFT+ALT+F9

Table 4-1: Formula Recalculations in Excel

Use External References in Formulas

You can *link* data using cell references to worksheets and workbooks other than the one you are currently working in. For example, if you are building a departmental budget, you could link to each division's budget workbook and have any changes made to formulas in those workbooks automatically applied to your total budget workbook. Changes made to the *external* references in the *source* workbooks are automatically updated in the *destination* workbook when the destination workbook is opened or when the source workbooks are changed and the destination workbook is open.

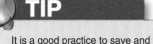

TIP

It is a good practice to save and close the source workbook before saving the destination workbook.

CREATE EXTERNAL REFERENCE LINKS

1. Open both the source and destination workbooks in your computer.

2. Arrange the workbooks so that they are all displayed. For example, in the View tab Window group, click **Arrange All**, click **Tiled**, and click **OK**. (See Chapter 3 for more information on arranging workbooks in the Excel window.)

3. In the destination worksheet, create the formula or open an existing formula.

4. Place the insertion point in the formula where you want the external reference.

5. In the source workbook, click the cell whose cell reference you want. The external reference is added to the formula, as shown in Figure 4-5.

6. Press **ENTER** to complete the entry.

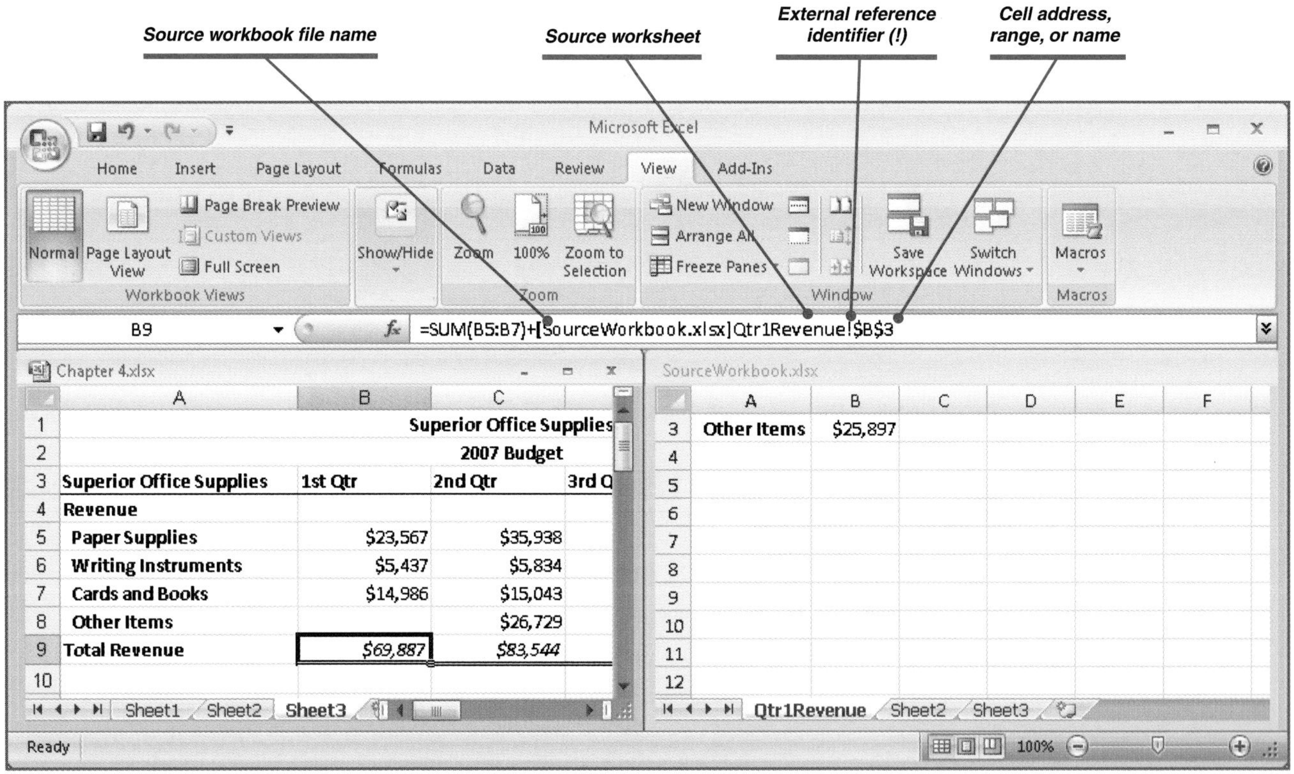

Figure 4-5: An external reference in a formula is comprised of several components.

CAUTION

If you break an external reference link in the Edit Links dialog box, all formulas using external references are converted to values. Broken links cannot be undone except by reestablishing the links.

QUICKFACTS

UNDERSTANDING THE TRUST CENTER

Microsoft Office 2007 recognizes the need to provide enhanced file security against the world of viruses and other malicious code that can compromise your data and impair your computer. To provide a unified approach in applying security settings for all Office 2007 programs installed on your system, Office 2007 includes a *Trust Center* to help you manage your security settings. It also provides information on privacy and general computer security (see Figure 4-7). The Trust Center security settings window (click **Trust Center Settings**) organizes security settings in eight categories. Taking a "better safe than sorry" approach, Microsoft errs on the side of caution by limiting any automatic updates or actions without user approval. You can change these defaults to allow more or less intervention. Security settings in the Trust Center are applicable to all workbooks and "trump" the automatic link updating behavior set for individual workbooks. To allow automatic link updating for individual workbooks, you must first enable automatic link updates in the Trust Center. (See Chapter 9 for more information on ways to protect workbooks.)

To open the Trust Center, click the **Office Button**, click **Excel Options**, and click the **Trust Center** option.

UPDATE AND MANAGE EXTERNAL REFERENCES

You can control how external references are updated, check on their status, and break or change the link.

1. Open the destination workbook.

2. In the Data tab Connections group, click **Edit Links**. The Edit Links dialog box appears, as shown in Figure 4-6.

3. Select a link and then use the command buttons on the right side of the dialog box to perform the action you want.

4. Click **Close** when finished.

UPDATE LINKS

When you open a destination workbook with external links to source workbooks, you are potentially providing a security risk to your computer by allowing data from other sources into your system. By default, automatic updating is disabled and the user opening a destination workbook needs to provide permission to enable the links (unless the source workbooks are open on the same computer as the destination workbook).

1. Open the destination workbook. Unless default settings have been changed, a Security Warning message displays below the ribbon notifying you that automatic link updating is disabled, as shown in Figure 4-8.

Figure 4-6: You can update and manage links in the Edit Links dialog box.

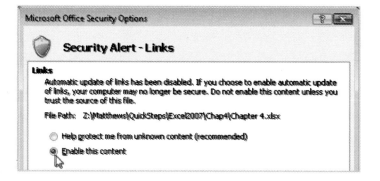

Help keep your documents safe and your computer secure and healthy.

Protecting your privacy

Microsoft cares about your privacy. For more information about how Microsoft Office Excel helps to protect your privacy, please see the privacy statements.

Show the Microsoft Office Excel privacy statement
Microsoft Office Online privacy statement
Customer Experience Improvement Program

Security & more

Learn more about protecting your privacy and security from Microsoft Office Online.

Microsoft Windows Security Center
Microsoft Trustworthy Computing

Microsoft Office Excel Trust Center

The Trust Center contains security and privacy settings. These settings help keep your computer secure. We recommend that you do not change these settings.

Figure 4-7:The Trust Center provides a focal point for accessing privacy and security information and settings for Office 2007 programs.

2. Click **Options**. In the Security Options dialog box, click **Enable This Content**, and click **OK**. The links will be updated.

TIP

If you are unsure of the origination of the source workbooks when updating links in a destination workbook, open the Edit Links dialog box to view the files involved in the links. See how in "Update and Manage External References."

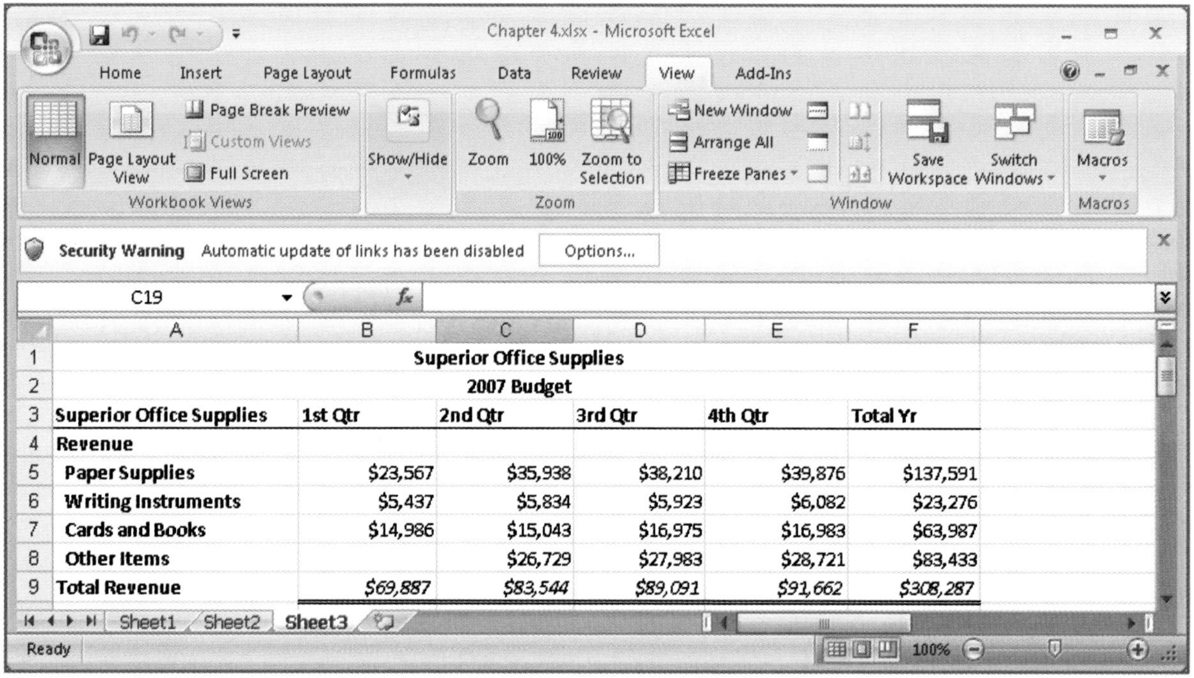

Figure 4-8: *To protect you from erroneous or malicious data, Office prompts you to enable link updates.*

CHANGE AUTOMATIC LINK UPDATING FOR ALL WORKBOOKS

You can change how links are updated in the Trust Center security settings window.

1. Click the **Office Button**, click **Excel Options**, and click the **Trust Center** option. In the Trust Center window, click **Trust Center Settings**.

–Or–

If opening a destination workbook and receiving a security warning, click **Options**, and click **Open The Trust Center** in the alert.

In either case, the Trust Center security settings window opens.

Trusted Publishers

Trusted Locations

Add-ins

ActiveX Settings

Macro Settings

Message Bar

External Content

Privacy Options

Security settings for Data Connections

○ Enable all Data Connections (not recommended)

◉ Prompt user about Data Connections

○ Disable all Data Connections

Security settings for Workbook Links

○ Enable automatic update for all Workbook Links (not recommended)

◉ Prompt user on automatic update for Workbook Links

○ Disable automatic update of Workbook Links

OK   Cancel

Figure 4-9: Trust Center privacy and security settings are organized in eight categories.

NOTE

Before you can allow automatic link updating in an individual workbook, you must enable it in the Trust Center for all workbooks. See how in "Change Automatic Link Updating for All Workbooks."

2. In the Trust Center security settings window, shown in Figure 4-9, click the **External Content** category.

3. In the Security Settings For Workbook Links area, select the automatic link updating behavior you want, and click **OK** twice.

CHANGE AUTOMATIC LINK UPDATING FOR INDIVIDUAL WORKBOOKS

You can choose to not display the security alert in a destination workbook that prompts users to update links. You can also choose to update links, or not, without user intervention.

1. Open the destination workbook whose security alert behavior you want to change.

2. In the Data tab Connections group, click **Edit Links**, and click **Startup Prompt**.

Startup Prompt

When this workbook is opened, Excel can ask whether or not to update links to other workbooks.

◉ Let users choose to display the alert or not

○ Don't display the alert and don't update automatic links

○ Don't display the alert and update links

OK   Cancel

Item:

Update: ◉ Automatic ○ Manual

Startup Prompt...

3. In the Startup Prompt dialog box, select the behavior you want, click **OK**, and click **Close**. The next time the workbook is opened, the new behavior will be enabled.

4	Revenue		
5	Paper Supplies		$23,567
6	Writing Instruments		$5,437
7	Cards and Books		$14,986
8	Other Items		$25,897
9	Total Revenue		*$69,887*

4	Revenue		
5	Paper Supplies		$23,567
6	Writing Instruments		$5,437
7	Cards and Books		$14,986
8	Other Items		$25,897
9	Total Revenue		*$69,887*

4	Revenue		
5	Paper Supplies	●	$23,567
6	Writing Instruments	○	$5,437
7	Cards and Books	◑	$14,986
8	Other Items	●	$25,897
9	Total Revenue		*$69,887*

Format Conditionally

Excel 2007 has greatly improved the ease and capabilities for identifying data in a worksheet based on rules you select. Rules are organized into several types that allow you to easily format cells that compare values against each other; meet specific values, dates, or other criteria; match top and bottom percentile values you choose; match values above or below an average; or identify unique or duplicate values. If no pre-existing rule accommodates your needs, you can use a formula to set up criteria that cells must match.

COMPARE CELLS AGAINST ONE ANOTHER

You can highlight the comparative value of selected cells by using one of three formatting styles:

- **Data bars** display in each cell colored bars whose length is proportional to their value as compared to the other values in the selection.

- **Color scales** blend two or three colors (such as a green-yellow-red traffic light metaphor) to differentiate among high to low values.

- **Icon sets** use from three to five similar icons (similar to the circles used in *Consumer Reports*) to differentiate among high to low values.

1. Select the cells that will be compared against one another.

2. In the Home tab Styles group, click **Conditional Formatting** and click the style you want to use to see a submenu of options.

3. Point to each option to see a live preview of its effect on your selected data, as shown in Figure 4-10. Click the option you want to use.

4. For more choices of each style, click **More Rules** at the bottom of each of their respective submenus.

5. In the New Formatting Rule dialog box, under Edit The Rule Description, you can change from one style to another and, depending on the style, change colors, change the values attributed to an icon or color, and make other customizations (see Figure 4-11). Click **OK** when finished.

Point to a conditional formatting style...   **...and see the effect on selected cells**

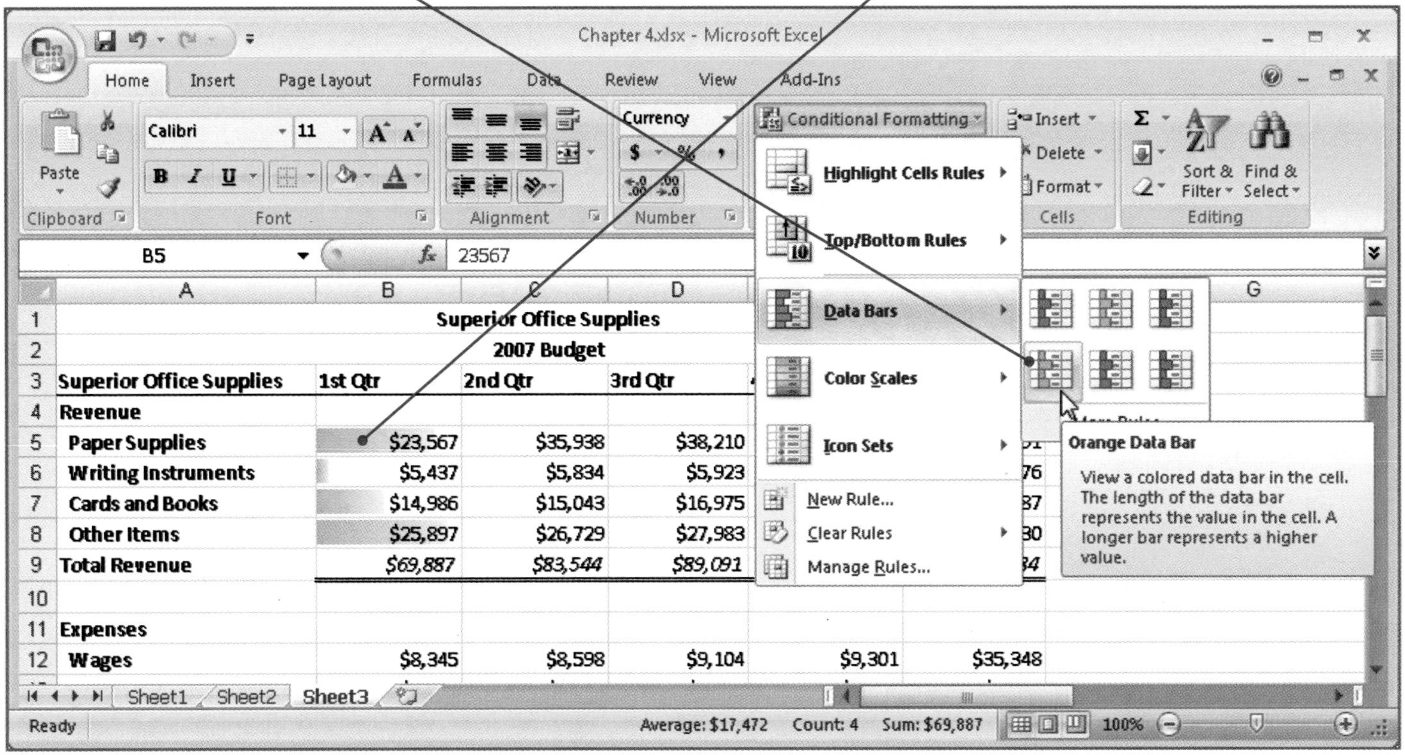

Figure 4-10: *You can see a live preview of each formatting style on your data before selecting one.*

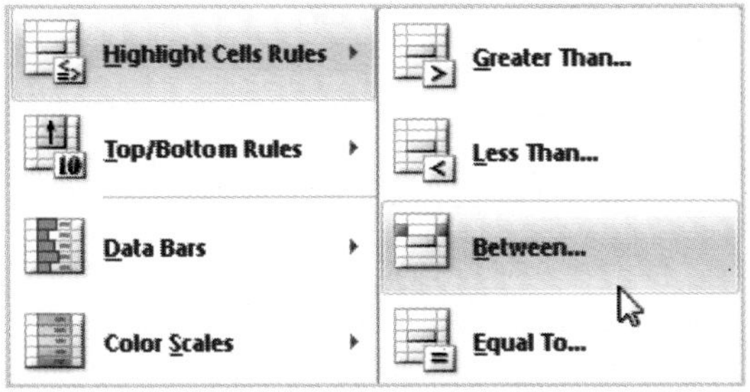

FORMAT CELLS THAT MATCH VALUES OR CONDITIONS

Excel provides several pre-existing rules that let you easily format cells that meet established criteria.

1. Select the cells that will be formatted if they meet conditions you select.

2. In the Home tab Styles group, click **Conditional Formatting** and click **Highlight Cell Rules** to view a submenu of rules that compare values to conditions.

–Or–

When changing values in dialog boxes for conditional formatting, as in the New Formatting Rule dialog box (and when setting up functions, described later in this chapter), you can type a value or formula in the associated text box, or you can select a cell that contains the value or formula you want and have it entered for you. When selecting a cell, click the **Collapse Dialog** button to shrink the dialog box so that you can see more of the worksheet. Click **Expand Dialog** to return to the full-size dialog box.

Value

67

New Formatting Rule

New Formatting Rule

Select a Rule Type:

► Format all cells based on their values
► Format only cells that contain
► Format only top or bottom ranked values
► Format only values that are above or below average
► Format only unique or duplicate values
► Use a formula to determine which cells to format

Edit the Rule Description:

Format all cells based on their values:

Format Style: 2-Color Scale

	Minimum	Maximum
Type:	Lowest Value	Highest Value
Value:	(Lowest value)	(Highest value)
Color:		

Preview:

OK   Cancel

Figure 4-11: Each style has a set of customization (or rules) that apply to how data is visually identified.

Icon Sets

New Rule...
Clear Rules
Manage Rules...

Text that Contains...

A Date Occurring...

Duplicate Values...

More Rules...

Click **Top/Bottom Rules** to view a submenu that lets you select cells based on top/bottom ranking or whether they're above or below the average of the selected cells.

3. For more choices, click **More Rules** at the bottom of each of the respective submenus.

4. In the New Formatting Rule dialog box, under Edit The Rule Description, you can change criteria and the formatting you want applied (see Chapter 3 for more information on using the Format Cells dialog box). Click **OK** when finished.

Top 10 Items...

Top 10 %...

Bottom 10 Items...

Bottom 10 %...

Above Average...

Below Average...

More Rules...

> **TIP**
>
> Excel 2007 increased the number of conditions that can be applied to a cell using conditional formatting from three to any number your system's memory will support.

MANAGE CONDITIONAL FORMATTING RULES

Using the Conditional Formatting Rule Manager, you can view any conditional formatting rules in a workbook as well as edit, delete, re-order, and create new rules.

1. In the Home tab Styles group, click **Conditional Formatting** and click **Manage Rules**. The Conditional Formatting Rule Manager appears, as shown in Figure 4-12.
2. Click the **Show Formatting Rules For** down arrow to select the scope of where you want to look for rules.
3. Select a rule and perform one or more of the following actions:
   - Click **Edit Rule** to open the Edit Formatting Rule dialog box and change criteria or conditions. Click **OK** to close the Edit Formatting Rule dialog box.
   - Click **Delete Rule** to remove it (alternatively, you can click **Clear Rules** on the Conditional Formatting drop-down menu to remove all rules in the selected cells or worksheet).
   - Click the up and down arrows to change the order in which rules are applied (rules are applied in order from top to bottom).
   - Click the **Stop If True** check box to discontinue further rules from being applied if the selected rule is satisfied as being True.

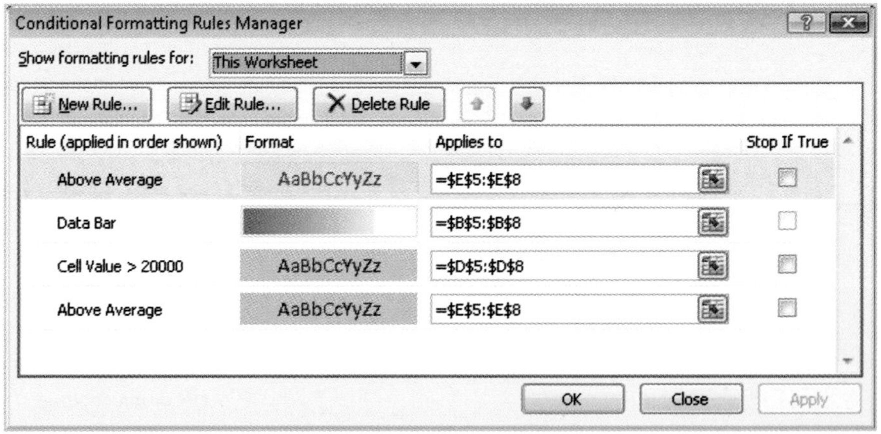

Figure 4-12: You can view and manage conditional formatting rules set up in a workbook.

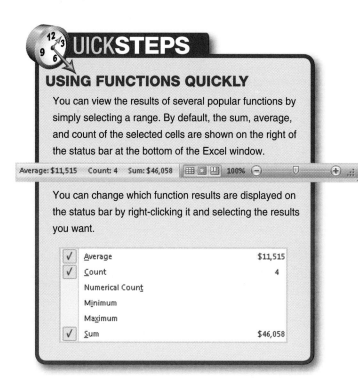

UICKSTEPS

USING FUNCTIONS QUICKLY

You can view the results of several popular functions by simply selecting a range. By default, the sum, average, and count of the selected cells are shown on the right of the status bar at the bottom of the Excel window.

Average: $11,515   Count: 4   Sum: $46,058   100%

You can change which function results are displayed on the status bar by right-clicking it and selecting the results you want.

√	Average	$11,515
√	Count	4
	Numerical Count	
	Minimum	
	Maximum	
√	Sum	$46,058

TIP

You do not need to type the closing parenthesis; Excel will add it for you when you complete the entry. However, it is good practice to include a closing parenthesis for each opening parenthesis. This is especially true if you use complex, nested functions that include other functions as arguments. (You may nest up to 64 levels!)

4. Click **New Rule** to open the New Formatting Rule dialog box and create a new rule. Click **OK** to close the New Formatting Rule dialog box.

5. Click **OK** when finished.

Use Functions

Functions are prewritten formulas that you can use to perform specific tasks. They can be as simple as =PI(), which returns 3.14159265358979, the value of the constant pi; or they can be as complex as =PPMT(rate,per,nper,pv,fv,type), which returns a payment on an investment principal.

A function is comprised of three components:

- **Formula identifier**, the equal sign (=), is required when a function is at the beginning of the formula.

- **Function name** identifies the function, and typically is a two- to five-character uppercase abbreviation.

- **Arguments** are the values acted upon by functions to derive a result. They can be numbers, cell references, constants, logical (True or False) values, or a formula. Arguments are separated by commas and enclosed in parentheses. A function can have up 255 arguments.

Enter a Function

You can enter functions on a worksheet by typing or by a combination of typing and selecting cell references, as described earlier in this chapter for formulas. In addition, you can search for and choose functions from Excel's library of built-in functions.

TYPE A FUNCTION

To type a function in a cell on the worksheet:

1. Select a blank cell, and type an equal sign (=). The equal sign displays in the cell and the Formula bar.

2. Start typing the function name, such as <u>AVERAGE</u>, <u>MAX</u>, or <u>PMT</u>. As you start typing, functions with related spellings are displayed. Click any to see a description of the function.

3. Double-click the function you want. The function name and open parenthesis are entered for you. Excel displays a tooltip showing arguments and proper syntax for the function.

4. Depending on the function, for each argument you need to do none, one, or both of the following:

   ● Type the argument.

   ● Select a cell reference.

5. Type a comma to separate arguments, and repeat steps 4 and 5 as necessary.

6. Type a closing parenthesis, and press **ENTER** or click **Enter** on the Formula bar to complete the entry. A value will be returned. (If a #code is displayed in the cell or a message box displays indicating you made an error, see "Find and Correct Errors" later in this chapter.)

INSERT A FUNCTION

You can find the function you want using the Insert Function tool or using the function category buttons on the ribbon.

In either case, Excel helps you enter arguments for the function you chose.

1. Select a blank cell. In the Formulas tab Function Library group, click the relevant function category button, and scroll to the function you want. Click the function and skip to step 5 to view its arguments.

   –Or–

   Click **Insert Function** in the Function Library group or its button *fx* on the Formula bar, or press **SHIFT+F3**. The Insert Function dialog box appears, as shown in Figure 4-13.

2. Type a brief description of what you want to do in the **Search For A Function** text box, and click **Go**. A list of recommended functions is displayed in the Select A Function list box.

   –Or–

   Open the **Select A Category** drop-down list, and select a category.

NOTE

You can create your own functions using Excel's built-in programming language, VBA (Visual Basic for Applications). Using VBA to programmatically customize Excel is beyond the scope of this book.

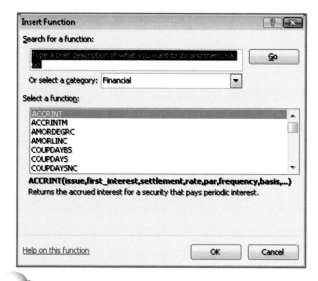

3. Click the function you want from the **Select A Function** list box. Its arguments and syntax are shown, as well as a description of what the function returns.

4. If you need more assistance with the function, click **Help On This Function**. A Help topic provides details on the function and an example of how it's used.

5. Click **OK** to open the Function Arguments dialog box, shown in Figure 4-14. The function's arguments are listed in order at the top of the dialog box, and the beginning of the function displays in the cell and in the Formula bar.

6. Enter values for the arguments by typing or clicking cell references. Click the **Collapse Dialog** button to shrink the dialog box so that you can see more of the worksheet. The formula on the worksheet is built as you enter each argument.

7. Click **OK** to complete the entry.

TIP

Using the AutoSum technique, you can apply other common functions to adjacent cells, such as averaging and getting a count. Click the **AutoSum** down arrow, and click the function you want; or click **More Functions** to open the Insert Function dialog box and access the full function library.

Σ AutoSum | Logi
Σ Sum
Average
Count Numbers
Max
Min
More Functions...

NOTE

The AutoSum button in the Function Library group can look different depending on whether the Excel window is maximized or sized smaller. This is true of most groups on the ribbon—that is, the width of the program window affects whether groups and their buttons/tools are fully displayed on the ribbon or condensed into a single button with an associated menu.

Function Arguments

PMT

Rate		📷	= number
Nper		📷	= number
Pv		📷	= number
Fv		📷	= number
Type		📷	= number

=

Calculates the payment for a loan based on constant payments and a constant interest rate.

Rate is the interest rate per period for the loan. For example, use 6%/4 for quarterly payments at 6% APR.

Formula result =

Help on this function | OK | Cancel

Figure 4-14: *Type or click cell references to enter argument values.*

Enter a Sum in Columns or Rows Quickly

AutoSum uses the SUM function to add contiguous numbers quickly.

1. Select a blank cell below a column or to the right of a row of numbers.

2. In the Formulas tab Function Library group, click **AutoSum**. The cells Excel "thinks" you want to sum above or to the left of the blank cell are enclosed in a border, and the formula is displayed in the cell and in the Formula bar.

3. Modify the cells to be included in the sum by dragging a corner sizing-box, editing the formula in the cell or the Formula bar, or by selecting cells.

4. Press **ENTER** or click **Enter** on the Formula bar to complete the entry. The sum of the selected cells is returned.

–Or–

1. Select a contiguous column or row of cells, including a blank cell at the end of the column or to the right of the row.

2. Click **AutoSum**. The sum is entered in the blank cell.

Find and Correct Errors

Excel provides several tools that help you see how your formulas and functions are constructed, recognize errors in formulas, and better locate problems.

Check for Errors

Excel can find errors and provide possible solutions.

1. In the Formulas tab Formula Auditing group, click **Error Checking**. If you have an error on the worksheet, the Error Checking dialog box appears, as shown in Figure 4-15.

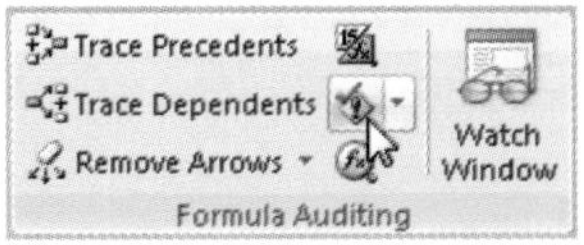

2. Use the command buttons on the right side of the dialog box to perform the indicated action. Click **Next** or **Previous** to check on other errors.

NOTE

You can perform the same actions and access the same dialog boxes from the Smart tag that is displayed next to a selected cell containing an error as you can using the Error Checking button on the Formula Auditing toolbar.

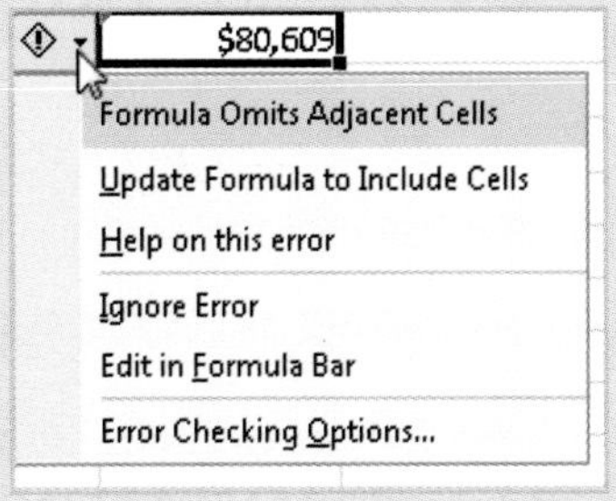

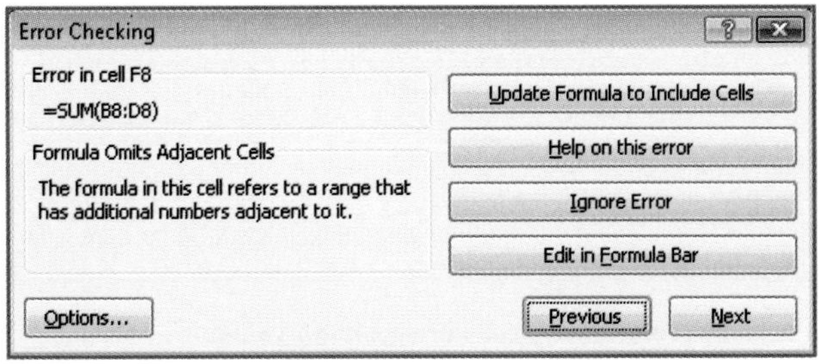

Figure 4-15: You can manage how errors are checked and locate cells that contain errors.

3. Click **Options** to view the Excel Options Formulas window (see Figure 4-16), where you can customize error checking:

- **Error Checking** lets you turn on or off error checking as you enter formulas and determines the color of flagged cells that contain errors. Errors are flagged in green by default.

- **Error Checking Rules** provides several criteria that cells are checked against for possible errors.

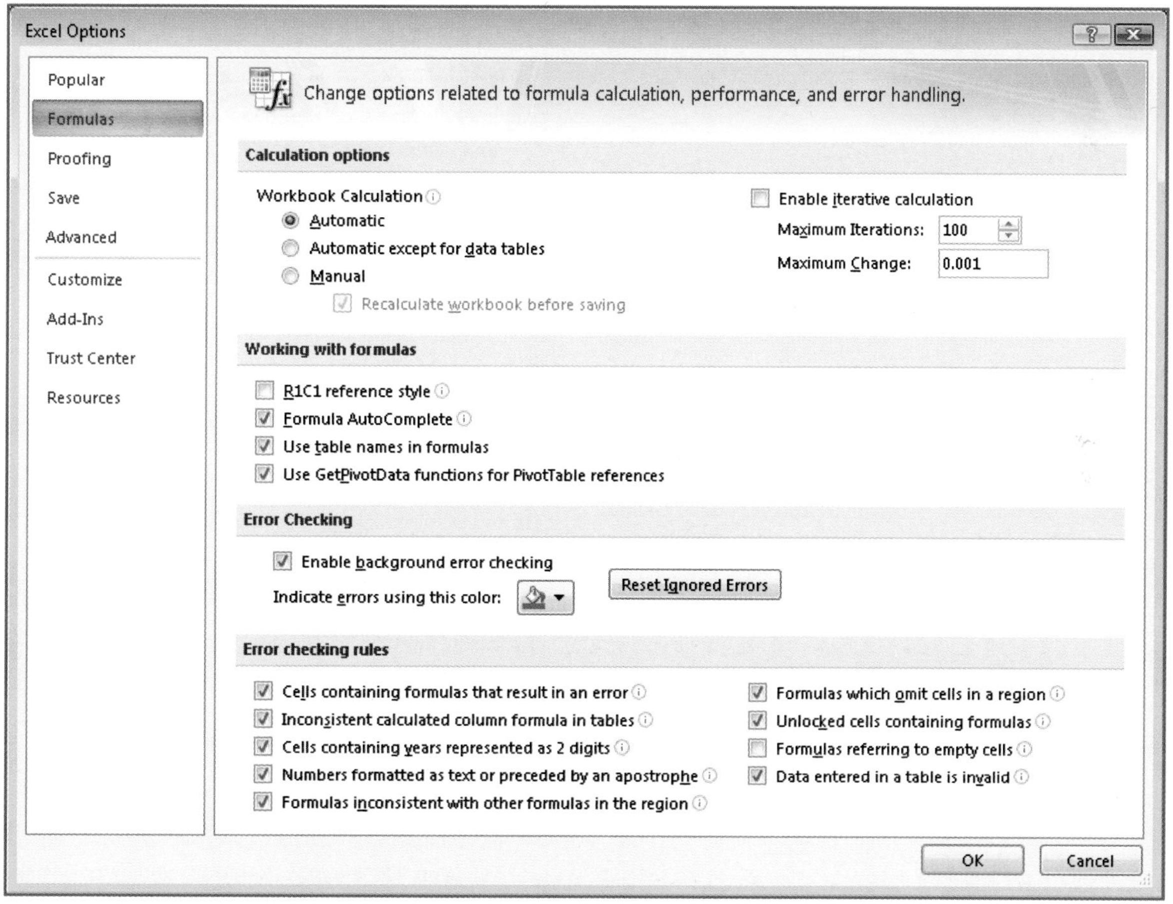

Excel Options

Popular	Change options related to formula calculation, performance, and error handling.
Formulas	
Proofing	
Save	
Advanced	
Customize	
Add-Ins	
Trust Center	
Resources	

Calculation options

Workbook Calculation ⓘ   ☐ Enable iterative calculation
  ⦿ Automatic   Maximum Iterations: 100
  ◯ Automatic except for data tables   Maximum Change: 0.001
  ◯ Manual
      ☑ Recalculate workbook before saving

Working with formulas

☐ R1C1 reference style ⓘ
☑ Formula AutoComplete ⓘ
☑ Use table names in formulas
☑ Use GetPivotData functions for PivotTable references

Error Checking

☑ Enable background error checking
Indicate errors using this color: 🎨 ▾   [Reset Ignored Errors]

Error checking rules

☑ Cells containing formulas that result in an error ⓘ   ☑ Formulas which omit cells in a region ⓘ
☑ Inconsistent calculated column formula in tables ⓘ   ☑ Unlocked cells containing formulas ⓘ
☑ Cells containing years represented as 2 digits ⓘ   ☐ Formulas referring to empty cells ⓘ
☑ Numbers formatted as text or preceded by an apostrophe ⓘ ☑ Data entered in a table is invalid ⓘ
☑ Formulas inconsistent with other formulas in the region ⓘ

[OK]   [Cancel]

Figure 4-16: You can customize how Excel performs error checking.

Trace Precedent and Dependent Cells

Precedent cells are referenced in a formula or function in another cell; that is, they provide a value to a formula or function. *Dependent* cells contain a formula or function that uses the value from another cell; that is, they depend on the value in another cell for their own value. This interwoven relationship of cells can compound one error into many, making a visual representation of the cell dependencies a vital error-correction tool.

1. Click a cell that uses cell references and/or is itself used as a reference by another cell in its formula or function.

2. In the Formulas tab Formula Auditing group, click **Trace Precedents** to display blue arrows that point to the cell from other cells.

   –Or–

   Click **Trace Dependents** to display blue arrows that point to other cells.

3. Click the **Remove Arrows** down arrow, and select whether to remove precedent, dependent, or all arrows.

Watch a Cell

You can follow what changes are made to a cell's value as its precedent cells' values are changed, even if the cells are not currently visible.

1. In the Formulas tab Formula Auditing group, click **Watch Window**. The Watch Window window opens.

2. Click **Add Watch** to open the Add Watch dialog box.

3. Select the cell or cells you want to watch, and click **Add**. Each selected cell will be listed individually in the Watch Window. As changes are made to a precedent cell, the value of the cells "being watched" will be updated according to the recalculation options you have set. (See "Recalculate Formulas" earlier in the chapter.)

4. Close the Watch Window when you are done.

Watch Window					
Book	Sheet	Name	Cell	Value	Formula
Chapt...	Sheet3	Other...	F8	$109,330	=SUM(B8:E8)
Chapt...	Sheet3		F9	$334,184	=F5+F6+63987...

Add Watch

Select the cells that you would like to watch the value of:

=Sheet3!$F$9

Evaluate a Formula in Pieces

You can see what value will be returned by individual cell references or expressions in the order they are placed in the formula.

1. Select the cell that contains the formula you want to evaluate.

2. In the Formulas tab Formula Auditing group, click **Evaluate Formula** 🔍 on the Formula Auditing toolbar. The Evaluate Formula dialog box, shown in Figure 4-17, appears.

3. Do one or more of the following:

   - Click **Evaluate** to return the value of the first cell reference or expression. The cell reference or expression is underlined.

   - Continue clicking **Evaluate** to return values for each of the cell references or expressions (again, underlined) to the right in the formula. Eventually, this will return the value for the cell.

   - Click **Restart** to start the evaluation from the leftmost expression. (The Evaluate button changes to Restart after you have stepped through the formula.)

   - Click **Step In** to view more data on the underlined cell reference.

   - Click **Step Out** to return to the formula evaluation.

4. Click **Close** when finished.

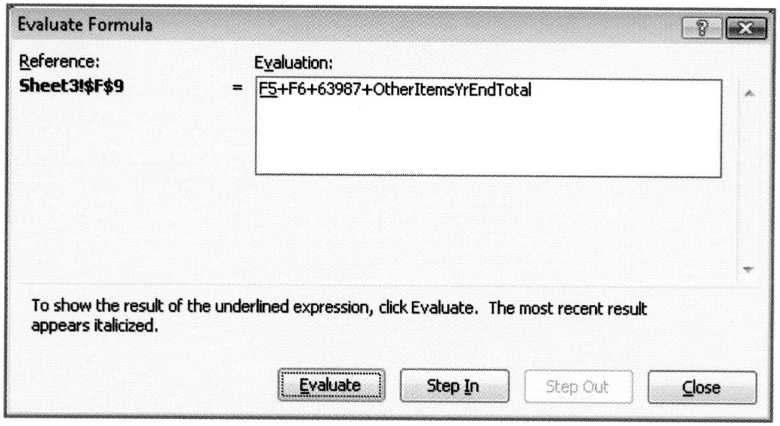

Evaluate Formula

Reference:
Sheet3!$F$9

Evaluation:

= F5+F6+63987+OtherItemsYrEndTotal

To show the result of the underlined expression, click Evaluate. The most recent result appears italicized.

Evaluate   Step In   Step Out   Close

Figure 4-17: You can dissect each expression or component of a formula to see its cell reference, its formula, and its value.

How to...

- 🚫 *Understanding Excel Views*
- *Add Headers and Footers*
- 🎨 *Adding Content to Headers and Footers*
- *Add Pictures to Headers and Footers*
- *Change Margins*
- *Select Page Orientation*
- *Use Headers as Page Titles*
- 🎨 *Working with Zoom*
- *Change the Order in Which Pages Print*
- 🎨 *Choosing Worksheet Print Options*
- *Print Comments*
- *Use Print Areas*
- 🎨 *Choosing What to Print*
- *Preview the Print Job*
- *Scale Your Data Before Printing*
- *Output the Print Job*

Chapter 5
Viewing and Printing Data

In this chapter you will learn how to organize a worksheet to better view the information it contains and print just the information you want. Excel provides several tools and options, such as headers, footers, and titles, that enhance a worksheet for viewing, distribution, or printing. Other features let you change the layout of your worksheet to better accommodate how you want to present the data, from changing the zoom level to dividing the worksheet into pages. Printing to page-sized dimensions is a prime consideration when modifying the layout of a worksheet, regardless if the pages are printed on paper or converted to digital formats such as Microsoft XPS or PDF documents, or Web pages. You can add or change printing features before you begin the final stages of printing. Besides making the printed pages easier to read and understand, you can save yourself time by saving the print options for subsequent use. Excel also provides a robust previewing feature so you can review your settings before actually distributing or printing your work.

Lay Out a Worksheet

You can transform an otherwise nondescript worksheet full of text and numbers into an easy-to-follow, organized report by adding or modifying features that assist viewing or printing. The following sections will show you how to add headers and footers, page titles, define pages, and change other organizational and visual enhancements to your worksheets.

Add Headers and Footers

Custom *headers* and *footers* that print on each page can greatly enhance the appearance of your printed data. Headers and footers (see Figure 5-2), are dedicated areas of the page—headers at the top and footers at the bottom—where you can place titles, page numbers, dates, and even add pictures.

CREATE A SIMPLE HEADER AND/OR FOOTER

Excel provides several prebuilt header and footer formats you can select. The formats contain ordinary text and formatting codes that automatically add information such as page numbers.

1. Display the worksheet where you want to add a header and/or footer.

2. In the Insert tab Text group, click **Header & Footer**. A contextual Header & Footer Tools Design tab displays on the ribbon, the worksheet appears in Print Layout view, and the insertion point is placed in the center header text box at the top of the page, as shown in Figure 5-3.

3. In the Header & Footer group, click either **Header** or **Footer**, and select one of the built-in formats from the drop-down list. Each format contains one, two, or three elements, separated by commas. Single-element formats are placed in the center header/footer text box on the worksheet; two-element formats are placed in the left

UNDERSTANDING EXCEL VIEWS (Continued)

the worksheet breaks into pages. You can work in Page Break Preview view as you do in Normal view to enter data, create formulas, and perform other standard Excel actions in any page that is represented in the view.

- **Full Screen** view provides the most "real estate" for viewing data by hiding screen elements such as the ribbon and status bar.

- **Custom** views allow you to retain multiple printing and viewing settings combinations so that you can quickly evoke the settings you want.

TIP

To remove content codes inserted by the Auto Header and Auto Footer formats, simply select the ampersand (&) preceding the code and the code itself–for example, &[File]–and press **DELETE**.

TIP

To see more of a worksheet, press **CTRL+F1** to collapse the ribbon groups and display only the tabs bar. Press the key combination a second time to return the ribbon to its full height.

and center or right and center text boxes; and three-element formats are placed in the left, center, and right text boxes.

4. To make changes to the default format, see "Customize a Header and Footer," next.

CUSTOMIZE A HEADER AND FOOTER

1. Display the worksheet where you want to add a header and/or footer.

2. In the Insert tab Text group, click **Header & Footer**. A contextual Header & Footer Tools Design tab displays on the ribbon, the worksheet appears in Print Layout view, and the insertion point is placed in the center header text box at the top of the page (see Figure 5-3).

3. If you want to start from a built-in format, select one from the Auto Header or Auto Footer drop-down lists (see "Create a Simple Header and/or Footer").

4. Click one of the three text boxes (left, center, or right) where you want to add text or objects to the header (top of the page) or footer (bottom of the page). The alignment in a text box is the same as the location of its section; for example, the left section is left-aligned.

5. If desired, place the insertion point where you want it, for example, within any existing characters. Then do one or more of the following:

   - Type characters.

   - Click a tool from the Header & Footer Elements group to add a format. (See the "Adding Content to Headers and Footers" QuickSteps for information on what the tools do.)

   - Use a combination of typing and features provided by the buttons.

   - Press **ENTER** at the end of a line to place text or objects on multiple lines.

When finished, click outside the text boxes or press **ESC** to see how the codes and text are displayed.

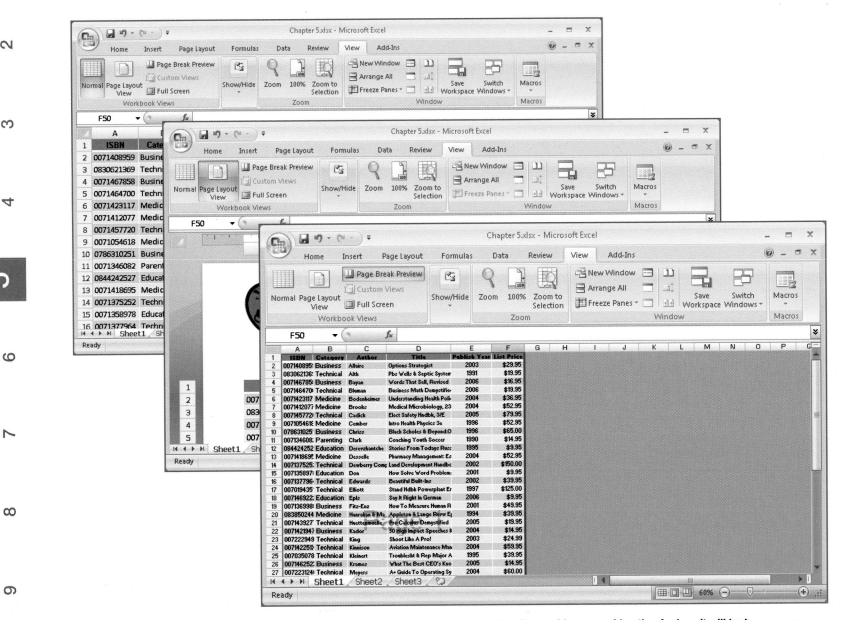

Figure 5-1: *Excel views allow you to see and use your data in the row-and-column matrix, with or without consideration for how it will look formatted to fit a page.*

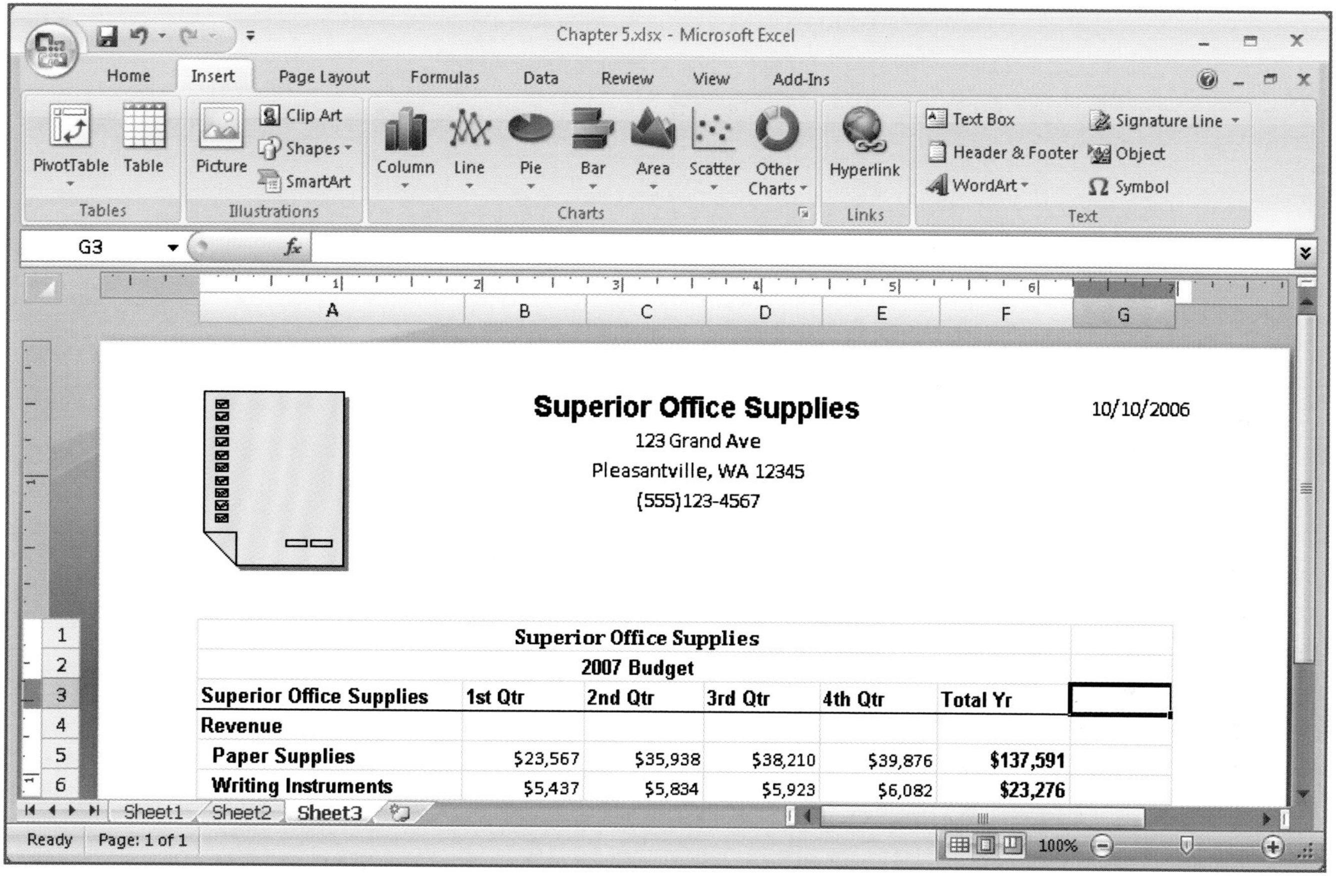

Figure 5-2: *Headers can be set up to look like letterhead.*

TIP

To quickly move back and forth between headers and footers when working in the Header & Footer Tools Design tab, click the respective button in the Navigation group.

Go to Header   Go to Footer

Navigation

6. To change to Normal view, click **Normal** ⊞ on the status bar

–Or–

In the View tab Workbook Views group, click **Normal**.

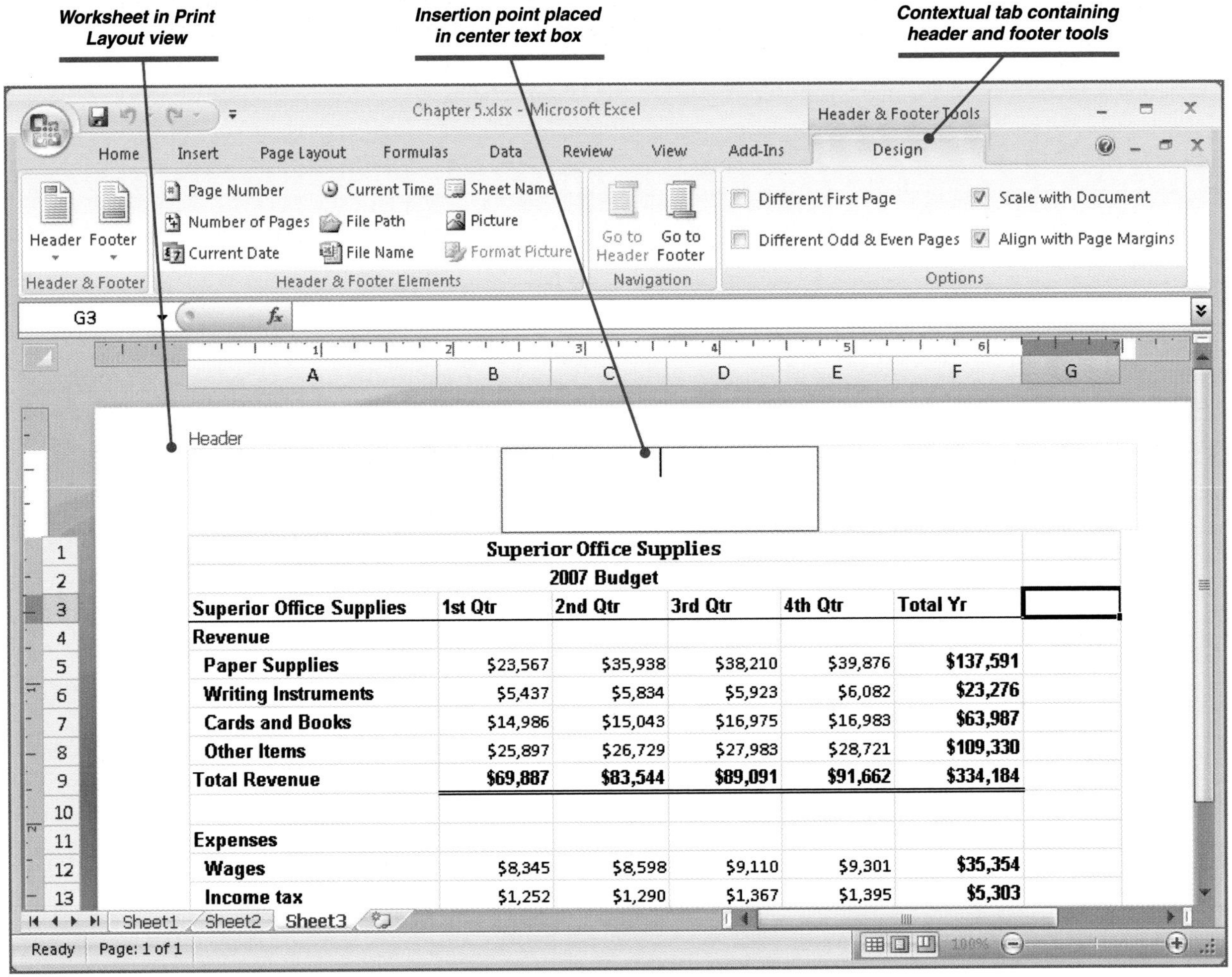

Worksheet in Print
Layout view

Insertion point placed
in center text box

Contextual tab containing
header and footer tools

Figure 5-3: *Choosing to add a header or footer switches Excel into Print Layout view with the tools you need to create or change them.*

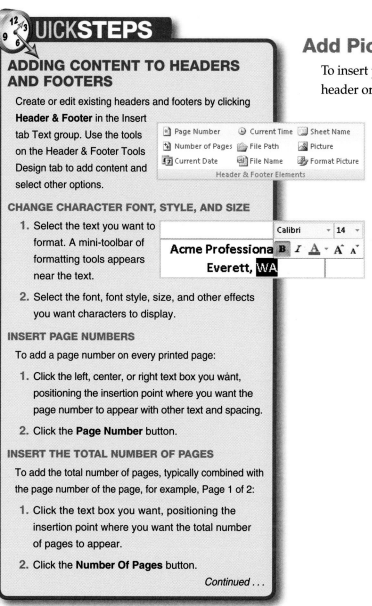
Add Pictures to Headers and Footers

To insert pictures, such as photos, clip art, and other digital graphic files, in the header or footer:

1. Display the worksheet where you want to add a header and/or footer.

2. In the Insert tab Text group, click **Header & Footer**. Click the text box you want, positioning the insertion point where you want the picture to appear.

3. In the Header & Footer Elements group, click **Picture**. In the Insert Picture dialog box, locate the picture you want, and click **Open**. A picture code is entered into the header or footer. Click outside the text box or press **ESC** to display the picture.

4. To change the picture's size, orientation, or other formatting, click the area where the picture code was placed, and click **Format Picture** in the Header & Footer Elements group. Make your changes in the Format Picture dialog box (see Figure 5-4), and click **OK** (see Chapter 7 for more information on formatting pictures).

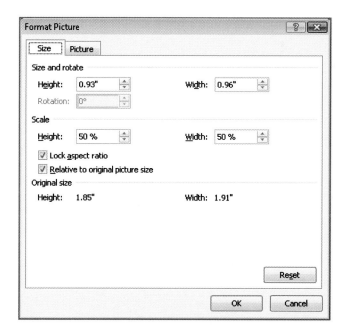

Figure 5-4: You can size, trim, and control other aspects of pictures placed in headers or footers.

INSERT THE DATE AND/OR TIME

To add the current date or time in the form mm/dd/yyyy or hh:mm (in this format, Excel omits AM and adds PM—see Chapter 2 for more information on date and time formats):

1. Click the text box where you want the date and/or time to appear.

2. Click the respective **Current Date** or **Current Time** buttons.

INSERT THE WORKBOOK'S PATH AND FILE NAME

To insert the path and file name of the workbook:

1. Click the text box you want, positioning the insertion point where you want the path and/or file name to appear.

2. Click the respective **File Path** or **File Name** buttons (File Path includes the file name).

INSERT THE WORKSHEET NAME

To insert the name of the worksheet:

1. Click the text box where you want the worksheet name to appear.

2. Click the **Sheet Name** button.

USE MORE THAN ONE HEADER AND/OR FOOTER

By default, the header and/or footer you create is displayed on each page of the worksheet. You can change this behavior from the Design tab (Header & Footer Tools) Options group. Select one or both of the following check boxes:

- **Different First Page** provides for a unique header and/or footer on the first page of a worksheet.

- **Different Odd & Even Pages** lets you alternate a header and/or footer on every other page.

Change Margins

You can change the distance between the edges of the page and where worksheet text and pictures start printing, as well as where headers and footer start printing.

1. In the Page Layout tab Page Setup group, click **Margins**. A drop-down menu lists standard settings for normal, wide, and narrow margins, as well as the last set of custom margins used.

2. Select one of the margin combinations or click **Custom Margins** for more options. The Margins tab of the Page Setup dialog box appears, as shown in Figure 5-5. (You can access this dialog box directly by clicking the **Dialog Box Launcher** in the lower-right corner of the Page Setup group.)

You cannot directly copy or insert clip art into a header or footer text box, but there is a way around this problem. Locate the clip art you want using the Clip Art task pane (see Chapter 7). Right-click the icon in the task pane and click **Preview/Properties**. At the bottom of the dialog box, note the File: path that identifies where the clip art file is stored on your system. Use that location in the Insert Picture dialog box and the "clip" will be inserted in the header or footer.

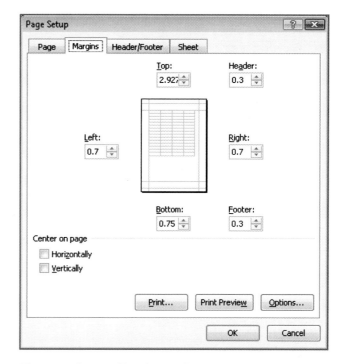

Figure 5-5: *Page and header margins are set in the Margins tab of the Page Setup dialog box.*

You can also adjust margins interactively by dragging them. See "Preview the Print Job" later in the chapter.

ADJUST PAGE MARGINS

1. Adjust the **Top**, **Bottom**, **Left** and/or **Right** spinners to change the distance that text and pictures start printing from the page edges. As you click a spinner, the preview area shows the location of the margin you are working on.

2. Click **OK** when finished making changes in the Page Setup dialog box.

CENTER PRINTED DATA BETWEEN MARGINS

Under Center On Page, select one or both check boxes:

- Click **Horizontally** to realign data centered between the left and right margins
- Click **Vertically** to realign data centered between the top and bottom margins

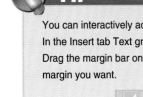
ADJUST HEADER AND FOOTER MARGINS

You can change the distance a header starts printing from the top edge of a page or the distance a footer starts printing from the bottom edge of the page.

1. Adjust the **Header** and/or **Footer** spinners to change the distance that header or footer text and pictures appear from the top or bottom page edge, respectively.

2. Click **OK** when finished making changes in the Page Setup dialog box.

Select Page Orientation

Pages can be laid out in *portrait* orientation, where a standard 8½ x 11-inch piece of paper is printed, with the sides being the longer dimension, or in *landscape* orientation, where the top and bottom edges are longer. You can also shrink or enlarge the data displayed in a worksheet, or *scale* it, to get more data to display and print on a page or focus in on a specific region.

In the Page Layout tab Page Setup group, click **Orientation** and click the layout (**Portrait** (tall) or **Landscape** (wide)) that works best for how your data is arranged in the worksheet.

Use Headers as Page Titles

You can retain text in the top rows or left columns of a worksheet for long lists of horizontal or vertical data so that the headers appear on every page in Page Layout view and, when printed, keeping you from having to return to the start of the worksheet to see what category of data is being displayed (see Figure 5-6).

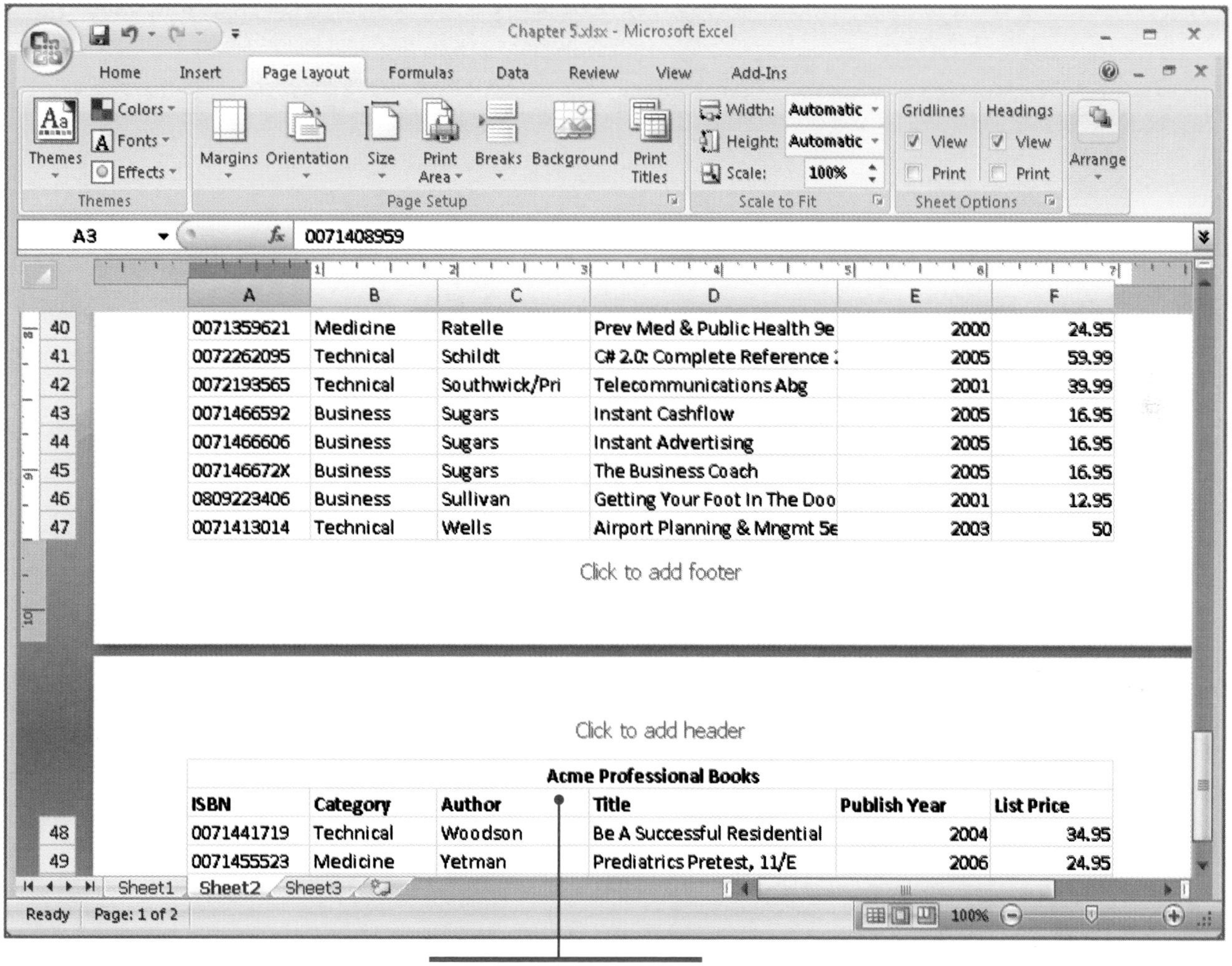

Repeated headers on every page

Figure 5-6: **Repeating headers on every page makes it easier to keep track of data in long worksheets.**

QUICKSTEPS

WORKING WITH ZOOM

You can change the magnification (or *zoom*) of a worksheet to see text and objects larger or smaller than the default size, as well as to see less or more of the worksheet on the screen. The worksheet will retain the new appearance until you change the zoom again.

SELECT A ZOOM PERCENTAGE

1. In the View tab Zoom group, click **Zoom**.

   –Or–

   Double-click the current zoom percentage on the right-side of the status bar.

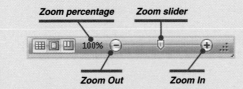

Zoom percentage   Zoom slider

Zoom Out   Zoom In

2. In either case, the Zoom dialog box appears. Click a preset magnification percentage (100% being the default).

   Zoom ? ✕

   Magnification
   ○ 200%
   ⦿ 100%
   ○ 75%
   ○ 50%
   ○ 25%
   ○ Fit selection
   ○ Custom: 100 %

   OK   Cancel

3. Click **OK** when finished.

Continued . . .

1. In the Page Layout tab Page Setup group, click **Print Titles**. The Page Setup dialog box appear with the Sheet tab displayed.

2. Under Print Titles, click the **Collapse Dialog** button to the right of:

   Print titles

   Rows to repeat at top: |

   Columns to repeat at left:

   - **Rows To Repeat At Top** to create horizontal titles at the top of every page

     –Or–

   - **Columns To Repeat At Left** to create vertical titles along the leftmost column of every page

3. Select the rows or columns you want to appear on each page. The rows or columns are outlined in a dotted rectangle, and the row/column numbers appear in the collapsed dialog box.

   Chapter 5.xlsx - Mi

   Home   Insert   Page Layout   Formulas   Data   Review

   Themes | Colors · A Fonts · Effects · | Margins Orientation Size Print Area · Breaks Background Pr Tit

   Page Setup - Rows to repeat at top: ? ✕

   $1:$2

	A	B	C	D
1				Acme Professional Books
⬏	ISBN	Category	Author	Title
3	0071408959	Business	Allaire	Options Strategist
4	0830621369	Technical	Alth	Pbs Wells & Septic System

4. Click **Close** in the collapsed dialog box. The row or column reference appears in the respective text box on the Sheet tab.

5. Click **OK** when finished.

QUICKSTEPS

WORKING WITH ZOOM (Continued)

SELECT A CUSTOM MAGNIFICATION

- In the View tab Zoom group, click **Zoom**, click **Custom**, and type a custom percentage.

–Or–

- Drag the **Zoom** slider on the status bar to the left for less magnification or to the right for greater magnification.

–Or–

- Click the **Zoom Out** and **Zoom In** buttons on the status bar.

MAGNIFY A SELECTION

Select a range or object on the worksheet whose size you want to increase to fill the worksheet window (the magnification percentage will vary depending on the size of your selection).

- In the View tab Zoom group, click **Zoom To Selection**.

–Or–

- From the Zoom dialog box, click **Fit Selection** and click **OK**.

NOTE

Zoom is similar to *scaling*, a feature that changes the size of a worksheet to fit on a specified number of pages. The major difference is that scaling is temporary, only affecting what prints (see "Scale Your Data Before Printing" later in the chapter).

Print the Data

In this section you will see how to print different segments of a workbook or worksheet, how to preview your settings and make adjustments, and how to change aspects related to the physical device(s) you use to print.

Change the Order in Which Pages Print

Excel assumes a portrait (tall) page orientation and logically prints down the worksheet as far as there is data. It then moves to the right one page width and prints data down that swath as far as there is data, and so forth. If you choose a landscape (wide) orientation, it will probably make more sense to first print pages across, then down.

1. In the Page Layout tab Sheet Options group, click the **Dialog Box Launcher**.
2. In the Sheet tab, under Page Order (see Figure 5-7), select the printing order that works best for the way you have data arranged on the worksheet.
3. Click **OK**.

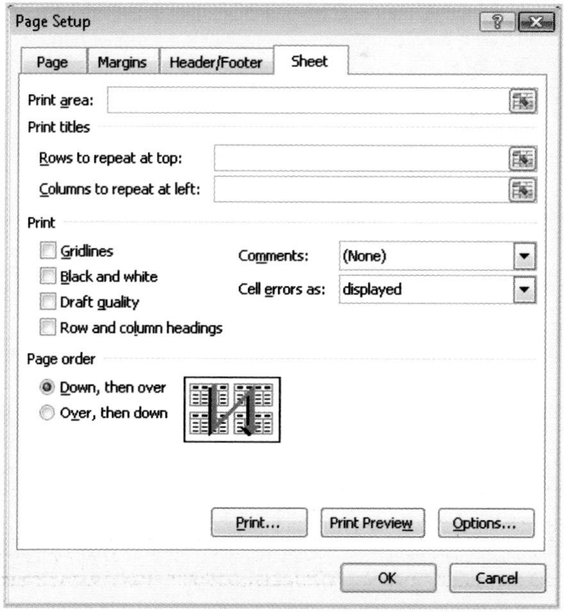

Figure 5-7: *The Sheet tab in the Page Setup dialog box contains several printing options.*

QUICKSTEPS

CHOOSING WORKSHEET PRINT OPTIONS

Prior to printing, you can choose several options for including or removing worksheet elements, as well as the quality of the print job. In the Page Layout tab Sheet Options group, click the **Dialog Box Launcher** to display the Sheet tab (see Figure 5-7) in the Page Setup dialog box (a few options are available directly on the ribbon).

Gridlines	Headings
☑ View	☑ View
☐ Print	☐ Print

Sheet Options

PRINT GRIDLINES

- To print the lines that outline the worksheet grid of rows, columns, and cells, under Print, click **Gridlines**.

–Or–

- In the Sheet Options group, under Gridlines, click **Print**.

PRINT IN BLACK AND WHITE

To save on color ink for draft prints or to otherwise print in monochrome, under Print, click **Black And White**.

PRINT USING LESS INK OR TONER

Under Print, click **Draft Quality**.

PRINT ROW NUMBERS AND COLUMN LETTERS

By default, the row numbers and column letters that define the addressing in a worksheet are not included when a worksheet prints. To include them both:

1. Under Print, click Row And Column Headings.

   –Or–

   In the Sheet Options group, under Headings, click **Print**.

2. Click **OK** when finished to close the Page Setup dialog box.

Print Comments

You can print comments in a list at the end of a worksheet, or you can print them as, and where, they appear on the worksheet.

1. In the Page Layout tab Sheet Options group, click the **Dialog Box Launcher**.

2. In the Print area of the Sheet tab, click the **Comments** down arrow, and choose where to print the comments:

Comments:	(None) ▼
	(None)
	At end of sheet
	As displayed on sheet

3. Click **At End Of Sheet** to print comments on a separate page, listed by cell, author, and comment, as shown in Figure 5-8.

   –Or–

   Click **As Displayed On Sheet** to print comments that are shown on the worksheet.

4. Click **OK**.

Use Print Areas

You can define a *print area* of a worksheet by selecting one or more ranges of cells that you want to print. Setting this area is especially useful if you print the same selected cells often. The print area is saved along with the other changes to the worksheet when the workbook is saved.

CREATE A PRINT AREA

1. Select the range of cells you want in the print area by dragging from the upper-leftmost cell to the lower-rightmost cell. To include multiple ranges, hold down CTRL while selecting them.

2. In the Page Layout tab Page Setup group, click **Print Area** and click **Set Print Area**.

Print Area | Breaks | Background

Set Print Area
Clear Print Area

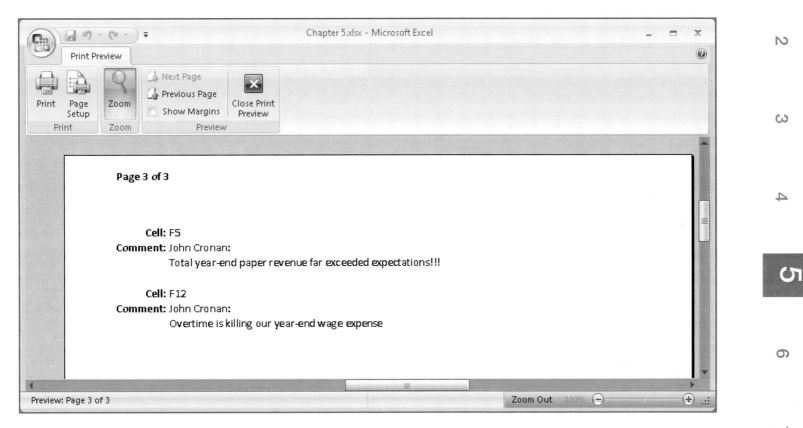

Chapter 5.xlsx - Microsoft Excel

Print Preview

Print | Page Setup | Zoom | Next Page | Previous Page | Show Margins | Close Print Preview

Print | Zoom | Preview

Page 3 of 3

Cell: F5
Comment: John Cronan:
Total year-end paper revenue far exceeded expectations!!!

Cell: F12
Comment: John Cronan:
Overtime is killing our year-end wage expense

Preview: Page 3 of 3   Zoom Out   100%

Figure 5-8: **You can print all comments on a worksheet on a separate page.**

ADD CELLS TO A PRINT AREA

1. Select the additional cells on the same worksheet you to want to print.

2. In the Page Layout tab Page Setup group, click **Print Area** and click **Add To Print Area**.

REMOVE ADDED CELLS FROM A PRINT AREA

1. In the View tab Workbook Views group, click **Page Break Preview**.

–Or–

Click **Page Break Preview** on the right-side of the status bar.

TIP

To display a comment, right-click the comment and click **Show/Hide Comments**. (See Chapter 3 for more information on working with comments.)

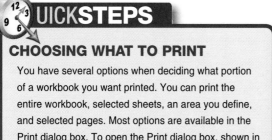

CHOOSING WHAT TO PRINT

You have several options when deciding what portion of a workbook you want printed. You can print the entire workbook, selected sheets, an area you define, and selected pages. Most options are available in the Print dialog box. To open the Print dialog box, shown in Figure 5-9, use any of the following methods:

- Click the **Office Button**, and click **Print**.

  –Or–

- Press **CTRL+P**.

  –Or–

- Click the **Print** button in the Page Setup dialog box.

  After choosing what to print, click **OK**.

PRINT A SELECTION

1. Select the cells you want to print.
2. Open the Print dialog box. Under Print What, click **Selection**.

PRINT SELECTED SHEETS

1. Select sheets to be printed by holding down the **CTRL** key and clicking the sheet tabs.
2. Open the Print dialog box. Under Print What, click **Active Sheet(s)**.

PRINT ALL SHEETS

In the Print dialog box, under Print What, click **Entire Workbook**.

PRINT SPECIFIC PAGES

1. In the Print dialog box, under Print Range, click **Page(s)**.

Continued...

Figure 5-9: **The Print dialog box provides options that control the physical aspect of printing.**

In either case, click **OK** in the Welcome dialog box (which appears every time you display a worksheet in Page Break Preview, unless you click **Do Not Show This Dialog Again**).

2. Select the previously added cells you want to remove from the print area.
3. Right-click the selection and click **Exclude From Print Area**, as shown Figure 5-10.

REMOVE A PRINT AREA

1. Click the sheet that contains the print area you want to remove to make it active.
2. In the Page Layout tab Page Setup group, click **Print Area** and click **Clear Print Area.**

QUICKSTEPS

CHOOSING WHAT TO PRINT *(Continued)*

2. To print a range of pages, use the **From** and **To** spinners to set the starting and ending pages to print.

–Or–

To print one page, set both the **From** and **To** spinners to the same page number.

–Or–

To print from a page to the last page, set only the **From** spinner.

NOTE

The easiest way work with print areas is to interactively select the cells you want printed and use the ribbon to set or change the print area.

Page Setup	? ✕
Page	Margins	Header/Footer	**Sheet**
Print area:	A4:F9
Print titles

However, you also can edit cell references in the Sheet tab of the Page Setup dialog box or right-click the sheet in Page Break Preview view and use context menu commands.

✂	Cu_t_
📋	_C_opy
📋	_P_aste
	Paste _S_pecial...
	_I_nsert...
	_D_elete...
	Clear Co_n_tents
	Insert Co_m_ment
	_F_ormat Cells...
	Insert Page _B_reak
	Reset _A_ll Page Breaks
	_S_et Print Area
	_R_eset Print Area
	Page Set_u_p...

PRINT A PRINT AREA

1. Set the print area and make active the worksheet it is on.

2. Click the **Office Button**, point to the **Print** side arrow, and click **Quick Print**.

Preview the Print Job

Before your printer actually starts printing paper, you can verify what you have set up to print. Print Preview displays replicas of the printed pages your data will produce, provides a hub for most printing features, and can be used as a printing starting point, as shown in Figure 5-11.

- To open Print Preview, click the **Office Button**, point to the **Print** side arrow, and click **Print Preview**.

  –Or–

- Click **Preview** in the Print or Page Setup dialog boxes.

  The buttons on the Print Preview tab provide tools to use in the window and links to other printing features:

- **Print** opens the Print dialog box.
- **Page Setup** opens the Page Setup dialog box.
- **Zoom** toggles between a full-page view and a magnified view of the current page. When viewing the full page, just click the Magnifier pointer anywhere to switch to the magnified view.
  - **Next Page** and **Previous Page** let you navigate between multiple pages.
  - **Show Margins** turns off or on visible margin lines that can be dragged to the position you want.
  - **Close Print Preview** returns the view to a full worksheet.

SET MARGINS IN PRINT PREVIEW

1. Open **Print Preview**.

2. Click **Zoom**, if necessary, to show the first page of the worksheet in full-page view.

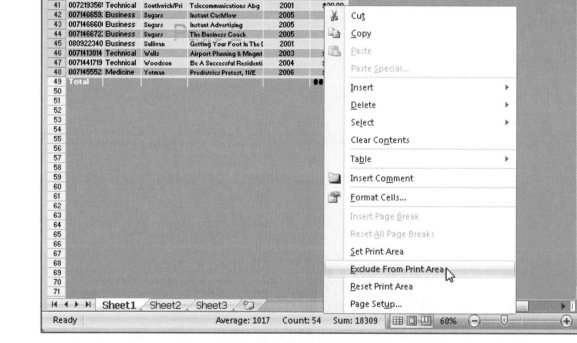

Figure 5-10: *Page Break Preview provides print area options on its context menu.*

TIP

If a worksheet has a print area, by default, it will print instead of the full worksheet (to print the full worksheet, click **Ignore Print Areas** under Print What in the Print dialog box). Also, if you have multiple ranges on your print area, each range will print on a separate page.

TIP

All pages in Print Preview use the same margin and column settings.

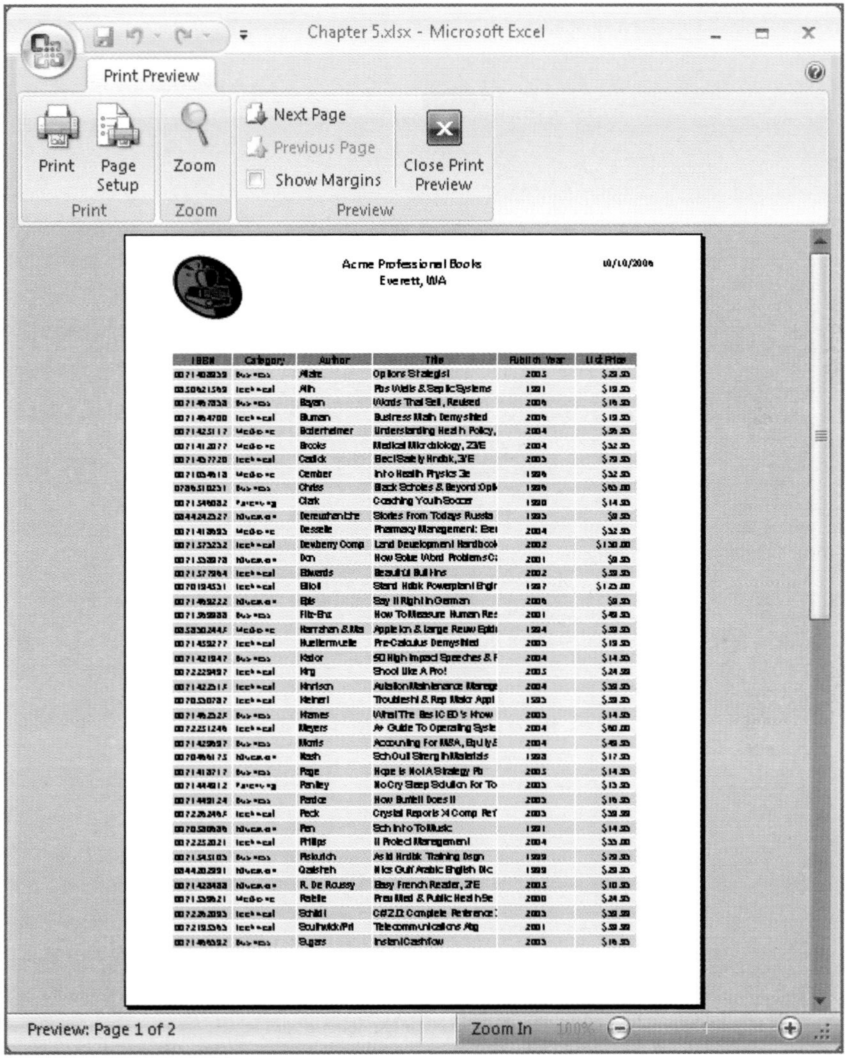

Figure 5-11: *Print Preview shows replicas of printer pages and provides a tab of tools to verify and modify print options before sending the job to a printer.*

ISBN	Category
2	0071408959	Business
3	0830621369	Technical
4	0071467858	Business
5	0071464700	Technical

Top Margin: 1.69 Inches

3. Click **Show Margins**, if necessary, to show six margin lines and handles as well as column width handles, as shown in Figure 5-12.

4. Point at a line or handle until the mouse pointer becomes a cross with either horizontal or vertical arrowheads, and drag the line or handle to set a new margin or column width.

5. Click **Close Print Preview** to return to the normal worksheet view.

SET PAGE MARGINS IN PAGE LAYOUT VIEW

1. Click **Page Layout** 🔲 view on the right-side of the status bar.

2. Point at the transition between dark and light areas on each end of the horizontal or vertical rulers until the mouse pointer becomes either horizontal or vertical arrowheads, and drag the transition to increase or decrease the top, bottom, left, or right margins.

ADJUST PAGE BREAKS

You can adjust page breaks using Page Break Preview.

1. To open Page Break Preview, click **Page Break Preview** on the right-side of the status bar.

   –Or–

   In the View tab Workbook Views group, click **Page Break Preview**.

   In either case, you see the Welcome message.

2. Click **Do Not Show This Dialog Again**, if that's what you want. In any case, click **OK**. The worksheet opens in a condensed format, as shown in Figure 5-13. Dashed lines show page breaks where Excel will separate data into pages; page break lines you move or add are shown as solid lines (outer boundary lines are also solid lines).

3. Do one or more of the following:

   - Adjust page breaks by dragging a page break line to where you want the page break. Dashed lines become solid after you move them from their default locations.

   - Insert a page break by selecting the row below or the column to the right of where you want the new page break, right-clicking, and clicking **Insert Page Break**.

   - Remove a page break by dragging it from the worksheet area to the dark gray area.

   - Remove all page breaks you added or changed by right-clicking the worksheet and clicking **Reset All Page Breaks**.

4. To close Page Break Preview, switch to either Normal or Page Layout view by clicking their respective buttons on the status bar or in the Workbook Views group on the ribbon.

Insert Page Break
Reset All Page Breaks
Set Print Area
Reset Print Area
Page Setup...

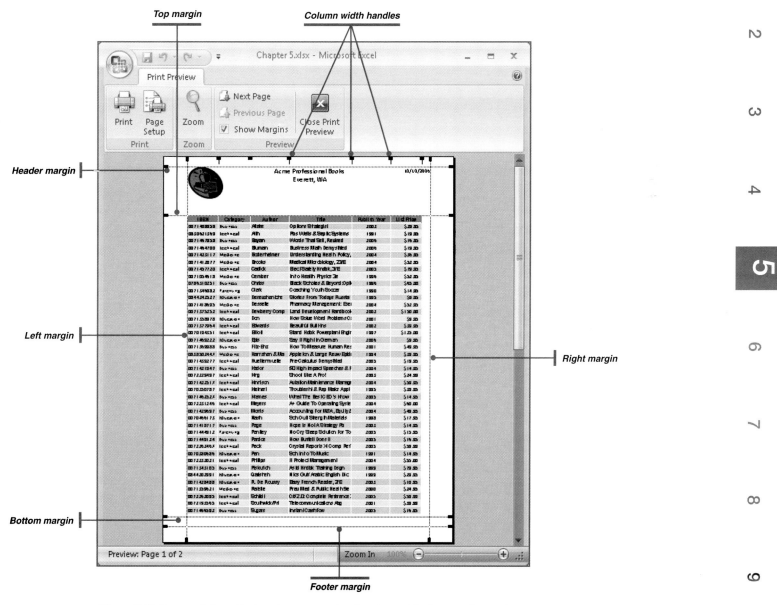

Figure 5-12: **You can interactively set page margins, header and footer margins, and column widths.**

	A	B	C	D	E	F	G	H	I	J	K	L	M	N	O
4	007146785	Business	Bayan	Words That Sell, Revised	2006	$16.95			Row Labels	Sum of List Price					
5	007146470	Technical	Bluman	Business Math Demystifie	2006	$19.95			Business	417.35					
6	0071423117	Medicine	Bodenheimer	Understanding Health Poli	2004	$36.95			Allaire	29.95					
7	0071412077	Medicine	Brooks	Medical Microbiology, 23	2004	$52.95			Bayan	16.95					
8	007145772	Technical	Cadick	Elect Safety Hndbk, 3/E	2005	$79.95			Chriss	65					
9	007105461	Medicine	Cember	Intro Health Physics 3e	1996	$52.95			Fitz-Enz	49.95					
10	078631025	Business	Chriss	Black Scholes & Beyond:O	1996	$65.00			Kador	14.95					
11	007134608	Parenting	Clark	Coaching Youth Soccer	1990	$14.95			Krames	14.95					
12	084424252	Education	Derevzhantche	Stories From Todays Russ	1995	$9.95			Morris	49.95					
13	007141869	Medicine	Desselle	Pharmacy Management: Es	2004	$52.95			Page	14.95					
14	007137525	Technical	Dewberry Comp	Land Development Handbc	2002	$150.00			Pardoe	16.95					
15	007135897	Education	Don	How Solve Word Problem:	2001	$9.95			Piskurich	79.95					
16	007137796	Technical	Edwards	Beautiful Built-Ins	2002	$39.95			Sugars	50.85					
17	007019435	Technical	Elliott	Stand Hdbk Powerplant Er	1997	$125.00			Sullivan	12.95					
18	007146922	Education	Epls	Say It Right In German	2006	$9.95			Education	103.65					
19	007136998	Business	Fitz-Enz	How To Measure Human R	2001	$49.95			Derevzhantche	9.95					
20	083850244	Medicine	Hanrahan & Ma	Appleton & Lange Revw Ep	1994	$39.95			Don	9.95					
21	007143927	Technical	Huettenmuelle	Pre-Calculus Demystified	2005	$19.95			Epls	9.95					
22	007142194	Business	Kador	50 High Impact Speeches &	2004	$14.95			Nash	17.95					
23	007222949	Technical	King	Shoot Like A Pro!	2003	$24.99			Pen	14.95					
24	007142251	Technical	Kinnison	Aviation Maintenance Man	2004	$59.95			Qafisheh	29.95					
25	007035078	Technical	Kleinert	Troublesht & Rep Major A	1995	$39.95			R. De Roussy	10.95					
26	007146252	Business	Krames	What The Best CEO's Kno	2005	$14.95			Medicine	338.6					
27	007223124	Technical	Meyers	A+ Guide To Operating Sy	2004	$60.00			Bodenheimer	36.95					
28	007142969	Business	Morris	Accounting For M&A, Equ	2004	$49.95			Brooks	52.95					
29	007046617	Education	Nash	Sch Outl Strength Material	1998	$17.95			Cember	105.9					
30	007141871	Business	Page	Hope Is Not A Strategy Pb	2003	$14.95			Desselle	52.95					
31	007144491	Parenting	Pantley	No Cry Sleep Solution For	2005	$15.95			Hanrahan & M	39.95					
32	007144912	Business	Pardoe	How Buffett Does It	2005	$16.95			Ratelle	24.95					
33	007226246	Technical	Peck	Crystal Reports Xi Comp	2005	$59.99			Yetman	24.95					
34	007038068	Education	Pen	Sch Intro To Music	1991	$14.95			Parenting	30.9					
35	007223202	Technical	Phillips	It Project Management	2004	$55.00			Clark	14.95					
36	007134310	Business	Piskurich	Astd Hndbk Training Dsgn	1999	$79.95			Pantley	15.95					
37	084420299	Education	Qafisheh	Ntcs Gulf Arabic English D	1999	$29.95			Technical	939.56					
38	007142848	Education	R. De Roussy	Easy French Reader, 2/E	2003	$10.95			Alth	19.95					
39	007135962	Medicine	Ratelle	Prev Med & Public Health S	2000	$24.95			Bluman	19.95					
40	007226209	Technical	Schildt	C# 2.0: Complete Referen	2005	$59.99			Cadick	79.95					
41	007219356	Technical	Southwick/Pri	Telecommunications Abg	2001	$39.99			Dewberry Com	150					
42	007146659	Business	Sugars	Instant Cashflow	2005	$16.95			Edwards	39.95					
43	007146660	Business	Sugars	Instant Advertising	2005	$16.95			Elliott	125					
44	007146672	Business	Sugars	The Business Coach	2005	$16.95			Huettenmuelle	19.95					

Figure 5-13: Dashed lines and superimposed page numbers show page breaks in Page Break Preview.

Scale Your Data Before Printing

You can automatically adjust data on a worksheet to fit the number of pages you select or to a percentage that will print on as many pages as needed using several different options.

- In the Page Layout tab Scale To Fit group, click the **Width** or **Height** down arrows, and select how many pages you want the worksheet to print. The worksheet will scale to accommodate your choice.

  –Or–

- Click the **Scale** spinner to increase (see text and objects larger, but fewer cells) or decrease (see text and objects smaller, but more cells) the percentage of magnification (the Width and Height option must both be set to Automatic).

Output the Print Job

You can print to printers attached to your computer or to printers on your network. You can also print to a file instead of to a printer and choose features provided by your printer manufacturer. All this is accomplished from the Print dialog box (see Figure 5-9).

Click the **Office Button**, and click **Print**, or press CTRL+P.

CHOOSE A PRINTER

- In the Printer area, click the **Name** down arrow, and select a printer that is installed on your computer from the drop-down list.

  –Or–

- If you are part of a domain with Active Directory, click the **Find Printer** button to locate a shared printer on your network. After choosing a printer, click **OK** to return to the Print dialog box.

  In either case, the printer name is displayed in the Name drop-down list box, and information about the printer is listed below it.

PRINT TO A FILE

You can print your printer information to a file instead of directly to a physical device. Print files are often used to create Adobe PDF documents (you must select a PDF printer in the Name box and follow its unique instructions) or when you want to create a file of the print job to send to another computer.

1. Click **Print To File**, and click **OK**.

2. In the Print To File dialog box, type the path and file name where you want the print file located, and click **OK**.

Print to File	
Output File Name:	OK
Chapter 5	Cancel

SELECT PRINTER-SPECIFIC OPTIONS

Most printers have additional printing options and features besides those provided in Excel.

- To display a printer's properties dialog box, as shown in Figure 5-14, click **Properties** in the Print dialog box.

  –Or–

- Click **Options** in the Page Setup dialog box.

Paper size:	Letter
Print quality:	
First page number:	Auto

Print...   Print Preview   Options...

OK   Cancel

PRINT MULTIPLE COPIES

1. In the Copies area, click the **Number Of Copies** spinner to reflect the number of copies you want.

2. Click **Collate** to print each copy from start to finish before starting to print the next copy.

–Or–

Deselect **Collate** to print each page the number of times set in the Number Of Copies spinner before printing the next page.

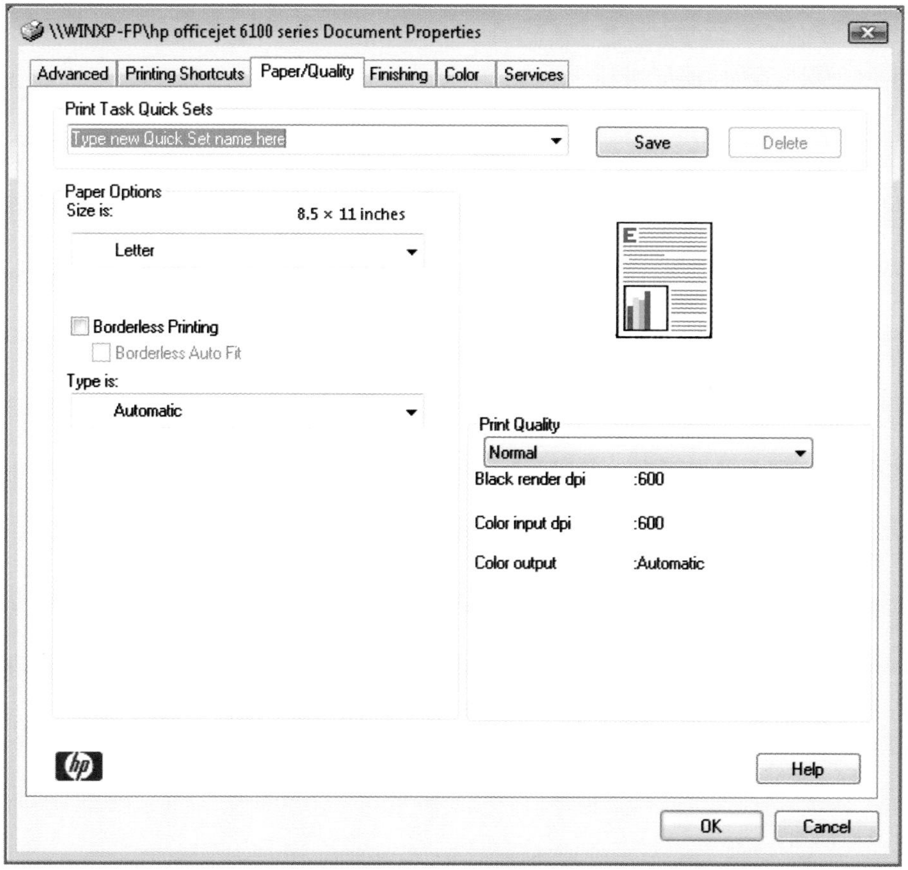

*Figure 5-14: **Printers have additional printing features besides those provide by Excel.***

How to...

- ☺ **Building a Chart**
- • *Choose a Chart Type*
- ✎ *Selecting Data for Charting*
- • *Choose a Chart Location*
- • *Modify How the Data Is Plotted*
- • *Apply a Chart Layout*
- • *Change a Chart's Style*
- ☺ *Selecting Chart Elements*
- • *Add Titles*
- • *Show or Hide Axes*
- • *Add or Remove Gridlines*
- ✎ *Identifying Chart Elements*
- • *Show or Hide a Legend*
- • *Add Data Labels*
- • *Display the Data Table*
- • *Create Your Own Chart Type*
- • *Add a Second Value Axis*
- • *Format Chart Elements*
- ☺ *Working with Charts*
- • *Add Charts Elsewhere*
- • *Analyze Charts*
- • *Print a Chart*

Chapter 6

Charting Data

In this chapter you will learn how to display worksheet data graphically in *charts*. Providing a more visual representation of data than a worksheet grid, charts show trends and comparisons at a quick glance. Figure 6-1 shows a column chart, typically used to compare the values of two or more categories, and many of the elements that can be used on a chart.

Charts in Excel follow the overall Office 2007 concept to quickly and easily produce a professional product that you can then modify if needed. After creating a simple chart, you can rely on Excel to provide several layout and style options, which you can use on their own or make further changes to. To fully integrate charts to the overall appearance of your workbook, many charting elements, such as color, font, and fills, take on the attributes of the current workbook theme. Display options are available that allow you to hide data

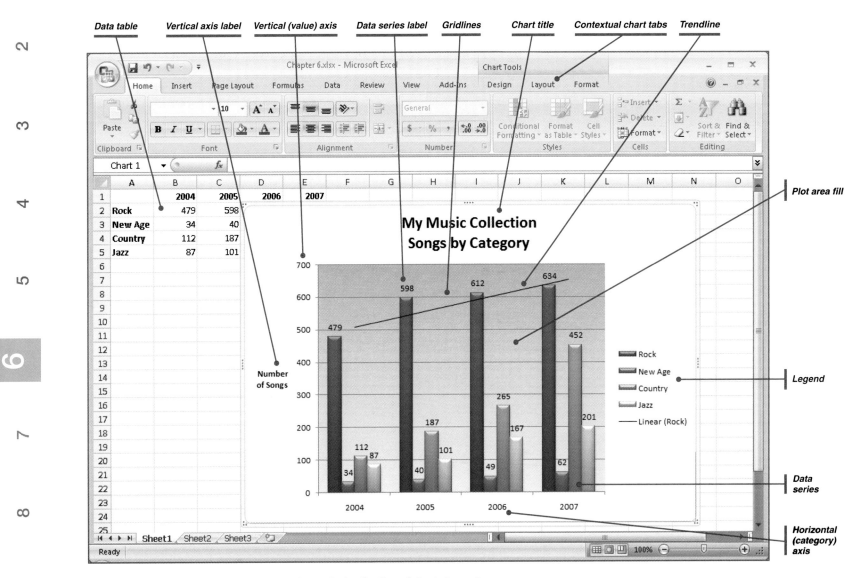

Figure 6-1: **This Excel chart demonstrates the typical collection of chart elements.**

QUICKSTEPS

BUILDING A CHART

You know that creating charts has gotten easier when Excel no longer provides a Chart Wizard to assist you. Excel 2007 now guides you through the process by assuming you'll move through one or more of the four tabs on the ribbon that contains chart-building tools. The tabs are essentially the steps to build a chart:

1. The **Insert** tab provides the means to initially create a chart from one of several chart types and subtypes. For many purposes, these charts are as far as you'll need to go.

2. The **Design** tab (under Chart Tools) lets you further refine the overall layout of the chart elements, change the chart type, and apply design styles.

3. The **Layout** tab (under Chart Tools) provides tools to add chart elements, such as axes, labels, and graphics. You can also add visual elements to help analyze data such as trendlines.

4. The **Format** tab (under Chart Tools) lets you fine-tune selected elements in terms of color, fills, and size.

Charts can be created in one of two forms:

- **Embedded charts** are objects that reside on a worksheet much like a drawing or picture, along with other objects and its underlying data. The chart is enclosed within a border and can be sized and moved similar to other graphic objects.

- **Chart sheets** are workbook sheets that contain a chart separated from its underlying worksheet. These charts also can be sized and moved within the sheet, and other graphic objects, such as pictures and SmartArt (professionally designed layouts combined with text entering capabilities), can be added to the chart sheet.

you may not want to display and that permit you to choose whether to show the chart on the same worksheet as its underlying data or in a separate chart sheet. These, along with other things you can do with charts, are covered in the following sections.

Create and Design a Chart

This section shows you how to create a chart and establish the basic design, or "infrastructure," of a chart. The topics in this section cover the tools involved in the first two basic steps in building a chart (see "Building a Chart" QuickSteps).

Choose a Chart Type

Excel organizes charts into 11 types, categorized by the function they perform. Within each chart type are from two to 19 variations called *subtypes*. For example, the Line chart type has seven ways to display trends, as shown in Figure 6-2. In total, you have 73 chart options to choose from and a virtually unlimited number of user-defined charts you can set up as *templates* (see "Create Your Own Chart Type" later in the chapter). The main chart types are summarized in Table 6-1.

SELECT A CHART TYPE FROM A GALLERY

1. Select the data range that you want to chart (see Chapter 2 for information on selecting ranges and "Selecting Data for Charting" QuickFacts in this chapter).

2. In the Insert tab Charts group, click the chart type you want (or click **Other Charts** to see more types). To see a description of the chart types or subtypes, point to a chart icon and a tooltip displays.

Though you do not have to select a range of data to create a chart (you can just click a cell within the range and Excel will do its best to assume the range), if you do, the chart initially displayed by Excel will give you a more accurate view of your data.

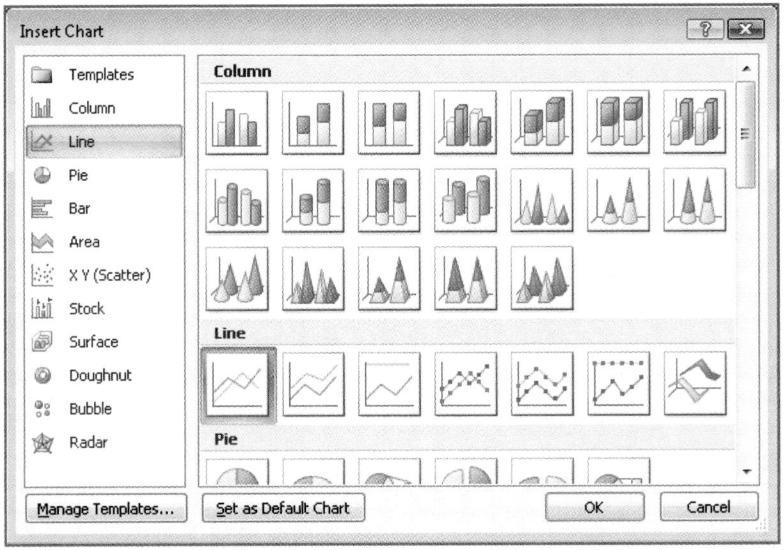

Insert Chart

		Column
📁	Templates	
📊	Column	
📈	Line	
🥧	Pie	
📊	Bar	
📉	Area	
🔲	X Y (Scatter)	**Line**
📊	Stock	
📊	Surface	
⊙	Doughnut	
🔵	Bubble	**Pie**
⭐	Radar	

Manage Templates... Set as Default Chart OK Cancel

Figure 6-2: *The Insert Chart dialog box displays all chart types in one venue.*

CHART TYPE	FUNCTION
Column, Bar, Line	Compare trends in multiple data series in various configurations, such as vertical or horizontal; available in several subtypes, such as 3-D line, cylinder, cone, and pyramid
Pie and Doughnut	Display one data series (pie) or compare multiple data series (doughnut) as part of a whole or 100 percent
XY (Scatter)	Displays pairs of data to establish concentrations
Area	Shows the magnitude of change over time; useful when summing multiple values to see the contribution of each
Radar	Connects changes in a data series from a starting or center point with lines, markers, or a colored fill
Surface	Compares trends in multiple data series in a continuous curve; similar to Line chart with a 3-D visual effect
Bubble	Displays sets of three values; similar to an XY chart with the third value being the size of the bubble
Stock	Displays three sets of values, such as a high, low, and closing stock prices
Templates	Charts that include formatting and unique settings that you might want to save to apply to future charts

Table 6-1: *Functional Types of Excel Charts*

3. Click the subtype you want from the respective gallery. A professionally designed chart is created and displayed on the worksheet.

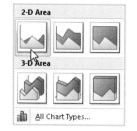

SELECT A CHART TYPE FROM A DIALOG BOX

1. Select the data range that you want to chart.

2. In the Insert tab Charts group, click the **Dialog Box Launcher** (the arrow in the lower-right corner of the group area). The Insert Chart dialog box appears (see Figure 6-2) with the default chart type selected (see "Change the Default Chart" if you want to change it).

3. Scroll through the complete inventory of Excel-provided chart types/subtypes in the large box to the right.

    –Or–

    Click a chart type in the left pane to auto-scroll to its chart subtypes.

4. To see an abbreviated description of the chart subtypes, point to a subtype icon and a tooltip displays.

5. Double-click the chart subtype you want. A professionally designed chart is created and displayed on the worksheet.

CREATE A CHART QUICKLY

1. Select the data range that you want to chart.

2. Press **ALT+F1** to create an embedded chart (Figure 6-1 shows an embedded chart).

    –Or–

    Press **F11** to create a chart sheet.

    In either case, a chart is created using the default chart type. See "Change the Default Chart," next, for steps to change the default chart type and see "Choose a Chart Location," later in the chapter, to switch a chart between embedded and a chart sheet.

TIP

Chart templates (referred to in previous versions of Excel as "custom types") are customized charts that extend your inventory of available chart types on which to base a new chart. You will have prebuilt templates available in the Insert Chart dialog box if you chose to install them when you set up Excel. You can add more templates by creating and saving your own custom charts (see "Create Your Own Chart Type" later in the chapter), or you can install them from outside sources, such as Office Online.

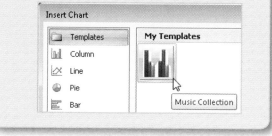

TIP

Chart sheets do not display their underlying data by default. You can add the range of cells that comprise the data, with or without legend keys. See "Display the Data Table" later in this chapter.

QUICKFACTS

SELECTING DATA FOR CHARTING

Charts are created from worksheet data. Excel makes assumptions on how to set up the plot area, assign axes, and make labels based on the data. Though you can change many of the chart elements after the chart is created and Excel will quickly reconfigure the chart, it speeds things along (and increases the likelihood of seeing what you want!) if the data is properly organized. Guidelines for setting up data for charting and assumptions Excel uses include:

- The selected data must be a rectangular *data range* or consist of multiple selections in a rectangular array.

- Text, which is used solely to create labels, should only be in the topmost row and/or the leftmost column; otherwise, text encountered within the range is charted as zero.

- Each cell must contain a *value* (or data point). Values in the same row or column are considered to be related and are called a *data series*. The first data series starts with the first cell in the upper-left area of the selected data that is not text or formatted as a date. Subsequent data series are determined by Excel, continuing across the rows or down the columns. Values are plotted on the vertical (generally, the Y, or value) axis.

- As Excel determines whether there are more rows or columns selected, it will assume the lesser number to be the data series and the greater number to be categories that are plotted on the horizontal (generally, the X, or category) axis. In Figure 6-3, three columns and four rows of data are selected; therefore, Excel plots the three years' values each as a data series and considers the rows to be categories.

Excel ships with the clustered column subtype as the default chart (see Figure 6-1). You can change it to any of the Excel chart types or to one you saved as a template.

1. In the Insert tab Charts group, click the **Dialog Box Launcher**.
2. In the Insert Chart dialog box (see Figure 6-2), click the chart type you want to be the new default chart type.
3. Click **Set As Default Chart**, and click **OK**.

| Manage Templates... | Set as Default Chart |

Choose a Chart Location

You can change where a chart is located, from an object on the worksheet (embedded chart) to a full, separate sheet (chart sheet, shown in Figure 6-4), and vice versa.

To relocate a chart:

1. Open either the worksheet that contains the embedded chart or the chart sheet whose position you want to change.
2. In the Design tab (Chart Tools), click **Move Chart**.
3. In the Move Chart dialog box, click **New Sheet** to move the chart to a chart sheet. You can change the name of the chart sheet that will be created to something other than the default.

–Or–

Click the **Object In** down arrow to select the sheet in the workbook where you want the chart to be added as an embedded chart.

Move Chart

Choose where you want the chart to be placed:

○ New sheet: Chart3

● Object in: Sheet3

OK   Cancel

4. Click **OK**. The chart is moved to the location you specified and removed from its original location.

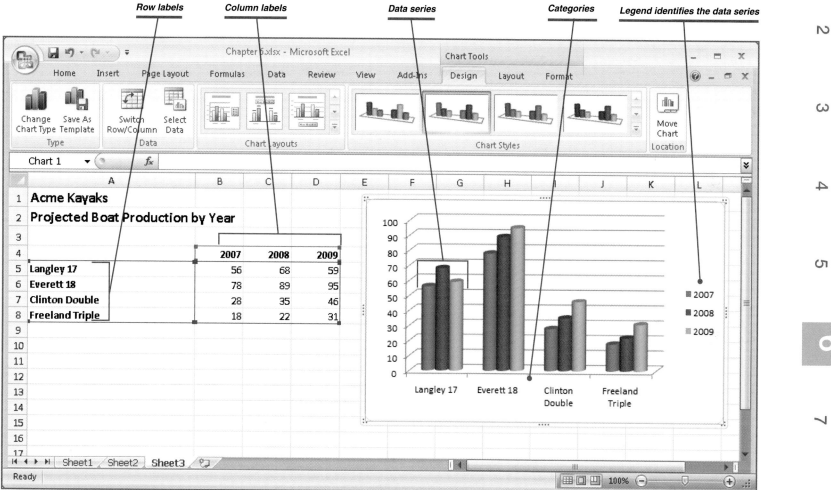

Figure 6-3: **Excel determines whether row or column labels become the plotted data series by choosing the lesser number for the data series and the greater for categories.**

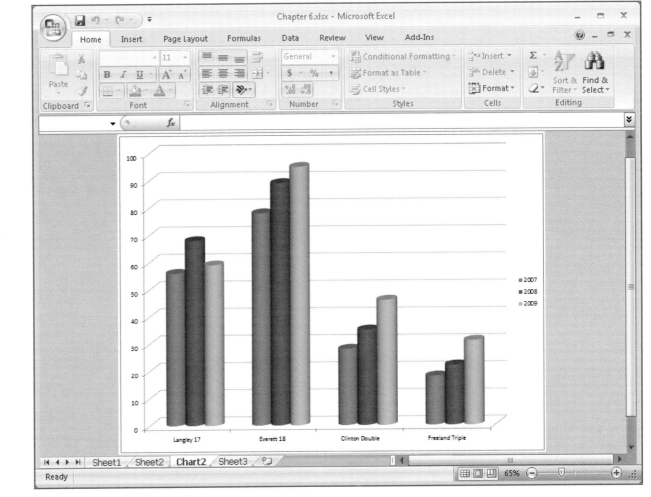

Figure 6-4: *You can create an embedded chart and easily move it to a chart sheet.*

NOTE

Charts also can be moved and copied to other workbooks and programs using the Copy, Cut, and Paste commands. See "Add Charts Elsewhere" later in the chapter.

Modify How the Data Is Plotted

Without affecting any of the underlying data, you can add or remove data series, select the cells that identify the data series' name and the data series' value, and change which cells are used for labels for the category (X) axis.

1. Display a worksheet with an embedded chart or open a chart sheet containing a chart. Click the chart to display the Chart Tools tabs.

2. In the Design tab Data group, click **Select Data**. The Select Data Source dialog box appears, shown in Figure 6-5. You can perform several actions from the dialog box:

- To change the range of data that is charted, click the **Collapse Dialog** button at the right end of the Chart Data Range text box. Select the range and click the **Expand Dialog** button in the shrunken dialog box to return to the full-sized Select Data Source dialog box.

    –Or–

    Type the range in the Chart Data Range text box.

- To switch between the row and column labels being used as the data series and horizontal (category) axis, select your data range, and click **Switch Row/Column**. (If this is all you want to do, you can click **Switch Row/Column** in the Data group.) The chart changes accordingly (see Figure 6-6).

- To include more data in the chart, click **Add** in the Legend Entries Series pane. In the Edit Series dialog box, click the applicable Collapse Dialog buttons to add cells for the data series name and its values. Click **OK** to return to the Select Data Source dialog box.

- To change existing data series, select the series you want to change, and click **Edit**. Make any changes and click **OK** to return to the Select Data Source dialog box.

- To remove a data series, select the series and click **Remove**.

- To change the order in which the data series is presented, select the data series you want to move, and click the up and down arrows to move it where you want it.

- To change the horizontal axis labels, select the label in the right pane, and click **Edit**. Select the range for the labels, and click **OK**.

- To change how empty and hidden cells are accounted for, click **Hidden And Empty Cells**. In the Settings dialog box, select the behavior you want, and click **OK**.

3. Click **OK** when you are finished with the Select Data Source dialog box.

TIP

Instead of clicking **Collapse Dialog**, dragging the area, and then clicking **Expand Dialog**, you can just start dragging the area, causing the dialog box to automatically collapse. It will expand again when you are done.

NOTE

The series name and values you choose can be from other worksheets or open workbooks. All you are really doing is adding more information to the chart that is not within your originally selected data.

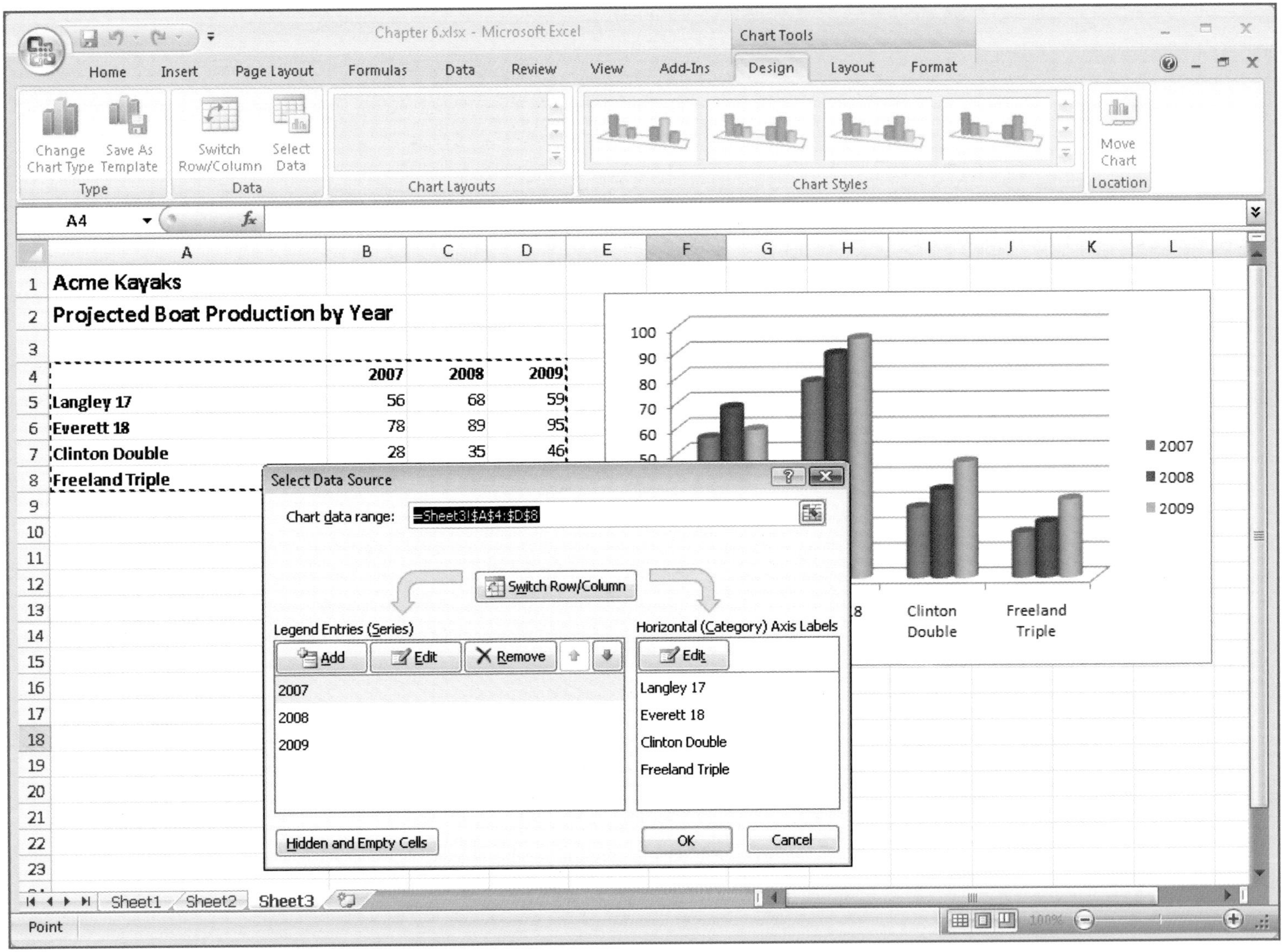

Figure 6-5: **You can change several parameters of your chart's data from one location and see the immediate effect on the chart.**

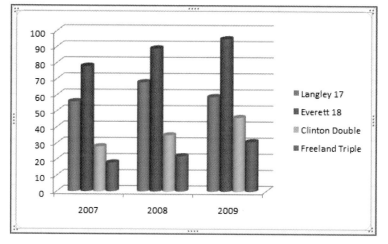

Figure 6-6: **Compare the switching of the data series and horizontal axis with the chart in Figure 6-5.**

Apply a Chart Layout

A chart *layout* allows you to quickly choose how chart elements are arranged within the boundaries of the chart window. For example, the default column layout places the legend on the right of the data series. Other layouts place the legend under the title, under axis labels (see Figure 6-7) or omit it altogether. As with selecting a chart type, you can easily modify any layout by moving or changing other chart element attributes.

1. Click the chart whose layout you want to change.

2. In the Design tab (Chart Tools) Chart Layout group, click the **Quick Layout** down arrow to view the gallery of layout icons available for your current chart type, if your window is small enough.

   –Or–

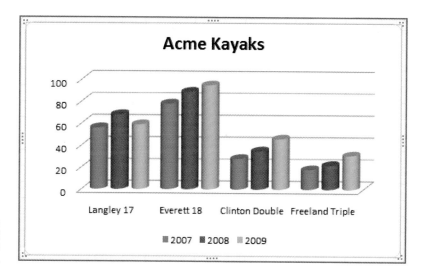

Figure 6-7: **Layouts allow you to rearrange and modify the chart elements on your chart with just a few mouse clicks.**

If your Excel window is large enough, click the up and down arrows to the right of the visible layouts to rotate through the layout icons, row by row; or click the **More** button to view all layouts at once.

Row by row buttons

More button

3. Click the layout you want. The chart changes to conform to your choice.

Change a Chart's Style

Styles change the color, fill, and special effects of several chart elements (for example, the rectangles or cylinders in a column chart or the color of plot area gridlines), including the background of the chart area window. A chart's initial style is derived from the workbook's theme (see Chapter 3 for more information on themes). You can change the current style by selecting a different combination of colors and shading from a gallery (or by changing the workbook's theme).

1. Click the chart whose style you want to change.

2. In the Design tab (Chart Tools) Chart Styles group, click the **Quick Styles** down arrow to view the gallery of style icons available for your current chart type, if your window is small enough (see Figure 6-8).

–Or–

If your Excel window is large enough, click the up and down arrows to the right of the visible layouts to rotate through the layout icons, row by row; or click the **More** button to view all layouts at once.

3. Click the style you want. The chart changes to conform to your choice.

NOTE

You can change the style-related attributes of individual chart elements to provide full flexibility in how you want your chart to appear. See the applicable section under "Modify Chart Elements" for the element you want to change.

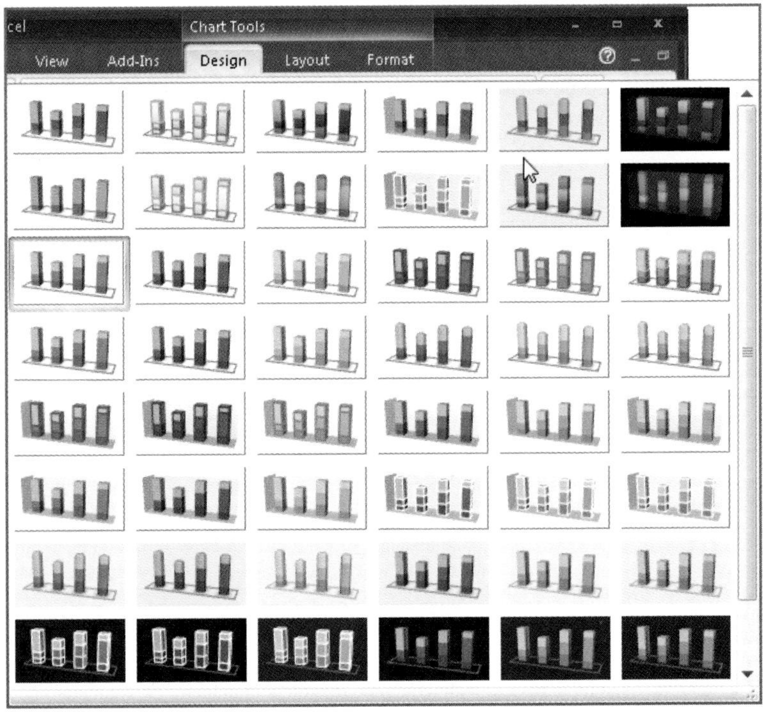

Figure 6-8: ***There is no shortage of styles for a given chart type.***

QUICKSTEPS

SELECTING CHART ELEMENTS

You can select chart elements using the keyboard or the mouse. When selected, elements will display small circular and/or rectangular handles (for some elements, these are sizing handles; for others, they just show selections) and the selected element's name appears in the Format tab (Chart Tools) Current Selection group on the ribbon.

Acme Kayaks

SELECT CHART ELEMENTS BY CLICKING

Place the mouse pointer over the element you want selected, and click it.

SELECT CHART ELEMENTS FROM THE RIBBON

1. Click the chart to display the Chart Tools tabs on the ribbon.

2. In the Format tab (Chart Tools) Current Selection group, click the Current Selection down arrow at the top of the group (labeled "Chart Area" if no element is selected).

3. Click the chart element you want selected from the drop-down list. Selection handles surround it.

SELECT CHART ELEMENTS USING THE KEYBOARD

1. Click the chart to select it.

2. Press the **UP ARROW** or **DOWN ARROW** key to cycle through the groups of elements.

   –Or–

   Press **RIGHT ARROW** or **LEFT ARROW** to cycle through the elements within a group.

REMOVE A SELECTION

Press **ESC**.

Modify Chart Elements

In addition to applying broad changes through styles, layouts, and themes, Excel allows you to treat each element of a chart uniquely; that is, each has its own set of formatting and other characteristics you can apply. Once you have a basic chart displayed, you can totally redesign it by selecting and changing each of its component elements.

Add Titles

Titles help readers quickly orient themselves to the data being presented. On an Excel chart, you can have chart and axis titles.

1. Click the chart.

2. In the Layout tab (Chart Tools) Labels group, click **Chart Title**.

3. Click one of the options to place the chart title where you want it, or click **None** to remove it.

4. In the Labels group, next to Chart Title, click **Axis Titles**.

5. Point to either the horizontal or vertical axis, and click one of the options to place the respective axis title where you want it; or click **None** to remove it.

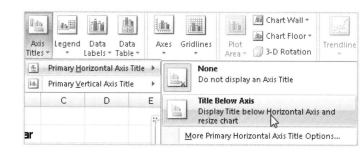

6. Select the default title text that appears on the chart ("Chart Title" or "Axis Title"), and type the title you want.

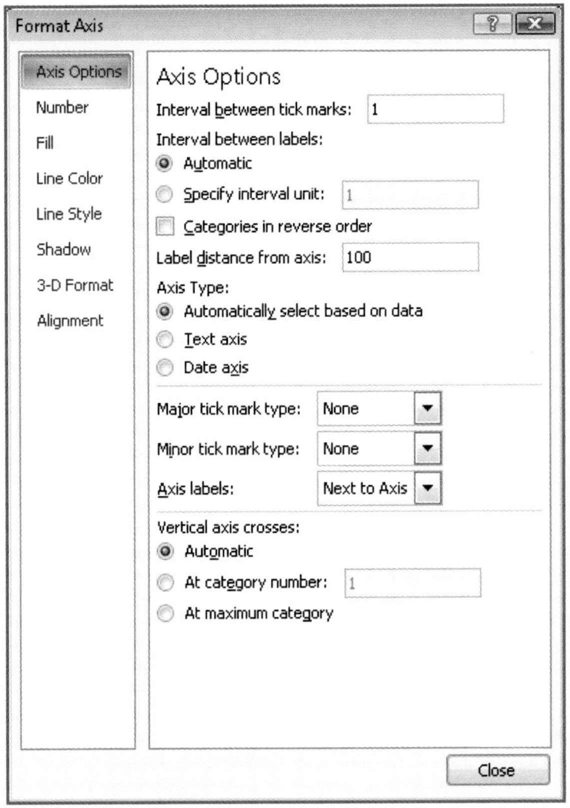

Format Axis

Axis Options

Interval between tick marks: `1`

Interval between labels:
- ⦿ Automatic
- ◯ Specify interval unit: `1`
- ☐ Categories in reverse order

Label distance from axis: `100`

Axis Type:
- ⦿ Automatically select based on data
- ◯ Text axis
- ◯ Date axis

Major tick mark type: | None ▾ |

Minor tick mark type: | None ▾ |

Axis labels: | Next to Axis ▾ |

Vertical axis crosses:
- ⦿ Automatic
- ◯ At category number: `1`
- ◯ At maximum category

[Close]

Figure 6-9: **You can modify horizontal and vertical axes to fit any unique set of data.**

TIP

You can add a second category and/or value axis with its own title. A second axis is typically used when the values in one data series is proportionately different from the others and needs a different scale of values. See "Add a Second Value Axis" later in the chapter.

Show or Hide Axes

The primary horizontal (category) and vertical (value) axes can be displayed or not depending on whether the information provided adds value to your chart.

1. Click the chart.
2. In the Layout tab (Chart Tools) Axes group, click **Axes**. Point to:
   - **Primary Horizontal Axis** and click one of the options to place the axis where you want it; or click **None** to remove it.
   - **Primary Vertical Axis** and click one of the options to choose a scale; or click **None** to remove it.
3. Select the horizontal or vertical axis, and click **More Primary Horizontal** (or **Vertical**) **Axis Options** at the bottom of the respective options drop-down list. Click **Axis Options** in the left pane of the Format Axis dialog box (shown in Figure 6-9) to see options related to:
   - Starting and ending scale values
   - Axis type (horizontal axis only); text or date
   - Locations for tick marks and where the axes intersect
   - Distance axis is from its label
4. Make any adjustments and click **Close**.

Add or Remove Gridlines

Gridlines provide a background reference to value and category axes intervals. You can choose to have a few gridlines at what Excel determines are the major intervals, such as every 10 values on a value scale of 0–100, and/or at minor intervals, such as at every other value on a value scale of 0–100, or not at all. Figure 6-10 shows minor and major gridlines.

1. Click the chart.
2. In the Layout tab (Chart Tools) Axes group, click **Gridlines**.
3. Point to **Primary Horizontal** (or **Vertical**) **Gridlines**, and click one of the options to display major, minor, or both sets of gridlines; or click **None** to remove them.

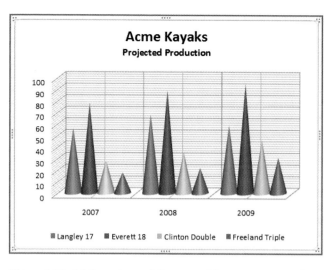

Figure 6-10: **Adding minor gridlines provides a more accurate determination of values, but they can clutter a chart.**

Show or Hide a Legend

A *legend* identifies the data series in a chart. You can choose to display the legend or not and where on the chart the legend is located.

1. Click the chart.
2. In the Layout tab (Chart Tools) Labels group, click **Legend**.
3. Click one of the options to place the legend where you want it, or click **None** to remove it.

Add Data Labels

The value of a data series can be interpolated using the vertical (value) axis and gridlines, but if you want the values shown directly on the plot area, you can add them.

1. Click the chart.
2. In the Layout tab (Chart Tools) Labels group, click **Data Labels**.

TIP

After data labels are displayed on your chart, you can edit any label by clicking it twice slowly. Do not double-click it, or you will open its Format dialog box.

Format Data Labels [?] [X]

Label Options	Label Contains
Number	☐ Series name
Fill	☐ Category name
Line	☑ Value
Line Style	
Shadow	[Reset Label Text]
3-D Format	
Alignment	☐ Include legend key in label
	Separator [,] [▼]

3. Click one of the placement options to add data labels to the chart, or click **None** to remove them.

4. Click **More Data Label Options** at the bottom of the Data Labels drop-down list. Click **Label Options** in the left pane of the Format Data Labels dialog box to see additional options:

- Under Label Contains, select whether to display a name instead of a value.
- Select **Include Legend Key In Label** to provide a color-coded rectangle near each data series that corresponds to the legend label.
- Click the **Separator** down arrow, and click the character you want used to separate multiple labels.

5. Click **Close**. (Figure 6-11 shows a chart with several data label possibilities.)

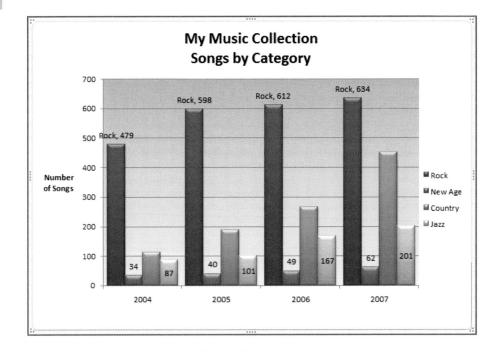

Figure 6-11: **Data labels can be positioned differently on the data series and can include series names and separators, such as commas.**

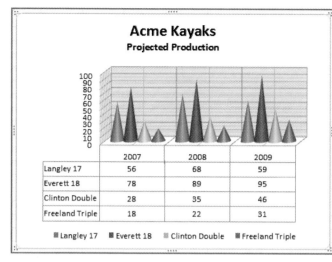

Acme Kayaks
Projected Production

	2007	2008	2009
Langley 17	56	68	59
Everett 18	78	89	95
Clinton Double	28	35	46
Freeland Triple	18	22	31

■ Langley 17   ■ Everett 18   ■ Clinton Double   ■ Freeland Triple

Figure 6-12: **A chart's data table can be added to a chart.**

Display the Data Table

You can add the underlying worksheet data, or *data table*, to the chart area.

1. Click the chart.

2. In the Layout tab (Chart Tools) Labels group, click **Data Table**.

3. Click one of the options to place the data table below the chart, with or without legend keys, or click **None** to remove it.

4. Click **More Data Table Options** at the bottom of the Data Table drop-down list. Click **Data Table Options** in the left pane of the Format Data Table dialog box to determine whether you want horizontal, vertical, or outline borders. Clear each check box if you don't want any borders.

5. Click **Close**. The data table is added to the chart area below the plot area (see Figure 6-12).

Create Your Own Chart Type

After you have applied formatting and added or removed chart elements, your chart may not resemble any of the standard or even custom chart types provided by Excel. To save your work so that you can build a similar chart at another time:

1. Build the chart and then select it.

2. In the Design tab (Chart Tools) Type group, click **Save Template**.

3. In the Save Chart Template dialog box, name the chart and click **Save**. The chart is saved in a Chart folder within your Excel Template folder and will be available in the Insert Chart and Change Chart Type dialog boxes.

4. Type a name and description for the chart, and click **OK**. The chart appears as a user-defined chart type that you can choose in the future (see "Use a Template" later in the chapter). Click **OK** to close the Chart Type dialog box.

NOTE

If you do not have chart templates available to you, they were not installed when Excel was set up. You can change your program configuration to add prebuilt templates in the Windows Programs And Features (Windows Vista) or Add Or Remove Programs (Windows XP) Control Panel features (click **Start** and then click **Control Panel** in either operating system to access these features). You can also add your own templates that will appear in the Template pane (see "Create Your Own Chart Type" earlier in the chapter).

Format Data Series

Series Options	Series Options
Fill	**Series Overlap**
Border Color	Separated ——○—— Overlapped
Border Styles	0%
Shadow	**Gap Width**
3-D Format	No Gap ——○—— Large Gap
	150%
	Plot Series On
	○ Primary Axis
	● Secondary Axis

My Templates

Column-Line

Add a Second Value Axis

When you have a data series that contains values (or data points) with disproportional or different types of values, you might need to create a second value axis to keep the scaling meaningful.

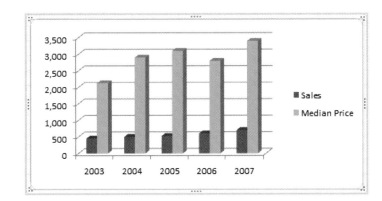

CREATE A SECOND AXIS MANUALLY (COLUMN-LINE CHART)

1. Create a column chart with two data series using one of the methods described earlier in the chapter.

2. Right-click one of the data series (this will be the series that changes from a column to a line), and click **Format Data Series**.

3. In the Format Data Series dialog box, click **Series Options**. Under Plot Series On, click **Secondary Axis**. Click **Close**.

4. In the Design tab (Chart Tools) Type group, click **Change Chart Type**. Click one of the line charts, and click **OK**. The two-data series column chart is converted to a column-line combination chart with a second value axis (see Figure 6-13).

Programs and Features

USE A TEMPLATE

1. Click the chart.

2. In the Design tab (Chart Tools) Type group, click **Change Chart Type**.

3. In the Change Chart Type dialog box (identical to Figure 6-2), click **Templates** in the left pane.

4. Under My Templates, click an applicable chart type, and click **OK**.

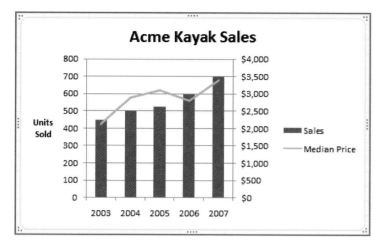

Figure 6-13: **Two value axes allow you to combine two different data series on one chart to ascertain relationships.**

Format Chart Elements

Each chart element has an associated Format dialog box with one or more categories that provide formatting options. Several of the chart elements have identical or a similar set of formatting options (unique options are described in other sections in this chapter). Table 6-2 shows the formatting options, organized by categories that display in the individual Format dialog boxes, and the chart elements that apply.

To format a chart element:

1. Click the chart.

2. In the Layout tab (Chart Tools), click the element whose formatting you want to change from the **Labels**, **Axes**, or **Background** groups. Click the **More** *element* **Options** command at the bottom of each element drop-down list.

–Or–

FORMATTING OPTIONS	DESCRIPTION	APPLY TO
Fill	Provides options for gradient, picture, or texture fill, as well as color choices, degrees of transparency, and gradient options	Axis, chart area, data labels/series, legend, plot area, titles, walls/floors
Line	Offers solid or gradient lines, as well as color choices, degrees of transparency, and gradient options	Axis, chart area, data labels/series, error bars, gridlines, legend, plot area, titles, trendlines, walls/floors
Line Style	Provides options for width, dashed, and compound (multiple) lines, as well as styles for line ends and line joins	Axis, chart area, data labels/series, error bars, gridlines, legend, plot area, titles, trendlines, walls/floors
Shadow	Provides preset shadow styles and controls for color, transparency, size, blur, angle, and distance	Axis, chart area, data labels/series, legend, plot area, titles, trendlines, walls/floors
3-D Format	Adds 3-D dimension to shapes; provides top, bottom, material, and lighting presets and controls for depth contours and color	Axis, chart area, data labels/series, legend, plot area, titles, walls/floors
3-D Rotation	Provides angular rotation and perspective adjustments, as well as positioning and scaling controls	Walls/floors
Number	Provides the same number formats as the Format Cells Number tab, such as currency, accounting, date, and time	Axis, data labels
Alignment	Vertically aligns, rotates, and stacks text	Axis, data labels, titles, legends

Table 6-2: **Chart Element Formatting Options**

NOTE

Graphics (including shapes, pictures, clip art, and text boxes) can be easily added to charts and formatted. See Chapter 7 for more information on working with graphics.

Select the element and, in the Format tab (Chart Tools) Current Selection group, click **Format Selection**.

–Or–

Right-click the element and click **Format *chart element***.

In any case, a Format dialog box appears similar to the one shown in Figure 6-14.

3. Select and/or adjust the formatting options, and click **Close**.

QUICKSTEPS

WORKING WITH CHARTS

Charts are highly flexible, and you can easily change several of their characteristics.

RESIZE A CHART

1. Click the chart. Eight sizing handles appear on the expanded border of the chart area.

2. Point to a sizing handle. The mouse pointer becomes a double-headed arrow.

3. Drag to increase or decrease the chart size. The plot area changes accordingly.

POSITION A CHART

You can move a chart to other programs by other means (see "Choose a Chart Location" and "Add Charts Elsewhere" in this chapter), but to adjust its location within the Excel window, simply drag it into the position you want.

1. Click the chart.

2. Point to the chart border (other than on a sizing handle). The mouse pointer becomes a cross with four arrowheads.

3. Drag the chart into the position you want.

Continued . . .

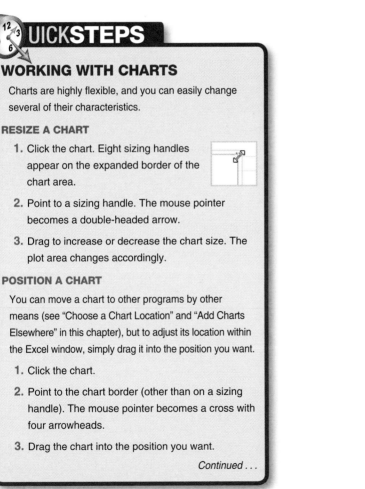

Figure 6-14: **You can get very detailed when making manual formatting changes.**

WORKING WITH CHARTS *(Continued)*

REMOVE A CHART

When removing a chart, make sure you click or right-click the chart area, not a chart element (verify this by clicking the **Format** tab (Chart Tools) and seeing Chart Area displayed in the Current Selection group).

Click the chart area, and press **DELETE**.

–Or–

Right-click the chart area, and click **Cut**.

INSERT A CHART SHEET

1. Right-click the worksheet tab to the right of where you want the new chart sheet, and click **Insert**.

2. In the General tab, double-click the **Chart** icon. The chart sheet is inserted and is named "Chart *x*."

3. Add a chart to the new chart sheet. (See "Choose a Chart Location" and "Add Charts Elsewhere" in this chapter for ways to move and copy charts.)

REVERT A CHART'S STYLING

Sometimes you can get carried away with visual customizations and want to start over with a basic appearance. You can quickly remove styling changes and reset a chart to match the attributes of the workbook's theme.

1. Click the chart.

2. In the Format tab (Chart Tools) Current Selection group, click **Reset To Match Style**.

   –Or–

   Right-click the chart and click **Reset To Match Style**.

Chart Area
Format Selection
Reset to Match Style
Current Selection

Use Charts

Charts can be moved, copied, printed, and enhanced with shapes, pictures, and text, and analyzed with trendlines and standard deviation indicators.

Add Charts Elsewhere

Charts used within Office 2007 programs (Microsoft Excel, Microsoft Word, and Microsoft PowerPoint) appear and behave almost identically, allowing you to easily share information among the three programs.

MOVE AND COPY A CHART WITHIN EXCEL

You can relocate both embedded charts and charts that have been placed on their own chart sheets. Any changes to the underlying data will be updated in the chart, according to calculations options selected for the workbook (see Chapter 4 for more information on recalculating).

1. Right-click the chart and click **Cut** to move it.

   –Or–

   Click **Copy** to copy the chart.

2. Right-click the upper-leftmost cell where you want the chart, either in the same or another workbook, and click **Paste**.

USE CHARTS IN WORD AND POWERPOINT

Excel is primarily a data collection and analysis program; Word and PowerPoint present data and other information. You can use Office 2007 to achieve the best of both worlds by using Excel to retain and manipulate the data and copying the charts to Word and PowerPoint for use in documents and presentations. You have several options as to the relationship between the data in Excel and the charts in other programs.

1. In Excel, right-click in a blank area of the chart, and click **Copy** (or use one of several alternative copying techniques).

2. Open Word 2007 or PowerPoint 2007. Right-click where you want the Excel chart inserted, and click **Paste**. The chart appears as it did in Excel.

TIP

Excel provides several tools to analyze data. See Chapter 9 for more information on using PivotTables and other data analysis tools.

3. Click the **Paste Options** SmartTag at the bottom right corner of the chart, as shown in Figure 6-15. There are two sets of options; the first set determines the relationship with Excel:

- **Paste As Picture** inserts the chart as a standalone picture. No changes to the structure are allowed by the destination program, and no data updates are provided by Excel.

- **Excel Chart (Entire Workbook)** embeds the chart and workbook data into the destination file so that both the chart and data can be changed independently of the source workbook.

- **Chart (Linked To Excel Data)** copies the chart and maintains a link with the source workbook so that changes made to the data are updated in the Word or PowerPoint chart as well (assuming the link isn't broken by removing the workbook or deleting the data). Updates are made automatically when both source and destination documents are opened, unless default settings have been changed.

4. The second set of options on the SmartTag menu control how the copied chart appears in the destination program:

- **Keep Source Formatting** copies the chart as it appears in Excel.

- **Use Destination Theme** resets the chart's styling to match the current theme in Word or PowerPoint, providing a more unified look.

Analyze Charts

"Past performance does not guarantee future results," as the saying goes, but Excel can analyze plotted data to predict possible trends and show errors.

ADD A TRENDLINE

Trendlines interpret a data series and establish trends for the existing data or project the current trend into the future (see Figure 6-1). To add one or more trendlines to your chart:

1. Click a data series in the chart that you want analyzed.

2. In the Layout tab (Chart Tools) Analysis group, click **Trendline** and click the type of trendline you want to apply. An addition is made to the legend, identifying the trendline.

3. Repeat step 2 to add additional trendline types.

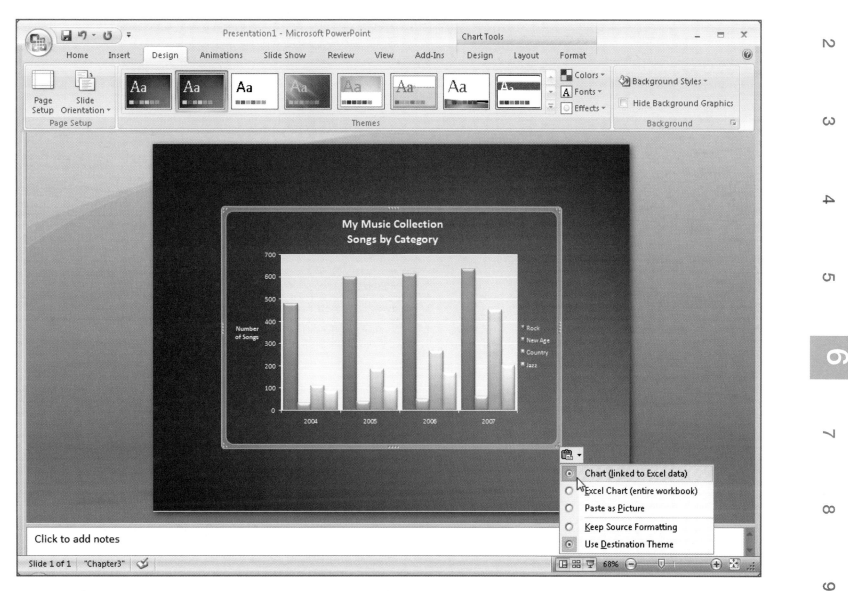

Figure 6-15: *Charts are easily copied from Excel to Word and PowerPoint, where you can link to the data or transfer the entire workbook into the destination file.*

4. To fine-tune trendlines, select the trendline you want to change (unless you only have one trendline), and click the **More Trendline Options** command at the bottom of the Trendline drop-down list.

–Or–

Right-click the trendline and click **Format Trendline.**

5. In the Format Trendline dialog box, click **Trendline Options**. Change any parameters, including type, the name as it appears in the legend, and forecast periods. Click **Close** when finished.

SHOW ERRORS

You can add indicators that show the margin of error of your data series, as shown in Figure 6-16.

1. Click a data series in the chart that you want to add error bars to.

–Or–

If you want to add error bars to all series, do not select any.

2. In the Layout tab (Chart Tools) Analysis group, click **Error Bars** and click the type of error bar that you want to apply.

![Error Bars menu showing options: None – Removes the Error Bars for the selected series or all Error Bars if none is selected; Error Bars with Standard Error – Displays Error Bars for the selected chart series using Standard Error; Error Bars with Percentage – Displays Error Bars for the selected chart series with 5% value; Error Bars with Standard Deviation – Displays Error Bars for the selected chart series with 1 standard deviation; More Error Bars Options...]

NOTE

Standard error and standard deviation are measures of spread (typically from the mean) used in statistical analysis.

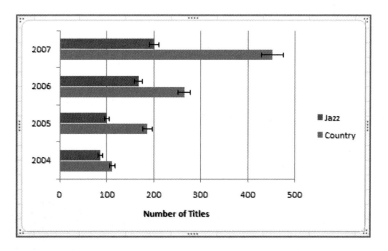

Figure 6-16: *These error bars show the margin of error to be plus or minus 5 percent of each data series value.*

3. To fine-tune error bars for a data series, select the error bar for the data series you want to change, and click the **More Error Bars Options** command at the bottom of the Error Bars drop-down list.

–Or–

Right-click the error bar, and click **Format Error Bars Options**.

4. In the Format Error Bars dialog box, click **Y Error Bars**. Change any parameters, including the amount of the error bar, whether the error bar represents a plus/minus amount, and whether the ends are capped or not.

5. Click **Close** when finished.

Print a Chart

You can print a chart, along with data and other worksheet objects (see Chapter 5), or you can choose to print just the chart.

1. Select the embedded chart or a chart located on a chart sheet.

2. Click the **Office Button**, and click **Print**. Under Print What, the **Selected Chart** option is chosen. Select a printer and any additional printing options. Click **OK** when ready.

TIP

Press **CTRL**+ **P** to quickly open the Print dialog box.

Print what
- ◯ Selection
- ◉ Selected Chart
- ☐ Ignore print areas
- ◯ Entire workbook
- ◯ Table

Preview

How to...

- *Understanding Shapes*
- Add Shapes
- *Working with Curves*
- Insert Pictures
- *Using Pictures*
- Organize Pictures
- Add Text
- Use SmartArt
- *Changing SmartArt*
- Select, View, and Delete Shapes
- *Using Handles and Borders to Change Shapes*
- Crop Pictures
- Position Shapes
- *Combining Shapes by Grouping*
- Use Styles
- Apply Styling Elements to Pictures
- *Changing a Picture's Attributes*
- Change a Shape's Fill
- Add WordArt Styling to Text
- Make Detailed Formatting Changes

Chapter 7
Working with Shapes and Pictures

Excel 2007 introduces *shapes*, which are built-in forms, such as rectangles and block arrows, that you can transform into professional-looking graphics by applying an incredible amount of styling, sizing, rotating, and 3-D special effects to achieve the results you seek. Shapes are containers that you can fill with any color or shading you can imagine, as well as textures and pictures. Integrated with *WordArt*, Microsoft's styling feature for text, shapes offer the full spectrum of visual and information tools to accentuate your worksheet data.

To achieve results right "out of the box," Excel 2007 (and its companion Office programs, Word, PowerPoint, and Outlook) combine shapes and an integrated text-entry tool to produce presentation-quality shapes, such as organization charts, process diagrams, and other related visuals. Shapes,

UNDERSTANDING SHAPES

Excel 2007 continues the trend of recent Office releases of blurring the distinction between various types of graphics and making working with them a more unified experience. The result is *shapes*, which share similar formatting, sizing, and other attributes. No need to wonder what sort of shape you are working on, simply select the shape, and contextual tabs are displayed on the ribbon, providing quick access to many galleries of prebuilt designs, styles, and other tools. You can achieve more control by changing the component elements of these prebuilt offerings (such as fill, outline, and special effects), or you can use a common Formatting dialog box that then lets you modify the formatting attributes in fine detail.

Drawing Tools	Picture Tools
Format	Format

SmartArt Tools	
Design	Format

Think of shapes in terms of bricks. For most of us, we see an example of a brick house someone else has designed and built, we buy it, and are satisfied with the results. Others approach this purchase as a starting point, rearranging rooms, repainting, and performing other significant modifications. And then, there are the few who build their own house from the ground up, brick by brick, making decisions for every conceivable aspect of the final product. Excel allows you to choose how you want to build your visual message with shapes in the same way.

either on their own or integrated into SmartArt, can make use of theme colors, styles, and other effects to provide a consistent look and feel with other aspects of your workbook.

In this chapter you will learn how to insert, modify, format, and manage shapes, as well as how to arrange, resize, and position them.

Add Shapes, Pictures, and Text

The first step to adding visual enhancements to your worksheet (and sometimes the last) is to simply insert the shape. This section shows you how to do that, along with demonstrating two main reasons to use shapes: to contain pictures and text.

Add Shapes

Shapes are initially added to the worksheet from the Insert tab. Once positioned on your worksheet, you can easily change the shape to any other shape in the gallery.

ADD A SHAPE

1. In the Insert tab Illustrations group, click **Shapes** to open the full shapes gallery. The shapes gallery displays dozens of shape icons, divided into several categories, as shown in Figure 7-1.

2. Click the shape you want. Your mouse pointer turns into a small cross.

NOTE

After you have at least one shape on your worksheet and have it selected, the contextual Drawing Tools Format tab is displayed on the ribbon. From here, you can access the primary tools for working on shapes, as well as insert additional shapes from its Insert Shapes group.

3. Drag your cross pointer to the approximate location and size you want. In the case of the freeform drawing shapes, see "Working with Curves" QuickSteps.

4. Release the mouse button when finished. The shape is surrounded by a selection border and handles (see "Working with Shapes" later in the chapter for information on selecting shapes and using handles), and is filled with a color determined by the workbook's theme (see Chapter 3 for more information on working with themes).

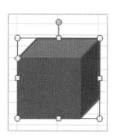

QUICKSTEPS

WORKING WITH CURVES

Freeform tools are available to draw curved shapes.

CREATE A CURVE

Open the shapes gallery from the Insert tab Shapes group or the Format tab (Drawing Tools) Insert Shapes group. The freeform tools are located on the right end of the Lines category:

- Click **Curve** and click the cross pointer to establish the curve's starting point. Move the pointer and click to set an inflection point, and then continue to move the pointer and click to create other curvatures. Double-click to set the end point and complete the drawing.

- Click **Freeform** and use a combination of curve and scribble techniques. Click the cross pointer to establish curvature points, and/or drag the pencil pointer to create other designs. Double-click to set the end point and complete the drawing.

- Click **Scribble** and drag the pencil icon to create the shape you want. Release the mouse button to complete the drawing.

Continued . . .

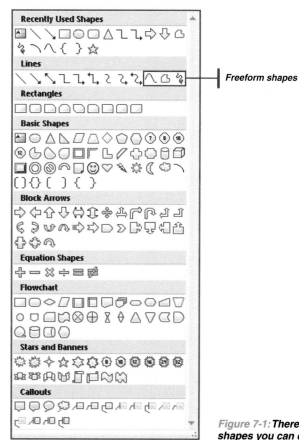

Freeform shapes

Figure 7-1: **There is no shortage of shapes you can choose from.**

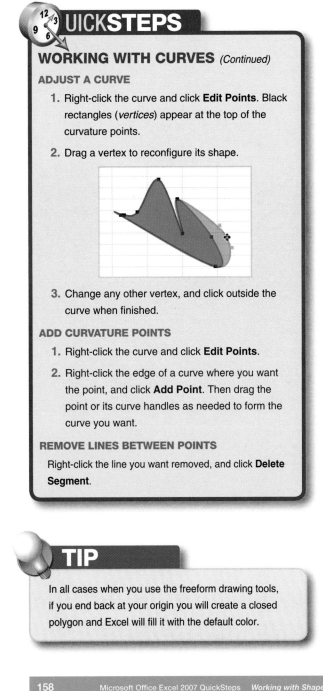

WORKING WITH CURVES *(Continued)*

ADJUST A CURVE

1. Right-click the curve and click **Edit Points**. Black rectangles (*vertices*) appear at the top of the curvature points.

2. Drag a vertex to reconfigure its shape.

3. Change any other vertex, and click outside the curve when finished.

ADD CURVATURE POINTS

1. Right-click the curve and click **Edit Points**.

2. Right-click the edge of a curve where you want the point, and click **Add Point**. Then drag the point or its curve handles as needed to form the curve you want.

REMOVE LINES BETWEEN POINTS

Right-click the line you want removed, and click **Delete Segment**.

TIP

In all cases when you use the freeform drawing tools, if you end back at your origin you will create a closed polygon and Excel will fill it with the default color.

CHANGE FROM ONE SHAPE TO ANOTHER

1. You can easily switch shapes once you have inserted one on a worksheet. There is no need to delete your initial choice and start over.

2. Click the shape to select it.

3. In the Format tab (Drawing Tools) Insert Shapes group, click **Edit Shape** and click **Change Shape**. The same shapes gallery displays as you saw when you inserted a shape (see Figure 7-1).

4. Click the new icon you want to use. Any formatting you may have applied to the original shape is retained, and the shape assumes the new look.

Insert Pictures

You can browse for picture files or use the Clip Art task pane to assist you.

BROWSE FOR PICTURES

1. Select the cell where you want the upper-leftmost corner of the picture. (Don't be too concerned with the exact placement; you can easily move the image where you want it.)

2. In the Insert tab Illustrations group, click **Picture**. The Insert Picture dialog box appears (see Figure 7-2).

3. Browse to the picture file you want, and select it. Click **Insert**. The image displays on the worksheet, as shown in Figure 7-3. (See "Using Handles and Borders to Change Shapes" QuickSteps later in the chapter to see how to move and resize the picture.)

SEARCH FOR PICTURES

1. Select the cell where you want the upper-leftmost corner of the picture.

The name of the Clip Art task pane is a bit of a misnomer. It is used to search for and organize conventional clip art (drawing) files, but also handles other media files, such as photos, sound, and video. In this chapter, clip art and/or photo files are referred to as "pictures." Strictly speaking, in Excel, pictures and clip art are distinguished by how they are inserted on the worksheet: pictures use the browse-style dialog box and clip art uses the Clip Art task pane.

If you do not see thumbnails of your picture files in the Insert Picture dialog box, or if you want to change the size of the ones you do see, click the **Views** down arrow on the dialog box toolbar, and click the size of icons you want. To view the Preview pane in Windows Vista, click **Organize**, click **Layout**, and click **Preview Pane**.

You can change the location and size of a task pane. To move the task pane, drag the pane's title bar to where you want the pane. To size the task pane, point to its border, and drag the double-headed arrow to increase or decrease the pane to the size you want (if the task pane is "docked" on either the left or right side, you can only drag the side closest to the worksheet).

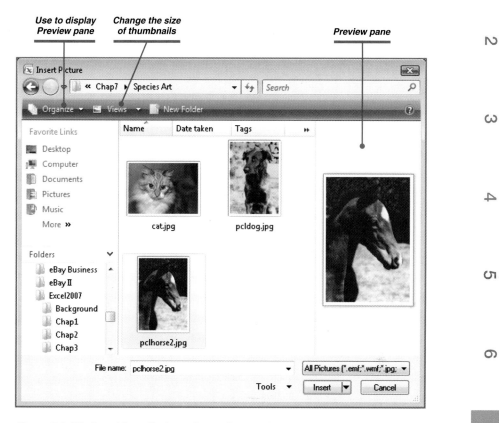

Figure 7-2: *Windows Vista displays picture files as thumbnails that you can select and preview.*

2. In the Insert tab Illustrations group, click **Clip Art**. The Clip Art task pane opens, similar to Figure 7-4, on the right side of the Excel window.

3. In the **Search For** text box, type a keyword, such as people or money.

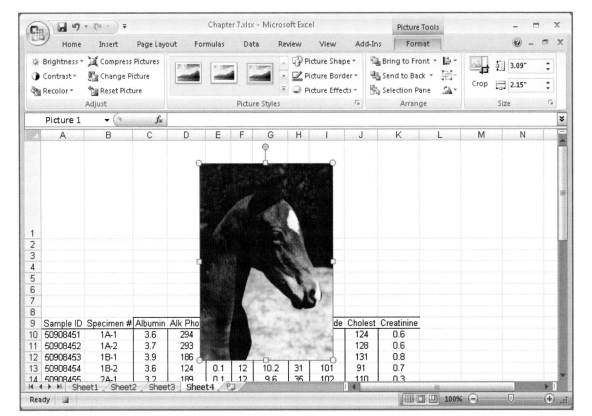

Figure 7-3: *Pictures appear on the worksheet with formatting and other tools.*

Clip Art

Search for:

money | Go

Search in:

Selected collections | ▼

Results should be:

Selected media file types | ▼

Organize clips...

Clip art on Office Online

Tips for finding clips

Figure 7-4: *The Clip Art task pane helps you find pictures and then organize them.*

4. Click the **Search In** down arrow, and refine your search to specific collections and categories of pictures. Place a check mark next to the categories you want to search, and deselect those items you do not want searched (see "Organize Pictures" for more information on working with collections):

Search in:

Selected collections | ▼

Office Collections
　Academic
　Agriculture
　Animals
　Arts
　AutoShapes
　Backgrounds
　Buildings
　Business
　Character Collection
　Communication

- **My Collections** is a library of pictures you have personally selected.
- **Office Collections** consists of pictures installed on your local computer when you installed Excel.
- **Web Collections** includes thousands of pictures maintained at Office Online (it can take considerable time to find what you're looking for using this option).

5. Click the **Results Should Be** down arrow, and deselect all file types *except* **Clip Art** and **Photographs**.

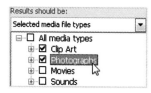

6. Click **Go**. In a few moments, thumbnails of the search results will appear (see Figure 7-4).

7. Click the thumbnail to insert it on your worksheet.

   –Or–

   Point to the thumbnail, click its down arrow, and click **Insert**.

ADD PICTURES FROM OFFICE ONLINE

1. Select the cell where you want the upper-leftmost corner of the picture.

2. In the Insert tab Illustrations group, click **Clip Art**. The Clip Art task pane opens.

3. Click the **Clip Art On Office Online** link at the bottom of the task pane. Assuming you have an active Internet connection, you are connected to the Clip Art And Media Home Page, shown in Figure 7-5.

4. Use the Search group to locate the selection of pictures you're looking for, or browse for a picture by clicking one of the listed categories. Each thumbnail contains three buttons under it. Click a thumbnail to see its details in a separate window, from which you can cycle through all the thumbnails in the category.

5. Click the **Add To Selection Basket** button for each picture you want. When finished, under Selection Basket on the page's left sidebar, click **Download x Items**. Review the items in your Selection Basket, and click **Download Now**. Wait while the files are downloaded. The files are copied to the Microsoft Clip Organizer folder in your user's Pictures folder and are added to your Clip Organizer (see the next section) in a Downloaded Clips collection.

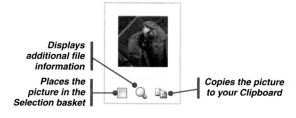

Displays additional file information

Places the picture in the Selection basket

Copies the picture to your Clipboard

NOTE

The first time you download clips, you might have to install an Internet Explorer add-in program. If prompted, click the Information Bar at the top of the Web page, and click **Run ActiveX Control**. Continue with the steps to allow the download to continue.

Figure 7-5: *Office Online offers tens of thousands of additional shape files for free download.*

USING PICTURES

Pictures, unlike shapes, are individual files with extensions such as JPG, GIF, and WMF that are stored on your computer or are available from other sources, such as a network, DVD, or the Internet. Pictures are photos produced by digital cameras or scanners, or clip art consisting of images created in drawing programs such as Abode Illustrator or Microsoft Paint. Table 7-1 lists the picture file formats supported by Excel.

While pictures have attributes that are unique to their file format origin (for example, brightness and contrast), it is easiest to think of them as simply a fill-like attribute for a shape. Once the picture is on the worksheet, you can easily replace its rectangular shape with any of the shape designs, or retain the rectangular shape and replace the picture that fills it with another image or with an assortment of colored and other fills. This concept is supported by the formatting dialog box for a picture—Excel considers a picture to be a shape with picture characteristics.

FILE TYPE	EXTENSION
Windows Bitmap	BMP, BMZ, RLE, DIB
Computer Shapes Metafile	CGM
CorelDRAW	CDR
Micrografx Designer/Draw	DRW
AutoCAD 2-D	DXF
Enhanced Windows Metafile/Compressed Enhanced Windows Metafile	EMF/EMZ
Encapsulated PostScript	EPS
FlashPix	FPX
Shapes Interchange Format	GIF, GFA
Joint Photographic Expert Group	JPG, JPEG, JFIF, JPE
Picture It!	MIX
Macintosh PICT/Compressed Macintosh PICT	PCT, PICT/PCZ
Portable Network Graphics	PNG
Tagged Image File Format	TIF, TIFF
Windows Metafile/Compressed Windows Metafile	WMF/WMZ
WordPerfect Graphics	WPG

Table 7-1: **Picture File Formats Supported by Excel**

Organize Pictures

The Microsoft Clip Organizer is a Windows Explorer-type window that lets you perform many typical file and folder activities on your own picture files and those provided by Microsoft Office.

1. Display the Clip Art task pane (in the Insert tab Illustrations group, click **Clip Art**).
2. Click **Organize Clips** at the bottom of the pane. The Microsoft Clip Organizer opens, as shown in Figure 7-6.

TIP

Actions you can perform on pictures (or clips) in the Clip Organizer only affect what you see in the Organizer; that is, the actual shape files located on your hard disks are not affected by what is done in the Organizer. What you see in the Clip Organizer are simply shortcuts to the files and folders themselves.

NOTE

You can display the Clip Organizer without being in a Microsoft application. Click **Start**, click **All Programs**, and click **Microsoft Office**. Click the **Microsoft Office Tools** folder, and click **Microsoft Clip Organizer**.

Figure 7-6: *The Clip Organizer creates shortcuts to pictures and organizes them in collections.*

ADD CLIPS TO EXISTING FOLDERS

In Figure 7-6 you can see that three categories are set up for you: My Collections, Office Collections, and Web Collections. Beneath My Collections, you have Favorites and Unclassified Clips and others you may have added. If you have clips you want in these categories, you can insert them into a collection folder.

1. Open the Microsoft Clip Organizer window as described previously.
2. Click the **File** menu, click **Add Clips To Organizer**, and click **On My Own**. The Add Clips To Organizer dialog box appears.
3. Select the clips you want, and click **Add**.

TIP

When you use the Add Clips To Organizer dialog box to insert the clips to the Clip Organizer, the clips will be added to the Favorites collection by default. If you want to add them to another collection, click **Add To** in the Add Clips To Organizer dialog box. In the Import To Collection dialog box, select another collection or click **New** to add a new one.

Import to Collection

Import clips to the selected collection:

- My Collections
  - Favorites
  - Unclassified Clips
  - Downloaded Clips
  - Species Collection

[New...] [OK] [Cancel]

New Collection

Name:

Excel 2007

Select where to place the collection:

- My Collections
  - Favorites
  - Unclassified Clips
  - Downloaded Clips
  - Species Collection

[OK] [Cancel]

AUTOMATICALLY CATALOG CLIPS

To have the Clip Organizer automatically catalog your clips:

1. Click the **File** menu, click **Add Clips To Organizer**, and click **Automatically**. An Add Clips To Organizer dialog box appears.

2. Click **OK** to start the process to search all your hard disks for shapes and other media files. It may take several minutes to complete.

   –Or–

   If you want to only catalog specific folders, click **Options**. Deselect check boxes next to those folders you do not want to be included in the catalog. Click **Catalog** to start the process.

Add Clips to Organizer

Add Media Clips

Clip Organizer can catalog picture, sound, and motion files found on your hard disk(s) or in folders you specify.

Click OK to catalog all media files. Click Cancel to quit this task. Click Options to specify folders.

[OK] [Cancel] [Options...]

ADD FOLDERS TO THE CLIP ORGANIZER

You can also add other folders to the initial set of folders to organize and establish pointers to other important clip folders.

1. Open the Microsoft Clip Organizer window.

2. Click the **File** menu, and click **New Collection**. The New Collection dialog box appears.

3. Type a name in the Name text box, and click the collection/folder in which the new collection will be placed. Click **OK**.

DELETE A CLIP FROM THE CLIP ORGANIZER

1. In the Clip Organizer, select the clip you want to delete.

2. Click the clip's down arrow, and click **Delete From *collection name*** to delete it only from that collection.

   –Or–

   Click **Delete From Clip Organizer** to delete it from everywhere in your Clip Organizer.

3. Click **OK** to complete the deletion.

MOVE AND COPY CLIPS

1. In the Clip Organizer, select a clip in the right pane (to move and copy multiple clips, hold down **CTRL** and click noncontiguous clips to select them; hold down **SHIFT** and click the first and last clip in a contiguous run).

2. Copy the selected clips by dragging them from the right pane to the destination collection in the left pane.

   –Or–

   Move the selected clips by holding down **SHIFT** while dragging them.

USE KEYWORDS AND CAPTIONS

Keywords make finding and organizing the pictures in Clip Organizer easier, and captions can provide identifying details.

1. In the Clip Organizer right pane, click the down arrow of the clip whose keywords or captions you want to add or change, and click **Edit Keywords**.

2. In the Keywords dialog box (see Figure 7-7), type new keywords in the Keyword text box, and click **Add**.

3. To change a keyword, select it under Keywords For Current Clip, make changes in the Keyword text box, and click **Modify**.

4. To remove keywords, select one or more keywords. You can select multiple keywords by holding down **CTRL** and selecting noncontiguous keywords or by holding down **SHIFT** and selecting contiguous keywords. Click **Delete**.

5. Type a caption, click the **Caption** down arrow, and select a caption or edit a current one. Click **OK** when finished.

NOTE

The clip is not deleted from your computer. It is only removed from the collection reference, or its shortcut is removed from the Clip Organizer. To delete the clip completely, you must delete it as you would any other file.

TIP

You can add multiple keywords by separating them with a comma.

![Keywords dialog box. Clip by Clip tab selected, showing Preview: Clip 5 of 5 with a photo of two people on a mountain. Caption: Bill and John Above the Dome. Keyword field contains "Volcano" with Add, Modify, Delete buttons. Keywords for current clip: Mt St Helens, Personal, JPG. Previous/Next buttons. OK, Cancel, Apply buttons.]

Figure 7-7: *Add keywords for easier searching and captions to better describe your pictures.*

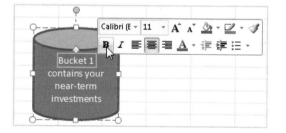

Add Text

You can add text to an existing shape or within its own shape (text box). You can use standard editing and formatting tools to modify text used in shapes (see Chapter 2). You can also apply WordArt styling to add some zing to your text (see "Add WordArt Styling to Text" later in the chapter for WordArt styling and formatting techniques).

ADD TEXT TO A SHAPE

Text added in this way is integral to the shape. If you have more than a few words or phrases to add, a separate text box (described next) may prove easier to work with.

1. Right-click the shape that you want to add text to (you cannot add text in this way to a shape that is filled with a picture).

2. Click **Edit Text**. An insertion bar is added to the approximate middle of the shape.

3. Start typing text. The text wraps to subsequent lines as necessary and is contained within a text area that conforms to the shape, with margins separating the text from the edges of the shape.

4. Highlight text to edit it. A selection box surrounds selected text.

5. To format the text, point at the selected text. A faint mini-toolbar displays above it. Move the mouse pointer over the toolbar to gain full use of its tools.

   –Or–

   Use the text tools on the Home tab to apply the formatting you want.

   In either case, see Chapter 2 for information on the individual text formatting tools you can use.

ADD A TEXT BOX

Text Box	Signature Line ▾
Header & Footer	Object
WordArt ▾	Symbol

Text

The 4th quarter results are inline with expectations but I would like to see better next quarter...|

A text box is simply a shape that contains text. You can move, size, or rotate the text box as you can with other shapes.

1. In the Insert tab Text group, click **Text Box**. The mouse pointer turns into an elongated cross.

2. Click in the approximate location where you want the text box (the mouse pointer changes to a standard crosshairs), and drag across and down the worksheet. Release the mouse button when you have the text box the approximate size you want.

3. Start typing text. The text wraps to subsequent lines as necessary and is contained within the sides of the text box, extending beyond the bottom of the border if necessary.

4. Highlight the text you want to edit.

5. To format the text, point at selected text, and a faint mini-toolbar displays above it. Move the mouse pointer over the toolbar to gain full use of its tools.

–Or–

Use the text tools on the Home tab to apply the formatting you want.

In either case, see Chapter 2 for information on the individual text-formatting tools you can use.

ADD WORDART

1. In the Insert tab Text group, click **WordArt** and click an initial style to apply to your text, shown in Figure 7-8. A text box with sample text displays on your worksheet.

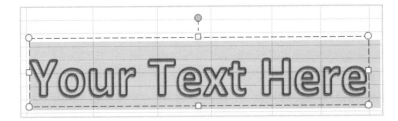

2. Type your text. See "Add WordArt Styling to Text" later in the chapter to apply additional WordArt styling.

TIP

To include text that extends beyond the boundaries of a text box within the text box, right-click the text box, and click **Format Shape**. Click **Text Box** in the left pane, and click the **Resize Shape To Fit Text** check box. Click **Close**.

Autofit
☑ Resize shape to fit text

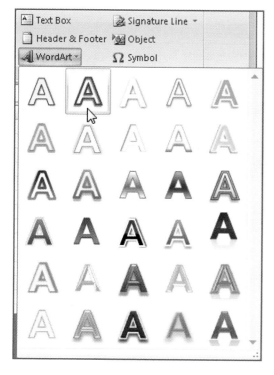

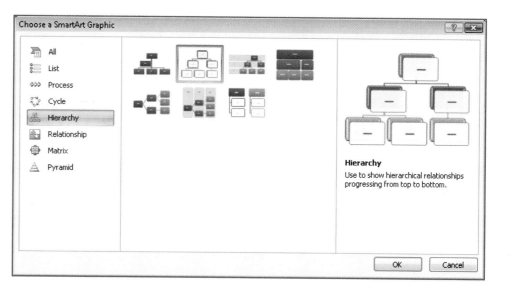

Figure 7-9: **SmartArt shapes offer you many choices for adding professional and complex "working" shapes to your worksheets.**

Use SmartArt

Excel provides predefined shapes for inserting many flexible and professional-looking diagrams and connecting symbols. Figure 7-9 shows the categories of SmartArt shapes that are available, including a description of the selected graphic.

To choose between the categories, you must be clear on what you are trying to show, what structure best displays the data, and how much data there is to display (some of the shapes do not hold a lot of text).

To insert a SmartArt shape:

1. In the Insert tab Illustrations group, click **SmartArt**. The Choose A SmartArt Shape dialog box appears.

2. Click the category on the left, and then select a shape in the middle. When you click a shape, a display of it is previewed on the right.

The Format tab (SmartArt Tools) contains many tools to change the shape, such as Shape Fill, Shape Outline, and Shape Effects. See "Formatting Shapes and Text" later in the chapter for information on formatting techniques. However, the Shapes group is a bit unique. It allows you to make selected graphic elements larger, smaller, or to change the shape. If your graphic is 3-D, you can edit it in 2-D in order to resize or move it.

3. When you find the shape you want, select it, and click **OK** to close the dialog box and insert the shape. The SmartArt Tools tabs, Design and Format, are now available, as shown in Figure 7-10.

4. In the Type Your Text Here text box, click a bullet and type your text. As you type, the text will be recorded in the appropriate shape.

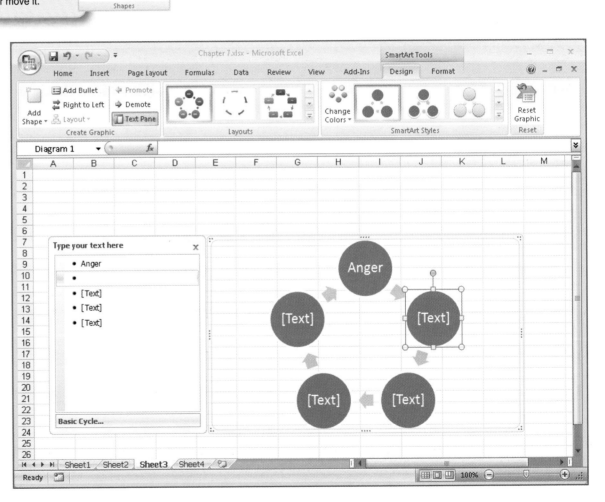

Figure 7-10: You can change the color, layouts, and styles of SmartArt shapes, as well as add or remove shape elements to make them fit your needs.

CHANGING SMARTART

The Design tab (SmartArt Tools) contains several ways to change your SmartArt:

- Click the **Add Shape** down arrow in the Create Graphic group to add another shape to the graphic. It may be another text box, circle, layer, bullet, or whatever element makes up the design. Click the placement option you want.

- Click **Add Bullet** in the Create Graphic group to add another label or bullet to the drawing. The bullet is initially added as a sub-bullet to an existing shape.

- Click **Right To Left** to orient the shape in the opposite direction.

- Click the **Promote** or **Demote** button in the Create Graphic group to move the selected text or shape to a higher or lower level, respectively. Promoting a sub-bullet will create a new shape; demoting a bullet generally removes its associated shape.

- Click a **Layouts** or **SmartArt Styles** thumbnail to change the layout or style of the shape, respectively (see "Use Styles" later in the chapter).

- Click **Change Colors** in the SmartArt Styles group, and click a color scheme to change the colors of the design.

- Click **Reset Graphic** to return the shape to its original state.

Working with Shapes

You can perform several actions on shapes, such as size, move, rotate, and combine with other shapes, to get them into just the right position and configuration you need to accentuate your Excel data.

Select, View, and Delete Shapes

How you select a shape depends on whether you're working with single or multiple shapes on a worksheet. When you select multiple shapes, you can perform actions that affect them all as group. To keep the selected shapes as a group, see the "Combining Shapes by Grouping" QuickSteps later in the chapter. In addition, you can hide shapes from view.

SELECT A SINGLE SHAPE

Select a single shape by clicking it. Handles will appear around the shape that allow you to perform interactive changes (see the "Using Handles and Borders to Change Shapes" QuickSteps).

SELECT MULTIPLE SHAPES

Hold down **CTRL** and click each shape.

–Or–

1. Select a shape and, in the Format tab Arrange group, click **Selection Pane**. The Selection And Visibility task pane displays on the right side of the worksheet, listing all shapes on the worksheet, as shown in Figure 7-11.

2. Hold down **CTRL** and click the shapes you want selected. Close the task pane when finished.

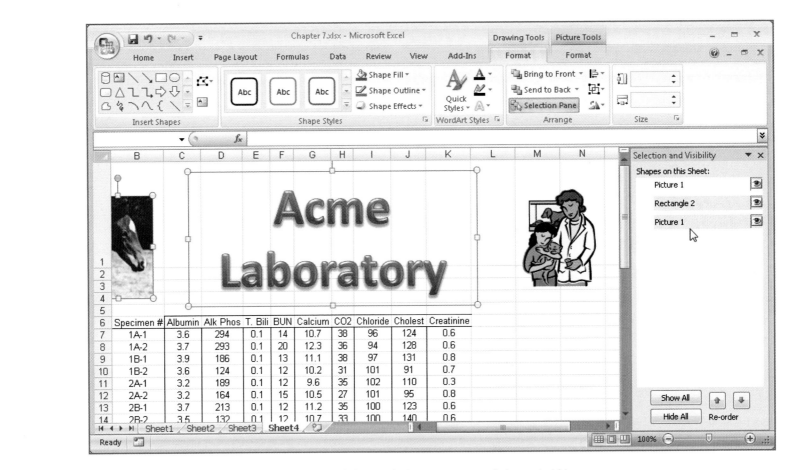

Figure 7-11: *You can see a list of all shapes on a worksheet, select one or more, and choose to hide any.*

HIDE AND SHOW SHAPES

Depending on your audience, you might want to show or hide visual enhancements you add to a worksheet. You can easily choose which ones you want to be visible.

1. Open the Selection And Visibility task pane (see the previous procedure).

QUICKSTEPS

USING HANDLES AND BORDERS TO CHANGE SHAPES

Once shapes are selected, you can interactively perform several useful actions by using the handles that surround the shape (see Figure 7-12).

MOVE A SHAPE

1. Point to any area on the border of the shape other than a handle. The mouse pointer changes to a cross with arrowheads on each end.

2. Drag the shape to the location you want.

ROTATE A SHAPE

Drag the green dot clockwise or counterclockwise. The green dot stays in place until you release the mouse button. Hold down **SHIFT** when dragging to rotate in 15-degree increments.

CHANGE A SHAPE'S PERSPECTIVE

If the shape supports interactive adjustment, a yellow diamond adjustment handle is displayed.

Drag the **yellow diamond** to achieve the look you want.

RESIZE A SHAPE

Drag one of the round corner sizing handles surrounding the shape—or at either end of it, in the case of a line—in the direction you want to enlarge or reduce the size of the shape in two dimensions.

–Or–

Drag a square sizing handle on the sides of the shape in the direction you want to enlarge or reduce the size of the shape in one dimension.

2. By default, all shapes are visible, denoted by the "eye" icon to the right of each shape listed in the pane. Click the **eye** icon for any shapes you want to be hidden.

–Or–

To hide all shapes, click **Hide All** at the bottom of the task pane.

3. To view hidden shapes, click the empty check boxes next to the shapes you want to become visible. The eye icon returns.

–Or–

To view all hidden shapes, click **Show All** at the bottom of the task pane.

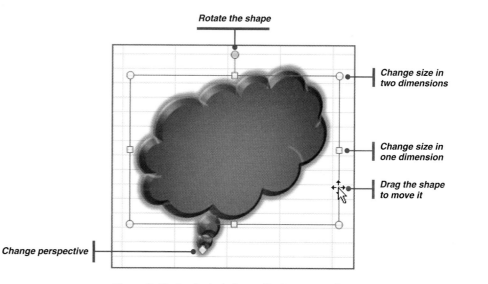

Figure 7-12: **A selected shape displays several handles that allow you to interactively change it.**

TIP

In order to delete a text box, the selection border must be solid. A dotted selection border signifies that the text within the text box is selected, not the text box itself. Click the dotted border to change the selection from the text to the text box, and press **DELETE**.

> There seems to be a quality control issue with our chloride results

TIP

Hold down **SHIFT** when dragging a corner sizing handle or corner cropping mark to make proportional changes to the height and length.

TIP

To size or rotate a shape more precisely, select the shape and, in the Format tab Size group, click the **Height** and **Width** spinners to adjust the shape's size. Alternatively, click the Size group **Dialog Box Launcher**. Under Size And Rotate and Scale, use the applicable spinners to make precise adjustments to rotation and size. Click **OK** when finished.

> **Size and Properties** [?] [X]
>
> **Size** | Properties | Alt Text
>
> Size and rotate
>
> Height: 1.52" Width: 2.03"
> Rotation: 0°
>
> Scale
>
> Height: 100% Width: 100%
> ☑ Lock aspect ratio
> ☐ Relative to original picture size

DELETE A SHAPE

Click the shape you want to delete, and press **DELETE**.

Crop Pictures

Pictures can be *cropped* (or trimmed) by removing area from the sides, either by dragging or precisely.

CROP BY DRAGGING

1. Select the picture.

2. In the Format tab (Picture Tools) Size group, click **Crop**. Cropping marks replace the standard handles surrounding the shape.

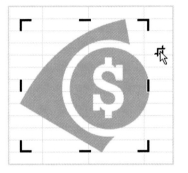

3. Place your mouse pointer over a cropping mark. Drag corner cropping marks inward to reduce the picture in two dimensions; drag a side cropping mark inward to reduce the picture in one dimension (drag a cropping mark outward to add white space to the picture). The mouse pointer turns into a cross.

4. Release the mouse button when the cutting line(s) is where you want it.

5. To remove the cropping marks and turn cropping off, click **Crop** in the Size group or press **ESC**.

CROP PRECISELY

1. Select the shape containing a picture.
2. In the Format tab (Picture Tools) Size group, click the **Dialog Box launcher**.

3. Click the **Crop From** spinners to crop the amount you want, or type a value. If necessary, drag the Size And Properties dialog box out of the way so that you can see the picture.

4. Click **Close** when finished.

Position Shapes

While shapes can be positioned by simply dragging them, Excel also provides a number of other techniques that help you adjust where a shape is in relation to other shapes and objects on the worksheet.

MOVE SHAPES INCREMENTALLY

Select the shape or group (see "Combining Shapes by Grouping" QuickSteps), and press the arrow key (for example, **UP ARROW**) in the direction you want to move.

REPOSITION THE ORDER OF STACKED SHAPES

You can stack shapes by simply dragging one on top of another.

CAUTION

There are a number of places in Excel (Picture Tools group and several dialog boxes, for example) where you can choose to reset a picture or shape to a previous state. Particularly for pictures, they can be reset to a state several actions from the most recent one. It's safer to click **Undo** on the Quick Access toolbar (next to the Office Button) to cancel the most recent action or click the **Undo** down arrow and select how far back you want to cancel from the list.

TIP

You can use the Selection And Visibility pane to re-order stacked shapes and pictures. Display the pane by clicking **Selection Pane** in the Format tab Arrange group. Select the object you want to re-order by clicking it on the worksheet or by clicking its name in the Shapes On This Sheet list. Click the **Bring Forward** or **Send Backward** buttons at the bottom of the pane to re-order the graphic.

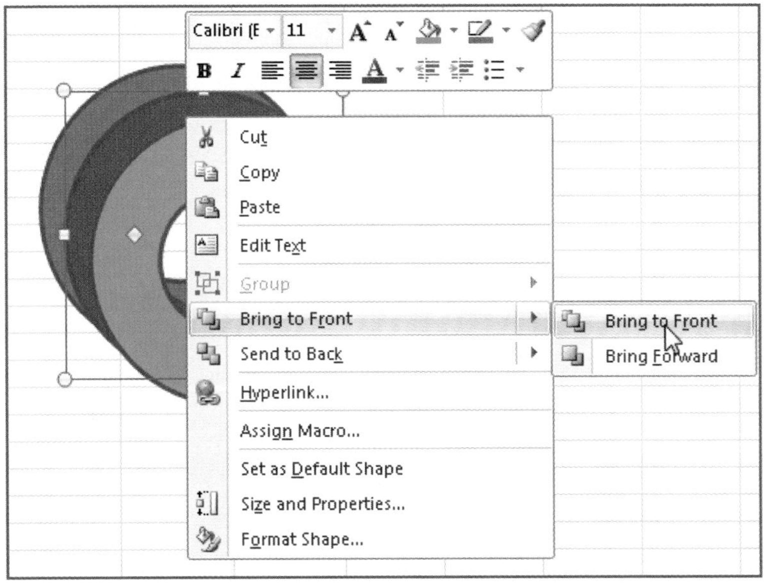

Figure 7-13: ***You can easily change the order of stacked shapes.***

Right-click the shape you want to change, and point to **Bring To Front** (see Figure 7-13):

- Click **Bring To Front** to move the shape to the top of the stack.
- Click **Bring Forward** to move the shape up one level (same as Bring To Front if there are only two shapes in the stack).

  –Or–

  Right-click the shape you want to change, and point to **Bring To Back**:

- Click **Send To Back** to move the shape to the bottom of the stack.
- Click **Send Backward** to move the shape back one level (same as Send To Back if there are only two shapes in the stack).

ALIGN SHAPES

You can align shapes to your worksheet's gridlines and use the lines as an aligning tool, as well as align shapes to one another:

- Select a shape and, in the Format tab Arrange group, click **Align**. Click **Snap To Grid** at the bottom of the menu to turn it on. When you move a shape near a gridline, it will "snap" to the line.

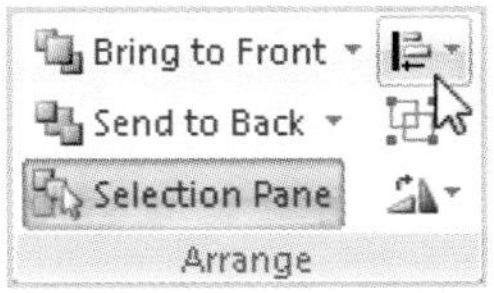

- To align shapes with one another, select the shapes and, in the Format tab Arrange group, click **Align** and click one of the vertical or horizontal alignment options on the menu.

EVENLY SPACE SHAPES

1. Select three or more shapes, and, in the Format tab Arrange group, click **Align**.
2. Click **Distribute Horizontally** or **Distribute Vertically**, depending on how you want the shapes oriented.

QUICKSTEPS

COMBINING SHAPES BY GROUPING

You can combine shapes for any number of reasons, but you typically work with multiple shapes to build a more complex drawing. To prevent losing the positioning, sizing, and other characteristics of these components, you can group them so that they are treated as one shape.

GROUP SHAPES

1. Select the shapes to be grouped by clicking the first shape and then holding down **CTRL** while selecting the other shapes.

2. Right-click any of the selected shapes, and click **Group**. Click **Group** again on the flyout menu. A single set of selection handles surrounds the perimeter of the shapes. Coloring, positioning, sizing, and other actions now affect the shapes as a group instead of individually (see Figure 7-14).

UNGROUP SHAPES

To separate a group into individual shapes:

Right-click one of the shapes in the group, click **Group**, and click **Ungroup** on the flyout menu. Selection handles appear on each shape that made up the group.

RECOMBINE A GROUP AFTER UNGROUPING

After making a modification to a shape that was part of a group, you don't have to reselect each component shape to reestablish the group.

Right-click any shape that was in the group, click **Group**, and click **Regroup** on the flyout menu. A group selection border and handles surrounded the originally grouped shapes.

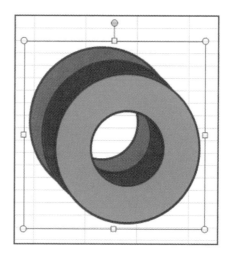

Figure 7-14: **Grouping lets you treat multiple selected shapes as one shape.**

Formatting Shapes and Text

This section describes how you can apply formatting. Start by being efficiently lazy, using themes (see Chapter 3) and styles provided on the ribbon. Next, make any adjustments to the constituent attributes of the style. Finally, delve into the details provided by a common shapes formatting dialog box.

Use Styles

The ribbon (assuming your Excel window is at a sufficient width) displays styling samples for pictures, shapes, and WordArt. With a click or two, you can apply a professional-looking design (and then spend all the time you saved working on formulas!).

1. Select the shape you want to apply a style to.

2. In the Format tab (the tab will be unique to Pictures, Shapes, or SmartArt tools), point to the style examples on the ribbon, shown in Figure 7-15. The shape or text will change to reflect the style attributes.

To cover every conceivable option for every type of shape in Excel would fill up a book all by itself. The examples provided in this section are not exhaustive; rather, they illustrate the methodology you can apply to formatting other types of shapes and text you will use.

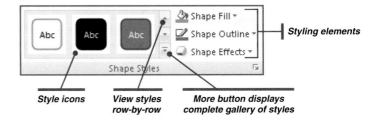

Style icons   *View styles row-by-row*   *More button displays complete gallery of styles*

Figure 7-15: **Styling options for shapes allow you to make quick choices or provide tools for more hands-on work.**

3. When you find a style that's close to want you want, click the style icon in the particular Styles group (click the **More** button to see the complete gallery, or click the row-by-row buttons).

–Or–

Click the particular **Styles** button if the style icons are hidden.

Apply Styling Elements to Pictures

You can alter the outward appearance of an inserted file by changing key elements: its overall shape; the color, weight, and style of a border or outline; and special effects, such as mirroring.

CHANGE A PICTURE'S SHAPE

Typically, pictures are rectangular in shape, conforming to conventions of uniformity, balance, and function. You can create some rather interesting and creative variations of these images by changing the original outline to one of dozens of prebuilt shapes (and you can further modify these prebuilt shapes by resizing and trimming them). See "Change a Shape's Fill" later in the chapter for information on working with shapes.

1. Click the picture to select it.

2. In the Format tab (Picture Tools) Picture Styles group, click **Picture Shape**. A gallery of shapes divides the available shapes library into seven categories (see Figure 7-1).

3. Click a shape that interests you. The selected picture assumes the new shape.

*Figure 7-16: **Your imagination is the only limit when working with multiple special effects.***

CHANGE A PICTURE'S BORDER

1. Click the picture to select it.

2. In the Format tab (Picture Tools) Picture Styles group, click **Picture Border**. The standard Office color gallery opens, along with options to change the border outline. (You will have to reopen the Picture Border menu each time you make one of the following selections.)

3. Click **Weight** and point to the border thickness options. The outline on your picture will change according to where your mouse pointer is placed. Click the weight you want to apply it to your picture.

4. Click **Dashes** and point to the line style you want, solid or dashed. The outline on your picture will change according to where your mouse pointer is placed. For more line options, click **More Lines**. Click the line style you want to apply it to your picture.

5. Point to a color on the color gallery, and see the immediate effect on the border. Click a color icon from Theme Colors (this changes according to the workbook theme applied) or Standard Colors, or click **More Outline Colors** for more options. (Chapter 3 describes the various color options available from the color gallery in detail.)

ADD EFFECTS TO PICTURES

To add some pizzazz to your pictures, you can apply special effects that add three-dimensional and other eye-catching elements (see Figure 7-16).

1. Click the picture to select it.

2. In the Format tab (Picture Tools) Picture Styles group, click **Picture Effects**.

3. Click one of the effects' categories, and point to the options in the gallery. The picture will change according to where your mouse pointer is placed. Click the effect you want to apply (you can apply multiple effects).

TIP

When setting a color to be transparent, choose solid colors in drawings instead of transitioning colors in a photo. Splotchiness can result otherwise.

Color gallery menu:

- Automatic
- **Theme Colors**
- **Standard Colors**
- No Outline
- More Outline Colors...
- Weight ▶
- Dashes ▶

QUICKSTEPS

CHANGING A PICTURE'S ATTRIBUTES

In Excel, you can use several tools to format the picture, instead of the shape that contains it. These tools are available in the Format tab (Picture Tools) Adjust group.

☼ Brightness ▾	🖼 Compress Pictures
◐ Contrast ▾	🖼 Change Picture
🖼 Recolor ▾	🖼 Reset Picture
	Adjust

CHANGE BRIGHTNESS AND CONTRAST

1. Click the picture to select it.

2. In the Adjust group, click **Brightness** or **Contrast** to view a gallery of options that change the respective effect by percentages that are greater than (+) or less (–) than the original setting. Point to the effects to see the changes on your picture. Click the effect you want.

3. To adjust brightness or contrast more precisely, click **Picture Correction Options** at the bottom of either gallery, and adjust the percentage of the desired effect by dragging its slider, typing a percentage, or using the respective spinner to find the value you want. Click **Close** when finished.

☼ Brightness ▾	🖼 Compress Pictures
☼	+ 40 %
☼	+ 30 %
☼	+ 20 %
☼	+ 10 %
☼	0 % (Normal)
☼	–10 %
☼	–20 %
☼	–30 %
☼	–40 %
🖐	Picture Corrections Options...

Continued . . .

Change a Shape's Fill

By default, shapes are filled with a color or with a combination of colors, determined by the workbook's theme. You can change the fill color and do much more with textures, gradient fills, and even by using a picture.

CHANGE FILL COLOR

1. Click the shape to select it.

2. In the Format tab (Drawing Tools) Shapes Styles group, click **Shape Fill**. A gallery of color options and other fill choices is displayed.

3. Point to a color on the color gallery, and see the immediate effect on the fill. Click a color icon from Theme Colors (they will change according to the workbook theme applied) or Standard Colors, or click **More Fill Colors** for more options. (Chapter 3 describes the various color options available from the color gallery in detail.)

USE A PICTURE

1. Click the shape to select it.

2. In the Format tab (Drawing Tools) Shapes Styles group, click **Shape Fill** and click **Picture**. The Insert Picture dialog box appears.

3. Browse to locate the picture you want, select it, and click **Insert**. The picture will be inserted into the background of the shape.

SET GRADIENTS AND TEXTURES

A gradient fill flows one or more colors within a shape, from lighter to darker shades, in varying directions, transparency, and other attributes. A texture provides a consistent weave or other pattern in varying colors and designs.

1. Click the shape to select it.

2. In the Format tab (Drawing Tools) Shape Styles group, click **Shape Fill**.

3. Click **Gradient** or **Texture** to see their respective galleries.

UICKSTEPS

CHANGING A PICTURE'S ATTRIBUTES *(Continued)*

RECOLOR A PICTURE

You can change the color of a picture by applying an overall solid tint. For example, you can change a colored or black-and-white photo to sepia or grayscale.

1. Click the picture to select it.

2. In the Adjust group, click **Recolor** to view a gallery of tinting options. Point to the effects to see the changes on your picture. Click the effect you want.

MAKE A COLOR TRANSPARENT

You can click a color in your picture and all instances of it within the picture will become transparent, allowing the worksheet or other objects beneath it to show through (this feature works best for solid colors).

1. Click the picture to select it.

2. In the Adjust group, click **Recolor** and click **Set Transparent Color**. The mouse pointer changes to a pen-like icon.

3. Click the color in the picture you want to become "see-through."

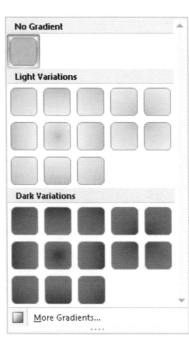

NOTE

Inserting a picture into a shape's fill achieves the same result as applying a shape to a picture (see "Change a Picture's Shape" earlier in the chapter). In either case, you can take a rectangular picture and change its boundaries.

4. If you need more control over either fill, click **More Gradients** or **More Textures** at the bottom of their respective galleries.

5. In the Format Shape dialog box, click **Fill** in the left pane, and click **Gradient** or **Picture Or Texture Fill** to access detailed options, as shown in Figure 7-17.

Add WordArt Styling to Text

WordArt styling used to be confined to text solely created by WordArt. In Excel 2007, you can apply WordArt effects, such as transforming text to follow a curved path, to all text used in shapes. WordArt provides an easy and effective graphic artist's professional touch (see Figure 7-18).

1. Select the text to which you want to apply WordArt styling (text can be in a shape, text box, or directly from WordArt). See "Add Text" earlier in the chapter.

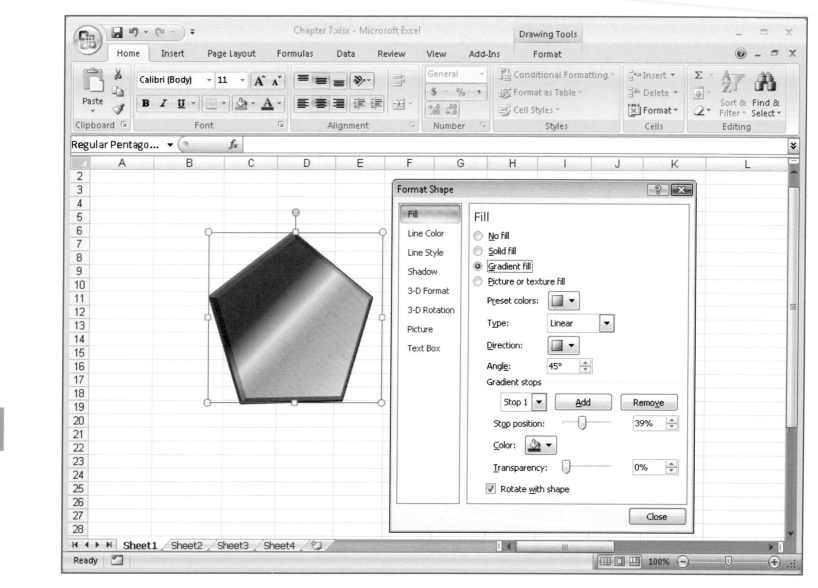

Figure 7-17: *You can get quite exact in your formatting.*

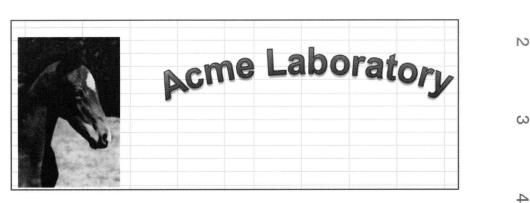

Figure 7-18: **WordArt effects can make a graphic artist out of you!**

2. In the Format tab (Drawing Tools) WordArt Styles group, click a style to apply a prebuilt style.

Text Fill

Text Outline

Text Effects

WordArt Styles

–Or–

Click **Text Fill** or **Text Outline** to apply color and other styling to the respective elements of the text (see "Change a Picture's Border" and "Change a Shape's Fill" earlier in the chapter for information on available options).

–Or–

Click **Text Effects** to view a menu of galleries that offer an abundance of special effects you can apply. Point to any option to view the effect on your text.

3. Click the effect you want.

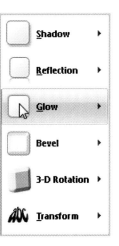

Shadow ▸

Reflection ▸

Glow ▸

Bevel ▸

3-D Rotation ▸

Transform ▸

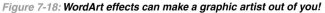

Make Detailed Formatting Changes

The Format Shape and Format Picture dialog boxes are the gateway for you to "tweak" formatting attributes to very fine detail (see Figure 7-17). Shapes and pictures share a common set of formatting categories, although a particular shape or picture might not have all options available. Table 7-2 lists the categories and a general description of the options each provides.

To access the Format dialog box, right-click the shape or picture, and click **Format Shape** or **Format Picture**.

FORMATTING OPTIONS	DESCRIPTION
Fill	Provides options for gradient, picture, or texture fill, as well as color choices, degrees of transparency, and gradient options
Line Color	Offers solid or gradient lines, as well as color choices, degrees of transparency, and gradient options
Line Style	Provides options for width, dashed, and compound (multiple) lines, as well as styles for line ends and line joins
Shadow	Provides preset shadow styles and controls for color, transparency, size, blur, angle, and distance
3-D Format	Adds a 3-D effect to shapes; provides top, bottom, and surface presets; and controls for depth contours and color
3-D Rotation	Provides angular rotation and perspective adjustments, as well as positioning controls
Picture	Provides controls to fine-tune brightness, contrast, and recoloring
Text Box	Vertically aligns, rotates, and stacks text; auto-fits text within a text box; allows you change margins and add columns

Table 7-2: *Formatting Categories Available for Shapes*

How to...

- *Understanding Excel Tables*
- Create a Table
- *Adding Rows and Columns to a Table*
- Delete Rows and Columns Within a Table
- Add a Total Row
- Apply Styles to a Table
- *Working with Tables*
- Validate Data
- *Locating Validation Data*
- Sort Data by Columns
- Sort Data by Rows
- *Removing Filters*
- Create an AutoFilter
- *Setting Up Criteria and Extract Ranges*
- Use Advanced Filtering
- Outline Data Automatically
- *Using Outlines*
- Outline Data by Manually Grouping
- Add Subtotals
- Add Styles to an Outline

Chapter 8

Managing Data

Excel, as you've seen in other chapters, "excels" at calculating and displaying information. An often overlooked aspect of what Excel has to offer is how well it works with more structured data. *Tables*, referred to as "lists" in previous releases, contain related data that's independent of other information on the worksheet (see "Understanding Excel Tables" QuickFacts). This chapter shows you how to create tables, how to work with them, and how to manage and organize data. In addition, you will learn how to validate data entered into a table, organize data by sorting it, retrieve just the data you want by setting up filters, and condense data by outlining and grouping. (See Chapter 10 for methods to acquire data from external sources.)

UNDERSTANDING EXCEL TABLES

Excel provides the ability to work with data in *tables*. Tables, like databases, consist of columns of similar data—the names of all the salespeople in a company, for example. Each salesperson covers a certain region, so this table would also need a Territory column. Each salesperson has a cell phone number; each has projected sales targets and actual sales, and so forth. You could say each salesperson has a collection of information pertaining just to them. In an Excel table, each row in the worksheet contains this collection of unique data—unique in the sense that while two or more salespeople might call Washington their territory, each row contains data for only one salesperson.

	A	B	C	D	E
1	**Last Name**	**First Name**	**Territory**	**Qtr Sales**	**Cell Phone**
2	Jones	Tom	Oregon	$6,876	(425) 555-1212
3	Smith	John	Washington	$4,567	(360) 555-4321
4	Brown	Sally	Washington	$3,475	(425) 555-2121

When you work with cells in, or adjacent to, a table, Excel automatically "comes to the table" with several tools and features to eliminate mouse clicks and keystrokes, and basically make your work in tables easier, faster, and more efficient.

In the days before Microsoft had a database product, such as Access or SQL (Structured Query Language) Server, an Excel *list* provided basic database functions. From its database roots, you may see database terms used when referring to tables—for example, in database terminology, columns are called *fields*, rows are called *records*, and the table itself is generally called a *datasheet*. So you can call a series of rows of related data that is organized into categories, a table, a list, a datasheet, or even (sometimes) a database.

Build Tables

Tables are easily created, allowing you to add new data from existing data (see Chapter 10 for information on importing data from external sources) or add data from scratch. In either case, once Excel recognizes data is within a table, it makes assumptions that help you to view, enter, format, and use the data in calculations.

Create a Table

Excel 2007 makes creating a table easier than ever. However, before you designate a range of data to be a table, you might want to consider reorganizing your data to better work with table features:

- **Column headings** (or *labels*) should be formatted differently from the data so that Excel can more easily differentiate one from the other. All data in a column should be similar. Avoid mixing dates and other number formats with text.

- **Clean up the data range** by eliminating any blank rows or columns within the range and removing extra spaces in cells.

- **Display all data** by showing any rows or columns you might have hidden. Hidden data can be inadvertently deleted.

- **Place values to be totaled** in the rightmost column. Excel's Total Row feature creates a total row, which you can toggle off or on, when it recognizes data that can be summed in the last column.

CREATE A BLANK TABLE

1. On the worksheet where you want a table, drag to create a range the approximate number of columns and rows you think you need for your data.

2. In the Insert tab Tables group, click **Table**. The Create Table dialog box displays your selected range, and the range is outlined within a selection border.

8

Use the Borders button ⊞ ▾ in the Home tab Font group to separate column headings from data instead of spacing or other separation techniques.

3. Click **OK**. The table is created (see Figure 8-1) with placeholder column headers that you can edit to fit your data, alternating row colors for better data differentiation, an AutoFilter down arrow to access easy filtering and sorting of data (see "Create an AutoFilter" later in the chapter for information on using filters), and a sizing arrow. In addition, a Design tab provides access to table-related tools.

Column header placeholders   AutoFilter   Table-related tools

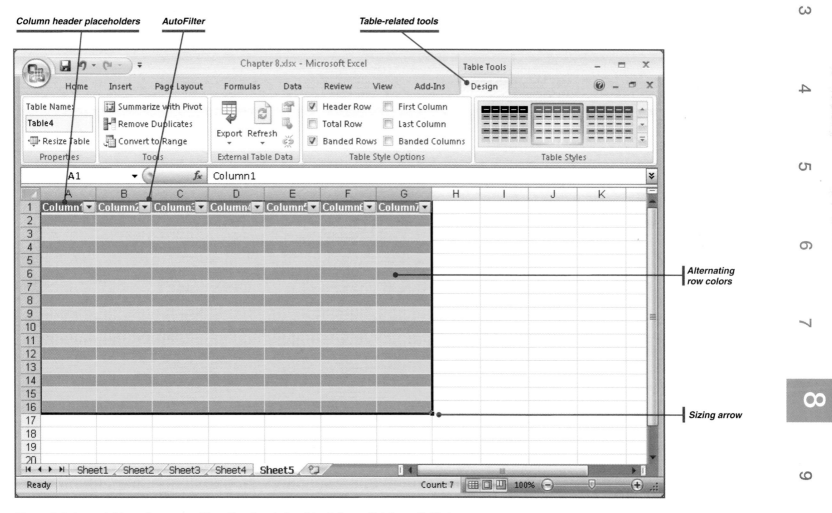

Alternating row colors

Sizing arrow

Figure 8-1: A new table makes several functional and visual tools immediately available to you.

TIP

Quickly create a table by selecting a range and pressing **CTRL+L**. Select whether the first row contains column headers, and click **OK**.

	A	B	C
1	ISBN ▼	Categor ▼	Author ▼
2	0071408959	Business	Allaire
3	0830621369	Technical	Alth

CREATE A TABLE FROM EXISTING DATA

1. Select the data you want to be included within a table.

2. In the Insert tab Tables group, click **Table**. The Create Table dialog box appears, and the range is outlined within a selection border.

3. Assuming your data is organized with column headers in the first row, select the **My Table Has Headers** check box, if Excel doesn't already recognize them. Click **OK**. The table is created similar to that shown in Figure 8-1, except the columns headers are created from the first row, as shown in Figure 8-2.

	A	B	C	D	E	F	G	H
1	ISBN ▼	Categor ▼	Author ▼	Title ▼	Publish Yea ▼	List Pric ▼		
2	0071408959	Business	Allaire	Options Strategist	2003	$29.95		
3	0830621369	Technical	Alth	Pbs Wells & Septic Sy	1991	$19.95		
4	0071467858	Business	Bayan	Words That Sell, Revis	2006	$16.95		
5	0071464700	Technical	Bluman	Business Math Demyst	2006	$19.95		
6	0071423117	Medicine	Bodenheimer	Understanding Health F	2004	$36.95		
7	0071412077	Medicine	Brooks	Medical Microbiology, 2	2004	$52.95		
8	0071457720	Technical	Cadick	Elect Safety Hndbk, 3/l	2005	$79.95		
9	0071054618	Medicine	Cember	Intro Health Physics 3e	1996	$52.95		
10	0786310251	Business	Chriss	Black Scholes & Beyor	1996	$65.00		
11	0071346082	Parenting	Clark	Coaching Youth Socce	1999	$14.95		
12	0844242527	Education	Derevzhantche	Stories From Todays R	1995	$9.95		
13	0071418695	Medicine	Desselle	Pharmacy Managemen	2004	$52.95		
14	0071375252	Technical	Dewberry Comp	Land Development Han	2002	$150.00		
15	0071358978	Education	Don	How Solve Word Proble	2001	$9.95		
16	0071377964	Technical	Edwards	Beautiful Built-Ins	2002	$39.95		
17	0070194351	Technical	Elliott	Stand Hdbk Powerplant	1997	$125.00		
18	0071469222	Education	Epls	Say It Right In German	2006	$9.95		
19	0071369988	Business	Fitz-Enz	How To Measure Huma	2001	$49.95		
20	083850244X	Medicine	Hanrahan & Ma	Appleton & Lange Rew	1994	$39.95		
21	0071439277	Technical	Huettenmuelle	Pre-Calculus Demystifi	2005	$19.95		
22	0071421947	Business	Kador	50 High Impact Speech	2004	$14.95		
23	0072229497	Technical	King	Shoot Like A Pro!	2003	$24.99		
24	007142251X	Technical	Kinnison	Aviation Maintenance M	2004	$59.95		
25	0070350787	Technical	Kleinert	Troublesht & Rep Major	1995	$39.95		
26	007146252X	Business	Krames	What The Best CEO's I	2005	$14.95		

Figure 8-2: Column headers "pulled" from the first row of data clarify and identify the information in an Excel table.

ADDING ROWS AND COLUMNS TO A TABLE

Tables are easily resized by adding rows and columns.

ADD ROWS TO THE END OF THE TABLE

Click the lower rightmost cell in the table (containing the sizing arrow), and press **TAB**. When you complete the entry, the sizing arrow moves to the next row below.

–Or–

Type in an empty row that is adjacent to the end of the table. The table will "annex" the row, unless the last row is empty or the last row is a total row.

–Or–

Drag the sizing arrow downward over the rows you want to add.

ADD COLUMNS TO THE SIDES OF A TABLE

Type in an empty column that is adjacent to the right side of the table. The table will "annex" the column.

–Or–

Drag the sizing arrow to the right over the columns you want to add.

Continued . . .

NOTE

If the last column contains data that cannot be summed, the Total row is still added and a count of the values in the column is displayed instead of a sum.

Delete Rows and Columns Within a Table

1. Click in the column or row within the table that you want to delete.

2. In the Home tab Cells group, click the **Delete** down arrow, and click **Delete Table Rows** or **Delete Table Columns**, depending on what you want removed.

–Or–

1. Right-click the column or row within the table you want to delete.

2. Click **Delete** and click **Table Columns** or **Table Rows**, depending on what you want removed.

Add a Total Row

Excel provides a nifty feature that sums the last column in a table and automatically creates a Total row at the bottom of the table. The Total row lets you perform other calculations on any of the columns in the table.

SUM THE LAST COLUMN

1. Select a cell in the table to display the Design tab (Table Tools), and select that tab.

2. Select the **Total Row** check box in the Table Style Options group. The rightmost column is summed within a new row, with the word "Total" in the leftmost cell, as shown in Figure 8-3.

3. To remove the Total row, click the **Total Row** check box to deselect it.

QUICKSTEPS

ADDING ROWS AND COLUMNS TO A TABLE *(Continued)*

ADD ROWS AND COLUMNS WITHIN A TABLE

1. Click in the column within the table to the right of or in the row below where you want to add more cells.

2. In the Home tab Cells group, click the **Insert** down arrow, and, depending on where you want the cells added, click **Insert Table Rows Above** or **Insert Table Columns To The Left**.

–Or–

1. Right-click the column within the table to the right of or the row below where you want to add more cells.

2. Click **Insert** and click **Table Columns To The Left** or **Table Rows Above**, depending on where you want the cells added.

CAUTION

To select rows and columns to be inserted or deleted, do not use (click) the numbered row headers and lettered column headings provided by Excel. Doing so will delete the entire row or column, including any data outside the table border. Instead, select just the portion of a row or column in the table by placing your mouse pointer just to the right of the left border of the leftmost cell or just below the top border of the topmost cell. When the pointer changes to a selection arrow, click to select one row or one column, or drag to select adjacent rows.

PERFORM FUNCTIONS IN A COLUMN

1. Add a Total Row (see "Sum the Last Column").

2. In the Total row at the bottom of the table, click the cell at the bottom of a column whose values you want to calculate. A down arrow appears to the right of the cell.

3. Click the cell's down arrow, and select the function you want performed (see Figure 8-3). The result is displayed in the cell.

Apply Styles to a Table

By default, table rows are banded in alternating shades from colors drawn from the workbook theme, with the header row in a darker shade. You can apply a Quick Style, modify table elements, or create a style of your own.

APPLY A QUICK STYLE TO A TABLE

1. Click a cell in the table to select it.

2. In the Design tab (Table Tools) Table Styles group, point to the style examples on the ribbon.

–Or–

Click the row-by-row buttons.

–Or–

Click the **More** button to see the complete gallery (as shown in Figure 8-4).

In all cases, pointing to a Quick Style icon will change the table to reflect the style attributes.

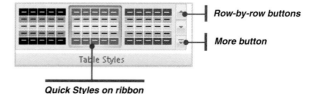

Quick Styles on ribbon

3. When you find a style that's close to want you want, click the **Quick Style** icon in the particular Styles group (Light, Medium, or Dark).

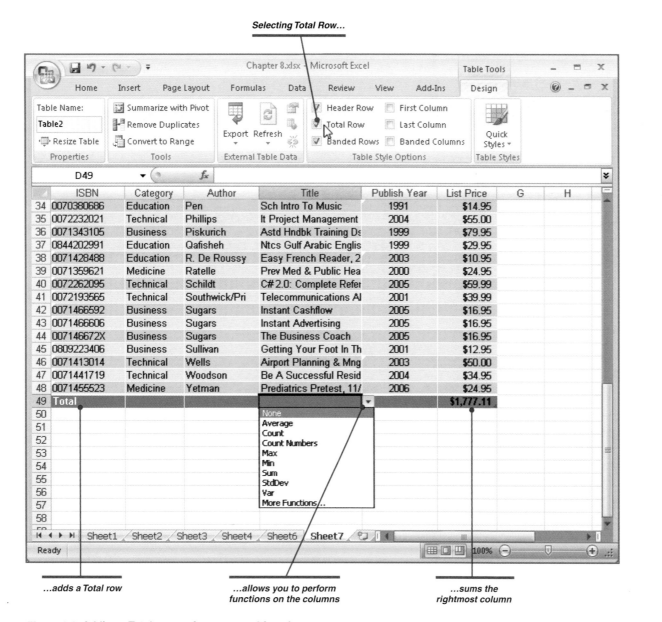

Selecting Total Row...

...adds a Total row

...allows you to perform functions on the columns

...sums the rightmost column

Figure 8-3: *Adding a Total row performs several functions.*

A feature of tables is that when you scroll through data beyond what's visible in the sheet window, the column headers replace the lettered Excel column headings at the top of the sheet (see Figure 8-3).

QUICKSTEPS

WORKING WITH TABLES

Tables provide a few features unique to themselves.

REVERT A TABLE TO A RANGE

1. Click a cell in the table.

2. In the Design tab (Table Tools) Tools group, click **Convert To Range**. Click **OK** to confirm that you want to convert the table to a normal range.

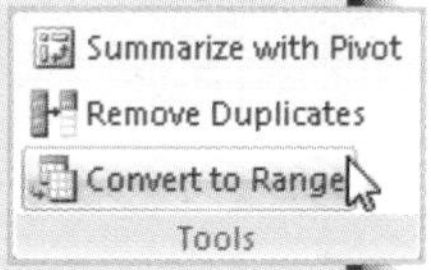

REMOVE DUPLICATES

You can delete rows (or records) that contain duplicate values on a column by column basis.

1. Click a cell in the table.

2. In the Design tab (Table Tools) Tools group, click **Remove Duplicates**. The Remove Duplicates dialog box appears, shown in Figure 8-5.

3. If your data does not have headers, deselect the **My Data Has Headers** check box.

4. To check for duplicate values in all columns, click **OK**.

   –Or–

   Click **Unselect All** and select the columns you want checked for duplicate values. Click **OK**.

   In either case, any row with a duplicate value is deleted from the table (see accompanying Caution).

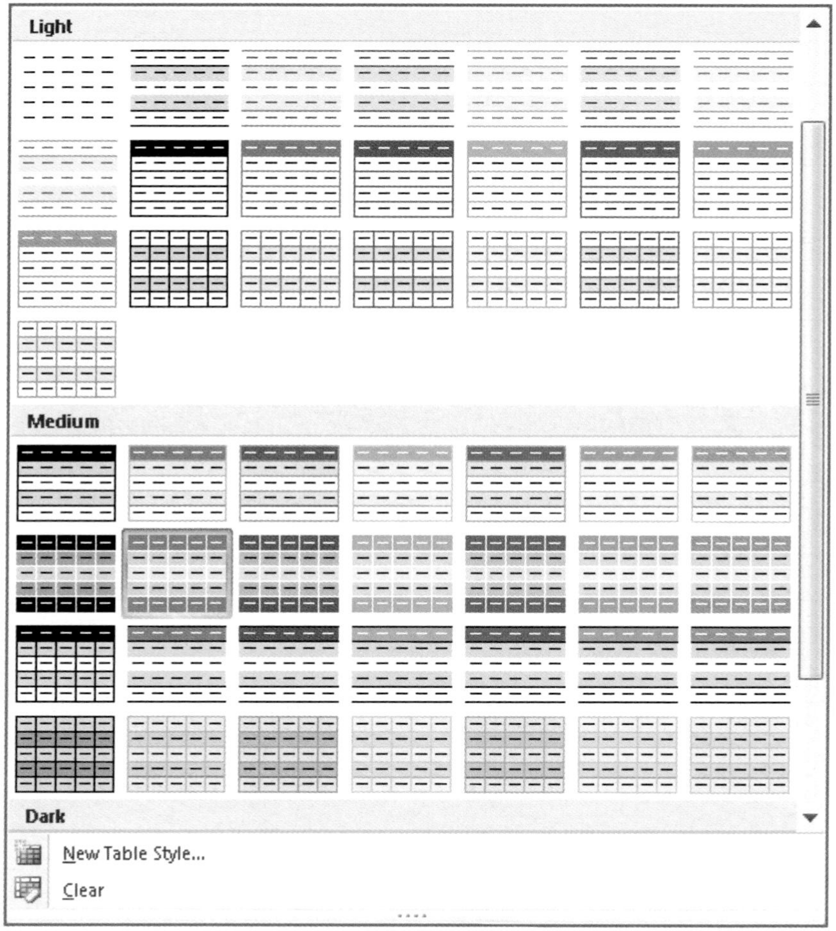

Figure 8-4: *The fastest way to style a table is to start with one of the several style samples.*

CAUTION

Removing duplicate values removes each row, or record, within a table. To ensure that you can recover data you might inadvertently delete, click the **Name Box** down arrow on the left of the Formula bar, and click the table name to select the table. Right-click the selected table, and click **Copy**. Paste the table to an empty area on the same or another worksheet.

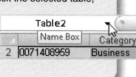

TIP

When referencing table data in a formula, use the Name Manager and AutoComplete to make life easier. In the Formulas tab Defined Names group, click **Name Manager**. Select your table (listed as Table x), and click **Edit**. Rename the table something more meaningful, click **OK**, and close the Name Manager. You can now use the table name, column names, and other arguments in formulas. For example, to reference a column sum in that table, type =SUM(*tablename* [*columnname*]). For the table name, after the open parenthesis, type the first letter of table name, and double-click the table from the AutoComplete list. For the column name, type the opening bracket. A list of the table column headers appears. Double-click the column header you want, type a closing bracket and parenthesis, and press **ENTER**. The sum of values in the column is returned.

Remove Duplicates

To delete duplicate values, select one or more columns that contain duplicates.

Select All   Unselect All   ☑ My data has headers

Columns
☑ ISBN
☑ Category
☑ Author
☑ Title
☑ Publish Year
☑ List Price

OK   Cancel

Figure 8-5: **You can choose on a column-by-column basis to remove rows that contain duplicate values.**

=SUM(Books[
SUM(**number1**, [number2], ...)
Category
Author
Title
Publish Year
List Price
#All
#Data
#Headers
#Totals
#This Row

CHANGE TABLE ELEMENTS

You can modify a table to show or hide elements that make the table data easier to view.

1. Click a cell in the table to select it.
2. In the Design tab (Table Tools) Table Styles Options group, select or deselect the option you want (Header Row and Total Row options are covered earlier in this chapter):
   - **Banded Rows/Banded Columns** displays alternating colors of rows and columns, respectively (the default is banded rows).
   - **First Column/Last Column** highlights the respective column in a darker shade.

TIP

If you don't see style examples on the ribbon in the Design tab (Table Tools) Table Styles group, increase the width of the Excel window until you do. Otherwise, click Quick Styles to open the full gallery of style examples.

TIP

You can create a new, blank table already prestyled. Drag the approximate range for the table. In the Home tab Styles group, click **Format As Table**, and select a table style. Click **OK** in the Format As Table dialog box.

CREATE YOUR OWN TABLE STYLE

You can save any changes you make to a Quick Style and have it available for future formatting within the same workbook.

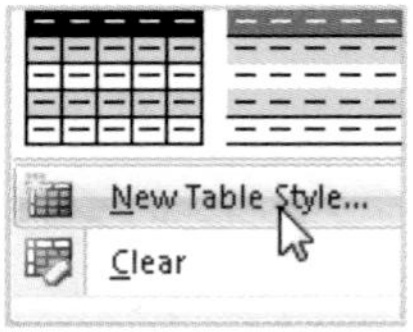

1. Apply a Quick Style and the styling options available on the Design tab (Table Tools), as described in "Apply a Quick Style to a Table."

2. Click the **More** button in the Table Styles group, and click **New Table Style**. The New Table Quick Style dialog box appears, as shown in Figure 8-6.

3. In the Name box, select the default name, and type a name of your own.

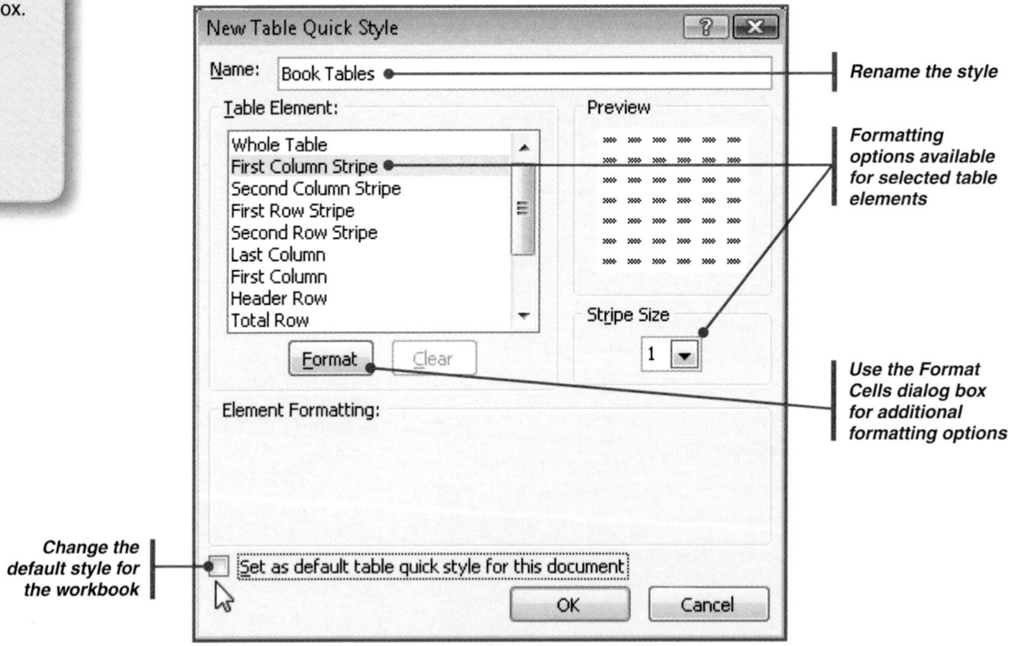

Figure 8-6: **You can create your own custom style to apply to other tables in the workbook.**

4. Select the table element to which you want to apply formatting, select any formatting attributes that display in the dialog box, and then click **Format**.

5. Select formatting options in the Format Cells dialog box (see Chapter 3 for more information on using the Format Cells dialog box), and click **OK**.

6. Repeat steps 4 and 5 for any other table elements you want to format, choose whether to make this table style your default (see Figure 8-6), and click **OK**. Your new table style is available at the top of the Quick Table Styles gallery.

REMOVE STYLING FROM A TABLE

1. Click a cell in the table to select it.

2. In the Design tab (Table Tools), click the **More** button in the Table Styles Options group.

3. Click **Clear** below the gallery. All table style formatting is removed from the table (individual formatting, such as bolding or selected cell fills, is not removed).

Validate Data

To prevent data entry errors, you can set validation criteria. Excel checks the entered data against the criteria you set and disallows the entry if the validation conditions are not met. You can use data validation in any cell on the worksheet; however, due to the quantity of data typically entered in a table, using data validation over an entire table is highly recommended.

In addition, you can choose to have Excel display a message when a user selects a validated cell, and you can choose to have Excel display an error message when an attempt is made to enter invalid data in the cell.

CREATE A VALIDATION

1. Select the cells you want validated. Typically, you would select a column (see the Caution).

2. In the Data tab Data Tools group, click **Data Validation**. The Data Validation dialog box appears with the Settings tab displayed, as shown in Figure 8-7.

3. Click the **Allow** down arrow, and select the validation criteria to use.

4. Click the **Data** down arrow, and select the comparison operator to use.

CAUTION

Do not select column or row headers when setting up data validation, since they are probably formatted as text and might cause compatibility problems with numbered data. In fact, Excel won't let you access the Data Validation dialog box if you do.

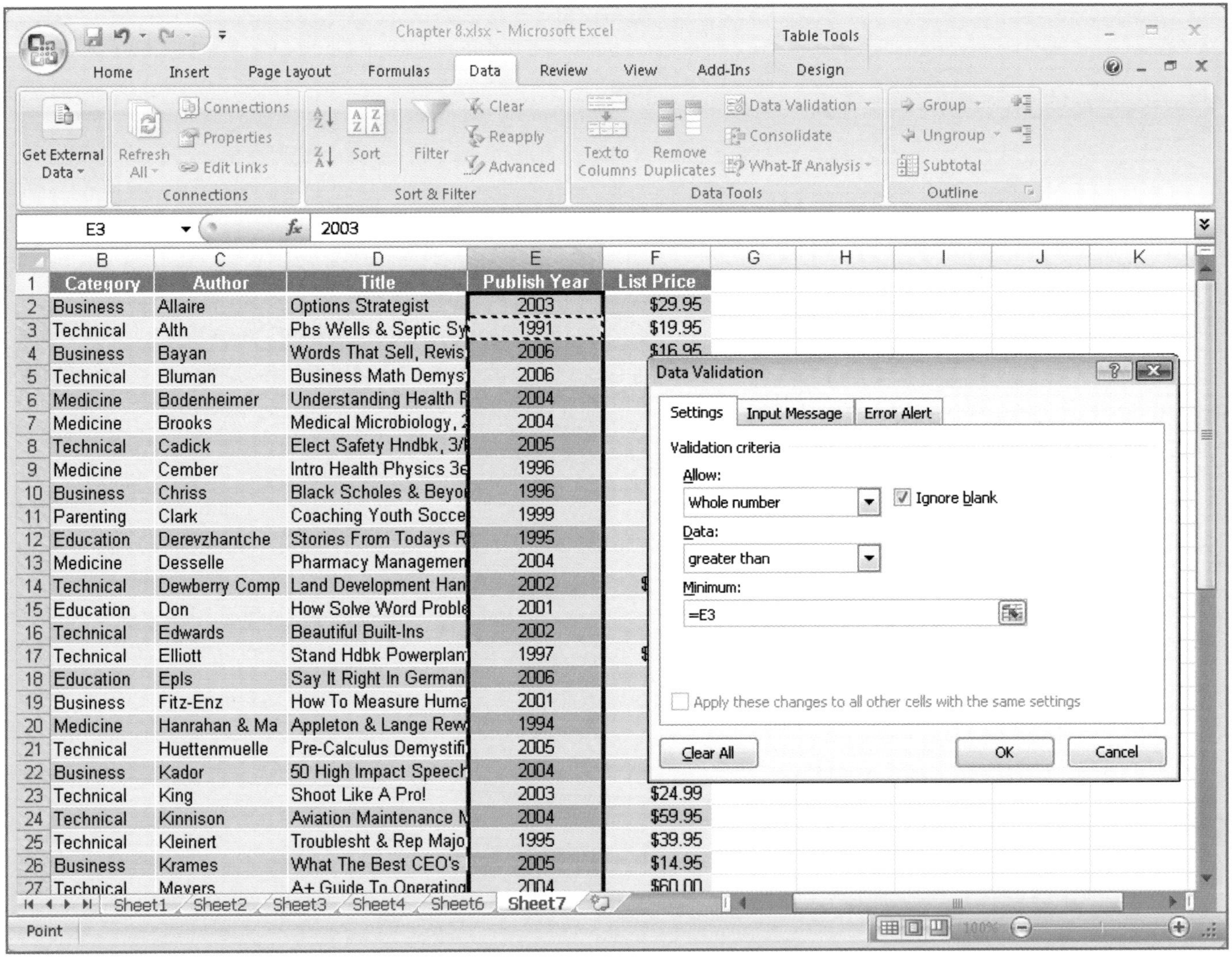

Figure 8-7: *The Data Validation dialog box provides comparison criteria you can use to establish conditions for data entry.*

QUICKSTEPS

LOCATING VALIDATION DATA

Excel easily identifies data you've selected to be validated, as well as data that doesn't fit validation criteria you've set.

FIND VALIDATED DATA

In the Home tab Editing group, click **Find & Select**, and click **Data Validation**. Data on the worksheet you had previously selected for data validation is highlighted.

FIND INVALIDATED DATA

In the Data tab Data Tools group, click the **Data Validation** down arrow, and click **Circle Validation Criteria**. To remove the circles, again click the **Data Validation** down arrow, and click **Clear Validation Circles**.

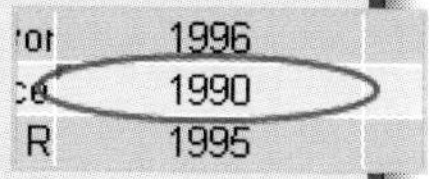

–Or–

Look for green error indicators in the upper-left corner of affected cells. Click the cell to view the Smart Tag and a tooltip provides the source of the error. Click the down arrow, and click **Display Type Information** to see an explanation of the validation, shown in Figure 8-8.

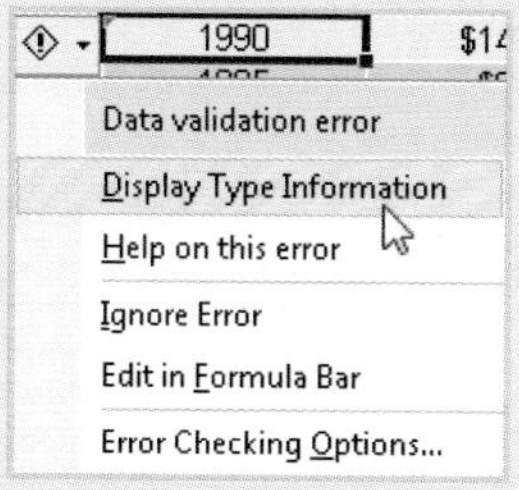

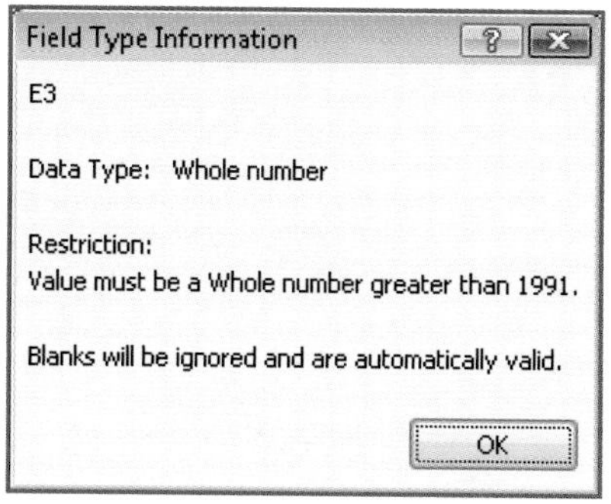

Figure 8-8: **Excel provides a full explanation for invalidated data.**

5. Type minimum/starting and maximum/ending values in the applicable text boxes, or locate them on the worksheet using the **Collapse Dialog** button. If using values on the worksheet, click the **Expand Dialog** button to return to the dialog box.

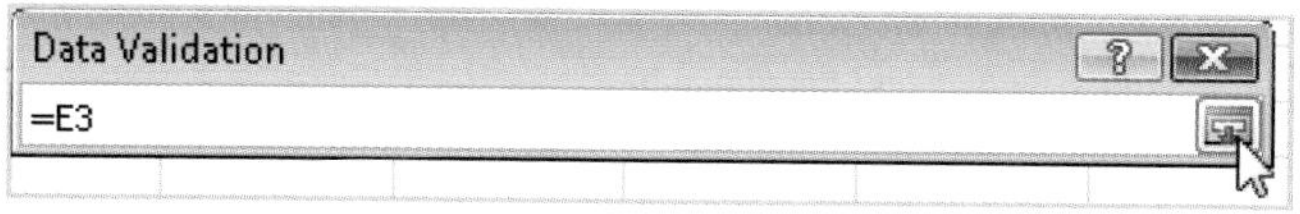

6. Click **OK** to apply the validation.

REMOVE VALIDATION CRITERIA

1. Select the cell(s) whose validation you want to remove. See "Locating Validation Data" QuickSteps to help you locate the validated cells.

2. In the Data tab Data Tools group, click **Data Validation**.

3. In the Data Validation dialog box Settings tab, click **Clear All** and then click **OK**.

CREATE A DATA ENTRY MESSAGE

You can forestall data entry mistakes by providing a message, similar to a tooltip, with information about a selected cell.

1. Set up a validation (see "Create a Validation), or select the range for an existing validation.

2. In the Data tab Data Tools group, click **Data Validation** and click the **Input Message** tab.

3. Verify that the **Show Input Message When Cell Is Selected** check box is selected.

TIP

Verify that data validation has been removed by doing the first set of procedures in "Locating Validation Data" QuickSteps.

TIP

You can create a message to appear when *any* cell is selected, not just those that have validation conditions applied—although comments are typically used for that purpose. See Chapter 3 for information on adding comments to a cell.

4. Type a title for the message and the message itself in their respective text boxes.

5. Click **OK** when finished. When a user selects a cell to enter data, a tooltip-type message will be displayed with the text you provided.

CREATE AN ERROR MESSAGE

When you (or anyone else!) try to add data that doesn't meet a cell's validation criteria, Excel returns a generic message box that informs you of your error. You can modify the type of alert that is displayed and the text that appears.

1. Set up a validation. See "Create a Validation."

2. In the Data tab Data Tools group, click **Data Validation** and click the **Error Alert** tab.

3. Verify that the **Show Error Alert After Invalid Data Is Entered** check box is selected.

4. Click the **Style** down arrow, and select the severity of the alert. The alert's associated icon is displayed below the selected style.

5. Type a title for the alert and the message itself in their respective text boxes.

6. Click **OK** when finished. When a user tries to complete an entry with data that doesn't meet the validation criteria, the alert you created will pop up, as shown in Figure 8-9.

41	0072193565	Technical	Southwick/Pri	Telecommunications Al	2001
42	0071466592	Business	Sugars	Instant Cashflow	2005
43	0071466606	ISBN Numbers			
44	007146672X				
45	0809223406	⊗ ISBN numbers are 10 digits. Please check your entry and try again.			
46	0071413014				
47	0071441719		Retry	Cancel	Help
48	0071455523				
49	007457659				
50	**Total**				
51					
52					

Figure 8-9: **You can create custom error messages to alert users that they are trying to enter invalid data.**

Organize Data

Data in a worksheet is often entered in a manner that doesn't lend itself well to being viewed or to being able to find specific data that you want. Excel provides several tools to assist you in organizing your data without permanently changing

Sort Warning

Microsoft Office Excel found data next to your selection. Since you have not selected this data, it will not be sorted.

What do you want to do?

○ Expand the selection
● Continue with the current selection

[Sort...]   [Cancel]

the overall structure of the worksheet. You can sort data on any column based on several criteria, filter data to view just the information you want to see, and outline data to streamline what you see.

Sort Data by Columns

You can sort data based on several criteria:

- **Ascending** or **descending** order according to the values in one or more columns. Excel sorts numbers "smallest to largest" and dates "oldest to newest," as well as their reverses.

- **Fill Color** or **Font Color** in a selected cell.

- **Cell icons** attached to cells.

- **Custom lists**, such as month or day names.

All data in the selected range (or table) is realigned so that the data in each row remains the same, even though the row might be placed in a different order than it was originally. You can also sort on dates and days of week, and use values tabled by rows instead of columns.

PERFORM AN ASCENDING/DESCENDING SORT

1. Click a cell in the range or table.

2. In the Data tab Sort & Filter group, click **Sort *ascending*** (the name changes according to the data type selected) to sort from smaller to larger numbers, newest to oldest dates, or from A to Z. (See the accompanying Note on sort orders.)

–Or–

Click **Sort *descending*** to sort from larger to smaller numbers, oldest to newest dates, or from Z to A.

SORT BY COLOR AND ICONS

1. Right-click a cell in the column that contains a color or an icon by which you want to sort the range or table.

2. In the Data tab Sort & Filter group, click **Sort** and click whether you want the data sorted based on the fill color, font color, or icon in the selected cell. The range or table is sorted, similar to what is shown in Figure 8-10.

⚊↓	Sort Smallest to Largest
⚊↓	Sort Largest to Smallest
	Put Selected Cell Color On Top
	Put Selected Font Color On Top
	Put Selected Cell Icon On Top
	Custom Sort...

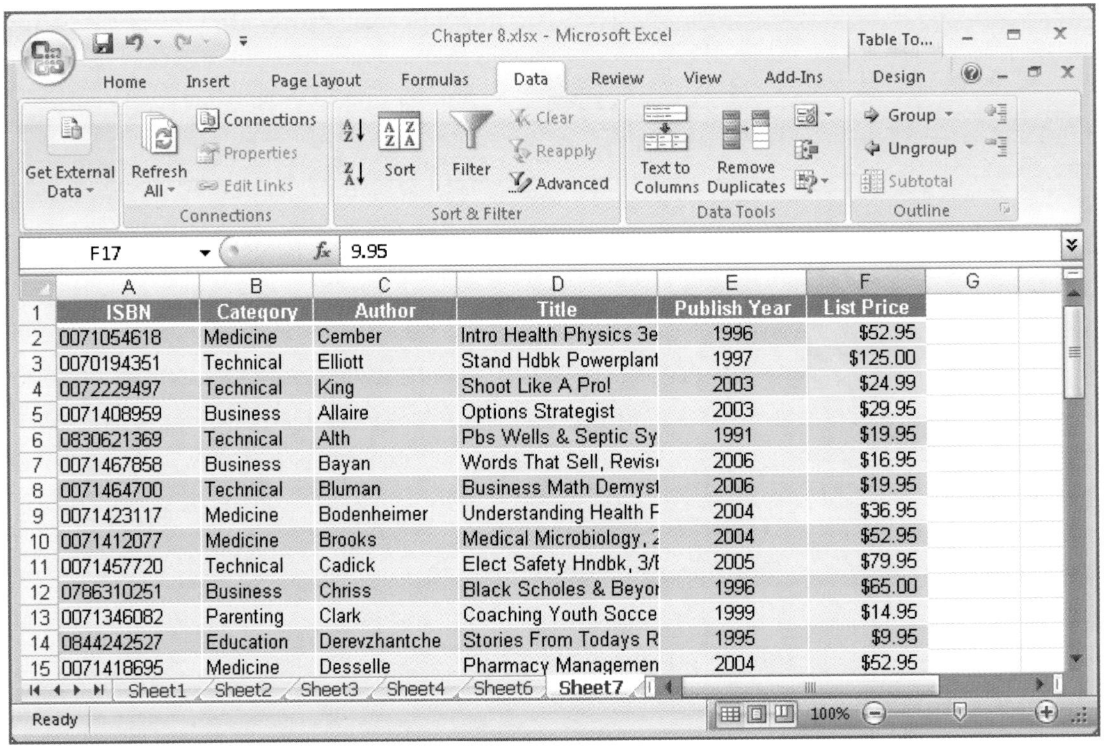

*Figure 8-10: **Using color or cell icons makes it easy to quickly bring data into view.***

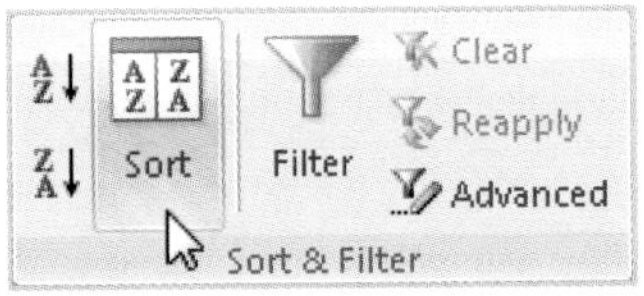

SORT BY MULTIPLE CRITERIA

You can nest levels of sorting criteria to refine a sort based on multiple criteria. For example, you could first sort a table based on a category of books, then the year they were published, and then by list price within each year.

1. Click a cell in the range or table you want to sort.

2. In the Data tab Sort & Filter group, click **Sort**.

    –Or–

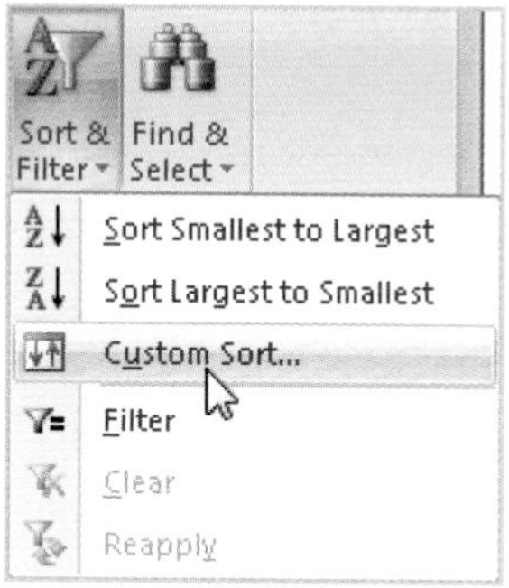

In the Home tab Editing group, click **Sort & Filter**, and click **Custom Sort**.

–Or–

Right-click a cell in the range or table you want to sort, click **Sort**, and click **Custom Sort**.

In any case, the Sort dialog box appear, shown in Figure 8-11.

3. If sorting data outside a table, select or deselect the **My Data Has Headers** check box, depending on whether your range has column headings or not.

4. Click the **Sort By (Column)** down arrow, and select the column of primary importance in determining the sort order.

5. Click the **Sort On** down arrow, and click the criteria you want to sort on.

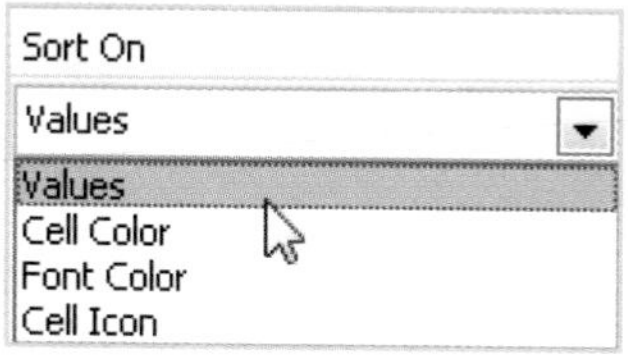

6. Click the **Order** down arrow, and click whether the sort is ascending or descending. Or click **Custom List** to sort on a prebuilt list or one of your own.

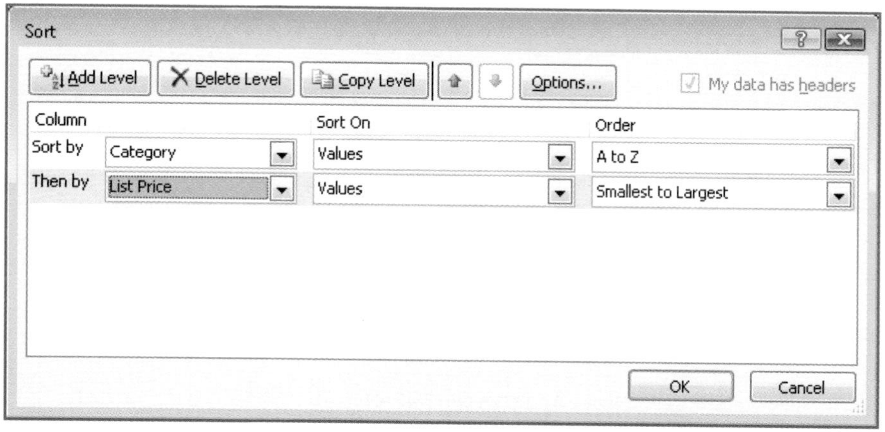

Figure 8-11: **The Sort dialog box allows you to set up 64 levels of sorting.**

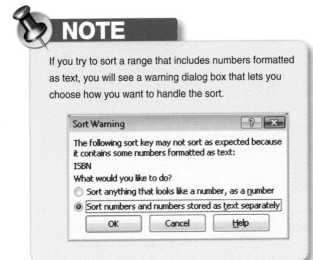

NOTE

If you try to sort a range that includes numbers formatted as text, you will see a warning dialog box that lets you choose how you want to handle the sort.

7. Click **Add Level** to create another set of sorting options (Figure 8-11 shows two levels). Repeat steps 4–6 for the next set of criteria to be sorted. Continue building sorting levels as deep and detailed as you need, using the available tools:

- Select a level and click **Copy Level** to create a copy of a previous level and minimize repetitious entries.
- Select a level and click **Delete Level** to remove a level from the list.
- Click the **Move Up** and **Move Down** arrows to re-order the priority of multiple levels.

8. Click **OK**. The data is sorted based on your criteria (see Figure 8-12).

Sort Data by Rows

1. Click a cell in the range you want to sort. (The range cannot be an Excel-defined table.)
2. In the Data tab Sort & Filter group, click **Sort**.

First-level sort organizes table by book categories

Second-level sort places books in ascending published order within each category

Third-level sort places prices of books in ascending order within each year

	A	B	C	D	E	F
1	ISBN	Category	Author	Title	Publish Year	List Price
2	0786310251	Business	Chriss	Black Scholes & Beyor	1996	$65.00
3	0071343105	Business	Piskurich	Astd Hndbk Training Ds	1999	$79.95
4	0809223406	Business	Sullivan	Getting Your Foot In Th	2001	$12.95
5	0071369988	Business	Fitz-Enz	How To Measure Huma	2001	$49.95
6	0071418717	Business	Page	Hope Is Not A Strategy	2003	$14.95
7	0071408959	Business	Allaire	Options Strategist	2003	$29.95
8	0071421947	Business	Kador	50 High Impact Speech	2004	$14.95
9	0071429697	Business	Morris	Accounting For M&A, E	2004	$49.95
10	007146252X	Business	Krames	What The Best CEO's I	2005	$14.95
11	0071449124	Business	Pardoe	How Buffett Does It	2005	$16.95
12	0071466592	Business	Sugars	Instant Cashflow	2005	$16.95
13	0071466606	Business	Sugars	Instant Advertising	2005	$16.95
14	007146672X	Business	Sugars	The Business Coach	2005	$16.95
15	0071467858	Business	Bayan	Words That Sell, Revisi	2006	$16.95
16	0070380686	Education	Pen	Sch Intro To Music	1991	$14.95
17	0844242527	Education	Derevzhantche	Stories From Todays R	1995	$9.95
18	0070466173	Education	Nash	Sch Outl Strength Mate	1998	$17.95
19	0844202991	Education	Qafisheh	Ntcs Gulf Arabic Englis	1999	$29.95
20	0071358978	Education	Don	How Solve Word Proble	2001	$9.95
21	0071428488	Education	R. De Roussy	Easy French Reader, 2	2003	$10.95

Figure 8-12: **Sorting on multiple levels allows you to finely tune how your information is organized and displayed.**

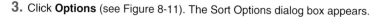

REMOVING FILTERS

When you apply filters, your data doesn't permanently disappear. Filtering only hides data that doesn't fit the criteria you select. You can return to the view of your data before you applied a filter.

REMOVE A FILTER FROM A COLUMN

1. Click the **AutoFilter** down arrow next to the column heading.

2. Click **Clear Filter From** *columnname*.

REMOVE FILTERS FROM ALL COLUMNS IN A RANGE OR TABLE

In the Data tab Sort & Filter group, click **Clear**. Filters are removed from the data, although AutoFilter down arrows are retained in the column headers.

TURN OFF AUTOFILTER

In the Data tab Sort & Filter group, click **Filter**. AutoFilter is turned off and the AutoFilter down arrows are removed from column headers.

TIP

You can apply filters to only one range or table on a worksheet at a time, but you can apply filters to more than one column in a range or table. Actually, you can nest filters by filtering on multiple columns, similar to sorting. For example, you could filter a table of books by category and then filter that list by author, displaying only those books by a given author with a certain category.

3. Click **Options** (see Figure 8-11). The Sort Options dialog box appears.

4. In the Orientation area, click **Sort Left To Right**. Click **OK**.

5. In the Sort dialog box, the Sort By element will change from "Column" to "Row." Perform steps 3–8 in "Sort by Multiple Criteria."

Create an AutoFilter

Filtering data allows you to quickly dismiss potentially thousands of rows (records) of data that you don't need at the moment so that only those rows of data that you want to see are displayed. The quickest and easiest way to filter data is to have Excel add AutoFilter to your column headings.

1. Click a cell in the range or table where you want to filter data.

2. If AutoFilter down arrows are not to the right of each column heading, in the Data tab Sort & Filter group, click **Filter** to add them.

3. Click the **AutoFilter** down arrow in the column that contains the values to which you want to apply a filter.

4. Decide what you want to filter from the menu (shown here) and follow the appropriate steps next.

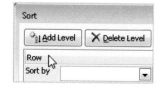

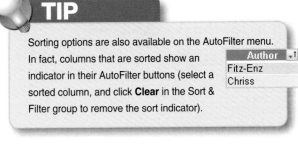

FILTER BY COLUMN VALUES

1. On the filter menu, click **Select All** in the values list to remove the check marks next to all values in the column.
2. Select the values whose rows you want to display. Click **OK**.

FILTER BY EMPTY CELLS

The Blanks option is only displayed if the column has at least one blank cell.

1. On the filter menu, click **Select All** to remove the check marks next to all values in the column.
2. Select **(Blanks)** at the bottom of the values list. Click **OK**.

FILTER BY CELL FILL

The Filter By Color option is available in columns that have at least one cell filled with a color or texture.

On the filter menu, click **Filter By Color**, and click the color you want to filter by.

–Or–

Click **No Fill** to display only those rows that do not have a fill.

FILTER BY NUMERIC VALUES

Excel provides several "quick" criteria you can choose from to quickly filter your data (most of these options simply open the Custom Filter dialog box prefilled with the criteria you chose).

1. On the filter menu, click **Number Filters**. A list of criteria options is displayed.

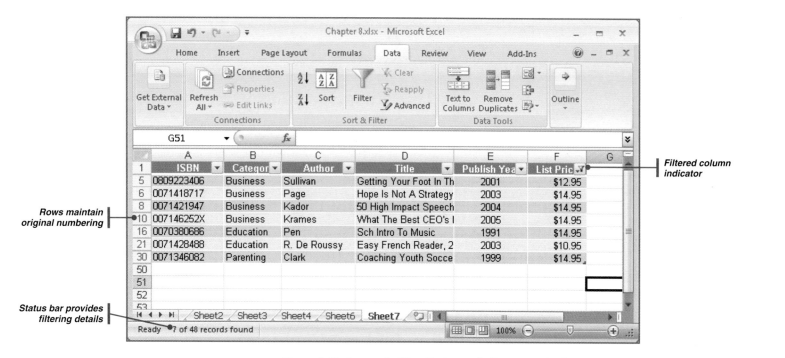

Figure 8-13: *A numeric filter displays only the range of values you specify.*

2. Click the comparison you want to filter by, type or select a value, and click **OK**. (Clicking **Above Average** or **Below Average** immediately performs the filter; clicking **Top 10** opens a dialog box, where you can filter for top or bottom values or percentages.) Figure 8-13 shows a filter on a book table of prices between $10 and $15.

–Or–

1. Click **Custom Filter** at the bottom of the Numeric Filters submenu to display the Custom AutoFilter dialog box, where you can add a second comparison to the criteria.

2. Click the first comparison operator down arrow, and select an operator. Type or select the value you want the operator to act upon. (See "Use Wildcards in Criteria" later in the chapter for information on using wildcards to represent single or multiple characters.)

3. Click **And** or **Or** to apply a logic operator.

SETTING UP CRITERIA AND EXTRACT RANGES

Before you perform an advanced filter to copy the results to a range outside your data range, you need to set up the criteria and extract ranges with column headers that match the column headers in the data range. For example, in a table containing several columns of book data, you could set up your *criteria* range to filter on "Sugars" in the Author column and extract only information from the ISBN and Title columns into a separate worksheet. In this case, your criteria range would include the Author label in one cell and Sugars in the cell below it. Your extract range would include two columns: ISBN and Title. When dragging the extract range, include the labels and as many rows as might be necessary. Also, copy the labels from the data range to the criteria and extract ranges by using Copy and Paste to reduce text entry errors (spoken from personal experience!).

Criteria:	Author	
	Sugars	
Extract:	ISBN	Title

4. Click the second comparison down arrow, select an operator, and then type or select its corresponding value.

5. Click **OK** when finished.

Use Advanced Filtering

You can set up an advanced filter where the criteria are located elsewhere than the table or data range. You can then have the results copied to a separate range on the worksheet. In addition, you can use wildcards in setting up your comparison criteria.

FILTER BASED ON EXTERNAL CRITERIA

1. Click a cell in the table, or select the range where you want to filter data.

2. In the Data tab Sort & Filter group, click **Advanced**. The Advanced Filter dialog box appears.

3. In the List Range text box, verify the range. If you need to make changes, click the **Collapse Dialog** button, reselect the range, and click the **Expand Dialog** button.

4. In the Criteria Range text box, click the **Collapse Dialog** button, select the cell that contains your criteria, and click the **Expand Dialog** button.

5. Click **Filter The List, In Place** if you want the rows that meet the filter to display within the current range.

   –Or–

   Click **Copy To Another Location** to extract the filter results to a range elsewhere. In the Copy To text box, click **Collapse Dialog**, select the range where you want the filter results copied (see "Setting Up Criteria and Extract Ranges" QuickFacts), and click the **Expand Dialog** button.

6. Click **OK** when finished. The data your criteria specified is copied to your extract range (see Figure 8-14).

Advanced Filter dialog box:

Action
- ● Filter the list, in-place
- ○ Copy to another location

List range: `$A$1:$F$48`

Criteria range:

Copy to:

☐ Unique records only

[OK] [Cancel]

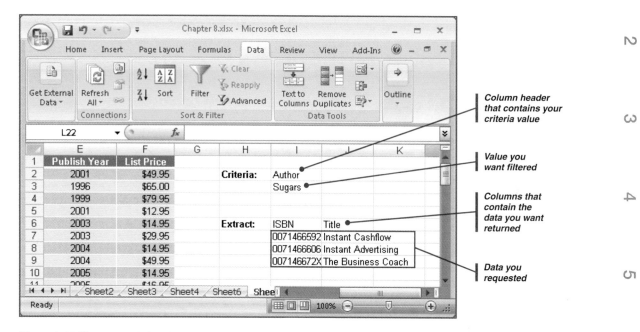

Figure 8-14: **You can pull data from a table and copy it to another range.**

USE WILDCARDS IN CRITERIA

You can use *wildcard* comparison criteria to help you find data:

- Type an asterisk (*) as a placeholder for any number of missing characters. For example, typing *son finds Robinson, Dobson, and bison.

- Type a question mark (?) as a placeholder for a single character. For example, typing Jo?n finds John and Joan.

- Type a tilde (~) before an asterisk, question mark, or tilde to find words or phrases containing one or more asterisks, question marks, and tildes. For example, typing msdos~~ finds msdos~.

Outline Data Automatically

You can display only summary rows and columns by outlining a range and hiding the details. The mechanics of creating the automatic outline involve

USING OUTLINES

Outlines are manipulated using a set of symbols on the row and column bars, as well as using commands in the Outline group (see Figure 8-15).

COLLAPSE ROWS AND COLUMNS

Click the Collapse symbol next to a group of rows or columns.

EXPAND COLLAPSED ROWS AND COLUMNS

Click the Expand symbol next to a hidden group of rows or columns.

COLLAPSE OR EXPAND ALL ROWS AND COLUMNS

1. Select the range where you want to show or hide all rows and columns.

2. In the Data tab Outline group, click **Show Detail** or **Hide Detail** .

COLLAPSE OR EXPAND BY LEVELS

Excel determines how many sets (or *levels*) of detail and summary data are in your outline and displays symbols you can use to expand and collapse accordingly.

Click the level symbols appropriate for the level of detail and summary data you want to see or hide.

REMOVE A GROUP

1. Select the rows or columns you want to ungroup.

2. In the Data tab Outline group, click **Ungroup**. (If you grouped by both rows and columns, select which to ungroup, and click **OK**.)

REMOVE AN OUTLINE

1. Select a cell in the outline.

2. In the Data tab Outline group, click **Ungroup** and click **Clear Outline**.

just a few clicks; however, there are a few things you should do to your data in advance of applying an automatic outline:

- **Column headings** should be in the first row if you are outlining by row; **row headings** should be in the first column if you are outlining by column.

- **Similar data** should be in the columns or rows you are outlining, and the data must be set up as a hierarchical summary.

- **Blank rows or columns** should be removed.

- **Sort the data** to get it into the groupings you want.

- **Create total or summary rows and columns** that sum the detail rows above them, or the detail columns to the left or right of them.

When you are ready to outline your data:

1. Click a cell in the range you want to outline.

2. In the Data tab Outline group, click the **Group** down arrow, and click **Auto Outline**. An outlining bar and outlining symbols are either added across the column headers and down the row headers, as shown in Figure 8-15, or across just one of the headers—depending on the structure of your data.

–Or–

Click the **Group** button (to the left of the down arrow). Click whether to group by rows or columns, and then click **OK**.

In either case, see "Using Outlines" QuickSteps for ways to manipulate your data.

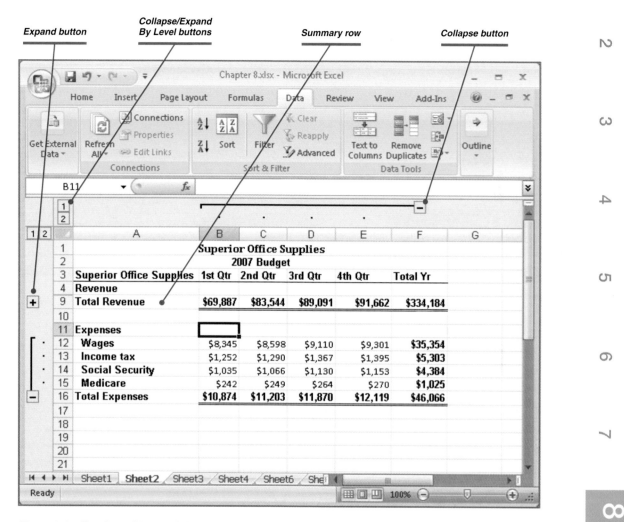

Figure 8-15: *Excel provides outlining tools to collapse and expand data by rows and columns.*

Outline Data by Manually Grouping

Grouping data allows you to create an outline of your data by selecting rows and columns that can be collapsed and hidden. You generally use this manual method of outlining when your data doesn't have the summary rows or columns used by the automatic outlining feature to recognize where to hide details.

1. Select the first set of rows or columns you want to be able to collapse and expand.

2. In the Data tab Outline group, click **Group**. An outlining bar is added to the left of the row headers or above the column headers, depending on whether rows or columns were selected.

	11	**Expenses**	
	12	**Wages**	$8,345
	13	**Income tax**	$1,252
	14	**Social Security**	$1,035
	15	**Medicare**	$242
	16		
	17		

3. Repeat steps 1 and 2 for as many sets of rows or columns you want to include in the outline.

Add Subtotals

You can add subtotals to your data grouping, assuming your data is properly set up (see the rules in "Outline Data Automatically" earlier in the chapter).

1. Select the range for which you want to add subtotals. If your data is not set up properly, Excel will provide suggestions you can use to get it in order.

Microsoft Office Excel

Microsoft Office Excel cannot determine which row in your list or selection contains column labels, which are required for this command.

- If you want the first row of the selection or list used as labels and not as data, click OK.
- If you selected a subset of cells in error, select a single cell, and try the command again.
- To create column labels, click Cancel, and enter a text label at the top of each column of data.
- For information about creating labels that are easy to detect, click Help.

OK   Cancel   Help

TIP

If you select only a cell or select rows and columns by dragging across cells, Excel will be "confused" and will display a Group or Ungroup dialog box. Choose whether you want to group or ungroup rows or columns, and click **OK**. To avoid this confusion, select rows and columns using their respective numbered and lettered headings.

2. In the Data tab Outline group, click **Subtotal**. The Subtotal dialog box appears.

3. Click the **At Each Change In** down arrow, and select which column the subtotals will be grouped on.

4. If you want to subtotal based on something other than a SUM, click the **Use Function** down arrow, and select the function you want.

5. In the Add Subtotal To list, select which columns will receive subtotals.

6. Select whether you want any of the features provided by the check boxes, and click **OK**.

Add Styles to an Outline

Excel can recognize summary rows and columns, and can add styling to differentiate them from other data.

1. Expand the outline to show any collapsed rows or columns.

2. Click a cell within the data range you want to add styling (bolding, font, and font size changes).

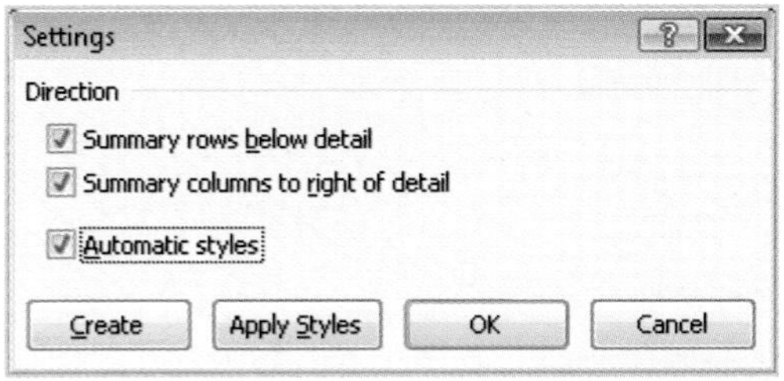

Settings

Direction

☑ Summary rows below detail

☑ Summary columns to right of detail

☑ Automatic styles

[Create] [Apply Styles] [OK] [Cancel]

3. In the Data tab, click the **Outline** group **Dialog Box Launcher** (the small arrow in lower-right corner).

4. In the Settings dialog box, select the **Automatic Styles** check box, and click **Create**. Bolding is applied to summary rows and/or columns, shown in Figure 8-16.

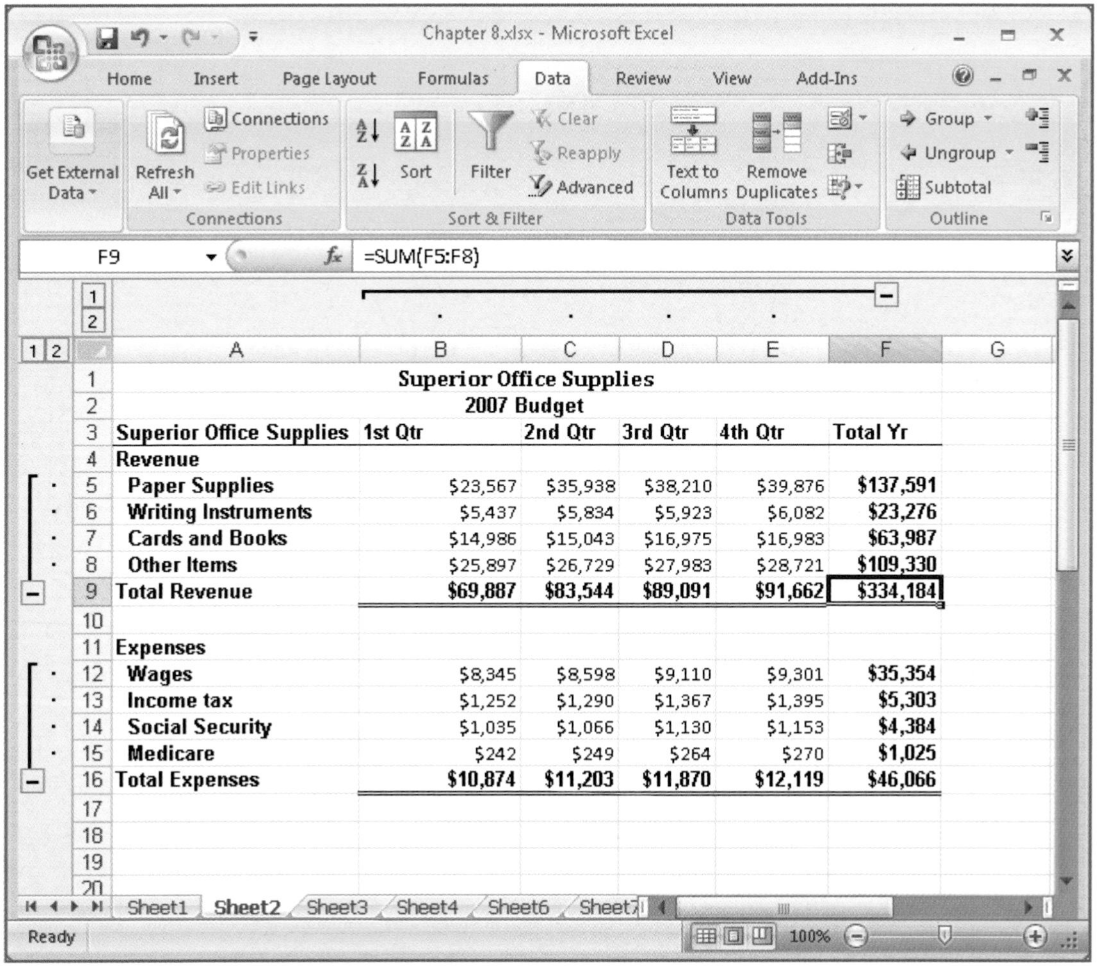

Chapter 8.xlsx - Microsoft Excel

F9   fx =SUM(F5:F8)

	A	B	C	D	E	F	G
1		Superior Office Supplies					
2		2007 Budget					
3	Superior Office Supplies	1st Qtr	2nd Qtr	3rd Qtr	4th Qtr	Total Yr	
4	Revenue						
5	Paper Supplies	$23,567	$35,938	$38,210	$39,876	$137,591	
6	Writing Instruments	$5,437	$5,834	$5,923	$6,082	$23,276	
7	Cards and Books	$14,986	$15,043	$16,975	$16,983	$63,987	
8	Other Items	$25,897	$26,729	$27,983	$28,721	$109,330	
9	Total Revenue	$69,887	$83,544	$89,091	$91,662	$334,184	
10							
11	Expenses						
12	Wages	$8,345	$8,598	$9,110	$9,301	$35,354	
13	Income tax	$1,252	$1,290	$1,367	$1,395	$5,303	
14	Social Security	$1,035	$1,066	$1,130	$1,153	$4,384	
15	Medicare	$242	$249	$264	$270	$1,025	
16	Total Expenses	$10,874	$11,203	$11,870	$12,119	$46,066	
17							
18							
19							
20							

Sheet1 **Sheet2** Sheet3 Sheet4 Sheet6 Sheet7

Ready   100%

Figure 8-16: You can add bolded styling to summary rows and columns.

How to...

- *Use Goal Seek*
- *Compare Alternatives Using Scenarios*
- *Use Multiple Variables to Provide a Result*
- *Save Solver Results and Settings*
- *Changing Solver Settings*
- *Create a PivotTable*
- *Understanding PivotTable Terms*
- *Create the PivotTable Layout*
- *Style a PivotTable*
- *Using PivotTables*
- *Create a PivotTable Chart*
- *Protect Workbooks with Passwords*
- *Share a Workbook*
- *Working with Changes in a Shared Workbook*
- *Protect a Shared Workbook*
- *Discontinue Sharing a Workbook*
- *Work with Views*
- *Protect Worksheet and Workbook Elements*

Chapter 9

Analyzing and Sharing Data

In this chapter you will learn how to use more advanced tools for manipulating your data to arrive at predetermined results that you want to achieve, how to reorient your data to give you different perspectives on how it is presented and interpreted, and how to protect your data when it is shared with others.

Get the Results You Want

Excel provides several features to help you find out how to arrive at a result by changing the underlying data. *Goal Seek* fills this requirement on a limited and temporary basis. *Scenarios* provide means to save and compare different sets of values that you can run to see how they affect your result. The most powerful feature in this suite of what-if analysis tools is *Solver*, an add-in program that extends the capabilities of Goal Seek and scenarios.

You must have a goal for the result of a formula and a variable that is part of the formula. For example, if you have a budget item that is the result of adding four quarters and you have three quarters complete, you could set a goal for the year and use Goal Seek to calculate what the fourth quarter must bring to accomplish the annual goal. The Set Cell would be the annual total, with a formula that sums the four quarters. The To Value would be the goal for the year, and the By Changing Cell will be the fourth-quarter number.

Use Goal Seek

With Goal Seek, you choose a cell whose results are derived from a formula that uses the values in other cells. By seeing the change required in the value in one of the referenced cells, you see what it would take to achieve the result. To provide the answer you are looking for, Goal Seek requires three inputs:

- **Set Cell** is the cell address for the result you want. The Set Cell must contain a formula.

> Microsoft Office Excel
>
> ⚠ Cell must contain a formula.
>
> OK

- **To Value** is the value (the goal) you want the formula in the Set Cell to achieve.

- **By Changing Cell** is the cell address for the value that you want to change in order to achieve the To Value (goal) you want. This cell must contain a value, not a formula, and must be referenced in the To Value's formula.

> Microsoft Office Excel
>
> ⚠ Cell must contain a value.
>
> OK

1. On a worksheet, enter a formula in a cell that will be your Set Cell.

2. Enter values needed in the formula in cells, one of which you'll chose to be the By Changing Cell.

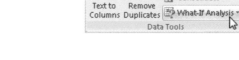

3. In the Data tab Data Tools group, click **What-If Analysis** and click **Goal Seek**.

4. In the Goal Seek dialog box, select the cell that will be the Set Cell. The cell will be surrounded by a blinking border.

5. In the To Value text box, type the new value you want the Set Cell to be.

Figure 9-1: *Find what a constituent value must be to meet a goal.*

6. Click the **By Changing Cell** text box, and then click the precedent cell on the worksheet that will need to change to accomplish your new Set Cell value. The cell will be surrounded by a blinking border, as shown in Figure 9-1.

7. Click **OK**. The cells will change value. The Goal Seek Status dialog box appears and shows that a solution was found.

8. Click **OK** to accept the changes to your worksheet.

–Or–

Click **Cancel** to return the worksheet to its original values.

TIP

If you click **OK** in the Goal Seek Status dialog box and change the values on your worksheet, you can revert to the original values by clicking the Undo button.

> **TIP**
>
> Before you create scenarios of what-if values, create a scenario of the present values for the cells you will be changing (*changing cells*) so you can compare alternatives to the original.

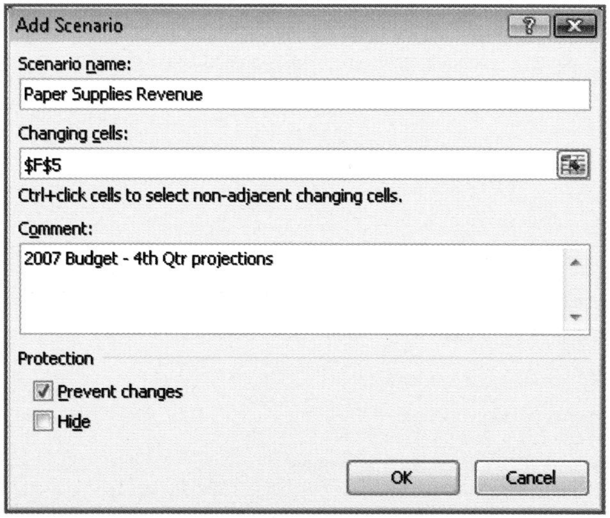

Figure 9-2: ***Set up each scenario with a unique name, changing cells, and a description.***

Compare Alternatives Using Scenarios

You use *scenarios* to create a set of situations where you can change the values for various cells, save the changed values, and evaluate how the scenarios compare against one another in a side-by-side summary report. For example, if you wanted to see how changes to upcoming fourth-quarter revenue and expenses might affect your year-end profit, you could create a scenario for each entry on the worksheet that you wanted to change.

IDENTIFY CHANGING CELLS

1. Name the cells whose values you will be changing by clicking a cell and typing a name in the **Name Box** at the left end of the Formula bar. Press **ENTER**. (It will be more meaningful to see descriptive names in the Scenario Values dialog box.)
2. Repeat for the other cells that you will be changing.

CREATE A SCENARIO

1. In the Data tab Data Tools group, click **What-If Analysis** and click **Scenario Manager**. In the Scenario Manager, click **Add**. The Add Scenario dialog box appears, similar to what is shown in Figure 9-2.
2. In the Scenario Name text box, name the scenario according to the type of changes it contains—for example, Revenue, Low Wages, or Current Values.
3. Click the **Changing Cells** text box, and then click the first cell where you will change a value. Hold down **CTRL** while clicking any other cells whose values you'll want changed in this scenario. Move the dialog box or click the **Collapse Dialog** button if the dialog box is in your way. Expand the dialog box by either clicking **Close** or clicking **Expand Dialog**.
4. In the Comment text box, edit the text by selecting the default text and entering your own.
5. Leave the **Prevent Changes** check box selected, unless you want the changes to replace the current values on the worksheet.
6. Click **OK**. If one of your selected cells contains a formula, you will be told that formulas in those cells will be replaced by constant values when you show the scenario. Click **OK** to continue.

Microsoft Office Excel

⚠ At least one of the changing cells you specified contains a formula. Formulas in changing cells will be replaced by constant values when you show a scenario.

[OK]

Figure 9-3: **The Scenario Manager provides a one-stop location to list, change, and run scenarios.**

7. Click **Add** to continue adding more scenarios.

   –Or–

   In the Scenario Values dialog box, change the values for one or more of the listed changing cells, and click **OK**.

RUN A SCENARIO

1. Open the Scenario Manager, if necessary. Select the scenario you want to run, and click **Show**, or double-click the scenario. The changing cells on your worksheet display any changed values, and any affected formulas recalculate and provide updated results.

2. To return your worksheet to its original state, close the Scenario Manager dialog box and then click **Undo** on the Quick Access toolbar.

EDIT A SCENARIO

1. Open the Scenario Manager (see Figure 9-3), if necessary, and select the scenario you want to edit. Click **Edit**.

2. In the Edit Scenario dialog box, change the name, add or remove changing cells, edit comments, and choose whether to change the protection status. Click **OK**.

3. In the Scenario Values dialog box, make any changes to the values for the changing cells. Click **OK**.

4. To delete the scenario, select it and click **Delete**.

COMPARE SCENARIOS

1. Open the Scenario Manager, if necessary, and click the **Summary** button.

2. In the Scenario Summary dialog box, leave the default option, **Scenario Summary**, selected.

3. Click the **Result Cells** box, and then click the first cell where you want to see the result of the change(s) you made in scenarios.

TIP

You can compare 251 scenarios in the Scenario Summary worksheet.

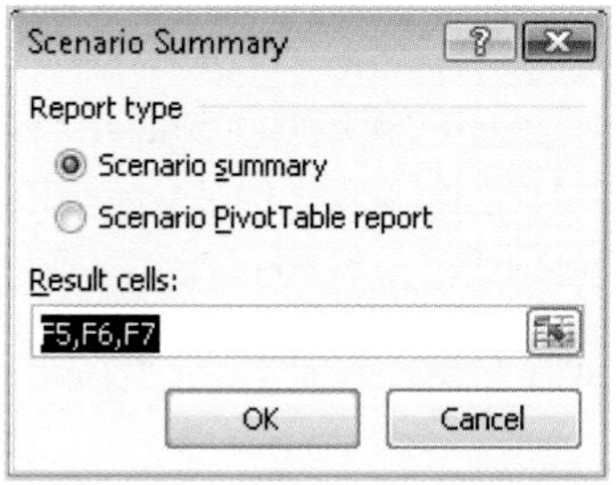
Scenario Summary
Report type
Scenario summary
Scenario PivotTable report
Result cells:
F5,F6,F7
OK
Cancel

4. If there is more than one results cell you want to see, type a comma (,) after the previous results cell before you click the subsequent cell.
5. Click **OK** when finished. A new worksheet named "Scenario Summary" is added to the workbook, similar to that shown in Figure 9-4.

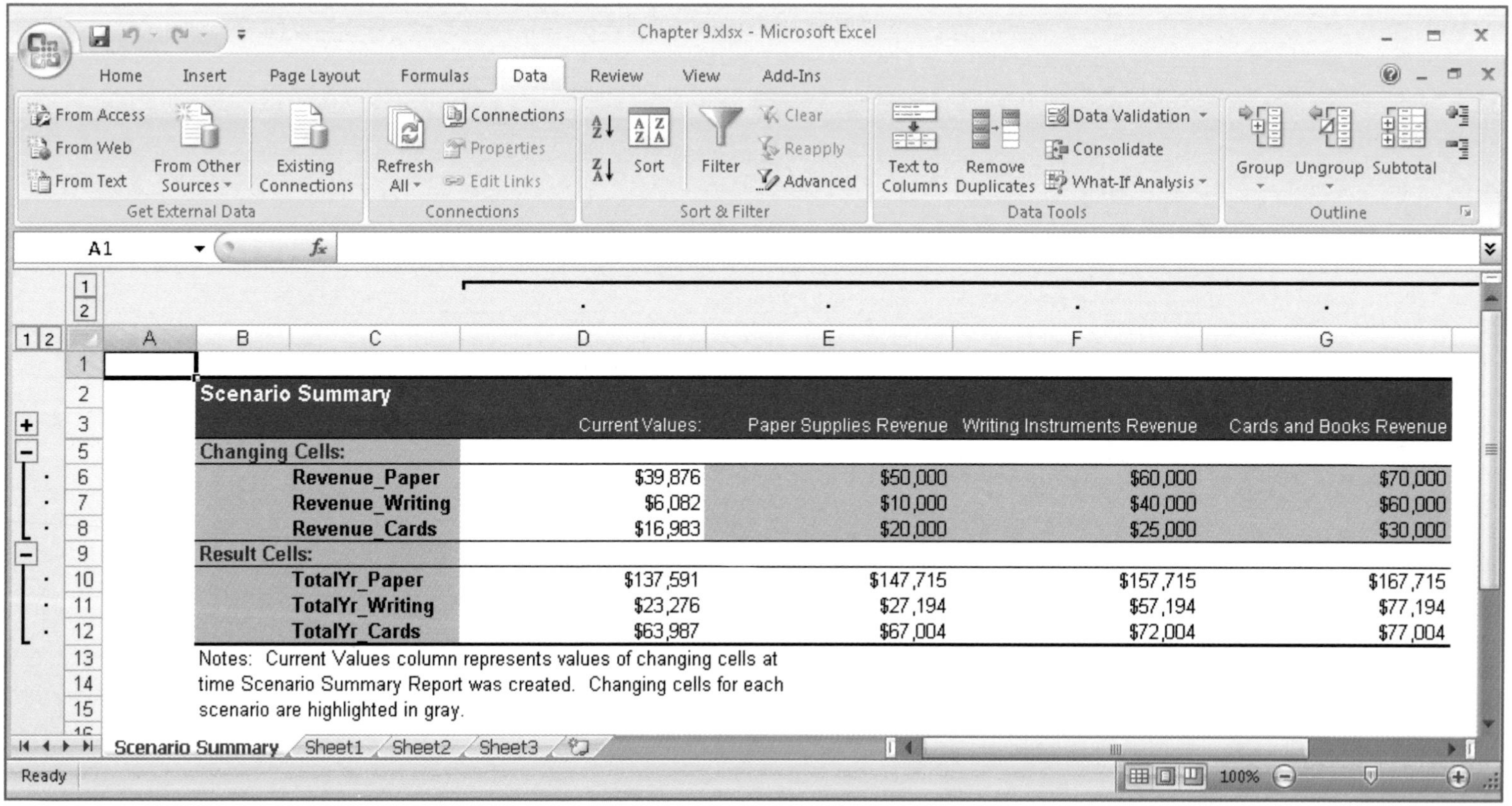
Chapter 9.xlsx - Microsoft Excel
Home Insert Page Layout Formulas Data Review View Add-Ins
From Access From Web From Text From Other Sources Existing Connections
Get External Data
Refresh All Connections Properties Edit Links
Connections
Sort Filter Clear Reapply Advanced
Sort & Filter
Text to Columns Remove Duplicates Data Validation Consolidate What-If Analysis
Data Tools
Group Ungroup Subtotal
Outline
A1
Scenario Summary
Current Values: Paper Supplies Revenue Writing Instruments Revenue Cards and Books Revenue
Changing Cells:
Revenue_Paper $39,876 $50,000 $60,000 $70,000
Revenue_Writing $6,082 $10,000 $40,000 $60,000
Revenue_Cards $16,983 $20,000 $25,000 $30,000
Result Cells:
TotalYr_Paper $137,591 $147,715 $157,715 $167,715
TotalYr_Writing $23,276 $27,194 $57,194 $77,194
TotalYr_Cards $63,987 $67,004 $72,004 $77,004
Notes: Current Values column represents values of changing cells at time Scenario Summary Report was created. Changing cells for each scenario are highlighted in gray.
Scenario Summary Sheet1 Sheet2 Sheet3
Ready
100%

Figure 9-4: ***The Scenario Summary lists changing cells from all scenarios and shows how each scenario changes the results cells.***

Use Multiple Variables to Provide a Result

Solver is Excel's most sophisticated tool for providing an answer to what-if problems. Figure 9-5 shows an example worksheet where Solver could be used. Solver is used by identifying the following cells and parameters:

- **Target cell** is the cell that contains a formula that you want to maximize, to minimize, or to return a specific value.

- **Changing (adjustable) cells** are related, directly or indirectly, to the target cell-by-cell references, and Solver will adjust them to obtain the result you want in the target cell.

- **Constraints** are limitations or boundaries you set for cells that are related, directly or indirectly, to the target cell.

INSTALL SOLVER

1. Click the **Office Button**, click **Excel Options**, and click **Add-Ins** in the left pane.

2. In the Excel Options dialog box Add-Ins list, verify that **Excel Add-Ins** is displayed in the Manage box. If not, select it. In either case, click **Go**.

   Manage: | Excel Add-ins | ▼ | Go...

3. In the Add-Ins dialog box (see Figure 9-6), select the **Solver Add-In** check box, and click **OK**. You might see a message informing you that Solver is not currently installed and giving you the opportunity to install it. Click **Yes**. You also might need your Microsoft Office CD or path to a network installation location to complete the installation.

4. After the installation is completed, a new Analysis group is added to the Data tab and the Solver add-in is added as an active application to the Excel Options dialog box.

View and manage Microsoft Office add-ins.

Add-ins

Name ▼
Active Application Add-ins
Solver Add-in
SnagIt Add-in

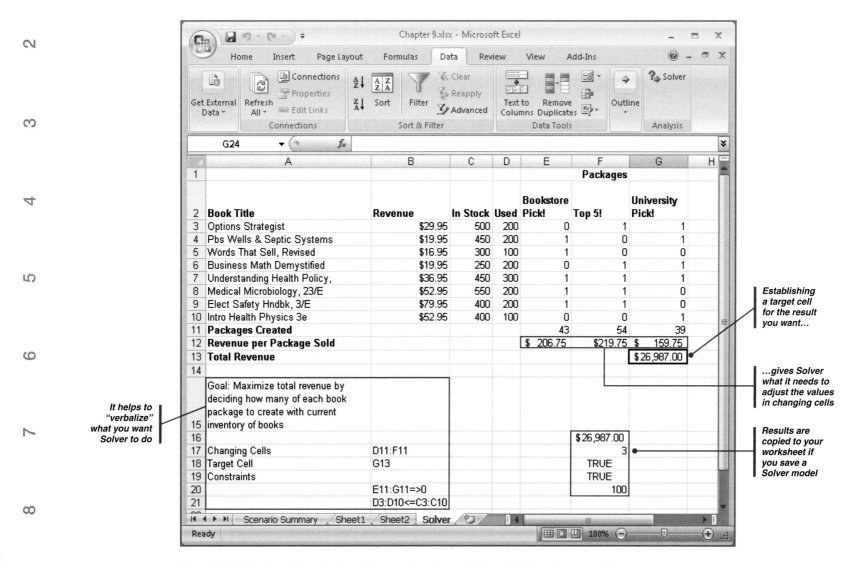

Figure 9-5: *Solver provides a solution to a problem with multiple variables and constraints.*

Establishing a target cell for the result you want...

...gives Solver what it needs to adjust the values in changing cells

Results are copied to your worksheet if you save a Solver model

It helps to "verbalize" what you want Solver to do

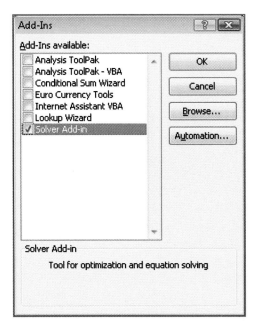

Figure 9-6: *The Add-Ins dialog box lists additional programs you can make available within Excel.*

TIP

If you're not sure which cells to select for changing cells, clicking **Guess** will have Solver return all nonformula cells referenced by the formula in the target cell.

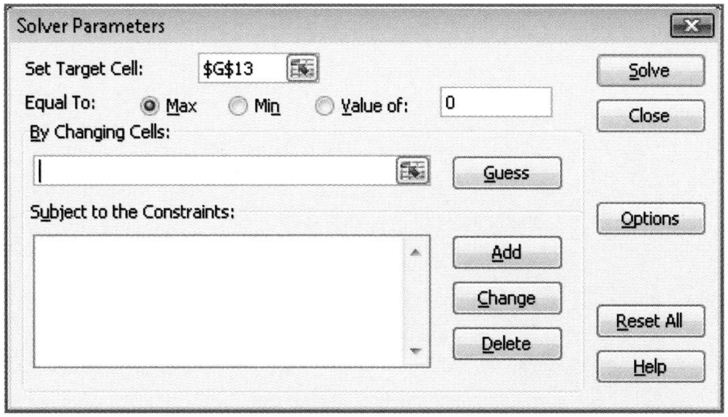

Figure 9-7: *Setting the target cell, indicating what cells are to be changed, and listing constraints in the Solver Parameters dialog box provides all that's needed to run Solver.*

SET UP SOLVER

1. In the Data tab Analysis group, click **Solver**. The Solver Parameters dialog box appears, as shown in Figure 9-7.

2. Click the **Set Target Cell** text box, and either type the address of the cell in which you want to see the result or click that cell on the worksheet. (If the dialog box is in your way, click the **Collapse Dialog** button, and then click the cell. Click **Expand Dialog** to return to the full-size Solver Parameters dialog box.)

3. In the Equal To area, select what type of value you want the target cell to return: maximized, minimized, or a value you enter.

4. Click the **By Changing Cells** text box. Type the address of the first cell whose value you want Solver to adjust, or click that cell on the worksheet. Hold down **CTRL** while clicking any other cells whose values you want Solver to adjust.

5. If you have constraints, click **Add** to open the Add Constraint dialog box.

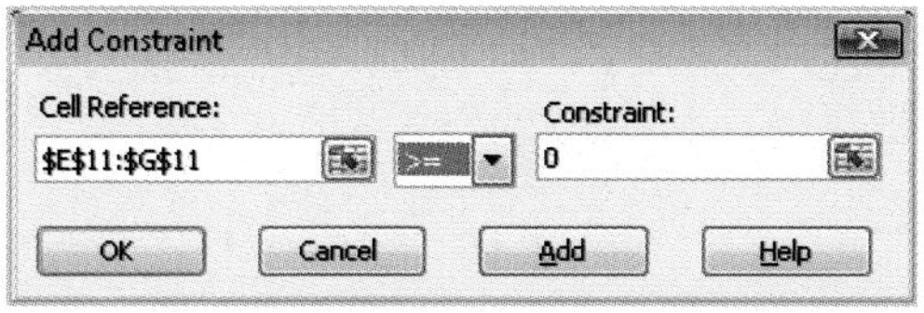

6. Click the **Cell Reference** text box. Type the cell reference that will be subject to your constraint, or select that cell reference on the worksheet.

7. Click the operators' down arrow to see a list of comparison operators, and select the one that matches your constraint. Choosing int (whole numbers) or bin (1 or 0) places integer or binary, respectively, in the Constraint text box.

8. Click **Add** to create another constraint, or click **OK** if you are done adding constraints. The constraints are displayed in the Subject To The Constraints list box.

9. Click **Solve**. The Solver Results dialog box lets you know (or not) that a solution was reached.

Save Solver Results and Settings

You can save the work you do in Solver in several ways.

SAVE VALUES

After running a Solver problem, in the Solver Results dialog box, click **Keep Solver Solution**. The values produced by Solver are added to the worksheet, replacing your original numbers. Save the worksheet by pressing **CTRL+S**.

SAVE AS A SCENARIO

You can save different sets of changing-cells values as scenarios, whose results you can then compare (see "Compare Scenarios" earlier in the chapter).

1. In the Solver Results dialog box, click **Save Scenario**. The Save Scenario dialog box appears.

2. Type a descriptive name for the scenario, and click **OK**.

3. In the Data tab Data Tools group, click **What-If Analysis** and click **Scenario Manager** to view and work with saved Solver and other scenarios.

SAVE SOLVER SETTINGS AS A MODEL

You can save the settings you've created in Solver as a *model*. These settings are copied onto the worksheet and are also made available for you to run at a later time. You can have more than one Solver model saved per worksheet.

1. In the Solver Parameters dialog box, enter your settings and click **Options**. In the Solver Options dialog box, click **Save Model**.

NOTE

To add the settings of a previously saved model in Solver, click **Options** in the Solver Parameter dialog box (see Figure 9-7). In the Solver Options dialog box, click **Load Model**. Select the range that contains the model settings you want to use, and click **OK** in any dialog boxes that might pop up until you return to the Solver Parameters dialog box.

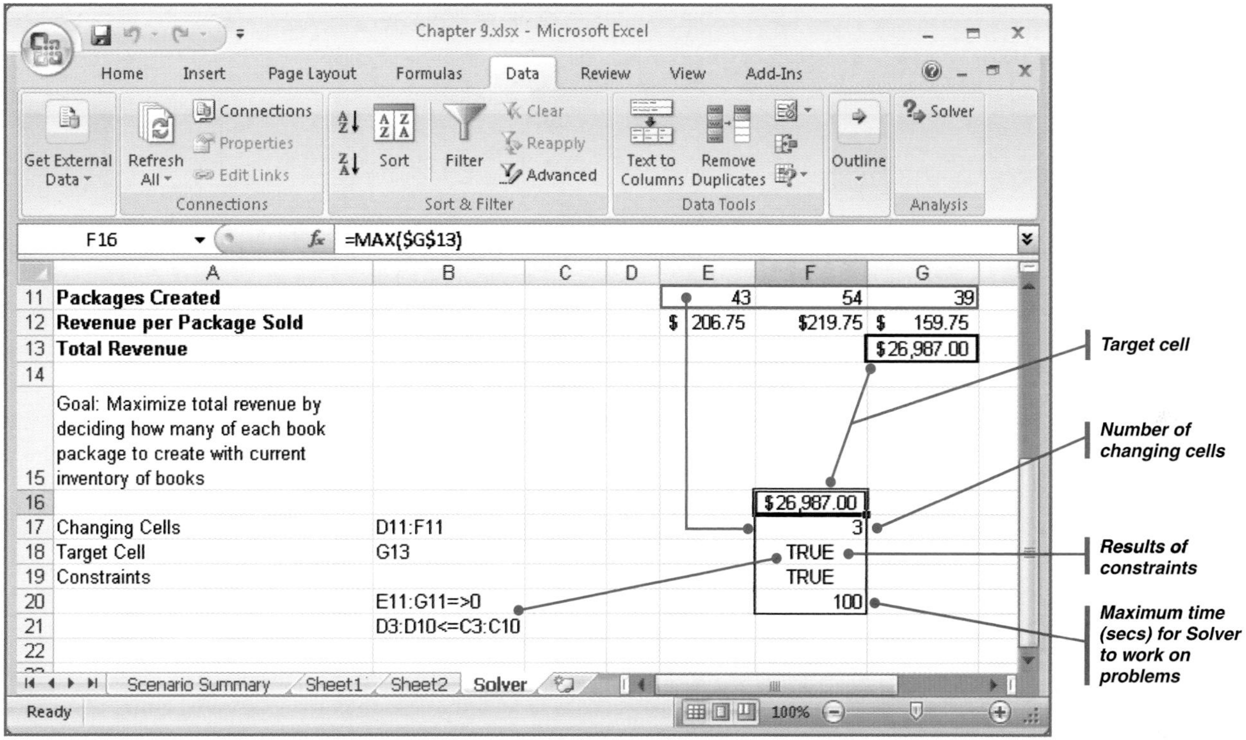

Figure 9-8: **Solver models save problem-solving settings directly on the worksheet.**

2. In the Save Model dialog box, accept or change the range on the worksheet to where the Solver settings will be copied. Each constraint evaluation and three other cells containing parameters of the model are displayed, as shown in Figure 9-8.

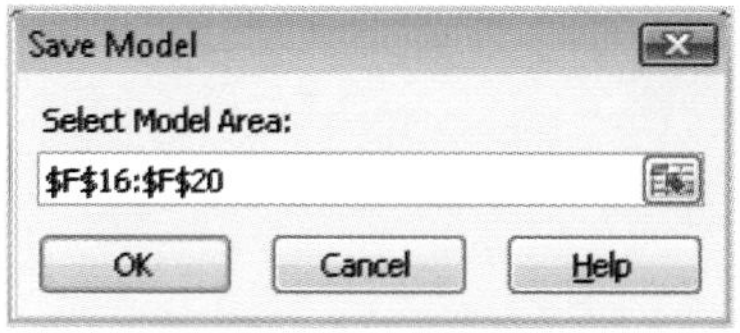

TIP

If you feel you need to give Solver more time or more attempts at reaching a solution, increase the **Max Time** and **Iterations** settings in the Solver Options dialog box. The maximum for each is 32,767 (seconds or interim calculations).

3. Click **OK**.

CHANGING SOLVER SETTINGS

In the Data tab Analysis group, click **Solver**. Perform the following procedures in the Solver Parameters dialog box.

CHANGE TARGET OR REFERENCED CELLS

Make changes to cell references in the Set Target Cell and By Changing Cells areas by typing in the text boxes or clicking cells on the worksheet. Change what the target cell is to be equal to.

CHANGE CONSTRAINTS

1. Select the constraint you want to change, and click **Change**.

2. Make changes in the Change Constraint dialog box, and click **OK**.

START ANEW

To remove all previous settings in the Solver Parameters dialog box, click **Reset All**.

SET ADVANCED OPTIONS

Click **Options**. Changing options in the Solver Options dialog box, as shown in Figure 9-9, should be done by only the most advanced users who work with complex worksheets.

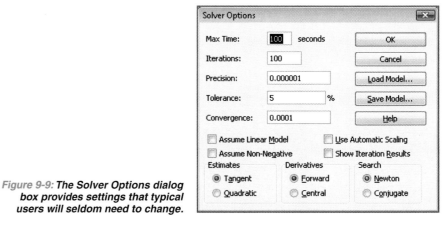

Figure 9-9: *The Solver Options dialog box provides settings that typical users will seldom need to change.*

NOTE

As shown in Figure 9-10, you can use a PivotTable to analyze external data. If you are unfamiliar with importing external data, see Chapter 10. You can also consolidate data from multiple ranges.

Work with PivotTables

PivotTables are Excel's "Swiss Army knife" solution for comparing and analyzing data, especially in larger worksheets. Excel helps you create the initial PivotTable report and lets you quickly make changes that pivot the table, rearranging the data for different solutions. In addition, you can create charts (*PivotCharts*) that graphically show the results of a PivotTable report.

Create a PivotTable

1. Select a cell in a range whose data you want to use in the PivotTable. In the Insert tab Tables group, click **PivotTable**.

   –Or–

   Click a cell in a table whose data you want to use in the PivotTable. In the Design tab (Table Tools) Tools group, click **Summarize With Pivot**.

   In either case, the Create PivotTable dialog box appears, shown in Figure 9-10.

2. Modify the range you want included in the PivotTable, if needed, or click **Use An External Data Source**.

3. Click **New Worksheet** to have Excel create a new worksheet for the report.

   –Or–

   Click **Existing Worksheet** and click the worksheet tab and upper-left cells for where you want the PivotTable report to begin.

QUICKFACTS

UNDERSTANDING PIVOTTABLE TERMS

PivotTables can be daunting at first. Knowing the terminology will get you started on a good footing:

- **Field** is a substitute term used for the column header label(s) in the table or range where your data is located.
- The **Report Filter** box holds fields that filter the PivotTable.
- The **Row Labels** box allows you to display each category of that item in its own row. Typically, these items are descriptive and identifying, not numerical—for example, Country, Salesperson, and Title.
- The **Column Labels** box allows you to display each category of the item in its own column. Typically, these items are descriptive and identifying, not numerical—for example, Population, Sales, and Pages.
- The **Values** box allows you to sum or otherwise perform calculations and display the results. Typically, these items are numerical and capable of being counted, summed, and calculated.

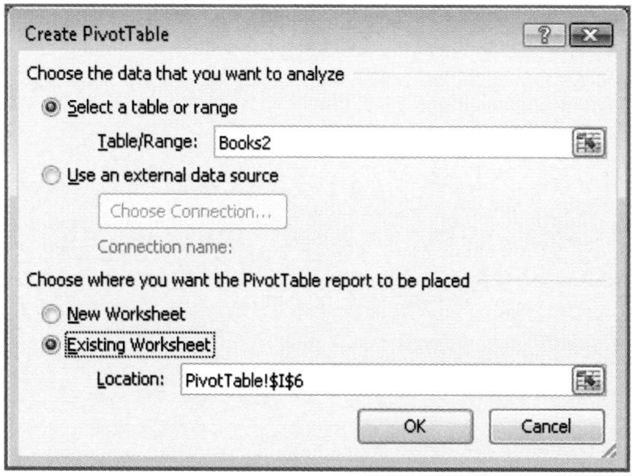

Figure 9-10: ***You need to supply minimal information to start a PivotTable.***

4. Click **OK** when finished. The Excel window changes in three major ways (see Figure 9-11): the framework of a PivotTable is inserted where you specified, a field list task pane is displayed on the right side of the worksheet window, and Options and Design tabs (PivotTable Tools) are added to the ribbon.

Create the PivotTable Layout

1. Create an initial PivotTable (see the previous procedure).
2. Click the check box next to a field (or column header from your table or range) from the PivotTable Field list at the top of the task pane. Depending on the type of data contained in the field, Excel will assign it to an area at the bottom of the task pane. Start by selecting fields that contain data that you want to display as row labels (see Figure 9-12). You can include more than one field in a box, and you can deselect a field's check box to remove it from an area.
3. Next, select a field that provides the initial summary information you are looking for. If the field contains numbers or formulas, Excel will initially place it in the Values area. This is the start of a meaningful PivotTable, as shown in Figure 9-13.

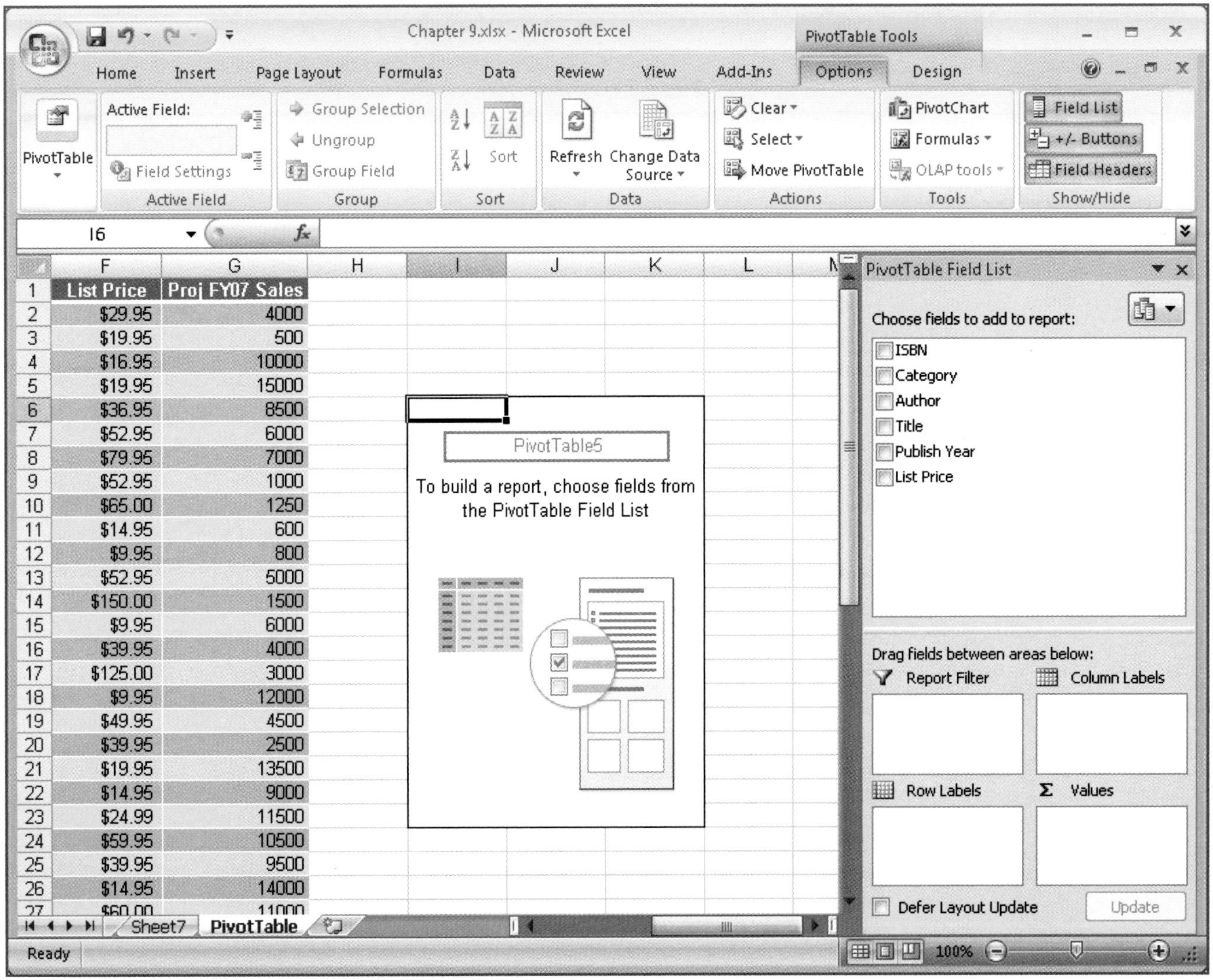

Figure 9-11: *Excel provides an Options tab and a task pane to facilitate your work with PivotTables.*

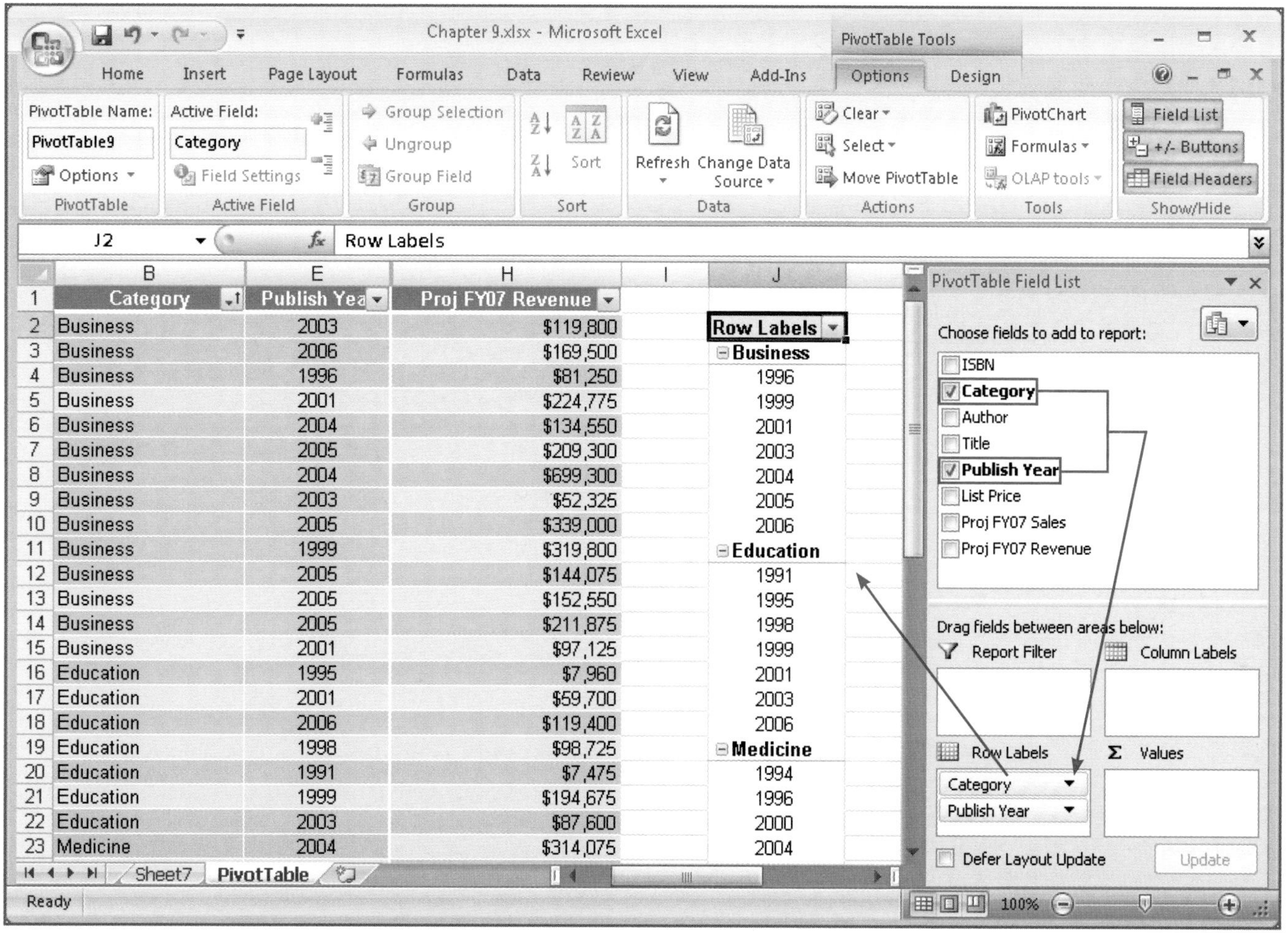

Figure 9-12: *Start a PivotTable by selecting the fields to be used as row or column labels.*

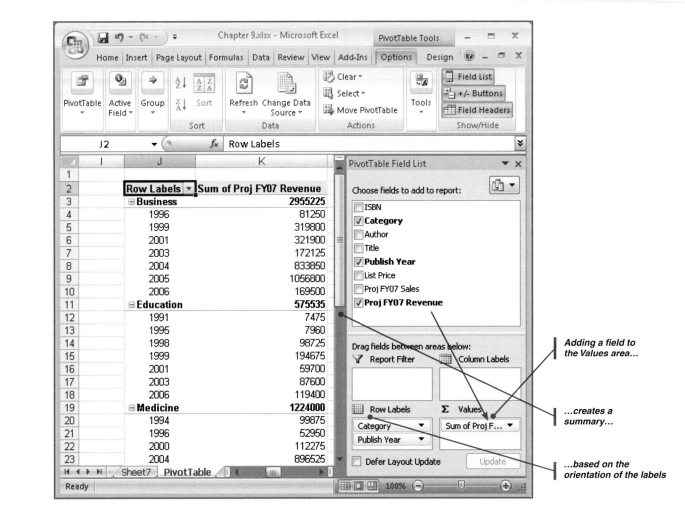

Figure 9-13: **This sample PivotTable shows sales summarized by years within a category using row labels.**

4. See your data in a different aspect by dragging a row label to the Column Labels area (or vice versa).

–Or–

Click the field icon down arrow of the field you want to move, and click one of the direction options.

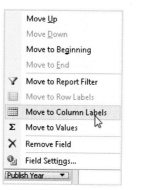

Figure 9-14 shows how the data in the PivotTable in Figure 9-13 changes when a field is moved from a row label to a column label.

Style a PivotTable

Excel offers a similar set of prebuilt styles to PivotTables as it does standard tables, along with styling and layout options.

SELECT A STYLE

1. Click a cell in the PivotTable

   –Or–

   In the Options tab (PivotTable Tools) Actions group, click **Select** and click **Entire Table**.

2. In the Design tab (PivotTable Tools) PivotTable Styles group, point to the style examples on the ribbon.

   –Or–

   Click the row-by-row buttons.

   –Or–

   Click the **More** button to see the complete gallery.

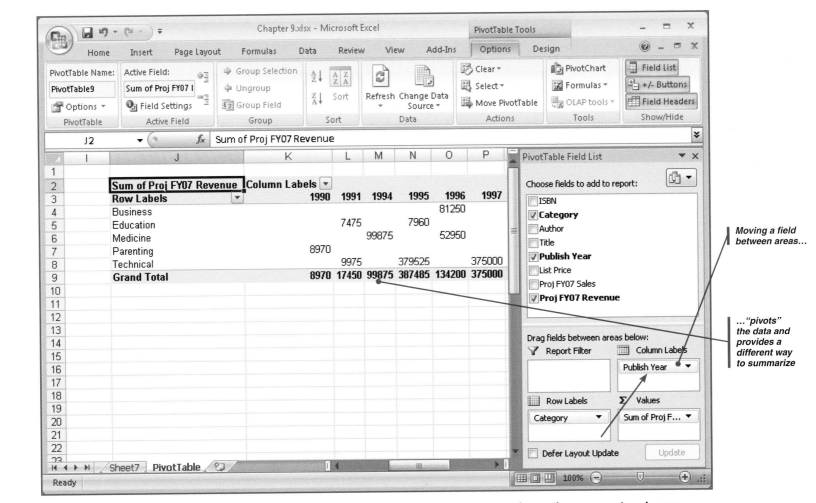

Figure 9-14: *By simply moving a field between the Row Labels and Column Labels area, you can change the summary to columnar year-by-year totals.*

USING PIVOTTABLES

PivotTables can utilize many features that are employed in tables, outlines, and in general worksheet usage. Access these features on the Options tab (PivotTable Tools) or by right-clicking specific PivotTable elements and selecting them from the context menu. Here is a sampling of the options you have available to you.

Start by selecting a cell in the PivotTable.

SORT AND FILTER PIVOTTABLES

1. Click the **AutoFilter** down arrow of the orientation header you want to sort or filter the data on.

2. Click the **Select Field** down arrow (only available if you have nested fields or labels), and click the field to sort or filter by.

3. Click one of the sort or filter options on the menu (see Chapter 8 for more information on sorting and filtering).

   –Or–

   Click the field you want to sort by directly on the PivotTable, and use the Sort group on the Options tab for the same sorting options.

HIDE OR SHOW THE PIVOTTABLE FIELD LIST TASK PANE

In the Options tab (PivotTable Tools) Show/Hide group, click Field List. Click it a second time to redisplay the task pane.

Continued . . .

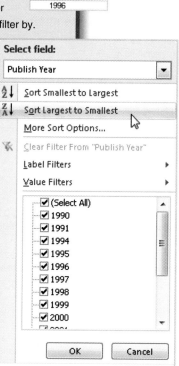

In all cases, pointing to a Quick Style icon will change the PivotTable to reflect the style attributes. (For more information on applying styles to PivotTables, see the discussion in Chapter 8 on applying styles to tables.)

CHANGE THE PIVOTTABLE'S LAYOUT

You can add some readability to a PivotTable by choosing a more expanded layout. For example, you can display the table in an outline or tabular layout.

1. Click a cell in the PivotTable.

2. In the Design tab (PivotTable Tools) Layout group, click **Report Layout**.

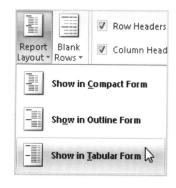

3. Click each of the layout options to see which one presents your data in the best form for your purposes. One example is shown in Figure 9-15.

Create a PivotTable Chart

1. Click a cell in the PivotTable.

2. In the Options tab (PivotTables Tools) Tools group, click **PivotChart**. The Insert Chart dialog box displays chart types (see Chapter 6 for information on building and working with charts).

QUICKSTEPS

USING PIVOTTABLES *(Continued)*

APPLY CURRENCY FORMATS TO A VALUE FIELD

PivotTables don't extract the cell formatting from the table or range where the data originates. To add currency (or other numbering formats):

1. Select a cell in a field to which you want to add currency formatting.

2. In the Options tab (PivotTable Tools) Active Field group, click **Field Settings**. Make any changes to how the field is calculated, and click **Number Format**.

3. In the Format Cells dialog box, click **Currency**, select the formatting you want, and click **OK**.

Category	Publish Year	Sum of Proj FY07 Revenue
⊟Business	1996	$81,250
	1999	$319,800
	2001	$321,900
	2003	$172,125
	2004	$833,850
	2005	$1,056,800
	2006	$169,500
Business Total		**$2,955,225**
⊟Education	1991	$7,475
	1995	$7,960
	1998	$98,725
	1999	$194,675
	2001	$59,700
	2003	$87,600
	2006	$119,400
Education Total		**$575,535**
⊟Medicine	1994	$99,875
	1996	$52,950
	2000	$112,275
	2004	$896,525
	2006	$62,375
Medicine Total		**$1,224,000**
⊟Parenting	1990	$8,970
	2005	$255,200
Parenting Total		**$264,170**

Figure 9-15: **You're just a few mouse clicks away from transforming your staid data into something you can use in presentations and other documents.**

TIP

If you do not have the PivotChart Filter Pane displayed (see Figure 9-16), you can easily turn it on. In the Analyze tab (PivotChart Tools) Show/Hide group, click **PivotChart Filter**.

Double-click the type you want. A chart area displays on the worksheet, a PivotChart Tools set of tabs displays on the ribbon, and a PivotChart Filter Pane is available, as shown in Figure 9-16.

3. Make any changes to the PivotTable using the PivotTable tools (for example, collapse fields by clicking the minus signs next to them), and then click the PivotChart to return to charting tabs and tools. The chart will change to reflect changes made to the PivotTable.

4. Use the PivotChart Filter Pane to filter your active fields. When finished, you can get your chart to display only the data you want, an example of which is in Figure 9-17.

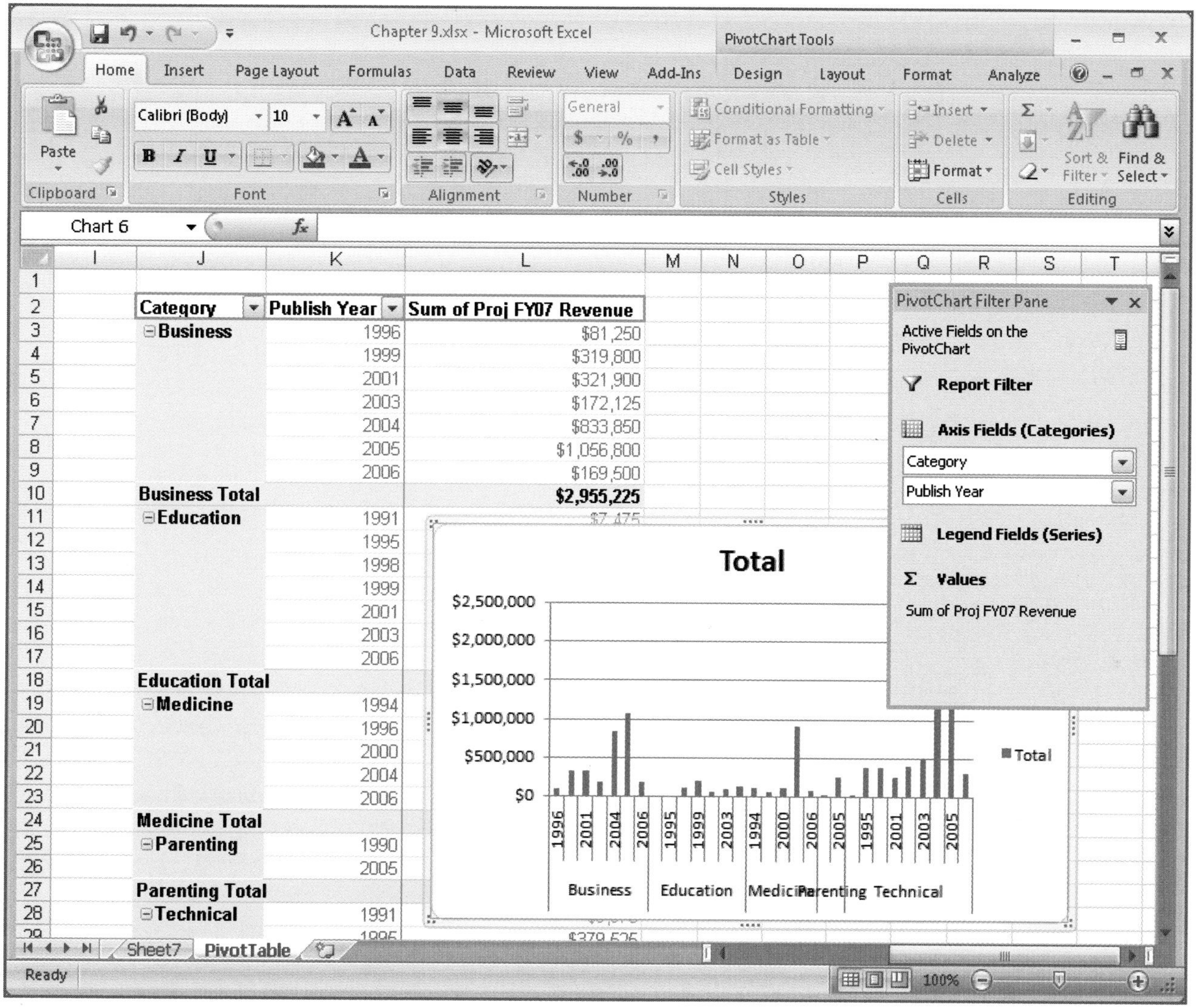

Figure 9-16: *Don't be concerned with how a PivotChart first displays—you can easily modify it to meet your needs.*

Category	Publish Year	Sum of Proj FY07 Revenue
⊕ Business		$2,955,225
⊕ Education		$575,535
⊕ Medicine		$1,224,000
⊕ Parenting		$264,170
⊕ Technical		$5,731,345
Grand Total		**$10,750,275**

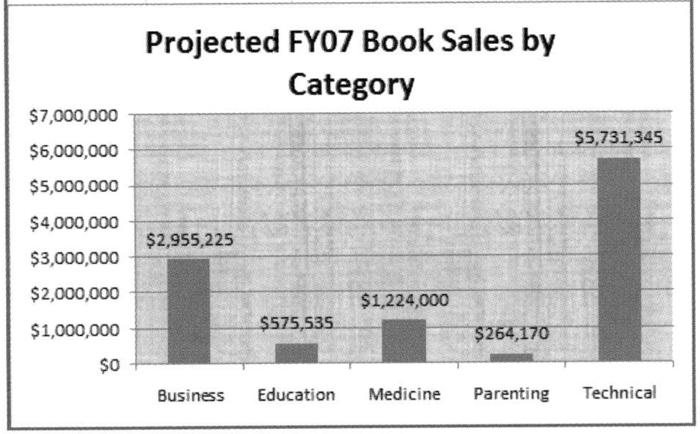

Projected FY07 Book Sales by Category

Business $2,955,225
Education $575,535
Medicine $1,224,000
Parenting $264,170
Technical $5,731,345

Figure 9-17: PivotTables and PivotCharts change dynamically as you modify layout and other options.

General Options

☐ Always create backup

File sharing

Password to open:

Password to modify:

☐ Read-only recommended

OK   Cancel

Work with Other Users

There are several ways to let others work with your data. One way is to control total access to the workbook file, choosing whether to allow others to open the file and/or make modifications. Another way is to provide access to the workbook and *protect* certain elements of the workbook and individual worksheets. You can also *share* the workbook so that all users can edit the same data, even simultaneously, while exercising limited protection.

Protect Workbooks with Passwords

The first level of security Excel offers is simple. If you know the correct password, you can open and/or modify the file.

ADD PASSWORD PROTECTION

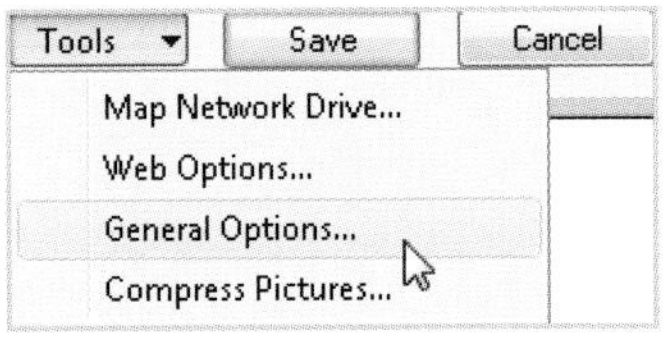

1. With an Excel workbook open, click the **Office Button**, and click **Save As**.

2. In the Save As dialog box, click the **Tools** down arrow (on the bottom next to Save), and click **General Options**.

Tools ▼	Save	Cancel
Map Network Drive...		
Web Options...		
General Options...		
Compress Pictures...		

3. In the General Options dialog box, in the File Sharing area:

   ● Type a password in the **Password To Open** text box to control who can open the workbook.

   ● Type a password in the **Password To Modify** text box to control who can modify contents. (Leaving this password blank allows everyone to make changes; adding a password effectively provides read-only access to those who do not have the password.)

   ● Select **Read-Only Recommended** to prevent changes without requiring a password.

4. Click **OK**. Type the password a second time (or third time if you select both password options), and click **OK**.

5. Click **Save**. If you are working with an existing workbook, click **Yes** to replace the current file.

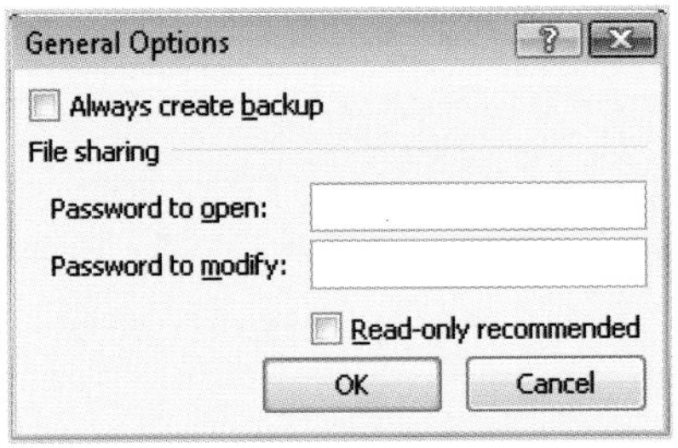

REMOVE A PASSWORD

Only the originator of a file can remove its passwords and thereby turn off access controls.

1. With an Excel workbook open, click the **Office Button** and click **Save As**.

2. In the Save As dialog box, click the **Tools** down arrow, and click **General Options**. In the General Options dialog box, delete the password(s) in the text boxes whose controls you want to remove.

3. Click **OK** and then click **Save**. Click **Yes** to replace the existing file.

Share a Workbook

Shared workbooks are particularly useful for users on a network when multiple people are adding and viewing data in tables (see Chapter 8 for more information on creating and using tables). However, Excel does impose several limitations on what can be accomplished in a shared workbook. Before the workbook is shared by you or by the originator, much of the "design work" of a worksheet should be completed. Shared workbooks are best used for entering and editing data, not making major structural changes. Many of the features that cannot be changed after a worksheet is shared are listed in Table 9-1.

Charts	Outlines
Conditional formats	PivotTables
Data tables	Scenarios
Data validation	Shapes (including pictures and clip art)
Hyperlinks	Subtotals
Macros	Workbook protection
Merged cells	Worksheet protection

Table 9-1: Features That Cannot Be Changed in a Shared Workbook

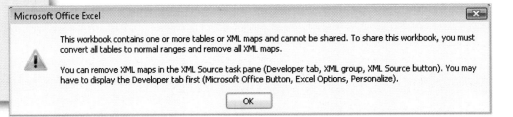

Microsoft Office Excel

This workbook contains one or more tables or XML maps and cannot be shared. To share this workbook, you must convert all tables to normal ranges and remove all XML maps.

You can remove XML maps in the XML Source task pane (Developer tab, XML group, XML Source button). You may have to display the Developer tab first (Microsoft Office Button, Excel Options, Personalize).

OK

1. In the Review tab Changes group, click **Share Workbook**.

2. In the Share Workbook dialog box, select the **Allow Changes By More Than One User At The Same Time** check box. Click **OK**.

Share Workbook

| Editing | Advanced |

☑ Allow changes by more than one user at the same time. This also allows workbook merging.

Who has this workbook open now:

John Cronan (Exclusive) - 9/23/2006 10:59 AM

3. Click **OK** in the confirmation dialog box to continue. You might see a warning dialog box related to replacing external structured references (cell names) with errors. Click **Yes** or **No** to continue, depending on whether that is acceptable to you. If Yes is clicked, the workbook is shared and is so indicated by the word *Shared* added next to the workbook name in the Excel window title bar.

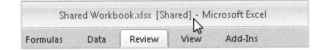

Shared Workbook.xlsx [Shared] - Microsoft Excel

| Formulas | Data | Review | View | Add-Ins |

WORKING WITH CHANGES IN A SHARED WORKBOOK

When sharing a workbook, you can adjust how often changes are kept, when they're updated, and how to resolve conflicts.

ENABLE TRACK CHANGES (IN UNSHARED WORKBOOKS)

When you enable Track Changes, you will also share the workbook.

1. In the Review tab Changes group, click **Track Changes** and click **Highlight Changes**.

2. Click **Track Changes While Editing**. Accept the default settings (the next procedures explains how to change these). Click **OK** to close the Highlight Changes dialog box. Click **OK** again to save the now-shared workbook. (If the workbook has not yet been saved, you will be given the opportunity to name it.)

MODIFY CHANGE ATTRIBUTES

In the Review tab Changes group, click **Track Changes** and click **Highlight Changes**.

- To highlight all changes, deselect the **When**, **Who**, and **Where** check boxes.

- To selectively highlight changes, select options from the When and/or Who drop-down list boxes, and/or click the **Where** text box, and select the range where you want changes highlighted.

Continued . . .

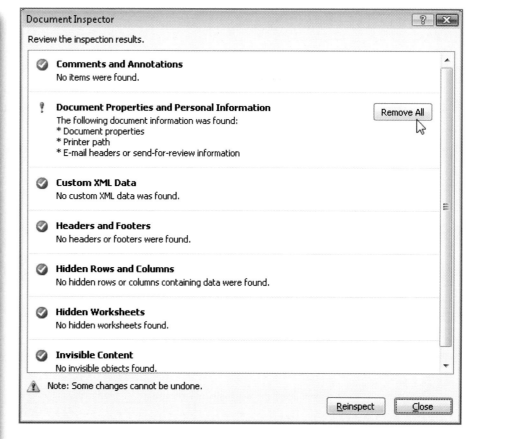

Figure 9-18: *Before you share a workbook (or otherwise provide a workbook to others), run a check for personal and other information you might want to remove.*

Protect a Shared Workbook

Shared workbooks are inherently not secure. (If you wanted them secure, you wouldn't share them.) However, you can protect against other users removing the shared workbook's Track Changes feature and require that a password be used to unprotect it.

1. In the Review tab Changes group, click **Protect Shared Workbook**.

QUICKSTEPS

WORKING WITH CHANGES IN A SHARED WORKBOOK *(Continued)*

- To view changes on-screen, select **Highlight Changes On Screen**.

| Change indicator | Placing mouse pointer on a changed cell... | ... opens a comment providing information on the change |

John Cronan, 9/23/2006 12:21 PM:
Changed cell D5 from '$16,975.00 ' to '$16,200.00 '.

- To view changes on a separate worksheet, select **List Changes On A New Sheet**. A History worksheet is added to the workbook, as shown in Figure 9-19.

WORKING WITH CHANGES IN A SHARED WORKBOOK

1. In the Review tab Changes group, click **Share Workbook** and click **Advanced**.

2. To change whether and for how long changes are tracked, change the settings in the Track Changes area.

3. To determine when changes are updated and whether to view changes by others, change the settings in the Update Changes area.

4. To determine how conflicting changes are handled, in the Conflicting Changes Between Users area, determine how conflicts will be resolved.

5. Click **OK** when finished.

ACCEPT OR REJECT CHANGES

1. In the Review tab Changes group, click **Track Changes** and click **Accept/Reject Changes**.

Continued . . .

2. In the Protect Shared Workbook dialog box, click **Sharing With Track Changes**.

3. Click **OK**. Click **OK** a second time to save the workbook.

   –Or–

   If the workbook is not shared at this time, type a password and click **OK**. In the Confirm Password dialog box, type the password a second time, and click **OK**. Click **OK** a third time to save the workbook. (If you are using a new workbook that hasn't yet been saved with a file name, you will be given that opportunity.)

Discontinue Sharing a Workbook

To stop sharing a workbook, you must first remove all users who may have the shared workbook open (contact any users and make sure they save any recent changes). In addition, if you need to keep a record of changes, save the data in the History worksheet (see Figure 9-19) to another workbook or other location before you try to stop sharing.

1. Open the shared workbook, and remove workbook protection by clicking **Unprotect Shared Workbook** in the Review tab Changes group, if enabled (see "Protect a Shared Workbook").

2. In the Review tab Changes group, click **Share Workbook**.

3. On the Editing tab, select any users other than yourself, and click **Remove User**.

4. Deselect the **Allow Changes By More Than One User At The Same Time** check box.

5. Click **OK**. Click **Yes** to accept losing the change history and any unsaved changes by other users.

UICKSTEPS

WORKING WITH CHANGES IN A SHARED WORKBOOK (Continued)

2. In the Select Changes To Accept Or Reject dialog box, select options from the When and/or Who drop-down list boxes, and/or click the **Where** text box, and select the range where you want changes highlighted. Click **OK**.

3. When a conflict arises due to different users changing the same data, accept either your own or the change(s) made by the other user(s) in the Accept Or Reject Changes dialog box.

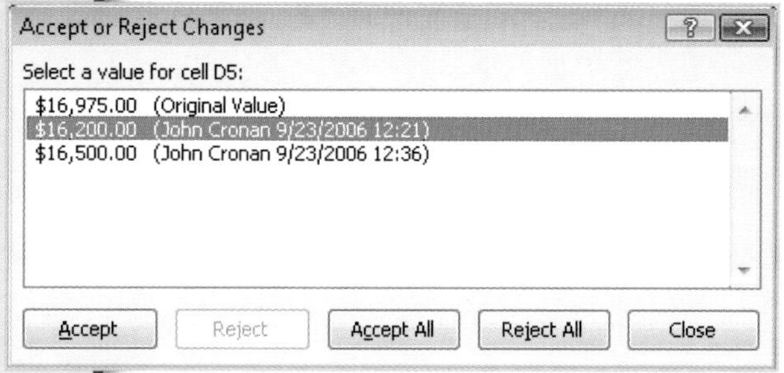

Accept or Reject Changes

Select a value for cell D5:

$16,975.00 (Original Value)
$16,200.00 (John Cronan 9/23/2006 12:21)
$16,500.00 (John Cronan 9/23/2006 12:36)

[Accept] [Reject] [Accept All] [Reject All] [Close]

*Figure 9-19: **In shared workbooks, you can opt to have changes recorded on a separate History worksheet.***

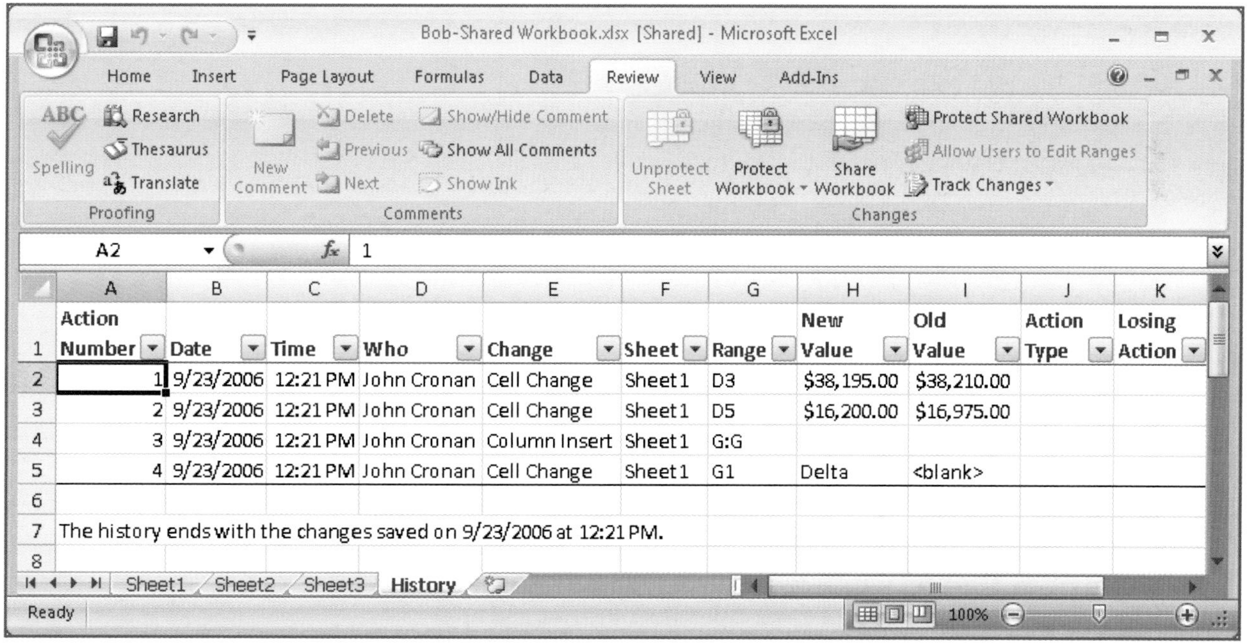

Bob-Shared Workbook.xlsx [Shared] - Microsoft Excel

Home   Insert   Page Layout   Formulas   Data   Review   View   Add-Ins

A2   fx   1

	A	B	C	D	E	F	G	H	I	J	K
1	Action Number	Date	Time	Who	Change	Sheet	Range	New Value	Old Value	Action Type	Losing Action
2	1	9/23/2006	12:21 PM	John Cronan	Cell Change	Sheet1	D3	$38,195.00	$38,210.00		
3	2	9/23/2006	12:21 PM	John Cronan	Cell Change	Sheet1	D5	$16,200.00	$16,975.00		
4	3	9/23/2006	12:21 PM	John Cronan	Column Insert	Sheet1	G:G				
5	4	9/23/2006	12:21 PM	John Cronan	Cell Change	Sheet1	G1	Delta	<blank>		
6											
7	The history ends with the changes saved on 9/23/2006 at 12:21 PM.										
8											

Sheet1 / Sheet2 / Sheet3 / **History**

Ready   100%

Not all changes are tracked. Tracked changes include changes to cell contents created by editing, moving and copying, and inserting and removing rows and columns.

Let's say you e-mail a workbook you have shared to three college-attending children and instruct each to update their spending according to the worksheet you provide. You get back three workbooks and want to reconcile the changes on your master copy. You would think Excel would provide a mechanism to do that—and as it turns out it does, but not without some effort on your part. The command is not available on the ribbon, so a little sleuthing is required to find it. Click the **Office Button**, click **Excel Options**, and click **Customize**. Click the **Choose Commands From** down arrow, and select **All Commands**. Scroll down the list of commands, and double-click **Compare And Merge Workbooks**. Click **OK** to close the Excel Options dialog box and add the command to the Quick Access toolbar. Place all four copies of the workbook in a folder, and open the master copy. Click **Compare And Merge Workbooks** on the Quick Access toolbar. Select the three other workbooks (click one file and hold down **CTRL** while clicking the other two), and click **OK**. Data in the master copy is updated according to any changes in the other files.

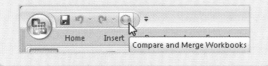

Work with Views

Although you can create custom views at any time, not just when working in a shared environment, the feature is especially useful when sharing a workbook. Each user's view can be saved with many personalized display settings, so the next time each user opens the workbook, the same worksheet that he or she was last working on will be displayed with the same print settings, filter settings, and other settings. Users can create other views and switch to them as well.

CREATE A CUSTOM VIEW

Set up any filters, print settings (including print areas), zoom magnifications, and other settings as you want them saved.

1. In the View tab Workbook views group, click **Custom Views**. The Custom Views dialog box lists your default *personal* view that appears when you open the workbook.

2. Click **Add**. In the Add View dialog box, type a descriptive name, and choose whether to include print settings, filter settings, and hidden rows and columns. Click **OK**.

3. Set up and add any other views. Click **OK** when done.

NOTE

If you are a member of a Microsoft Windows domain, you can allow other users to edit specific areas of a worksheet and set permissions for each user. In addition, you can restrict access to users until their credentials are verified by a Microsoft verification service (see Figure 9-20). Though both of these features are beyond the scope of this book, it's interesting to see what level security is at in larger organizations.

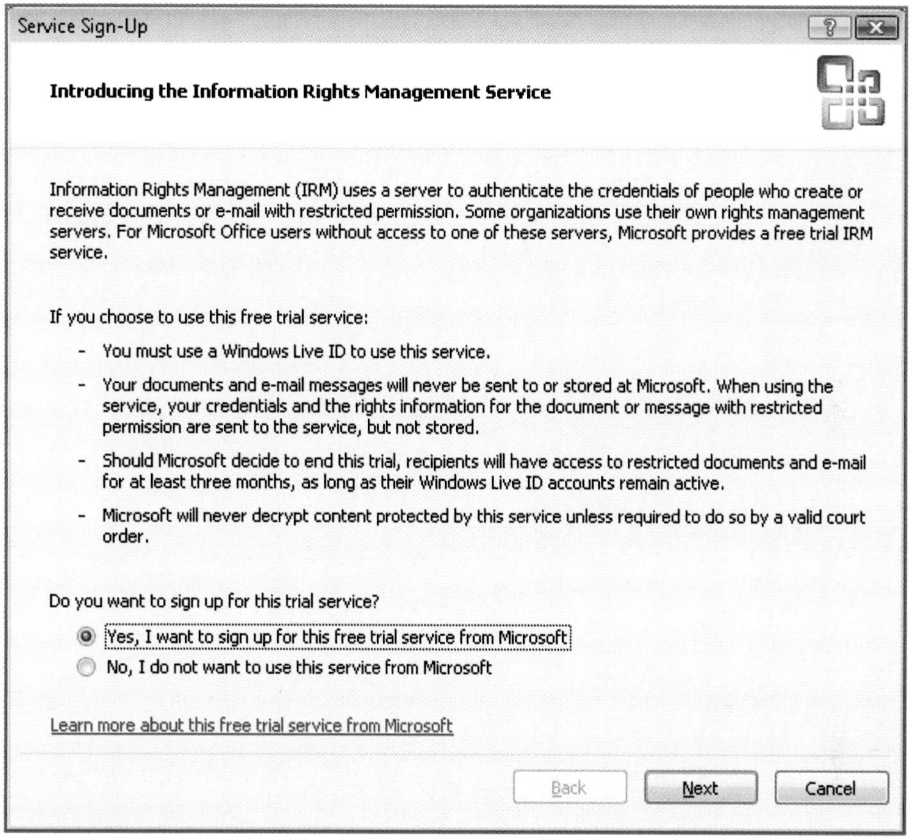

Service Sign-Up

Introducing the Information Rights Management Service

Information Rights Management (IRM) uses a server to authenticate the credentials of people who create or receive documents or e-mail with restricted permission. Some organizations use their own rights management servers. For Microsoft Office users without access to one of these servers, Microsoft provides a free trial IRM service.

If you choose to use this free trial service:

- You must use a Windows Live ID to use this service.

- Your documents and e-mail messages will never be sent to or stored at Microsoft. When using the service, your credentials and the rights information for the document or message with restricted permission are sent to the service, but not stored.

- Should Microsoft decide to end this trial, recipients will have access to restricted documents and e-mail for at least three months, as long as their Windows Live ID accounts remain active.

- Microsoft will never decrypt content protected by this service unless required to do so by a valid court order.

Do you want to sign up for this trial service?

⊙ Yes, I want to sign up for this free trial service from Microsoft

○ No, I do not want to use this service from Microsoft

Learn more about this free trial service from Microsoft

Back   Next   Cancel

*Figure 9-20: **You can subscribe to a verification service and restrict workbook access only to vetted users.***

CHANGE VIEWS

In the View tab Workbook views group, click **Custom Views**. In the Custom Views dialog box, select the view you want to display, and click **Show**. To remove a view, select it and click **Delete**.

Protect Worksheet and Workbook Elements

If you generally "share" workbooks with others without formally creating a shared workbook, you can control whether several elements of both worksheets and workbooks can be changed.

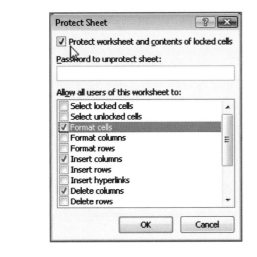

Figure 9-21: **You can protect worksheet elements selectively without sharing a workbook.**

PROTECT WORKSHEET ELEMENTS

Worksheet protection applies only to the currently active worksheet.

1. In the Review tab Changes group, click **Protect Sheet**.

2. Ensure that the **Protect Worksheet And Contents Of Locked Cells** check box is selected (see Figure 9-21). Optionally, type a password that will be needed to unprotect the worksheet.

3. Select the check boxes in the Allow All Users Of This Worksheet To list box for only those actions you want others to be able to perform. Click **OK**. If necessary, confirm the password and click **OK**.

PROTECT WORKBOOK ELEMENTS

1. In the Review tab Changes group, click **Protect Workbook** and click **Protect Structure And Windows**. In the Protect Structure And Windows dialog box:

- Select **Structure** to prevent changes to noncontent aspects of the workbook, which include viewing hidden worksheets; inserting, moving, deleting, renaming, or hiding worksheets; moving and copying worksheets; and creating a scenario summary report.

- Select **Windows** to prevent resizing and repositioning workbook windows.

2. Optionally, enter a password. Click **OK**. If necessary, confirm the password and click **OK**.

How to...

- Convert Text to Data
- Add a Table from an Access Database
- Get Data from the Web
- Add External Data from Existing Connections
- Setting External Data Range Properties
- Manage Connections
- Understanding the Difference Between Save and Publish
- Save a Workbook as a Web Page
- Publish Workbook Items as a Web Page
- Understanding Excel Services
- Use Hyperlinks
- Use Recorded Macros
- Edit a Macro

Chapter 10
Extending Excel

In the final chapter of this book, you will learn several techniques that you can use to extend Excel beyond the desktop. Chapter 8 described how you could manage data of your own. In this chapter you will have to connect to data from several disparate sources, including Web pages from the Internet. Excel maintains a record of these connections, which you will see how to manage. You will also learn how to publish data to Web pages for use on Web sites of your own, and will be introduced to Excel Services, a server product for distributing your work to anyone, anywhere, with an Internet connection and a Web browser. Finally, you'll see how you can automate steps you take in Excel by creating macros.

Connecting to external data sources to import data can quickly become an involved and complicated endeavor. System and database administrators might need to get involved to ensure that you have the proper authorization to access the network, the servers involved, and the data itself. If you need to connect to data beyond the three types described in this section, contact your technical support resources.

From SQL Server
Create a connection to a SQL Server table. Import data into Excel as a Table or PivotTable report.

From Analysis Services
Create a connection to a SQL Server Analysis Services cube. Import data into Excel as a Table or PivotTable report.

From XML Data Import
Open or map a XML file into Excel.

From Data Connection Wizard
Import data for an unlisted format by using the Data Connection Wizard and OLEDB.

From Microsoft Query
Import data for an unlisted format by using the Microsoft Query Wizard and ODBC.

Acquire Data

In addition to typing data directly onto a worksheet or entering data by using a form—both of which are time-consuming and prone to error—you can import data from an external source into Excel. Once the data is "safely" on an Excel worksheet, you have all the tools and features this book describes to format, organize, analyze, or otherwise whip the data into the shape you want. You can import data from several *data sources*, including text files, the Web, and databases. Data sources include the *connections* to source data, and are comprised of the information needed to locate the data (or database server), as well as information needed to access the data, such as user names and passwords.

Convert Text to Data

Text files are files with file extensions such as TXT and CSV (comma-separated values) that can be formatted using commas, spaces, tabs, and other separators to organize data. Though the data might not appear to be structured, as shown in Figure 10-1, Excel can correctly place the data into columns and rows as long as it is separated in a consistent and recognizable format.

1. Select the cell into which you want to place the beginning of the range of imported data.

2. On the Data tab Get External Data group, click **From Text**. In the Import Text File dialog box, locate the text file you want, select it, and click **Import**. Step 1 of the Text Import Wizard opens.

Figure 10-1: Text files might look like a jumble of unrelated data, but Excel can "see through" the clutter to properly format files.

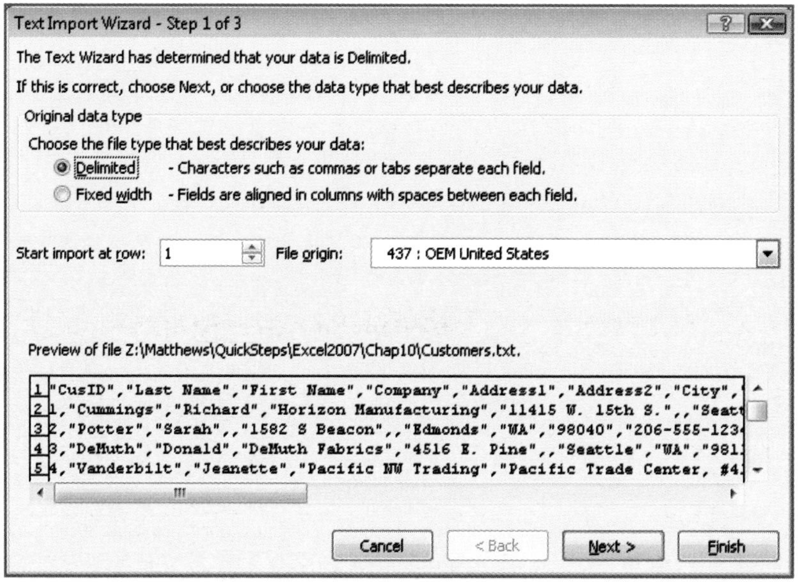

Figure 10-2: Excel provides an educated guess as to how the data in a text file should be divided.

3. Preview the file in the lower half of the dialog box. If all appears to be in order, Excel has done a good job so far. If needed, make the following choices or decisions (see Figure 10-2), which immediately change the preview:

   - Determine if the file is delimited (separated) by characters or if it is a fixed width. You can further refine your choice in Step 2 of the wizard.

   - Decide from where in the text file you want to start importing data. You may not want the headers row if the file already contains one. In that case, you would change the Start Import At Row spinner to 2.

   - Choose a file origin that matches the text language used in the file.

4. Click **Next** or—if you feel "lucky"—click **Finish**. (You can always delete and start over again).

5. Step 2 of the wizard lets you fine-tune the delimiter used or set field widths (depending on your choice in Step 1) and preview how the changes align the data. Experiment with the delimiter option or column widths, and see which makes the preview most representative of how you want the data organized. Click **Next** or **Finish**.

6. Step 3 of the wizard lets you apply data formats on a column-by-column basis. You can also format the columns in the worksheet. Click **Finish**.

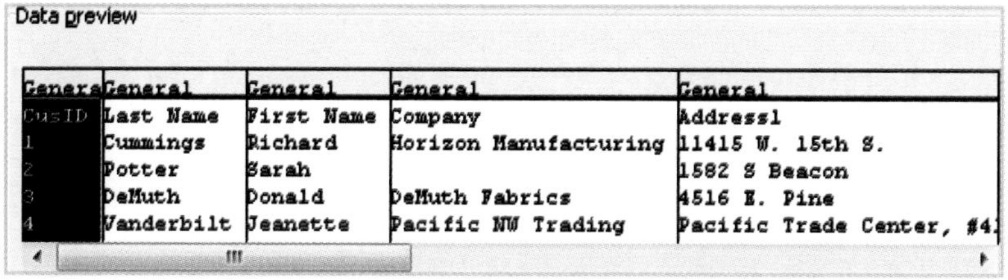

7. Verify where you want the data placed—either in the current worksheet or in a new worksheet. Make your choice and click **OK**. The data is displayed in Excel, as shown in Figure 10-3.

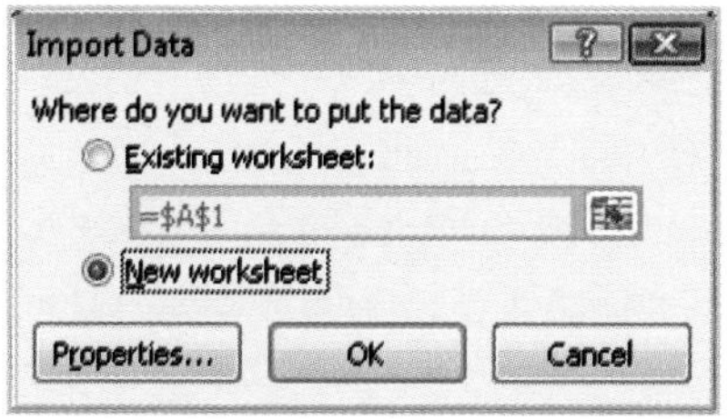

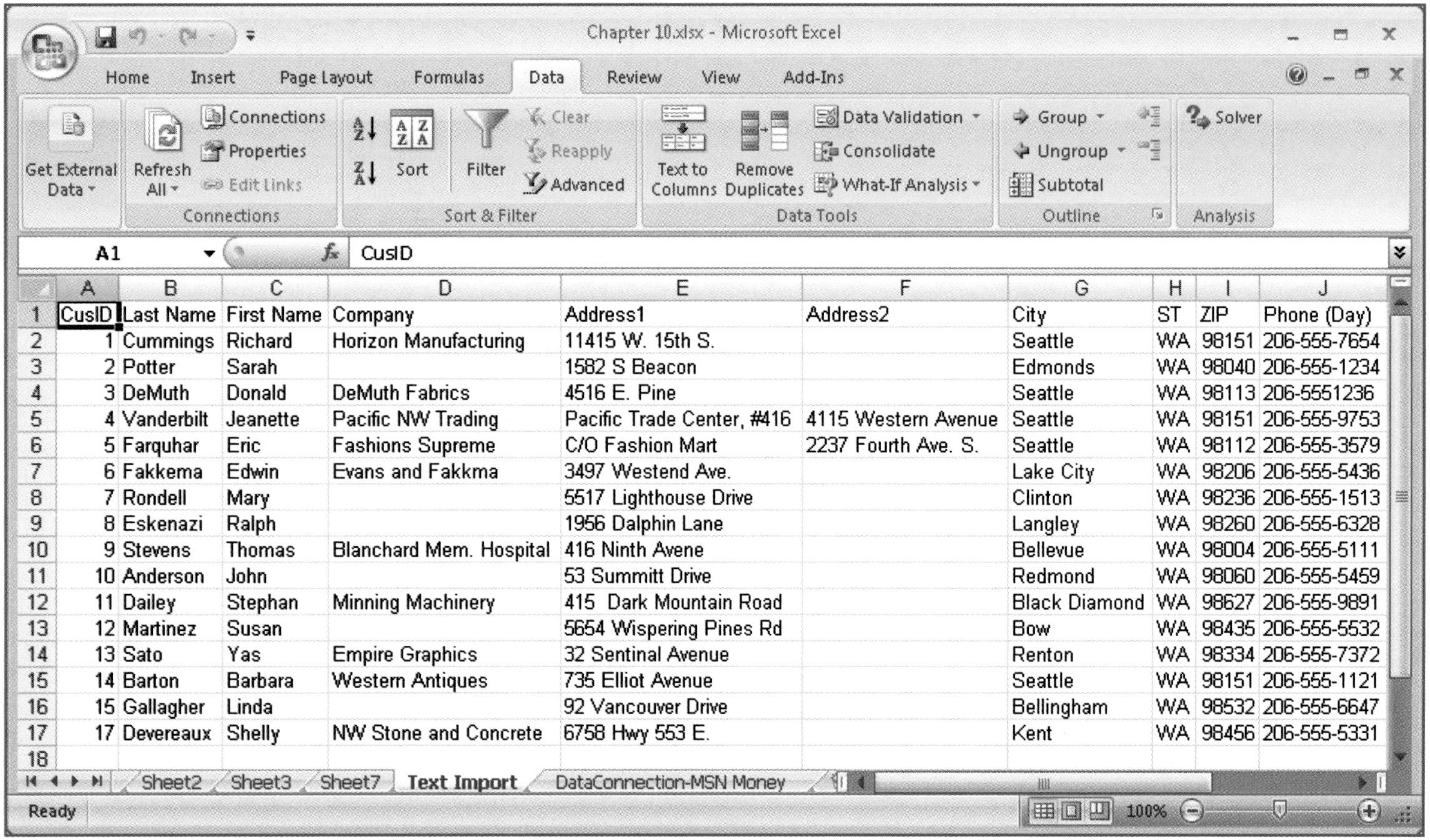

	A	B	C	D	E	F	G	H	I	J
1	CusID	Last Name	First Name	Company	Address1	Address2	City	ST	ZIP	Phone (Day)
2	1	Cummings	Richard	Horizon Manufacturing	11415 W. 15th S.		Seattle	WA	98151	206-555-7654
3	2	Potter	Sarah		1582 S Beacon		Edmonds	WA	98040	206-555-1234
4	3	DeMuth	Donald	DeMuth Fabrics	4516 E. Pine		Seattle	WA	98113	206-5551236
5	4	Vanderbilt	Jeanette	Pacific NW Trading	Pacific Trade Center, #416	4115 Western Avenue	Seattle	WA	98151	206-555-9753
6	5	Farquhar	Eric	Fashions Supreme	C/O Fashion Mart	2237 Fourth Ave. S.	Seattle	WA	98112	206-555-3579
7	6	Fakkema	Edwin	Evans and Fakkma	3497 Westend Ave.		Lake City	WA	98206	206-555-5436
8	7	Rondell	Mary		5517 Lighthouse Drive		Clinton	WA	98236	206-555-1513
9	8	Eskenazi	Ralph		1956 Dalphin Lane		Langley	WA	98260	206-555-6328
10	9	Stevens	Thomas	Blanchard Mem. Hospital	416 Ninth Avene		Bellevue	WA	98004	206-555-5111
11	10	Anderson	John		53 Summitt Drive		Redmond	WA	98060	206-555-5459
12	11	Dailey	Stephan	Minning Machinery	415 Dark Mountain Road		Black Diamond	WA	98627	206-555-9891
13	12	Martinez	Susan		5654 Wispering Pines Rd		Bow	WA	98435	206-555-5532
14	13	Sato	Yas	Empire Graphics	32 Sentinal Avenue		Renton	WA	98334	206-555-7372
15	14	Barton	Barbara	Western Antiques	735 Elliot Avenue		Seattle	WA	98151	206-555-1121
16	15	Gallagher	Linda		92 Vancouver Drive		Bellingham	WA	98532	206-555-6647
17	17	Devereaux	Shelly	NW Stone and Concrete	6758 Hwy 553 E.		Kent	WA	98456	206-555-5331
18										

***Figure 10-3:* Data imported from a text file is indistinguishable from other data in a worksheet.**

> **TIP**
>
> After you have imported data from a data source, such as an Access database, a data source *connection* is created and saved in a new folder under your user Documents folder, titled My Data Sources. The next time you want to import data from that source, click **Connections** in the Connections group on the Data tab.

Add a Table from an Access Database

You can add data from a Microsoft Access database by choosing from a list of tables that the database contains.

1. Select the cell into which you want to place the beginning of the range of imported data.
2. On the Data tab Get External Data group, click **From Access**. In the Select Data Source dialog box, locate and select the Access database that contains the table of data you want. Click **Open**.

3. In the Select Table dialog box, select the table you want, and click **OK**.

4. In the Import Data dialog box, select in which form you want the data and where you want the data placed—either in the current worksheet or in a new worksheet. Make your selections and click **OK**.

Get Data from the Web

More and more data is being offered on the Web sites of companies and individuals. In the past, you were limited to copying and pasting, which tended to provide inconsistent formatting and, often, just plain strange results. Excel now lets you select what pieces of data you want from a Web page and import them in a few clicks.

1. Select the cell into which you want to place the beginning of the range of imported data.

2. On the Data tab Get External Data group, click **From Web**. The New Web Query dialog box appears.

3. Type the address of the Web site from which you want to retrieve data, and then navigate to the page where the data is located.

4. Click the table selection arrow in the upper-leftmost corner of each table whose data you want. The arrow changes to a check mark when selected (see Figure 10-4).

5. Click **Options** on the toolbar to open the Web Query Options dialog box. Make any formatting or other importing changes, and click **OK**.

TIP

You can select more than one table when you import data from the Web, but all the selected data must be on the current Web page.

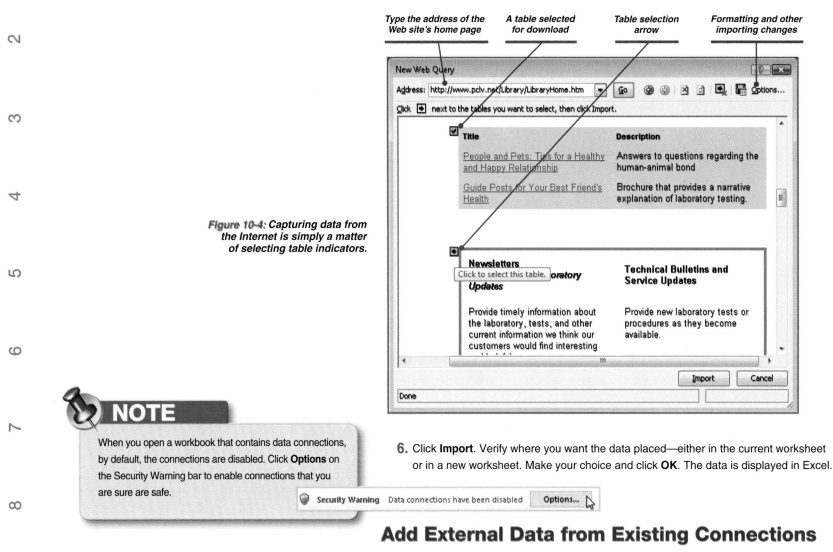

Type the address of the Web site's home page

A table selected for download

Table selection arrow

Formatting and other importing changes

Figure 10-4: *Capturing data from the Internet is simply a matter of selecting table indicators.*

6. Click **Import**. Verify where you want the data placed—either in the current worksheet or in a new worksheet. Make your choice and click **OK**. The data is displayed in Excel.

Add External Data from Existing Connections

You can import data from any existing connection files that are available on your computer or network. If you have not yet added data connections (see "Add Connections" later in the chapter), you might be able to add prebuilt

SETTING EXTERNAL DATA RANGE PROPERTIES

You can change several parameters that affect an external data range. You can change when the data is refreshed, the name of the connection, and formatting properties.

Click a cell in an external data range. In the Data tab Connections group, click **Properties**. The External Data Range Properties dialog box appears, shown in Figure 10-5.

SET WHEN TO REFRESH

In the Refresh Control area, select whether you want to enable background (automatic) refreshes and when you want them, either by time and/or when the workbook is opened.

DETERMINE HOW IMPORTED DATA APPEARS

In the Data Formatting And Layout area, select the formatting and layout options that you want. Avoid including row numbers, unless you absolutely need them. It only tends to confuse things with the row numbering provided by Excel.

CONTROL HOW NEW ROWS ARE ADDED

In the area under If The Number Of Rows, decide if, when refreshing, you want to add new cells, new rows, or overwrite existing cells when there are more rows in the source data than in the worksheet.

connections provided by others. Excel provides sample connections you can use to download information from Microsoft Web sites.

1. Click the cell in a worksheet that will be the upper-left corner of the range for the external data.

2. In the Data tab Get External Data group, click **Existing Connections**. In the Existing Connections dialog box, select the connection you want from your network or computer, and click **Open**.

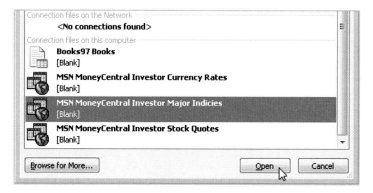

3. Verify where you want the data placed in the Import Data dialog box, and click **OK**. The data is imported.

Manage Connections

Connections information—such as the path to source data, what form the data is in, and what portions of the data to retrieve—is typically stored in connection files, such as Office Database Connections (.odc), or queries, such as Web Queries (.iqy) and Database Queries (.dqy). You can modify the parameters of these connections, refresh data in the workbook from these sources, add or remove them, as well as use other features.

VIEW CONNECTIONS

1. In the Data tab Connections group, click **Connections**. The Workbook Connections dialog box, shown in Figure 10-6, shows any connections in the workbook.

External Data Range Properties

Name: LibraryHome

Query definition
☑ Save query definition
☐ Save password

Refresh control
☑ Enable background refresh
☐ Refresh every   60 ↕ minutes
☐ Refresh data when opening the file
☐ Remove external data from worksheet before closing

Data formatting and layout
☑ Include field names   ☐ Preserve column sort/filter/layout
☐ Include row numbers   ☑ Preserve cell formatting
☑ Adjust column width

If the number of rows in the data range changes upon refresh:
◉ Insert cells for new data, delete unused cells
○ Insert entire rows for new data, clear unused cells
○ Overwrite existing cells with new data, clear unused cells

☐ Fill down formulas in columns adjacent to data

[OK]   [Cancel]

Figure 10-5: Control refresh and formatting options for imported data in the External Data Range Properties dialog box.

Workbook Connections

Name	Description	Last Refreshed
Books-Bestsellers		
Publications		
Customers		
MSN MoneyCentral Investor Stock Quotes		

[Add...] [Remove] [Properties...] [Refresh ▾]

Locations where connections are used in this workbook

Click here to see where the selected connections are used

[Close]

Figure 10-6: You can view and manage data connections within a workbook.

2. To quickly locate where a connection is used within the workbook, click a connection to select it, and click **Click Here To See**. The sheet and range where the data is located in the workbook are displayed, along with other details, as applicable.

Locations where connections are used in this workbook		
Sheet	Name	Location
Web Page Import	LibraryHome	$A$1:$D$53

REMOVE CONNECTIONS

1. In the Data tab Connections group, click **Connections**.

2. Select the connection and click **Remove**. Read the message that tells you removing the connection will separate the data from its source (the data itself is not removed from the workbook or source) and that refreshes will no longer work. Click **OK** to remove the connection.

Microsoft Office Excel

⚠ Removing connection(s) will separate this workbook from its data source(s), and data refresh operations in the workbook will no longer succeed. Click Cancel to keep connection(s), or click OK to proceed with connection removal.

[OK]   [Cancel]

10

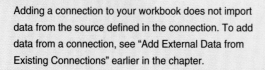
ADD CONNECTIONS

1. In the Data tab Connections group, click **Connections** and click **Add**. The Existing Connections dialog box shows any connection files it finds on your computer or network.

2. Click a connection you want to add, and click **Open**. The connection is added to your workbook.

REFRESH DATA

External data can be updated, or *refreshed*, to transfer any changes in the source data to the data you imported into Excel. You can refresh an individual connection or all connections in the workbook in sequence.

- Refresh options include:
  - **Refresh** connects to the source data and updates it in Excel.
  - **Cancel Refresh** interrupts the updating of your original data with the changes in the source data.
  - **Refresh All** updates all external data ranges in the workbook (it doesn't matter which cells are selected).
  - **Refresh Status** displays the External Data Refresh Status dialog box and the status of in-progress refreshes.

- To refresh an individual connection, in the Data tab Connections group, click **Connections**, select the connection you want to refresh, and click **Refresh**.

  –Or–

  Click a cell in the external data range, and, in the Data tab Connections group, click the top half of **Refresh All**.

- To refresh all connections in the workbook, click the **Refresh** down arrow in the Workbook Connections dialog box.

  –Or–

  Click the **Refresh All** down arrow in the Connections group.

  In either case, click **Refresh All**. A connection dialog box will appear for each connection and allow you to update the external data.

EDIT A QUERY

You can change the specifics of the data you are requesting from a source. For example, when selecting tables on a Web page, you are setting up a *query* that tells Excel which of the available tables you want.

1. In the Data tab Connections group, click **Connections**, select the connection whose query you want to change, and click **Properties**.
2. In the Connection Properties dialog box, click the **Definition** tab. At the bottom of the tab, click **Edit Query**. The dialog box that appears depends on the type of connection you are editing. For example, when changing a query from a text file, the Text Import Wizard opens (see Figure 10-2).
3. Make changes to the data you want imported, and close the query dialog box.

Use Excel with Web Technology

The work you do in Excel is not confined to your computer. You can share workbooks, as described in Chapter 9, but you can extend well beyond that in breadth, as well as in capabilities, by making your work available to be displayed in Web browsers such as Microsoft Internet Explorer. You can save or publish to Web pages what you create in Excel—from entire workbooks to individual elements—such as worksheets, charts, ranges, and PivotTable reports. Excel converts your work to *HTML*, the *Hypertext Markup Language* used to display text, graphics, and other items on the Internet and intranets. In addition, you can choose to publish many elements to Web pages with *interactive* capabilities, allowing users to not only view your work, but also to *use* your work to enter, change, sort, filter, and otherwise manipulate data. (This capability requires you to transfer workbooks to an Excel Services–enabled server, which is introduced later in this section.)

Save a Workbook as a Web Page

Workbooks can be saved for use on the Internet or within a local intranet (see "Understanding the Difference Between Save and Publish" QuickFacts for more information on the meaning of *save* and *publish*).

1. Open the workbook you want to put on a Web page.

2. Click the **Office Button**, and click **Save As**.

3. In the Save As dialog box, click the **Save As Type** down arrow, and click **Single File Web Page** to save the workbook data and all elements (such as shapes and tables) within one file.

   –Or–

   Click **Web Page** to save the workbook as a "mapping" Web page that links to an associated folder containing workbook elements.

   In either case, a few added options for saving are added to the dialog box.

4. In the Save area of the Save As dialog box, verify that **Entire Workbook** is selected.

5. Click **Change Title**. In the Set Page Title dialog box, type a descriptive title for the Web page. This title appears in the title bar of the user's browser and helps to quickly identify the nature of the material on the page. Click **OK**.

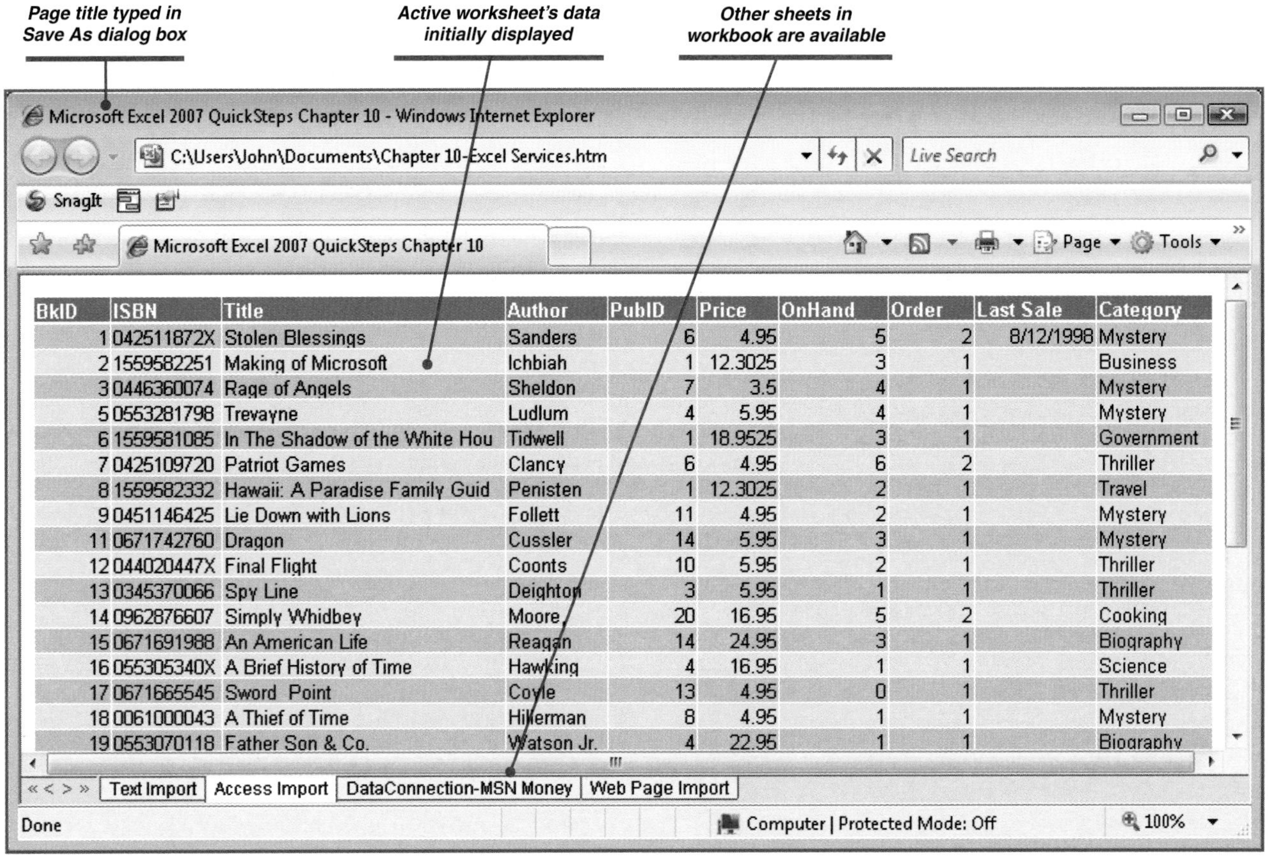

Page title typed in
Save As dialog box

Active worksheet's data
initially displayed

Other sheets in
workbook are available

Figure 10-7: A worksheet displays well in a Web browser,
although it does not include any interactive elements,
such as AutoFilter buttons.

6. Browse to where you want the Web page located, type the file name, and click **Save**.
A dialog box informs you that incompatible features will not be retained. Click **Yes**
to continue. The workbook version in Excel is now in the Web page format. Figure 10-7
shows a worksheet saved as a Web page in Internet Explorer version 7.

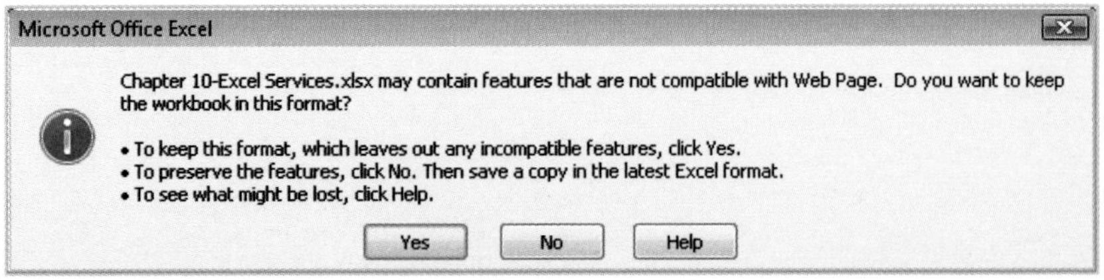

10

NOTE

While there are benefits to saving or publishing your Excel work in HTML, you do run the risk that your worksheets will not display as fully intended. This is especially true for many of the latest Excel 2007 features. To provide the closest representation of your original work, your best option is simply to provide a copy of the workbook by disk, e-mail, or other means. For broader access, publish a copy to an Excel Services–enabled Web site, though, again, there are limitations to using only a Web browser (see "Understanding Excel Services" QuickFacts later in the chapter). Perhaps the best compromise of true representation and broad access is to save the content as a PDF (Portable Document Format) or XPS (XML Paper Specification) file. Anyone with a free reader program can view the more popular PDF file in whatever venue it is delivered to them. You can save workbooks, tables, sheets, and selected cells as a PDF or XPS file if you install a free add-in program available from the Microsoft Office 2007 Web site.

	Save As ▶		**Excel 97-2003 Workbook** Save a copy of the workbook that is fully compatible with Excel 97-2003.
	Print ▶		**PDF or XPS** Publish a copy of the workbook as a PDF or XPS file.

Publish Workbook Items as a Web Page

You can choose to publish the entire workbook, individual worksheets, or just selected objects and cells.

1. Open the workbook you want to put on a Web page, and select the item or range you want placed on the Web page (you'll have the opportunity to fine-tune your choice later).

2. Click the **Office Button**, and click **Save As**.

3. In the Save As dialog box, click the **Save As Type** down arrow, and click **Single File Web Page** to save the workbook data and all elements (such as shapes and tables) within one file.

   –Or–

   Click **Web Page** to save the workbook as a "mapping" Web page that links to an associated folder that contains workbook elements.

4. In the Save area of the Save As dialog box, click **Entire Workbook**.

   –Or–

   Click **Selection:*your selected element***.

   > Save: ○ Entire Workbook
   > ● Selection: $A$1:$E$17

5. Click **Change Title**. In the Set Page Title dialog box, type a descriptive title for the Web page. This title appears in the title bar of the user's Web browser and helps to quickly identify the nature of the material on the page. Click **OK**.

6. Browse to where you want the Web page located, type the file name, and click **Publish**. The Publish As Web Page dialog box appears, as shown in Figure 10-8.

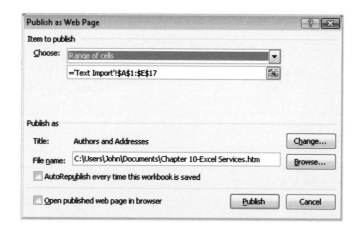

Figure 10-8: You can select what workbook item you want to publish, as well as other publishing parameters.

UNDERSTANDING EXCEL SERVICES

The gold standard for sharing Excel information using Internet technology is Excel Services, a technology that allows Excel 2007 to integrate with server-based Office SharePoint Server 2007 (SPS) and provide interactive access to workbooks using only a web browser. (SPS is a platform for prebuilt Web sites that supports team collaboration and document sharing).

The process starts in Excel 2007 using the Publish command on the Office Button menu (you can also use the Save As command, although you cannot selectively choose which workbook items are made available, as described next). In the Publish version of the Save As dialog box, click **Excel Services Options**, and select what parts of the workbook you want others to view (users only see cell values, not the underlying formulas), as shown in Figure 10-9.

When a user clicks the workbook in a SPS document library, Excel Services loads the sheets and items you made available, refreshes any external data, recalculates, and returns the data to the user's Web browser. The user cannot edit the data (or create a new workbook) within the browser; he or she would also need Excel 2007. Security is paramount. Access to the file is protected by a logon password, and any interaction with the workbook can be logged and an audit trail established to satisfy regulatory rules.

Excel Services Options

Show | Parameters

Only the selected items are shown by Excel Services in the browser. The entire workbook is always shown in Excel.

Items in the Workbook ▾

☑ All Tables
  ☑ Table_Books97.accdb
☐ All Named Ranges
  ☐ Text Import!Customers
  ☑ Web Page Import!LibraryHome
  ☐ DataConnection-MSN Money!MSN_MoneyCentral_Investor_Stock_Quotes

OK | Cancel

Figure 10-9: You can selectively publish workbook content to an Excel Services–enabled Web site, and users can interactively work with your data in a browser.

☑ Open in Excel Services
Excel Services Options...

7. Verify that the item or range you want saved to a Web page is displayed in the Choose text box. If it is not correct, click the down arrow to select another worksheet and see the individual items on each sheet.

8. Select the **AutoRepublish Every Time This Workbook Is Saved** check box to automatically update the published range or item when the workbook is saved.

9. Select the **Open Published Web Page In Browser** check box to view the page in your default browser.

10. Click **Publish** when finished.

Use Hyperlinks

Hyperlinks (or *links*) are items in documents that, when clicked, take you to other documents, different locations in the same document, other programs, and other locations. The Internet has brought links to mainstream use ("surfing the Web" is really just following a trail of several links), but hyperlinking is not just confined to Web pages. For example, for each company in a worksheet, you could create a hyperlink that would open Internet Explorer with that company's Web site home page (see Figure 10-10). In addition, you could create a link to a Microsoft Word document that provides narrative support for a value in a balance sheet, or you could create a bookmark to take you to a specific cell.

Figure 10-10: Creating a hyperlink in a worksheet connects your data with other resources.

Create a hyperlink...   ...to link to supporting material

CREATE A HYPERLINK

1. Select the cells, pictures, or other items you want to serve as the hyperlink.

2. In the Insert tab Links group, click **Hyperlink**.

–Or–

Right-click the selected item, and click **Hyperlink**.

3. In the Insert Hyperlink dialog box (shown in Figure 10-11), under Link To, select where the destination of the link will be:

- **Existing File Or Web Page** opens a set of controls you can use to find a Web address or file. Click the **Browse The Web** button to open your default browser to your home page. Click the **Browse To File** button to open a dialog box similar to the Open dialog box.

- **Place In This Document** opens a text box where you can type a cell address and opens a list box where you can choose a cell reference or named reference.

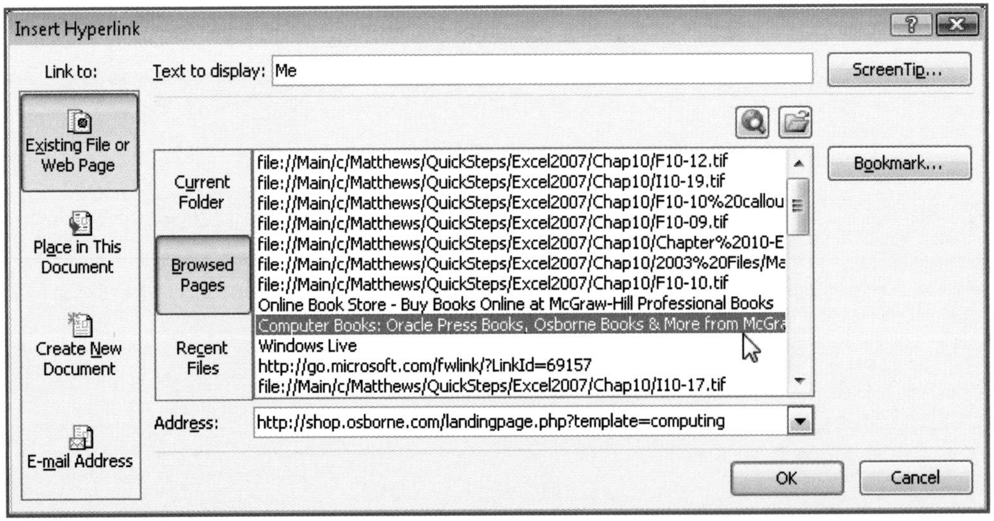

Figure 10-11: The Insert Hyperlink dialog box provides controls that allow you to tailor the destination of a hyperlink.

- **Create New Document** lets you name and locate a new Office document. It opens the blank document in its parent program if you select **Edit The New Document Now**.

- **E-mail Address** displays text boxes that you use to enter e-mail address(es) and the subject of the message. When clicked, a new message dialog box appears in the default e-mail program with the address(es) displayed in the To box and the subject filled in. (You can send to multiple addressees by using a semicolon (;) to separate each address.)

4. Click **OK**.

CREATE A BOOKMARK

Bookmarks are locations within the current workbook that you can "jump" to.

1. Select the cells, pictures, or other items you want to serve as the hyperlink.

2. In the Insert tab Links group, click **Hyperlink**.

   –Or–

   Right-click the selected item, and click **Hyperlink**.

3. In the Insert Hyperlink dialog box, under Link To, select **Existing File Or Web Page**, and click **Bookmark** (on the far right of the dialog box).

4. In the Select Place In Document dialog box, shown in Figure 10-12, type a cell reference or select a named place that you want as the hyperlink destination (or bookmark).

5. Click **OK** twice.

EDIT A HYPERLINK

1. Right-click the cell that contains the hyperlink you want to change, and click **Edit Hyperlink**. The Edit Hyperlink dialog box appears, similar to the Insert Hyperlink dialog box (see Figure 10-11).

2. Make changes to the hyperlink destination (see "Create a Hyperlink").

   –Or–

   Click the **Remove Link** button to remove the hyperlink.

3. Click **OK**.

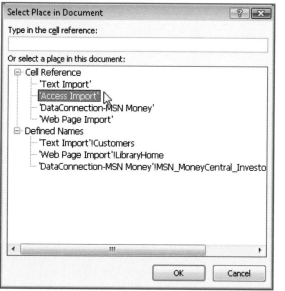

Figure 10-12: You can designate where in a workbook a hyperlink will land the user.

Automate Excel

You can automate repetitive tasks in Excel by using *macros*. Macros are recorded either by keyboard and mouse actions or by using Microsoft Visual Basic for Applications (VBA), a programming language.

Use Recorded Macros

Repetitive tasks you perform in Excel can be *recorded* as a macro and re-run at later times. For example, if you formatted a worksheet differently for each of your division heads, you could record the formatting sequence for each. For next quarter's report, simply run each macro in turn to quickly get the tailored results you want. Though macros are small programs written in the VBA programming language, you don't have to know VBA or be a programmer to record and run macros.

NOTE

To record and run macros, you might be interrupted to enable them in the workbook (see Figure 10-13). By default, macros are disabled (as are data connections, described earlier in the chapter). Macro security is important, because macros are executable programs and can bring havoc to your system when used by hackers for malicious purposes. Though you can change the default settings in the Trust Center (see Chapter 4), it's a safer bet to go along with Excel and simply enable the actions as they are presented to you.

Macro Settings

For macros in documents not in a trusted location:
- ○ Disable all macros without notification
- ◉ Disable all macros with notification
- ○ Disable all macros except digitally signed macros
- ○ Enable all macros (not recommended; potentially dangerous code can run)

Figure 10-13: Excel protects you from multiple points of security breaches.

TIP

If you record a step in the macro you don't want, you can open the macro in the Visual Basic Editor and remove the unwanted code. However, it might be easier to delete the macro and start over.

TIP

To use relative cell references in the cell addresses, click **Relative References** on the Macro menu before you start recording a macro. (See Chapter 4 for information on relative and absolute cell references.)

RECORD A MACRO

1. In the View tab Macros group, click **Macros** and click **Record New Macro**.

2. In the **Macro Name** text box, create a name to identify the macro. Macro names must begin with a letter and must not contain spaces or be the same name as a cell reference.

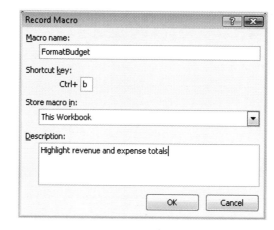

3. In the **Shortcut Key** text box (creating a shortcut key is optional), type a letter (no numbers) to use in combination with CTRL that will run the macro. To use an uppercase letter, the key combination will be CTRL+SHIFT+*your letter*. (If you choose a shortcut key combination that Excel uses for other purposes, your shortcut will override Excel's when the workbook that contains the macro is open.)

4. In the **Store Macro In** drop-down list box, choose whether you want to store it in the current workbook, in a new workbook, or in your Personal Macro Workbook, which makes the macro available to workbooks other than the workbook in which it was created.

5. In the **Description** text box (this step is optional), type a description that helps you identify the nature of the macro. Click **OK**.

6. Perform the steps involved to do the repetitive task. These steps might include opening dialog boxes, selecting settings, creating formulas, and applying formatting.

7. Click **Macros** in the View tab Macro group, and click **Stop Recording** to finish recording your actions as part of the macro and return to normal use.

Figure 10-14: *The Macro dialog box lists available macros and provides the tools to run, edit, configure, and remove them.*

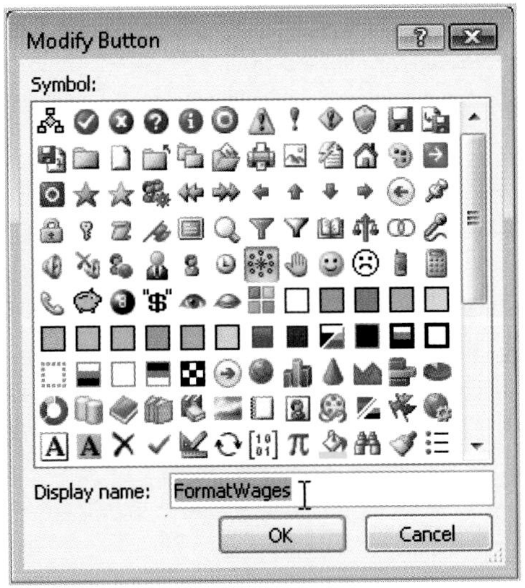

DELETE A RECORDED MACRO

1. In the View tab Macros group, click **Macros** and click **View Macros**.
2. In the Macro dialog box, shown in Figure 10-14, select the macro you want deleted, and click **Delete**.

ADD A MACRO TO THE QUICK ACCESS TOOLBAR

1. Open the workbook that contains the macro you want to add unless the macro is stored in your Personal Macro Workbook.
2. Click the **Office Button**, click **Excel Options**, and click the **Customize** option. In the Customize The Quick Access Toolbar dialog box, click the **Choose Commands From** down arrow, and click **Macros**.

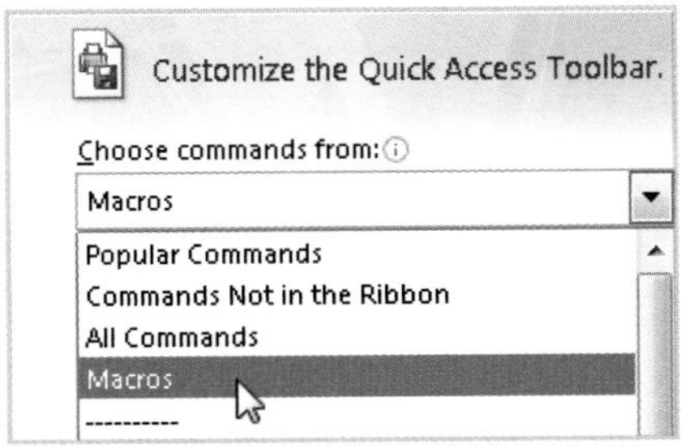

3. Click the macro you want to add to the toolbar, and click **Add**. The macro names appear in the right pane of the dialog box.
4. Click **Modify**. Select a new button, and select the text in the Display Name text box. Type the name you want for toolbar button. Click **OK**.
5. Click **Close** when finished.

Edit a Macro

You can change minor attributes of a macro such as its shortcut key without using VBA. (To edit the code that defines the actions of the macro, you will have to use the Microsoft Visual Basic Editor, shown in Figure 10-15, a discussion of which is beyond the scope of this book.)

10

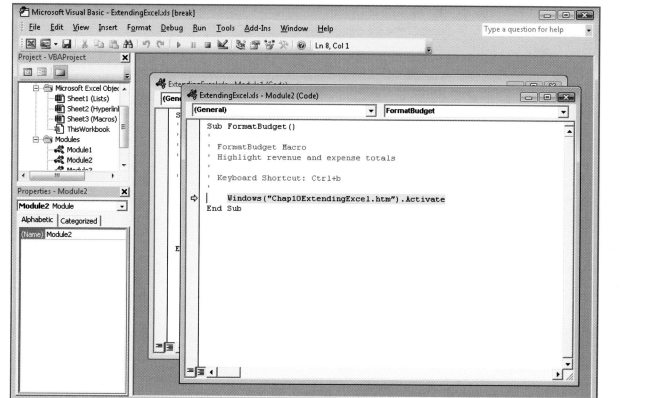

Figure 10-15: The Microsoft Visual Basic Editor provides a graphical palette for working on macros and other VBA code.

1. In the View tab Macros group, click **Macros** and click **View Macros**.
2. Select the macro you want to change, and click **Options**.
3. In the Macro Options dialog box, change the shortcut key and/or the macro description.
4. Click **OK** when finished.

Numbers

3-D Format option
  using with charts, 147
  using with shapes, 184
3-D Rotation formatting option
  using with charts, 147
  using with shapes, 184

Symbols

& (ampersand), selecting to remove content codes, 105
' (apostrophe), using with numbers, 29
() (parentheses), using with functions, 95
* (asterisk) wildcard, using with filters, 207
? (question mark) wildcard, using with filters, 207
\ (backslash), using with cell names, 78
_ (underscore), using with cell names, 78
~ (tilde) wildcard, using with filters, 207
= (equal) sign
  using with functions, 95–96
  using with formulas, 80–81

A

A1 cell referencing scheme, changing, 76
absolute cell references
  explanation of, 76
  using, 78
Access databases, adding tables from, 246–247
active cell. *See also* cells
  changing direction of, 31
  identifying, 27
  moving, 30
  staying in, 30
active sheet, printing, 117
ActiveX control, running for downloaded clips, 161
Add To Dictionary feature, using, 42
address, finding cells and ranges by, 42
address bar, identifying, 10. *See also* cell addresses
alignment, changing, 65–66

Alignment formatting option, using with charts, 147
alignment options, overview of, 67
ALT key. *See* keyboard shortcuts
ampersand (&), selecting to remove content codes, 105
apostrophe ('), using with numbers, 29
area chart, function of, 132
arguments, using with functions, 96–97
ascending sort, performing, 199
asterisk (*) wildcard, using with filters, 207
AutoComplete feature, adding data with, 36
AutoCorrect feature, using, 43
AutoFilter. *See also* filters
  creating, 203–206
  identifying, 187
  sorting options available to, 204
  turning off, 203
automatic link updating, changing, 89–90
AutoRecover file location, explanation of, 20
AutoSum feature
  using SUM function with, 98
  using with functions, 97
axes
  adding second value axis to charts, 146
  showing and hiding in charts, 142

B

Back button, using with Help feature, 17–18
background color, applying patterns to, 68
backgrounds, adding, 66, 68
backslash (\), using with cell names, 78
bar chart, function of, 132
black and white, printing in, 116
BMP extension, file type for, 163
BMZ extension, file type for, 163
body font, explanation of, 57
bookmarks, creating, 259
borders. *See also* cell borders
  changing picture borders, 179
  changing shapes with, 173
  separating column headings from data with, 187

brightness of pictures, changing, 180
bubble chart, function of, 132
bullets, adding to drawings, 171
buttons, using with Help feature, 17

C

captions, using with Clip Organizer, 166
case, searching by, 41
CDR extension, file type for, 163
cell addresses. *See also* address bar
  explanation of, 26
  identifying, 26, 86
  using relative cell references in, 261
cell borders. *See also* borders
  drawing, 51
  picking, 50
  previewing, 50–51
cell contents
  editing, 35–36
  fitting row height to, 47
  removing, 36–37
  replacing, 36
  using to change row height, 46–47
cell editing, canceling, 36
cell fill, filtering by, 204
cell names
  changing, 80
  identifying, 86
  rules for, 78
cell ranges. *See also* ranges
  identifying, 86
  naming directly, 77–78
  naming in dialog boxes, 78–79
  referencing, 79
cell references. *See also* external reference links
  changing, 76
  operators used with, 79
  types of, 76
  using, 81

cell styles. *See also* styles
   adding from other workbooks, 64
   applying, 61
   basing on existing styles, 63
   changing, 63
   features of, 60
   removing, 63
Cell Styles gallery, using, 62–63
cells. *See also* active cell
   adding, 47–48
   adding to print areas, 117
   applying conditions to, 91
   attaching formatting to, 69
   comparing, 91
   copying formulas to, 84
   deleting, 39
   entering current date in, 34
   entering current time in, 35
   explanation of, 26
   filling data into, 36–37
   fitting column width to, 48
   formatting, 31
   formatting to match values or conditions,
      92–93
   going to named cells, 79
   identifying changing cells for scenarios, 216
   location of beginning cell, 29
   merging, 48, 67
   naming directly, 77–78
   naming in dialog boxes, 78–79
   removing, 48
   removing from print areas, 117–118
   tracing precedent and dependent cells, 100
   watching, 100
cells and ranges
   finding by address, 42
   selecting, 39–41
center alignment, applying to text, 67
CGM extension, file type for, 163
Change Font Size button, using with Help feature,
      17–18
chart area, adding data tables to, 145

chart elements
   formatting, 147–148
   identifying, 143
   selecting, 141
chart layouts, applying, 139–140
chart sheets
   example of, 130
   explanation of, 131
   inserting, 149
chart styling
   changing, 140
   reverting, 149
chart templates. *See also* templates
   function of, 132–133
   using, 145
chart title, example of, 130
chart types
   creating, 145
   functions of, 132
   selecting from dialog boxes, 133
   selecting from gallery, 131, 133
charts
   adding data labels to, 143–144
   adding gridlines to, 142
   adding second value axis to, 146
   adding titles to, 141
   analyzing, 150–153
   building, 131
   changing defaults for, 134
   creating PivotCharts, 231–233
   creating quickly, 133
   error bars in, 152
   forms of, 131
   including more data in, 137
   modifying plotting of data for, 137
   moving and copying within Excel, 149
   positioning, 148
   printing, 153
   relocating, 134
   removing, 149
   removing gridlines from, 142
   removing selections from, 141

   resizing, 148
   selecting data for, 134
   showing and hiding axes in, 142
   using Hidden and Empty Cells option with, 137
   using in Word and PowerPoint, 149–150
Clip Art task pane, displaying, 159–160
clip art
   inserting into headers and footers, 111
   versus pictures, 159
Clip Organizer
   adding folders to, 165
   deleting clips from, 166
   using, 163–166
clips
   adding to existing folders, 164
   cataloging automatically, 165
   deleting from Clip Organizer, 166
   inserting in Clip Organizer, 165
   moving and copying, 166
Close button
   description of, 6
   identifying, 5
Collapse button, identifying for outlines, 209
Collapse/Expand By Level buttons, identifying for
      outlines, 209
Collate option, using in printing, 127
color scales, using to compare cells, 91
colored backgrounds, using, 66, 68
coloring worksheet tabs, 74
colors
   changing custom colors, 58
   changing themed colors, 57–58
   making transparent, 181
   sorting by, 199
Colors dialog box, displaying, 55, 57
column headers
   explanation of, 26
   identifying, 27
   placeholders for, 187
column headings
   explanation of, 26
   separating from data, 187

column chart, function of, 132
column letters, printing, 116
column values, filtering by, 204
column width, adjusting, 47–48
column-line chart, creating, 146
columns
  adding, 47
  adding to tables, 189
  attaching formatting to, 69
  collapsing in outlines, 208
  deleting in tables, 189
  entering sums in, 98
  as fields, 186
  hiding, 48
  identifying, 27
  locking and unlocking, 70
  maximum availability of, 46
  performing functions in, 190
  removing, 48
  removing filters from, 203
  selecting, 40, 190
  sorting data by, 199–202
  unhiding, 49
commands, accessing, 10–11
comment colors and borders, changing, 53
comment text, changing appearance of, 53
comments
  adding, 51
  changing default behavior for, 52
  changing user names for, 51
  copying, 53
  deleting, 52
  displaying, 115
  editing, 52
  formatting, 53
  moving, 52
  printing, 116
  resizing, 52
  viewing, 51–52
Compare And Merge Workbooks feature, using, 240
"Compatibility Mode," explanation of, 23
Conditional Formatting feature, using, 92–93

Conditional Formatting Rule Manager, using, 94–95
conditions, applying to cells, 91
connection options, using with Help feature, 16
connections
  adding, 251
  adding external data from, 248–249
  removing, 250
  viewing, 249–250
constraints, changing in Solver, 224
content codes, removing, 105
contextual chart tabs, examples of, 130
contrast of pictures, changing, 180
copies of workbooks, saving, 22
copying and pasting data, 38
corrections, making automatically, 43
Create Table dialog box, displaying, 186
cropping pictures, 174–175
CTRL key. *See* keyboard shortcuts
currency formats, adding to value fields in
  PivotTables, 232
currency symbols, adding, 33
curvature points, adding, 158
curves
  adjusting, 158
  creating, 157
Custom Views feature, using, 240

D

data
  adding from existing connections, 248–249
  adding quickly, 36–38
  continuing series of, 37
  converting text to, 243–247
  copying and pasting, 38
  deleting, 36
  entering from lists, 38
  filling into active cell, 35
  filling into adjoining cells, 36–37
  finding, 39–41
  getting from Web, 247–248
  importing, 243–247

modifying plotting of, 137
moving, 36–37
organization of, 27
refreshing, 251
replacing, 41
scaling before printing, 125
selecting for charting, 134
sorting, 199
validating, 195–198
data labels
  adding to charts, 143–144
  editing, 144
  positioning on data series, 144
data range properties, setting, 249
data series in charts, plotting, 134–135
data tables, adding to chart area, 145
data bars, using to compare cells, 91
data entry messages, creating, 197–198
data groupings, adding subtotals to, 210–211
data series in charts
  changing, 137
  changing presentation order of, 137
  combining with two value axes, 146–147
  example of, 130
  positioning data labels on, 144
  showing margin of error in, 152
data series label in chart, example of, 130
data table in chart, example of, 130
data types, overview of, 26
databases, adding tables from Access databases, 246–247
data-removal action, undoing, 38
date formats, examples of, 30
dates
  changing default display of, 31
  determining short date settings, 31
  entering in cells, 34
  formatting, 31
  inserting in headers and footers, 110
  overview of, 34
decimal places, adding and decreasing, 32
decimals, converting to fractions, 34
dependent cells, tracing, 100

descending sort, performing, 199
Design tab, using with charts, 131
Dialog Box Launcher, identifying, 8, 65
dialog boxes
  collapsing for charts, 137
  naming cells and ranges in, 78–79
  selecting chart types from, 133
  shrinking, 93
DIB extension, file type for, 163
Document Inspector, using with shared workbooks, 236
documents, sharing, 22
doughnut chart, function of, 132
.dqy extension, explanation of, 249
DRW extension, file type for, 163
duplicates, removing from tables, 192–193
DXF extension, file type for, 163

E

Edit Links dialog box, opening, 87
effects, adding to pictures, 179
embedded chart
  explanation of, 131
  example of, 136
EMF extension, file type for, 163
EMZ extension, file type for, 163
encrypting workbooks, 235
entries, completing, 30–31
EPS extension, file type for, 163
equal (=) sign
  using with functions, 95–96
  using with formulas, 80–81
Error Checking feature, using, 98–99
error messages, creating, 197–198
Evaluate Formula button, identifying, 101
Excel, opening, 3–4
Excel Services, overview of, 256
Excel sessions, exiting, 23
Excel window
  description of, 5–6
  minimizing, maximizing and restoring, 5
  minimizing and maximizing, 5

Expand button, identifying for outlines, 209
external (3-D) cell reference, explanation of, 76
external data, adding from existing connections, 248–249
external data range properties, setting, 249
external reference links. *See also* cell references
  breaking, 87
  creating, 86
  updating, 87–88

F

F keys. *See* keyboard shortcuts
fields
  explanation of, 26
  moving in PivotTables, 229–230
Figures
  Add-Ins dialog box, 221
  alignment group tools, 65
  Alignment tab in Format Cells dialog box, 66
  argument values for functions, 97
  AutoCorrect feature, 43
  AutoRecover setting, 20
  Border tab, 50
  cell selection, 40
  chart elements, 130
  chart layout, 139
  chart parameter changes, 138
  chart styles, 140
  charts copied to Word and PowerPoint, 151
  Clip Art task pane, 160
  Clip Organizer, 164
  color and cell icons, 200
  Colors dialog box, 57
  column headers, 188
  column width settings, 123
  conditional formatting rules, 94
  content published to Excel Services–enabled
    Web site, 256
  data imported from text file, 246
  data labels positioned on data series, 144
  data series and horizontal axis changes in charts, 139
  data table added to chart, 145

Data Validation dialog box, 196
date display options, 33–34
duplicate values removed from table, 192
Edit Links dialog box, 87
embedded chart, 136
error bars for chart, 152
Error Checking dialog box, 98
Error Checking feature, 99
error message customization, 198
Evaluate Formula dialog box, 101
external reference, 86
Fill tab, 68
Find tab, 41
font group tools, 64
Font tab in Format Cells dialog box, 65
Format Axis dialog box for charts, 142
Format Cells Number tab, 32
Format Picture dialog box, 109
formatting capabilities, 54
formatting chart elements, 148
formula components, 82
Goal Seek, 215
gradient effects, 68
grid layout of worksheets, 27
headers and footers, 108
headers repeated on pages, 113
headers set up like letterhead, 107
heading and body fonts, 58
Help window, 15
hiding rows and columns, 49
hyperlink in worksheet, 257
identifying data added to locate workbook, 24
Insert Chart dialog box, 134
Insert Function dialog box, 97
Insert Hyperlink dialog box, 258
keywords added to clips, 167
link updates enabled, 89
live preview of formatting styles, 92
Macro dialog box, 262
margin settings, 123
Margins tab, 111
Microsoft Visual Basic Editor, 263

Microsoft technical support, 14
Name Manager, 80
New Formatting Rule dialog box, 93
New Workbook dialog box, 9
numeric filter, 205
Office Online, 61
Office Online offers shape files, 162
Open dialog box, 10
outline with styles, 212
outlining tools, 209
Page Break Preview feature, 120
page breaks in Page Break Preview, 124
Paste Special dialog box, 40
pictures appear on worksheet, 160
PivotTable creation, 225
PivotTables, 226–228
plotted data series, 135
Print dialog box, 118
Print Preview, 121
printing comments, 117
printing features for printers, 127
printing options, 115
Publish as Web Page dialog box, 255
Quick Access toolbar, 12
relative references, 77
ribbon, 8
Save As dialog box, 21
Scenario Manager, 217
scenario setup for Goal Seek, 216
Scenario Summary, 218
Security Alerts dialog box, 260
Series dialog box, 37
shape selection with handles, 173
shapes, 157, 172
SmartArt, 169
SmartArt shapes, 170
Solver models, 223
Solver Options dialog box, 224
Solver Parameters dialog box, 221
Solver provides solution to problem, 220
Sort dialog box, 201
sorting on multiple levels, 202

Spelling dialog box, 43
split worksheet, 73
stacked shapes reordered, 176
styles, 62
styling options for shapes, 178
summary changed for PivotTable, 230
table style customization, 194
table styles, 192
tables, 187
technical support, 14
text box with WordArt, 169
text in cell, 28
theme colors, 57
theme customization, 60
themes, 56
Total row for table, 191
Trust Center, 88, 90
value axes, 147
verification subscription service, 241
views, 106
Windows Vista displays picture files as
     thumbnails, 159
WordArt effects, 183
workbook creation, 11
workbook default file format, 19
worksheet displayed in Web browser, 254
worksheet comparisons, 71
worksheet elements, 5
worksheet element protection, 242
files
   AutoRecover location for, 20
   compatibility of, 23
   listing, 10
   printing to, 125–126
   saving automatically, 18–20
   saving legacy files, 23
fill color, changing for shapes, 180–181
Fill formatting option
   using with charts, 147
   using with shapes, 184
fill handle, removing, 38
filtering PivotTables, 231–232

filtering options, using with Help feature, 16
filters. See also AutoFilter
   applying and nesting, 203
   basing on external criteria, 206
   removing, 203
   setting up criteria and extract ranges for, 206
Find & Select drop-down menu, objects in, 42
Find and Replace dialog box, displaying, 40
folders
   adding clips to, 164
   adding to Clip Organizer, 165
font tools, accessing, 64
fonts
   changing, 64
   changing custom fonts, 58
   changing for headers and footers, 109
   changing themed fonts, 57–59
footer margins, adjusting, 112
footers
   adding content to, 109–110
   adding pictures to, 109
   changing behavior of, 110
   creating, 104–105
   customizing, 105, 107
   inserting clip art into, 111
   inserting date and time in, 110
   inserting workbook path and file name in, 110
   inserting worksheet name in, 110
footers and headers, moving between, 107
Formal tab, using with charts, 131
Format Painter, using, 69
Format Cells dialog box, using with fonts, 64–65
Format Shape dialog box, managing, 184
formatting, attaching to inserted cells, rows, and
     columns, 69
formatting categories, availability to shapes, 184
formatting hierarchy, explanation of, 54–55
formatting rules, managing conditional rules, 94–95
formatting styles, performing live preview of, 91–92
Formula bar
   identifying, 5
   contents of, 26

formulas
being careful with, 83
calculation of, 80
canceling entering and editing of, 84
copying, 84
definition of, 79
deleting, 84
editing, 82–83
entering, 80
evaluating in pieces, 101
moving, 83
recalculating, 85
referencing table data in, 193
replacing portions of, 84
replacing with values, 84
turning off automatic calculation of, 85
viewing, 77
Forward button, using with Help feature, 17–18
FPX extension, file type for, 163
fractions, converting decimals to, 33
Freeform tool, using with curves, 157
Freeze Panes feature, using, 70
Full Screen view, explanation of, 105
functions
components of, 95
finding, 96–97
inserting, 96–97
typing, 95–96
using AutoSum technique with, 97
using parentheses with, 95
viewing results of, 95

G

gallery
identifying, 8
selecting chart type from, 133
GFA extension, file type for, 163
GIF extension, file type for, 163
Goal Seek, inputs required for, 214
gradients, setting, 180–181
grid. *See* worksheet grid

gridlines
adding to and removing from charts, 142
example of, 130
printing, 116
Group or Ungroup dialog box, appearance of, 210
groups
identifying, 8
organization of, 7
removing from outlines, 208
Guess option, using with Solver, 221

H

handles
changing shapes with, 173
dragging, 174
header margins, adjusting, 112
headers
adding content to, 109–110
adding pictures to, 109
changing behavior of, 110
creating, 104–105
customizing, 105, 107
inserting clip art into, 111
inserting date and time in, 110
inserting workbook path and file name in, 110
inserting worksheet name in, 110
using as page titles, 112–114
headers and footers, moving between, 107
heading font
availability of, 58
explanation of, 57
Help window
opening, 15
searching for information in, 16
help, browsing for, 17
Help feature
navigating, 17
using, 14–18
using Keep On Top tool with, 17
Help headings, displaying, 17
Help tools, using, 17–18

Highlight Changes feature, using with workbooks, 237–238
Highlight Cell Rules feature, using, 92–93
History worksheets, saving changes in, 238–239
Home button, using with Help feature, 17–18
horizontal alignment buttons, identifying, 65
horizontal axis in chart, example of, 130
horizontal axis labels in charts, changing, 137
horizontal text alignment, description of, 67
HTML (Hypertext Markup Language), saving and publishing Excel work in, 255
hyperlinks. *See also* links
creating, 258–259
editing and removing, 259
features of, 256–257

I

icon sets, using to compare cells, 91
icons, including on Quick Launch toolbar, 4
identifying information, adding to workbooks, 22–23
Ignore Print Areas option, using, 121
Import Data dialog box, displaying, 247
imported data, controlling refresh and formatting options for, 249–250
indents
creating left and right indents, 67
increasing and decreasing, 65
ink, saving, 116
Insert Hyperlink dialog box, displaying, 258
Insert Function tool, using, 96–97
Insert tab, using with charts, 131
Internet, capturing data from, 247–248
Internet Explorer version 7, opening workbooks in, 252
intersections, referencing, 79
.iqy extension, explanation of, 249

J

JFIF extension, file type for, 163
JPE extension, file type for, 163

JPEG extension, file type for, 163
JPG extension, file type for, 163
justification, applying to text, 67

K

Keep On Top tool, using with Help feature, 17
Key Tips, using, 29
keyboard
  loading Excel from, 3
  selecting chart elements with, 141
keyboard shortcuts. *See also* shortcuts
  for accessing help, 15
  for copying comments, 53
  for copying data, 38
  for copying formulas to nonadjacent cells, 84
  for creating charts, 133
  for creating tables, 188
  for displaying more of worksheets, 105
  for entering current date in cells, 34
  for filling data into active cell, 35
  for finding data, 39
  for inserting functions, 96
  for moving formulas, 83
  for opening Print dialog box, 153
  for pasting data, 38
  for printing, 125
  for printing portions of workbooks, 118
  for replacing data, 41
  for saving Solver values, 222
  for saving workbooks, 21
  for selecting all cells, 39
  for undoing actions, 38
  for verifying spelling, 42
keywords, using with Clip Organizer, 166

L

landscape orientation, explanation of, 112
Layout tab, using with charts, 131
legacy files, saving, 23

legends in charts
  example of, 130
  moving, 143
  showing and hiding, 143
letterhead, setting up headers as, 107
Line Color formatting option, using with shapes, 184
line chart, function of, 132
Line formatting option, using with charts, 147
Line Style formatting option
  using with charts, 147
  using with shapes, 184
lines between points, removing, 158
link updating, changing automatic updates for
  workbooks, 89–90
links. *See also* hyperlinks
  creating external reference links, 86
  editing, 87
lists
  adding and removing tools from, 10–11
  entering data from, 38
Live Preview
  identifying, 8
  turning on, 91
Live zoom
  description of, 6
  identifying, 5
locking rows and columns, 70
Lotus 1-2-3, transitioning from, 83
lowercase text, searching by, 41

M

Macro dialog box, opening, 262
macros
  adding to Quick Access toolbar, 262
  deleting, 262
  editing, 262–263
  recording, 261
  removing unwanted code from, 261
magnification, scaling, 125
margins
  adjusting for headers and footers, 112

centering printed data between, 111
changing, 110–112, 122–123
setting in Page Layout view, 122
setting in Print Preview, 119, 122
menus. *See* ribbon
Merge & Center button, identifying, 65
MIX extension, file type for, 163
mixed cell reference, explanation of, 76
models, saving Solver settings as, 222–223
mouse
  adjusting column width with, 47
  changing row height with, 46–47
Move Chart dialog box, opening, 134

N

Name A Range option, using, 78
Name Box
  accessing, 77
  contents of, 26
  increasing width of, 78
Name Manager
  increasing column width in, 81
  increasing width of dialog boxes in, 81
  opening, 79–80
named cells
  deleting, 80
  going to, 79
  sorting and filtering, 81
names
  changing user names for comments, 51
  rules for cell names, 78
navigation pane, identifying, 10
Normal template, resetting font attributes to defaults
  in, 65
Normal view
  explanation of, 104
  switching to, 107
Number formatting option, using with charts, 147
Number Of Copies feature, using in printing, 126–127
Number Of Pages feature, using, 109
Number tab, displaying, 32

numbers
  converting to scientific notation, 30
  entering, 29
  interpreting as text, 29
  using apostrophe (') with, 29
numeric values, filtering by, 204–206

O

objects, finding, 42
.odc extension, explanation of, 249
Office button
  description of, 6
  features of, 10
  identifying, 5, 8
Office Online
  adding pictures from, 161–162
  finding themes on, 60
orientation. *See also* page orientation
  changing, 65–66
  description of, 67
outlines
  adding styles to, 211–212
  removing, 208
  using, 208
outlining
  of data automatically, 207–208
  of data by grouping manually, 210

P

Page Break Preview feature
  explanation of, 104
  using, 117
page breaks
  adjusting, 122
  appearance of, 124
Page Layout view
  explanation of, 104
  setting margins in, 122
page margins, changing, 110–112
page numbers, adding to headers and footers, 109

page orientation, selecting, 112. *See also* orientation
page ranges, printing, 119
page titles, using headers as, 112–114
pages. *See also* Web pages
  adding total number to headers and footers, 109
  changing print order of, 115
  printing, 118–119
panes, dividing worksheets into, 71, 73
parentheses (()), using with functions, 95
password protection, adding, 234–235
passwords, removing, 235
Paste Special feature, using, 39
patterned backgrounds, using, 66, 68
PCT extension, file type for, 163
PCZ extension, file type for, 163
PDF (Portable Document Format) files, saving content as, 255
PDF format, saving workbooks in, 22
phone numbers, formatting, 33
PICT extension, file type for, 163
Picture formatting option, using with shapes, 184
picture attributes, changing, 180–181
picture borders, changing, 179
picture files
  displaying as thumbnails, 159
  file formats for, 163
picture icons, sizing, 159
picture shapes, changing, 178
pictures
  adding effects to, 179
  adding from Office Online, 161–162
  adding to headers and footers, 109
  browsing for, 158
  changing brightness and contrast of, 180
  changing shape fill with, 180
  versus clip art, 159
  cropping, 174–175
  organizing, 163–166
  recoloring, 181
  resetting, 175
  searching for, 158–161
  using, 163
pie chart, function of, 132

PivotChart Filter Pane, displaying, 234
PivotCharts, creating, 231–233
PivotTable field list task pane, hiding and showing, 231
PivotTables
  adding currency formats to value fields in, 232
  changing categorization of data in, 229
  changing layouts for, 231
  creating, 224–225
  creating layouts for, 225, 229
  moving fields in, 229–230
  sorting and filtering, 231
  styling, 229–231
  terminology for, 225
  using, 231–232
plot area fill in chart, example of, 130
plotting of data, modifying method of, 137
PNG extension, file type for, 163
points, adding curvature points, 158
portrait orientation, explanation of, 112
PowerPoint, using charts in, 149–150
precedent cells, tracing, 100
Print dialog box, opening, 153
print areas
  adding cells to, 117
  creating, 116
  printing, 119
  removing, 118
  removing cells from, 117–118
  working with, 119
Print button, using with Help feature, 17–18
print jobs
  previewing, 119, 122
  running, 125–127
print options, choosing, 116
print order, changing, 115
Print Preview feature, accessing, 122
printers, choosing, 125
printer-specific options, selecting, 126
printing
  charts, 153
  multiple copies, 126–127
  page ranges, 119
  portions of workbooks, 118–119

Protect Shared Workbook feature, using, 237–238
Publish as Web Page dialog box, displaying, 255
publishing versus saving Web pages, 253

Q

queries, editing, 252
question mark (?) wildcard, using with filters, 207
Quick Access toolbar
　adding macros to, 262
　customizing, 10–14
　customizing for workbooks, 13
　description of, 6
　identifying, 5, 8
　rearranging tools on, 13–14
　relocating, 13
Quick Launch toolbar, including icons on, 4
Quick Styles, applying to tables, 190, 192
QuickFacts
　Identifying Chart Elements, 143
　Selecting Data for Charting, 134
　Setting Up Criteria and Extract Ranges, 206
　Understanding Cell Referencing Types, 76
　Understanding Data Types, 26
　Understanding Excel Dates and Times, 34
　Understanding Excel File Compatibility, 24
　Understanding Excel Formatting, 54–55
　Understanding Excel Services, 256
　Understanding Excel Tables, 186
　Understanding Excel Views, 104–105
　Understanding Excel's XML File Formats, 18–19
　Understanding PivotTable Terms, 225
　Understanding Shapes, 156
　Understanding the Ribbon, 7–8
　Understanding the Difference Between Save and
　　Publish, 253
　Understanding the Trust Center, 87
　Using Cell Reference Operators, 79
　Using Pictures, 163
QuickSteps
　Adding and Removing Rows, Columns, and Cells,
　　46–48

Adding Content to Headers and Footers, 109–110
Adding Data Quickly, 36–38
Adding Rows and Columns to a Table, 189–190
Building a Chart, 131
Changing Solver Settings, 224
Changing a Picture's Attributes, 180–181
Changing SmartArt, 171
Choosing What to Print, 118–119
Choosing Worksheet Print Options, 116
Combining Shapes by Grouping, 177
Completing an Entry, 30–31
Formatting Comments, 53
Formatting Numbers, 32–33
Locating Validation Data, 197
Opening Excel, 3–4
Removing Filters, 203
Searching for Themes, 60–61
Selecting Cells and Ranges, 39–40
Selecting Chart Elements, 141
Setting External Data Range Properties, 249
Using PivotTables, 231–232
Using Formulas, 84
Using Functions Quickly, 95
Using Handles and Borders to Change Shapes, 173
Using Outlines, 208
Working with Changes in a Shared Workbook,
　237–239
Working with Cell Names, 80–81
Working with Charts, 148–149
Working with Curves, 157–158
Working with Tables, 192
Working with Worksheets, 72–74
Working with Zoom, 114–115

R

R1C1 references, changing to, 76
radar chart, function of, 132
ranges, reverting tables to, 192. *See also* cell ranges
recorded macros, deleting, 262
refresh options, controlling, 249–250
Refresh button, using with Help feature, 17–18

refreshing data, 251
relative references
　explanation of, 76
　using in cell addresses, 261
ribbon
　features of, 7–8
　hiding tools on, 13
　minimizing, 13
　selecting chart elements from, 141
ribbon, appearance of, 4
RLE extension, file type for, 163
row header, identifying, 27
row and column labels for charts, switching
　between, 137
row heading, explanation of, 26
row height, adjusting, 46–47
row numbers, printing, 116
rows
　adding, 46
　adding to tables, 189
　attaching formatting to, 69
　collapsing in outlines, 208
　deleting in tables, 189
　entering sums in, 98
　hiding, 48
　identifying, 27
　locking and unlocking, 70
　maximum availability of, 46
　as records, 186
　removing, 48
　selecting, 40, 190
　sorting data by, 202–203
　unhiding, 49

S

Save Model dialog box, displaying in Solver, 222–223
Save Workspace feature, using, 3, 70
Save As dialog box, displaying, 21
saving versus publishing Web pages, 253
scaling data before printing, 125
scatter chart, function of, 132

Scenario Manager, opening, 216
scenarios
  comparing, 217–218
  creating, 216–217
  creating for present values, 216
  editing, 217
  running, 217
  saving Solver results as, 222
scientific notation
  converting numbers to, 30
  entering numbers as, 30
Scope down arrow, using with cells and ranges, 78
Scribble tool, using with curves, 157
scroll bars
  description of, 6
  identifying, 5
Search feature, using with Help feature, 16
searches, refining, 39–41
security. See Trust Center
Selection And Visibility task pane, using with shapes,
    171–172, 176
selections
  magnifying, 115
  printing, 118
  removing from charts, 141
Series dialog box, displaying, 37
Shadow formatting option
  using with charts, 147
  using with shapes, 184
shape fill, changing, 180–181
shape perspective, changing, 173
shapes
  accessing tools for, 157
  adding, 156–157
  adding text boxes to, 168
  adding text to, 167–168
  aligning, 176
  applying styles to, 177–178
  changing, 173
  changing from one to another, 158
  changing picture shapes, 178
  combining by grouping, 177
  conceptualizing, 156

deleting, 174
formatting categories for, 184
hiding and showing, 172–173
inserting SmartArt shapes, 169–170
moving, 173
moving incrementally, 175
removing WordArt from, 183
repositioning stacked shapes, 175–176
resetting, 175
resizing, 173–174
rotating, 173–174
selecting, 171
shapes gallery, opening, 157
Shapes group, using, 172
Share Workbook feature, using, 236
shared workbooks
  accepting and rejecting changes in, 238–239
  discontinuing sharing of, 238
  protecting, 237–238
  using Track Changes feature with, 237–238
  working with changes in, 237–239
sheet navigator
  description of, 6
  sizing handle, 5
sheets versus spreadsheets and worksheets, 3
shortcuts, starting Excel from, 4. See also keyboard
    shortcuts
Show Formulas button, identifying, 77
Show/Hide Table of Contents button, using with Help
    feature, 17–18
size orientation, changing, 109
sizing arrow for tables, identifying, 187
sizing handles
  changing shapes with, 173
  dragging, 174
SmartArt shapes
  changing, 171
  inserting, 169–170
Solver
  adding settings from saved models to, 222
  giving more time to reach solutions, 223
  installing, 219
  saving values produced by, 222

setting up, 221–222
using Guess option with, 221
Solver Parameters dialog box, removing settings in, 224
Solver results, saving as scenarios, 222
Solver settings
  changing, 224
  saving as models, 222–223
Sort dialog box, displaying, 201
Sort Warning dialog box, appearance of, 199, 202
sorting
  by color and icons, 199
  by columns, 199–202
  by multiple criteria, 200–202
  PivotTables, 231
  by rows, 202–203
  using with AutoFilter, 204
source workbooks
  identifying, 86
  determining origination of, 88
spelling, verifying, 42–43
Spelling dialog box, displaying, 42–43
Split feature, using with worksheets, 71, 73
spreadsheets versus sheets and worksheets, 3
SPS (SharePoint Server 2007), relationship to Excel
    Services, 256
SSNs (Social Security Numbers), formatting, 33
Start menu, opening Excel from, 3
Startup Prompt feature, using with automatic link
    updating, 90
stock chart, function of, 132
Stop button, using with Help feature, 17–18
style examples, displaying for tables, 194
styles. See also cell styles
  adding to outlines, 211–212
  applying to PivotTables, 229, 231
  applying Quick Styles to tables, 190, 192
  applying to shapes, 177–178
  changing for charts, 140
  changing for headers and footers, 109
  customizing, 62–63
  definition of, 53
  features of, 55
  removing from tables, 195

subtotals, adding to data groupings, 210–211

summary rows, using with outlines, 211–212

sums, entering in columns and rows, 98

surface chart, function of, 132

Synchronous Scrolling feature, using with
  workbooks, 74

system date and time formats, changing, 35

T

table styles, creating, 194–195

table data, referencing in formulas, 193

table elements, changing, 192

Table of Contents for Help feature, showing, 17

tables

  adding from Access databases, 246–247

  adding rows and columns to, 189

  adding Total row to, 189–190

  applying Quick Styles to, 190, 192

  converting to standard data ranges, 236

  creating, 186–188

  creating blank prestyled tables, 194

  creating quickly, 188

  as data sheets, 186

  deleting rows and columns in, 189

  displaying style examples for, 194

  features of, 186

  removing duplicates from, 192–193

  removing styling from, 195

  reverting to ranges, 192

  showing and hiding elements in, 192

  summing last column in, 189–190

tabs, identifying, 8

task pane

  changing location and size of, 159

  description of, 6

  identifying, 5

technical support, getting assistance from, 14

templates. *See also* chart templates

  accessing, 4

  adding, 146

  adding second value axis to charts with, 146

  saving workbooks as, 22

text

  adding to shapes, 167–168

  adding WordArt styling to, 183

  aligning, 28, 67

  constraining on multiple lines, 28–29

  converting to data, 243–247

  entering continuously, 28

  extending beyond text–box boundaries, 168

  formatting for comments, 53

  interpreting numbers as, 29

  shrinking to fit, 67

  wrapping, 65, 67

  wrapping on multiple lines, 28

text boxes

  adding to shapes, 168

  deleting, 174

Text Box formatting option, using with shapes, 184

text selection, identifying, 174

textures, setting, 180–181

themed colors, changing, 55, 57–58

themed fonts, changing, 57–59

themed graphic effects, changing, 59

themes

  changing current theme, 54

  customizing, 59

  definition of, 53

  determining, 57

  features of, 54

  finding on Office Online, 60

  locating and applying, 60

thousands separator, adding, 32

thumbnails, displaying picture files as, 159

TIF extension, file type for, 163

TIFF extension, file type for, 163

tilde (~) wildcard, using with filters, 207

times

  changing default display of, 33–34

  conventions for, 31–32

  entering, 32–33

  entering in cells, 35

  inserting in headers and footers, 110

  overview of, 34

title bar

  description of, 6

  identifying, 5

titles

  adding to charts, 141

  using headers as, 112–114

toner, saving, 116

toolbar, adding and removing tools on, 12

tools

  accessing with Key Tips, 29

  adding and removing from lists, 10–11

  hiding on ribbon, 13

  rearranging on Quick Access toolbar, 13–14

Top/Bottom Rules feature, using, 93

Total row, adding to and removing tables, 189

Track Changes feature, using with shared workbooks,
  237–238

transparency, applying to colors, 181

trendlines, adding to charts, 130, 150, 152

Trust Center

  overview of, 87

  changing link updates with, 89–90

typefaces, examples of, 64

U

underscore (_), using with cell names, 78

Undo feature

  using, 38

  using with Goal Seek, 215

  using with pictures, 175

Unfreeze Panes feature, using, 70

unions, referencing, 79

updates, checking for, 14

uppercase text, searching by, 41

user names, changing for comments, 51

V

validation, creating for data, 195–197

validation criteria, removing, 197

validation data, locating, 197

value axes, adding to charts, 146

vertical alignment buttons, identifying, 65
vertical axis in chart, example of, 130
vertical axis label in chart, example of, 130
vertical text alignment, description of, 67
views
  changing, 241
  customizing, 105, 240
  Full Screen view, 105
  Normal view, 104
  Page Break Preview, 104
  Page Layout view, 104
  returning to, 105

W

Watch Window, opening, 100
watches, removing, 100
Web, getting data from, 247–248
Web pages. *See also* pages
  modifying, 256
  saving versus publishing of, 253
  saving workbooks as, 253–254
Web-friendly colors, accessing, 57
what-if problems. *See* Solver
wildcards, using with filters, 207
window arrangement, saving, 70
WMF extension, file type for, 163
WMZ extension, file type for, 163
Word, using charts in, 149–150
WordArt
  adding, 168–169
  removing from shapes, 183
WordArt styling, adding to text, 181, 183
workbook elements, protecting, 242
workbook windows, scrolling simultaneously, 74
workbook name
  description of, 6
  location of, 5

workbook path and file name, inserting in headers and
  footers, 110
workbook views
  description of, 6
  identifying, 5
workbooks
  adding cell styles from, 64
  adding identifying information to, 22–23
  browsing, 10
  changing appearance of, 8–10
  changing automatic link updating fro, 89–90
  closing, 23
  comparing, 73–74
  comparing and merging, 240
  creating, 3–4, 6, 9
  creating outside Excel, 7
  customizing Quick Access toolbar for, 13
  encrypting, 235
  identifying source workbooks, 86
  opening in Internet Explorer version 7, 252
  opening existing workbooks, 7–8
  printing portions of, 118–119
  protecting shared workbooks, 237–238
  saving, 85
  saving as templates, 22
  saving automatically, 18–20
  saving as Web pages, 253–254
  saving changes in History worksheets, 238–239
  saving copies of, 22
  saving manually, 21–22
  sharing, 235–236
  viewing worksheets from, 73
worksheet elements, protecting, 242
worksheet grid
  description of, 6
  identifying, 5
worksheet name, inserting in headers and footers, 110
worksheet tabs, coloring, 74

worksheets
  adding, 73
  deleting, 73
  displaying more of, 105
  dividing into independent panes, 71, 73
  grid layout of, 27
  moving and copying, 73
  navigating, 74
  printing active sheets, 117
  printing in entirety, 121
  printing selected sheets, 118
  renaming, 74
  splitting, 71, 73
  viewing from multiple workbooks, 73
WPG extension, file type for, 163
Wrap Text button, identifying, 65

X

.xls file format, explanation of, 23
.xlsm file format, explanation of, 260
.xlsx file format, explanation of, 23
.xltm file format, explanation of, 260
.xlw file format, explanation of, 70
XML (eXtensible Markup Language) formats, overview
  of, 18–19
XPS (XML Paper Specification) files, saving content
  as, 255
XPS file format, saving workbooks in, 22
XY chart, function of, 132

Z

zip codes, formatting, 33
Zoom magnification, customizing, 115. *See also*
  magnification
Zoom percentage, selecting, 114